Reprints of Economic Classics

THE COSTS OF THE WORLD WAR

TO THE AMERICAN PEOPLE

THE

COSTS

OF THE

WORLD WAR

TO THE

AMERICAN PEOPLE

BY

JOHN MAURICE CLARK

[1931]

WITH AN INTRODUCTORY ESSAY

Some Documentary Notes on the Relations Among
J. M. Clark, N. A. L. J. Johannsen and J. M. Keynes

BY JOSEPH DORFMAN

REPRINTS OF ECONOMIC CLASSICS

Augustus M. Kelley · Publishers
NEW YORK 1970

First Edition 1931

(New Haven: Yale University Press, 1931)

Reprinted 1970 by
AUGUSTUS M. KELLEY · PUBLISHERS
REPRINTS OF ECONOMIC CLASSICS
New York New York 10001

. . . .

I S B N 0 678 00662 8
L C N 68 55507

. . . .

PRINTED IN THE UNITED STATES OF AMERICA
by SENTRY PRESS, NEW YORK, N. Y. 10019

SOME DOCUMENTARY NOTES ON THE RELATIONS AMONG J. M. CLARK, N. A. L. J. JOHANNSEN AND J. M. KEYNES

The late Professor J. M. Clark (1884-1963) of Columbia University ranked among the most creative economists that the United States has produced. He was in the forefront of the modernization of economic science, including the development of tools and theories which are now popularly called Keynesianism. Not least of the merits of *The Costs of the World War to the American People* (1931),[1] which is reprinted below, is that it contains some of the most original parts of his pioneering work in the analysis of economic fluctuations. Here appeared his first explicit statements of the principle of economic "multipliers." The multiplier was a powerful instrument in the effective questioning of a basic orthodox doctrine; namely, that there could be no general overproduction of goods, a doctrine whose acceptance, Clark pointed out, "became one of the prime tests of a competent economist."[2] The historian of the multiplier doctrine has defined the concept as follows: "All expenditures give rise to subsequent income effects and their aggregated sum can always be expressed as a multiple of the original disbursement. If this aggregated sum is larger than the original stream of expenditure, one usually speaks of multiplying effects, though it may seem more appropriate to use this term when the marginal propensity to spend is larger than unity or induced effects appear."[3]

Clark in *The Costs of the World War to the American People* made clear the view that the volume of production may vary more widely than economists had generally conceived, as a result of changes in aggregate effective demand. In discussing the nation's productivity in 1916 he had already presented the idea of the cumulative effect of an increase of the country's trade balance. In *The Costs of the World War* he developed this analysis with the aid of the mathematical precision of "multipliers." He not only developed a foreign-trade multiplier, but also an investment multiplier; that is, the multiplicative effect of capital investment on na-

[1] Clark completed the manuscript for *The Costs of the World War to the American People* in March 1930.

[2] *Alternative to Serfdom* (New York: Knopf, 1948) p. 95.

[3] Hugo Hegeland, *The Multiplier Theory* (1954; reprint, New York: Augustus M. Kelley · Publishers, 1966) p. 251.

tional income. In 1935 he presented his comprehensive development of the idea in the now famous *Economics of Planning Public Works*.[4] The study was published by the Government Printing Office for the National Planning Board, on whose staff Clark served at the time. There were unsuccessful attempts originally to secure a commercial publisher. It has since become a classic.

As I have noted elsewhere, "Clark was one of several students who, working independently at about the same time, began a quantitative formulation of this idea. While the exact formal statement of the principle became associated . . . with R. F. Kahn and [J. M.] Keynes, Clark, in typical fashion, felt that the multiplier was useful chiefly as a model. An empirical investigation, he believed, would indicate that an exact formulation did not fit the real world; for the consumption function was probably a variable, not the constant required by the Keynes-Kahn formula."[5]

Since I wrote the above, information has become available that throws light on an important source of Clark's ideas in this area, and on his relation to Keynes. Much of this involves N. A. L. J. Johannsen (1844-1928), a self-taught or "amateur" economist, who is now recognized as an outstanding leader in the systematic development of the modern form of "the multiplying (or cumulative) principle," as he called it, as a basic mechanism of his pioneering use of the income approach to the theory of money, and to business cycles.[6]

Espousing as he did the greatest of economic heresies, Johannsen found little open sympathy outside of a few adventurous minds, such as W. C. Mitchell, John A. Hobson and J. M. Clark. How and when Clark became acquainted with Johannsen we do not precisely know. We do know that his father, John Bates Clark, had corresponded at least as early as 1908 with Johannsen, and had reviewed his chief book, *A Neglected Point in Connection with Crises* (1908), in *The Bankers' Magazine*, where he gave encouragement to the author but was rather cautious as to the con-

---

[4] It was reprinted in 1965 by Augustus M. Kelley · Publishers.

[5] *The Economic Mind in American Civilization*, 5 volumes (New York: The Viking Press, 1946-1959; reprint, Augustus M. Kelley · Publishers, 1966, 1969, 1970) V, p. 762.

[6] For the first comprehensive account of Johannsen's life and work, see Dorfman, *The Economic Mind in American Civilization*, III, 408-413; IV, 15.

Hegeland in referring to Johannsen as a "German writer" was doubtless confused by the fact that he published in both German and English. Johannsen was born in Berlin, Germany, but he wrote practically all his works in the United States, in Brooklyn and Staten Island, New York City.

The most recent contribution to the history of the multiplier continues the confusion by describing Johannsen as "the German pioneer in multiplier theory." (Mogens Boserup, "A Note on the Prehistory of the Kahn Multiplier," *The Economic Journal*, September 1969, p. 667.

tribution of his theory.[7] And we now know that the correspondence was renewed in 1925, as Johannsen showered the elder Clark and others with his almost endless pamphlets and leaflets. The elder Clark was dubious about the attribution of depression to general overproduction, but like the orthodox at large he would be willing to accept partial overproduction as a cause. He proposed in one letter that Johannsen should submit a note to an economics journal ''stating your views as to the partial cessation of building and equipping industrial plants as a cause of crises. If I may suggest, the argument would have to show a kind of overproduction due to some cause—not universal overproduction—then a lessened demand for plant, which will affect the general market for labor—a considerable element in the general disturbance.''[8]

In that same year, it appears that Johannsen sent to J. M. Clark a manuscript ''Business Depressions,'' which contained the substance of his argument, for submission to *The Journal of Political Economy*, of which Clark then at the University of Chicago was an editor as a member of the university's department of political economy. In August, Johannsen wrote Clark: ''I received at the time, your lines of June 6, relating to a manuscript 'Business Depressions' which you turned over to an editorial reader. On July 11, I mailed you a copy of the article printed *here* [privately in New York]. Today I enclose another copy with a card giving some additional points. Would be glad to hear from you regarding progress, and would still more appreciate an *opinion of your own*.''[9] Several months later, he received from *The Journal of Political Economy* the following comment: ''The article 'Business Depressions, Their Cause' which you submitted for printing in *The Journal of Political Economy* met with a

[7] See Dorfman, *The Economic Mind in American Civilization*, III, p. 411.

According to Johannsen, J. B. Clark got in touch with him after he appealed to the ''men of highest reputation as economists,'' to examine his theory and either accept it as correct, or show him why it is wrong. He made this appeal through a broadside titled *An Open Letter to Prof. J. B. Clark, Prof. J. Laurence Laughlin, Prof. E. R. A. Seligman, Prof. F. W. Taussig*, dated September 1, 1908.

Professor Mitchell began reading the book in March 1911, while preparing *Business Cycles* (1913).

[8] J. B. Clark to Johannsen, December 15, 1925. Letter in possession of Joseph Dorfman.

[9] Johannsen to J. M. Clark, August 3, 1925. Letter in possession of Joseph Dorfman.

The full title of the eight-page leaflet is *Business Depressions; Their Cause. A Discovery in Economics;* it appeared in July 1925. The card, which was published the following month, was titled *Business Depressions; Their Cause, A Discovery in Economics. Additional.* Here he saluted Professor Mitchell's theory as being in the right direction. ''Even without the need of complicated statistics, [he] brought out the fact that, at prosperous times, business men are likely to go into over-production, which automatically engenders a subsequent under-production and unemployment. While such over-production, if confined to consumptibles, seldom amounts to much, it becomes serious when extending to factors *and means of production*.''

very long delay in the hands of one of our readers. Mr. Clark has informed us that you decided to publish elsewhere. I am very sorry so much time has elapsed before returning your manuscript to you.''[10]

Clark's interest in Johannsen's work by no means ceased. It is revealed in striking fashion in his heavily marked copy of Keynes's *The General Theory of Employment, Interest and Money* (1936). In the closing lines of the next to last chapter—"Notes on Mercantilism, the Usury Laws, Stamped Money and Theories of Underconsumption"—Keynes paid tribute to that "brave army of heretics . . . who following their intuitions, have preferred to see the truth obscurely and imperfectly rather than to maintain error, reached indeed with clearness and consistency and by easy logic, but on hypotheses inappropriate to the facts" (p. 371). Johannsen's name was not listed there but Clark added it in his copy and wrote: "Cf., Johannsen, *A Neglected Point in Connection with Crises* 1908 (the point being 'impair savings'; [that is, savings] invested in buying existing equities not in creating new capital goods). Seems to be the American pioneer, to have preceded Keynes, and communicated with him, probably in 1925.''[11] And he added to the index at the appropriate place: "N. Johannsen not mentioned.''[12]

Clark's statement that Johannsen communicated with Keynes prob-

---

[10] M. McKugo to Johannsen, October 27, 1925. Letter in possession of Joseph Dorfman.

[11] Clark's copy is in the possession of Joseph Dorfman. "Impair savings" was Johannsen's own term and he attributed them "to the saturation of productive capital." (Johannsen to Professor J. W. Martin, Emory University, Georgia, March 5, 1928; from transcript of Johannsen's letterbooks.) He said in one of his broadsides that they consist "of such savings as, though extracted from the people *as income* for the savers, and though not withdrawn from the general circulation, do not in the course of such circulation reach the people *as income for the people* (by calling for work to be done) and do not replace what the savers extracted from them; thus impairing their income and their purchasing power." He noted rather sharply that "Recently much has been made of the habit of corporations to withhold and accumulate an unnecessary share of their profits. The habit is wrong, but stopping it would not prevent impair savings from terminating a period of prosperity." (*To Whom It May Concern*, broadside attached to *Business Depressions; Their Cause, A Discovery in Economics*, revised edition, December 1925).

In the conclusion of the pamphlet he explained that thrift was a virtue only "if the savings funds are invested (directly or indirectly) so as to become income for others in payment for new constructions (especially of new productive or useful capital) or in the expansion of existing business. If not so invested, the saving process causes a slackening of the general demand. This leads to unemployment; this to the impoverishment of the working classes; this to retrenchment on the part of the latter; this to a multiplication of the lack of demand, and to a spreading of the baneful effects over all classes of the people." (p. 12).

[12] P. 393.

Clark included Johannsen in his own published list of heretics "on the doctrine of general overproduction," in *Alternative to Serfdom* (p. 91), but he too forgot to include his name in the index.

ably in 1925 is doubtless based in part on Keynes's reference to that date in *A Treatise on Money* and on Johannsen's reference to a communication from Keynes in the leaflet of June, 1926, *Two Depression Factors: The Minor One Known, Not the Other*. In *A Treatise on Money*, Keynes wrote: "Johannsen originally published his theory in *A Neglected Point in Connection with Crises*, 1908, and followed up with pamphlets in 1925, 1926 and 1928."[13] In *Two Depression Factors*, Johannsen wrote: "When, owing to saturation, the investment of savings in the creation of *new* capital goods falls off, they will not to the same degree as now, be turned into income for others. And as a consequence, lack of income, unemployment and lack of demand will follow. The consequence, due to oversaving is admitted by England's great economist, Dr. J. M. Keynes, as correct, and as being long neglected by orthodox economics." In the opening pages, he wrote that Keynes "editor of *The Economic Journal* [like J. B. Clark] did not accept his view unconditionally" and "asked for more clearness, showing the theory's right relation to orthodox theory."[14]

J. M. Clark placed checks, denoting significance, against the following passage in his copy of *Two Depression Factors:* "A depression seems due within an early year, of a character different from those which occurred in recent decades. It may set in despite the splendid condition now ruling [1926] in business and despite the belief that the bugaboo of overbuilding is dead. Likely it will not begin with a panic, but will come in gradually with a spread of unemployment, reducing the people's purchasing power by many billions of dollars and creating a jobless proletariat more or less permanent."

In his last publication, a leaflet, *A Depression Manifest . . . . by an Aged Outsider* (February 1928), Johannsen wrote: "The fundamental cause—the saturation of productive and useful capital—is not admitted by the economic world, who contend that the opportunities for the creation of such capital are unlimited. But if they had to count up such opportunities, they would not get far. . . . Owing to such saturation many of the savings become 'impair savings,' causing unemployment and a decline

[13] *A Treatise on Money*, 2 volumes (New York: Harcourt Brace, 1930) II, p. 100. Beginning in the very same year as the publication of his book, *A Neglected Point*, Johannsen followed it up with a continuous series of pamphlets presenting digests of his theory.

[14] In the extant papers there is one note from Keynes, in his capacity as secretary of the Royal Economic Society. It reads: "The revised list of the addresses of members of the Royal Economic Society is being prepared. A copy will be sent you when it is ready. The assistant secretary asks me to remind you that you are now three years in arrears with your subscription." (Keynes to Johannsen, April 18, 1925. Letter in possession of Joseph Dorfman).

Most of Johannsen's papers were destroyed by a fire.

of business activity. If we could find a suitable way to make savings unprofitable (favoring luxury, pleasure, enjoyments, education, charity, especially of such grand style as Rockefeller charity, raising the standard of life and of health, not only at home but the world over), unless they can be employed constructively, and devise a means to enforce such measure[s] automatically, without inquiring, argument, or expense,—this ought to put our business activity permanently on a prosperous, salient basis.''[15]

Two years after Johannsen's death in 1928, Keynes in *A Treatise on Money* commented that Johannsen's ''doctrine of 'Impair Savings', i.e., of savings withheld from consumption expenditure but not embodied in capital expenditure and so causing entrepreneurs who have produced goods for consumption to sell them at a loss, seems to me to come very near to the truth.'' And then he continued along J. B. Clark's line: ''But Mr. Johannsen regarded the failure of current savings to be embodied in capital expenditure as a more or less permanent condition in the modern world due to a saturation of the capital market, instead of as a result of a temporary but recurrent failure of the banking system to pass on the full amount of the savings to entrepreneurs, and overlooks the fact that

---

[15] Johannsen noted also in the pamphlet that ''John A. Hobson, the well-known English economist, referred to me as the first man who had given a clear exposition of the process of investment (partial at least) in trade depressions.'' [See Hobson, *The Industrial System. An Inquiry into Earned and Unearned Income* (2nd edition, London: Longmans Green, 1910; reprint, Augustus M. Kelley · Publishers, 1969) p. 300 ft.]
He did feel, however, that: ''Hobson's own theory as to the investment of 'over-savings' is hardly tenable; namely, that these keep on creating new productive capital, the latter turning out unable to meet its running expenses and getting into financial difficulties. The fact is, so long as oversavings are used for erecting new constructions, workers remain employed and there can be no depression.'' [*Business Depressions, Their Cause. A Discovery in Economics* (New York: privately printed, 1925) no page numbers]. Johannsen had presented this critique of Hobson and Uriel Crocker more elaborately in July 1909, and then went on to say: ''I do not wish to belittle the useful work these men have done in disclosing the evil tendencies of the saving process whenever the latter is carried on beyond healthy limits. Nor do I wish to discredit any of the numerous other points of economic research, unique as they are, which secure to Hobson a prominent place in economic literature.'' He reiterated that Hobson's ''views on the saving process . . . in their general drift follow the same directions as mine.'' [*To the Economists of America. The New Depression Theory as Against the Views of Hobson, Crocker and a Prominent Banker* (New York: privately printed, 1909) no page numbers]. There is a copy of the pamphlet in the Seligman Papers, Special Collections, Columbia University Libraries. Hobson's theory of the time was given scant consideration by the profession, especially in his native England. One of his few admirers, William Smart of the University of Glasgow, wrote the eminent American economist, E. R. A. Seligman: ''I hear from [Henry] Higgs you have been talking to him about Hobson's theory. If you have any ideas on the subject I should be very glad to hear from you about it. I am distinctly taken with it, but, so far as I can see, nobody will look at what he says because he is Hobson.'' (June 23, 1895, Seligman Papers).

a fall in the rate of interest would be a cure for the malady if it were what he diagnoses it to be.''[16]

As an historian of economic thought has pointed out, Johannsen had already given the answer in his earlier German version, *Depressionsperioden* (1903) : '' 'The argument is one of those which are not based on practical experience but which are derived solely from theories, without regard to whether these theories agree with actual conditions. In fact the activity of saving is very little affected by the rate of interest.' ''[17]

As another writer noted, ''Keynes did not mention Johannsen in the *General Theory*, but actually Johannsen's ideas were much more relevant to the latter book than to the *Treatise*.''[18] For example, as Johannsen stated in one of his numerous appeals *To the Economists of America*, ''The 'accepted views' now ruling on the subject of saving do not go far enough to give us a clear conception of the scope of the savings process. They hinge on the erroneous assumption that, inasmuch as saving is inseparable from investing, and as the investment usually leads to a good, useful end, the saving activity, too, must lead to a good useful end. . . . Instead of treating saving and investing 'both in one,' because inseparable, we should consider and define each one of these two elements by itself, then we would arrive at no such fallacies.''[19]

As the end approached for the octogenarian in 1928, he became increasingly concerned that ''the economic world do[es] not believe in a saturation of productive capital, considering that saving funds always find investment.''[20] But he staunchly continued to fight for his theory.

---

[16] *A Treatise on Money*, II, p. 100.

[17] T. W. Hutchison, *Review of Economic Doctrines 1870-1929* (Oxford: Oxford University Press, 1953) p. 395.

[18] Lawrence R. Klein, *The Keynesian Revolution* (New York: Macmillan, 1947) pp. 143.

In a sense, Lord Robbins made the appropriate acknowledgement for Keynes in 1968. After dismissing ''what Keynes called the underworld of heresy'' as of little importance, he added in a footnote: ''An exception should be made for N. Johannsen whose *A Neglected Point in Connection with Crises* (New York, 1908) seems to have got very near what is now held to be the truth of the matter''; that is, ''the macroeconomic effects of saving or the benefit to development of accumulation.'' [*The Theory of Economic Development in the History of Economic Thought* (London: Macmillan, 1968) p. 66. In the ''Select Index of Proper Names,'' he enters Johannsen as follows: ''Johannsen, N. An anticipator of Keynes and [D. H.] Robertson'' (p. 79)].

[19] *To the Economists of America. The New Depression Theory Presented in* [*the*] *Form of an Illustration* (Rosebank, N. Y.: privately printed, June 1909) no page numbers.

In this pamphlet Johannsen quoted the following from a letter from F. W. Taussig on his theory: ''Nor could my opinion or that of any economist be regarded as conclusive on a subject about which there is so much controversy. We differ among ourselves. And it will take much time and discussion to reach a settled conclusion.''

[20] Johannsen to Martin, March 15, 1928.

He wrote in a private letter ''I still hope my saving theory will be considered, the great expert on the depression theme, Prof. Mitchell, having promised me that in his next issue on that subject he would more thoroughly go into my studies.''[21]

So much for the relations of Johannsen, Clark and Keynes, but not for Clark and Keynes. Another World War brought them together at least on one occasion, at a high level conference, July 23, 1941, in Washington, a conference which lead to a revealing exchange amid circumstances almost the reverse of the days of the Great Depression. Then the question had been how to get out of deflation, now the problem was to prevent the inflation threatened by the American national defense program, and its deleterious consequences on the war effort for the survival of democracy and on the post war economy. Both were engaged on government service: Keynes at the British Treasury, Clark at the Office of Price Control and Civilian Supply. The day after the conference, Clark in a postscript to a letter to Keynes wrote: ''It has seemed to me that what I call the 'income-flow analysis,' of which yours is the most noted presentation, has done something which has not been done in comparable degree since Ricardo and Marx: namely, constructed a coherent logical theoretical system or formula having the quality of a mechanism, growing directly out of current conditions and problems which are of paramount importance and furnishing a key for working out definite answers in terms of policy. On this a 'school' has grown up. All that has tremendous power; and is also exposed to the dangers of too-undiscriminating application, from which classical economics suffered, and of which I think the [Richard V.] Gilbert-[Don] Humphrey attitude is one illustration.

I am myself enough of an 'institutionalist' (whatever that may mean)

---

[21] Johannsen to Professor D. S. Tucker, Massachusetts Institute of Technology, April 7, 1928. Transcript from Johannsen's letterbooks.

Tucker and other correspondents intimate quite rightly that there was a good deal of similarity between the works of Johannsen and the writings, especially *Profits* (1925), of the very popular team of William Trufant Foster and Waddill Catchings. In the same letter Johannsen wrote: ''You refer to Foster & Catchings and ask me if I ever have been in touch with them. They have brought out several publications going very minutely into the cause of depressions as far as they look for that cause within the course and routine of regular business, but I have brought out a factor not lying within the realm of that routine, but outside of it—in the saving process. In regard to that, Mr. Foster wrote me that 'rightly or wrongly, my factor was fallacious'—without stating where the fallacy comes in. Years ago he sent me a batch of proof matter for one of his own publications, asking me to scrutinize and make comments where feasible —which I did. No thanks for this—not even an acknowledgement.''

To another correspondent he wrote at the time: ''In their book *Profits*, they refer to me, p. 433.'' He felt, however, that the authors of *Profits* completely distorted his theory. (Johannsen to Professor Joseph Mayer, Tufts College, March 20, 1928; from transcript of Johannsen's letterbooks). The team claimed in *Profits* that Johannsen's theory was ''directly contrary to theirs.''

to have more than a lurking distrust of formulas and equations! But not enough of an institutionalist to ignore their importance: merely to want to think all round them and reckon with the imponderables that modify their action; and the other factors which no single formula can comprehend—for instance, the long-run incidence of continued large deficit-spending.'"[22]

Two days later in his reply, Keynes said: ". . . As you will have gathered the other evening, I agree with what you say about the danger of a 'school,' even when it is one's own. There is great danger in quantitative forecasts which are based exclusively on statistics relating to conditions by no means parallel. I have tried to persuade Gilbert and Humphrey and [Walter S.] Salant that they should be more cautious. I have also tried to persuade them that they have tended to neglect certain theoretical considerations which are important, in the interests of simplifying their statistical task.'"[23]

[22] Clark to Keynes, July 24, 1941. Copy in J. M. Clark Papers, Special Collections, Columbia University Libraries.

Clark in 1926 characterized his objective as seeking a ''social-institutional-dynamic economic theory'' (Clark to Seligman, April 8, Seligman Papers). This to him was the third division of the field of economics. The first two, which comprised ''value theory,'' were ''1. Static value—(or price)—economics. 2. Dynamic value—(or price)—economics.'' The last was ''Dynamic social or institutional economics or realistic economics.'' (Clark to Professor Roche-Agusoll, September 14, 1918, copy in possession of Joseph Dorfman.)

This view was in good part due to the influence of Professor Charles Horton Cooley of the University of Michigan, a sociologist trained in economics, and his foremost student in economics, Walton Hale Hamilton. Clark had great respect for the people generally considered the founders of institutional theory—Thorstein Veblen, John R. Commons and Wesley C. Mitchell, but he thought that Cooley should be added to the list. He dedicated *Alternative to Serfdom* ''To the Memory of Charles Horton Cooley.'' He wrote as late as 1953 that ''Cooley performed the great service of showing that the mechanism of the market, which dominates the values that purport to be economic, is not a mere mechanism for neutral recording of people's preferences, but a social institution with biases of its own, different from the biases of the institutions that purport to record, for example, aesthetic and ethical valuations. Policy-wise, his theories looked largely in the direction of making the market responsive to a more representative selection of the values actually prevalent in the society.'' [''Aims of Economic Life as Seen by Economists,'' 1953, reprinted in his *Economic Institutions and Human Welfare* (New York: Knopf, 1957) p. 57.]

I have stated elsewhere that: ''Were it not for the fact that only a small part of his [Cooley's] work dealt directly with economic theory in general and institutional theory in particular, he might well be considered a fourth founding father of institutional theory.'' [''The Background of Institutional Economics,'' in Dorfman *et al*, *Institutional Economics; Veblen, Commons and Mitchell Reconsidered* (Berkeley and Los Angeles: University of California Press, 1963) p. 4.]

[23] Keynes to Clark, July 26, 1941, in J. M. Clark Papers.

The Clark-Keynes episode is obliquely referred to in Herbert Stein *The Fiscal Revolution in America* (Chicago: University of Chicago Press, 1969) p. 489, ft. 23: ''When Keynes visited Washington in June 1941, on behalf of the British government, he was surprised at the extent to which the Washington economists had absorbed his thinking and the sophistication with which they applied it. At the same time he was critical of some of the procedures used, for reasons which suggested that he was still more classical than his Washington followers (John M. Keynes to Walter S. Salant, July 9, 1941, July 24, 1941, July 27, 1941 [in possession of W. S. Salant, Washington, D. C.]).''

What disturbed Clark, as becomes clear from subsequent publications that same year, was that as he saw the situation, Keynes's American disciples were not seriously concerned with the problem of inflation that the national defense effort threatened. They appeared to him to believe that there was no need to worry about it at least until full employment had been reached, a view which Keynes seemingly taught. As Clark put it in an article the following month : '' [The pressure] toward general inflation . . . finds support in economic theories of expansion through increased consumer buying power. These theories have been developed in years of depression, during which consumer buying power constituted the effective limit on physical production, and their momentum carries over into a situation in which this is, to a large extent, no longer the case. These theories tend to regard inflation as beginning when 'full employment' is reached, and to that extent are misleading in a condition in which the effective limitations are of 'bottleneck' variety.''[24]

At the end of the year in an address before the American Economic Association on the theme of post-war economic adjustment, Clark elaborated the postscript with the benefit of Keynes's reply: ''Among other things, we appear to be in for a period of government by statistics and econometrics. This is a little better than chartless fumbling with essentially quantitative problems; and it would be a great deal better if only those who use the statistics could manage to keep constantly and vividly in mind how unreliable many of the figures are, including the estimates of unemployment and the derived concept of full employment, which are so central to the present problem. There is real danger that, in certain sectors, government's immediate objective will be not a realistic picture of the lives of its citizens but figures in tables or lines on charts which leave out vital imponderables and are not even accurate as figures. One wonders if there is anyone who can use the same statistical guess for the twentieth time without being hypnotized into a belief in its reliability, even against his better judgment. If the figure fits in with his own wishful thinking, the case is often hopeless.

An enormously important element in the attitudes of government will consist of certain economic consequences of Mr. Keynes (for which Mr. Keynes himself should not be held too closely responsible).[25] These

---

[24] ''Further Remarks on Defence Financing and Inflation,'' *The Review of Economic Statistics*, August 1941, p. 108. Clark indicated in his letter to Keynes that the article was to appear ''next month'' (August).

[25] ''These consequences are the more important because certain central problems cannot be successfully handled without the use (which does not imply exclusive reliance) of the income-flow method of analysis of which Keynes's studies are the most prominent form, but presumably not the definitively final one. Keynes offers a reversed Ricardianism, of similar power and exposed to similar dangers, including that of undue dogmatism on the part of disciples.''

consequences include a propensity to intervene at any point short of something called full employment on a chart, representing a condition probably quite unattainable in actual life by the measures advocated. They also include a propensity to obliviousness of the importance of wage and price adjustments, and an insolvency-preference—to give a Keynesian name to the philosophy of unlimited deficit spending as the one tested and reliable way to secure full employment. They also include a dogma, the purport of which appears to be that deficit spending will take effect in sustaining or increasing physical output and employment, and will not tend to be dissipated in increased prices and wage rates, until 'general full employment' is reached. I hesitate to present this doctrine, feeling that I must have misinterpreted it, because as I have presented it, it is unsupported by reason and flies in the face of experience. My conjecture is that in any attempt to approach full employment by this route, the tendency of money wages and prices to swallow up a major part of the benefits would prove to be one of the chief difficulties.'"[26]

The issues that are raised in the correspondence between Clark and Keynes are still central, not only as respects the multiplier of Johannsen, Clark and Keynes, but also as respects such other vital questions as the role and character of the economic theorist and economic theory in public policy.

JOSEPH DORFMAN

Columbia University
January 1970

---

[26] ''The Theoretical Issues,'' *The American Economic Review*, March 1942, supplement no. 1, pp. 8-9.

THE
COSTS OF THE WORLD WAR
TO THE
AMERICAN PEOPLE

BY

JOHN MAURICE CLARK

PROFESSOR OF ECONOMICS IN COLUMBIA UNIVERSITY

NEW HAVEN : YALE UNIVERSITY PRESS
LONDON : HUMPHREY MILFORD : OXFORD UNIVERSITY PRESS
FOR THE CARNEGIE ENDOWMENT FOR INTERNATIONAL
PEACE : DIVISION OF ECONOMICS AND HISTORY
1931

EDITOR'S PREFACE

In the autumn of 1914, when the scientific study of the effects of war upon modern life passed suddenly from theory to history, the Division of Economics and History of the Carnegie Endowment for International Peace proposed to adjust the program of its researches to the new and altered problems which the war presented. The existing program, which had been prepared as the result of a conference of economists held at Berne in 1911, and which dealt with the facts then at hand, had just begun to show the quality of its contributions; but for many reasons it could no longer be followed out. A plan was therefore drawn up at the request of the Director of the Division in which it was proposed, by means of an historical survey, to attempt to measure the economic cost of the war and the displacement which it was causing in the processes of civilization. Such an 'Economic and Social History of the World War,' it was felt, if undertaken by men of judicial temper and adequate training, might ultimately, by reason of its scientific obligations to truth, furnish data for the forming of sound public opinion, and thus contribute fundamentally toward the aims of an institution dedicated to the cause of international peace.

The need for such an analysis, conceived and executed in the spirit of historical research, was increasingly obvious as the war developed, releasing complex forces of national life not only for the vast process of destruction, but also for the stimulation of new capacities for production. This new economic activity, which under normal conditions of peace might have been a gain to society, and the surprising capacity exhibited by the belligerent nations for enduring long and increasing loss—often while presenting the outward semblance of new prosperity—made necessary a reconsideration of the whole field of war economics. A double obligation was therefore placed upon the Division of Economics and History. It was obliged to concentrate its work upon the problem thus presented, and to study it as a whole; in other words, to apply to it the tests and disciplines of history. Just as the war itself was a single event, though penetrating by seemingly unconnected ways to the remotest parts of the world, so the analysis of it must be developed according to a plan at once all embracing and yet adjustable to the practical limits of the available data.

During the actual progress of the war, however, the execution of this plan for a scientific and objective study of war economics proved impossible in any large and authoritative way. Incidental studies and surveys of portions of the field could be made and were made under the direction of the Division, but it was impossible to undertake a general history for obvious reasons. In the first place, an authoritative statement of the resources of belligerents bore directly on the conduct of armies in the field. The result was to remove as far as possible from scrutiny those data of the economic life of the countries at war which would ordinarily, in time of peace, be readily available for investigation. In addition to this difficulty of consulting documents, collaborators competent to deal with them were for the most part called into national service in the belligerent countries and so were unavailable for research. The plan for a war history was therefore postponed until conditions should arise which would make possible not only access to essential documents, but also the coöperation of economists, historians, and men of affairs in the nations chiefly concerned, whose joint work would not be misunderstood either in purpose or in content.

Upon the termination of the war, the Endowment once more took up the original plan, and it was found with but slight modification to be applicable to the situation. Work was begun in the summer and autumn of 1919. In the first place, a final conference of the Advisory Board of Economists of the Division of Economics and History was held in Paris, which limited itself to planning a series of short preliminary surveys of special fields. Since, however, the purely preliminary character of such studies was further emphasized by the fact that they were directed more especially toward those problems which were then fronting Europe as questions of urgency, it was considered best not to treat them as part of the general survey, but rather as of contemporary value in the period of war settlement. It was clear that not only could no general program be laid down *a priori* by this conference as a whole, but that a new and more highly specialized research organization than that already existing would be needed to undertake the Economic and Social History of the War, one based more upon national grounds in the first instance, and less upon purely international coöperation. Until the facts of national history could be ascertained, it would be impossible to proceed with comparative analysis; and the different national histories were themselves of almost baffling intricacy and variety. Consequently the former European Committee of Research was dissolved, and in its place it was decided to erect an Editorial Board in each of the larger countries and to nominate special editors in the smaller ones, who should concentrate, for the present at least, upon their own economic and social war history.

The nomination of these boards by the General Editor was the first step taken in every country where the work has begun. And if any justification was needed for the plan of the Endowment, it at once may be found in the lists of those, distinguished in scholarship or in public affairs, who have accepted the responsibility of editorship. This responsibility is by no means light, involving as it does, the adaptation of the general editorial plan to the varying demands of national circumstances or methods of work; and the measure of success attained is due to the generous and earnest coöperation of those in charge in each country.

Once the editorial organization was established there could be little doubt as to the first step which should be taken in each instance toward the actual preparation of the history. Without documents there can be no history. The essential records of the war, local as well as central, have therefore to be preserved and to be made available for research in so far as is compatible with public interest. But this archival task is a very great one, belonging of right to the governments and other owners of historical sources and not to the historian or economist who proposes to use them. It is an obligation of ownership; for all such documents are public trust. The collaborators on this section of the war history, therefore, working within their own field as researchers, could only survey the situation as they found it and report their findings in the form of guides or manuals; and perhaps, by stimulating a comparison of methods, help to further the adoption of those found to be most practical. In every country, therefore, this was the point of departure for actual work; although special monographs have not been written in every instance.

The first stage of the work upon the war history, dealing with little more than the externals of archives, seemed for a while to exhaust the possibilities of research, and had the plan of the history been limited to research based upon official documents, little more could have been done, for once documents have been labelled 'secret' few government officials can be found with sufficient courage or initiative to break open the seal. Thus vast masses of source material essential for the historian were effectively placed beyond his reach, although much of it was quite harmless from any point of view. While war conditions thus continued to hamper research, and were likely to do so for many years to come, some alternative had to be found.

Fortunately, such an alternative was at hand in the narrative, amply supported by documentary evidence, of those who had played some part in the conduct of affairs during the war, or who, as close observers in privileged positions, were able to record from first or at least second-hand knowledge the economic history of different phases of the Great War, and of its effect upon society. Thus a series of monographs was planned consisting for the most part of unofficial yet authoritative statements, descriptive or historical, which may best be described as about half-way between memoirs and blue-books. These monographs make up the main body of the work assigned so far. They are not limited to contemporary war-time studies; for the economic history of the war must deal with a longer period than that of the actual fighting. It must cover the years of 'deflation' as well, at least sufficiently to secure some fairer measure of the economic displacement than is possible in purely contemporary judgments.

With this phase of the work, the editorial problems assumed a new aspect. The series of monographs had to be planned primarily with regard to the availability of contributors, rather than of source material as in the case of most histories; for the contributors themselves controlled the sources. This in turn involved a new attitude toward those two ideals which historians have sought to emphasize, consistency and objectivity. In order to bring out the chief contribution of each writer it was impossible to keep within narrowly logical outlines; facts would have to be repeated in different settings and seen from different angles, and sections included which do not lie within the strict limits of history; and absolute objectivity could not be obtained in every part. Under the stress of controversy or apology, partial views would here and there find their expression. But these views are in some instances an intrinsic part of the history itself, contemporary measurements of facts as significant as the facts with which they deal. Moreover, the work as a whole is planned to furnish its own corrective; and where it does not, others will.

In addition to the monographic treatment of source material, a number of studies by specialists are already in preparation, dealing with technical or limited subjects, historical or statistical. These monographs also partake to some extent of the nature of first-hand material, registering as they do the data of history close enough to the source to permit verification in ways impossible later. But they also belong to that constructive process by which history passes from analysis to synthesis. The process is a long and difficult one, however, and work upon it has only just begun. To quote an apt characterization, in the first stages a history like this one is only 'picking cotton.' The tangled threads of events have still to be woven into the pattern of history; and for this creative and constructive work different plans and organizations may be needed.

In a work which is the product of so complex and varied coöperation as this, it is impossible to indicate in any but a most general way the apportionment of responsibility of editors and authors for the contents of the different monographs. For the plan of the History as a whole and its effective execution the General Editor is responsible; but the arrangement of the detailed programs of study has been largely the work of the different Editorial Boards and divisional editors, who have also read the manuscripts prepared under their direction. The acceptance of a monograph in this series, however, does not commit the editors to the opinions or conclusions of the authors. Like other editors, they are asked to vouch for the scientific merit, the appropriateness, and usefulness of the volumes admitted to the series; but the authors are naturally free to make their individual contributions in their own way. In like manner, the publication of the monographs does not commit the Endowment to agreement with any specific conclusions which may be expressed therein. The responsibility of the Endowment is to History itself—an obligation not to avoid but to secure and preserve variant narratives and points of view, in so far as they are essential for the understanding of the war as a whole.

The present volume treats of a subject of outstanding importance, not only for the understanding of the economic consequences of the World War, but for the history of the succeeding years and, above all, of the present economic and financial disturbances. It is a subject which was unfortunately obscured for almost a decade by the inflation following upon the first recovery after the War. But civilization apparently learns its major lessons by catastrophe, and the present crisis brings once more to mind the significance of the earlier one. It was originally intended that Professor Clark's volume should be buttressed by detailed studies of the elements of the problem with which he deals. But for practical reasons it was necessary to abandon this plan, leaving this statement of the costs of the War to the United States as the final volume in the American Series, and placing an added burden upon the author, who has to work single-handed in a field as vast in size as it was baffling in complexity. The achievement speaks for itself.

J. T. S.

AUTHOR'S PREFACE

A STUDY of war costs is either a relatively simple matter of tabulation and fiscal allocation, or else it is an economic problem of insoluble difficulty, one which no volume can master and no series of volumes exhaust. Outlays of money are definite facts, and are nearly all recorded. There are questions of allocation, but they hardly justify very extended research. But once we go behind the money outlays and ask what they represent in the way of burdens on the whole national economy, we open up endless problems. The war debt settlements, for example, represent a fiscal asset to the United States Government, but are they an economic asset to the nation as a whole? Responsible financiers have lately been expressing the view that these debts disorganize and hamper trade to such an extent that we ourselves are among the sufferers: that they are a liability for us and not an asset. Such testimony is weighty, even though the question is not susceptible of proof: the ultimate economic effects of war lie outside the realm of absolute measurement.

In this volume, the fiscal payments are regarded as of little significance in themselves, their chief importance being as evidence of the outpouring of goods, the diversions of productive power from peace to war uses, and the sacrifices of the people, all of which constitute the more important realities behind the various sums of money which serve to call them forth. The money outlays are far from perfect measures of the underlying costs. And since measurement of a more valid sort is so often impossible, it becomes necessary to tell the main facts of the story, that the reader may judge for himself the bearing and weight of the different phases of war's impact. The writer, of course, does not forego the privilege of judgment, but he has taken some pains to exercise it conservatively.

In the early chapters the war experience is viewed as a whole and its story is told as a connected chronicle; after which particular subjects or particular sections of the evidence are taken up more intensively. The story is, of course, unfinished, since the effects of the War are yet far from spent. Some attempt has been made at prophecy with regard to the main continuing items in the account, always recognizing that such prophecy must be predicated on conditions and policies which are certain to see some change. For instance, the assumption that the present debt settlements are carried out to 1987, and that veterans' benefits continue substantially as at present: these represent rather hopes and apprehensions than expectations. As to which are hopes and which are apprehensions, the reader will, of course, form his own conclusions.

Aside from government reports, the most generally used sources of material have been the studies of the national income made by the National Bureau of Economic Research. Professor W. I. King has courteously answered various inquiries, as have the officials of the Veterans' Bureau and the Legislative Reference Service of the Library of Congress. Miss Estella B. Weeks has assisted in analyzing the material bearing on the costs of death and disability. On this subject acknowledgment is due to the studies of the economic value of human life made by Dublin and Lotka. While their results were not followed, their data were used, and a variation of their general method permitted results which could not otherwise have been reached. For these results, as for all conclusions in the study, the author is wholly responsible.

*　　　*　　　*　　　*　　　*

Events have moved so rapidly while this study has been under way that it has not proved practicable to bring every part of it completely up to date as of the moment of final completion. Parts of the work were done at the height of the post-war prosperity, in a period when approximate price stability appeared to have been reached. Other parts were done in the midst of the subsequent depression, when this temporary stability of prices had been shattered and prices were moving rapidly downward. A final revision, made in July, 1931, has taken account of some of the current developments; but it has not seemed wise further to delay publication by bringing all figures, tables, and charts down to that date. The failure to do so does not materially affect the final estimates.

J. M. C.

Westport, Connecticut
    July, 1931.

CONTENTS

INTRODUCTION

To the most casual observer of the effects of the World War one out-standing fact is evident: the greatest catastrophe of modern times touched the United States relatively lightly, compared to its effects on other countries. Whatever are the economic burdens of modern war, the recent experience of this country does not afford a sample comparable to that of the countries which felt the full impact. The aggregate costs of our participation were enormous, as was the economic effort they represented, but the burden has been borne with comparative ease—until the coming of the present depression.

This was the richest country in the world before the invasion of Belgium, and in the years from 1922 to 1929 it became vastly richer than ever before. Even now, in the midst of a depression of the first magnitude, with unemployed workers estimated at six to eight millions, we are still a rich nation, and while recovery, when it comes, may start from a level representing a temporary loss of many years' progress, and may not for a long time restore the prosperity of 1928 or 1929, there is no real doubt that this level will ultimately be regained. We are in a "new era," as every generation is, but not one of permanent stagnation.

And by contrast with the impoverished condition of our chief companions in the family of nations after the War, our post-war prosperity exhibited a discrepancy which was one of the most out-standing phenomena of the new period which the end of the War ushered in. The rebuilding of the economic life of Europe has reduced that discrepancy, but the major fact remains. And the stresses produced by it are among the causes of the present depression, and may well constitute one of the most serious problems which the War has brought to America, and to the world at large.

To enumerate a few of the evils which we escaped: our territory was not invaded and we were spared the destruction of factories, mines, homes, and of the very soil itself, which visited France and Belgium. Our loss of life due to the War has been at least 170,000 and is still growing, in addition to which the numbers receiving disability compensation at any one time have mounted to totals of over 260,000; but this represents a small burden compared to that borne by the European participants. It has not, as in Europe, so trenched

upon the best of our man-power as to leave us with a working population obviously depleted and grossly impaired and warped in age-
constitution and efficiency. We have not, like other countries, lost a
large part of that generation which should now be coming into positions of national leadership. Malnutrition was never a serious evil
with us, as it was in Germany; and the interruption of normal education for those just coming into manhood was shorter and less serious than with either our Allies or our adversaries. Losses of capital
and other permanent wealth have not been such as to leave the productive system in seriously weakened condition and thus to aggra-
vate the burden of making the losses good by reducing the productive power available for the purpose. Instead, we were apparently in
a condition in which increased demands of this sort could be met by
increased production, with a wide margin to spare for meeting the
more pressing needs of Europe on a credit basis.

The War found us a debtor nation, and left us a creditor nation
on a huge scale, and in an economic position which has rapidly increased our credit margin until it almost rivals that of Great Britain. Our aftermath of taxation has not remotely approached the
weight—which we would consider intolerable and crippling—of that
borne by the chief countries of Europe. Our economic demobilization involved one sharp depression in 1921 and some continuing unemployment, but nothing approaching the problem of England. In
the present depression we suffer in common with the whole industrial
world. We have our legacy of handicapped industries, especially
agriculture, but, again, no such crippling illnesses as that of the
British coal industry. The War has brought disturbances in the distribution of American wealth, making some richer and others poorer,
but no such phenomenon as the utter ruin of a large section of the
"middle class."

So easily was the burden borne, and so great was our subsequent
prosperity, that intelligent observers, even on this side of the water,
were led to the conclusion that the United States "made a profit out
of the War": that when the stimulus to trade and industry was
taken into account the ultimate net costs to the country would
prove to be less than nothing. Or it has been urged that the War was
fought with no demonstrable decrease in consumption at the time,
and no more than a temporary setback in our subsequent power to

produce; a claim which gives ground for the view that the War called forth its own means of support. Such a view, of course, looks at the aggregate social income of the country rather than at the financial outlays of the Government; and implies that this social income was somehow increased sufficiently to offset the social wastage of which the financial outlays are the most obvious economic index. These contentions must be kept in mind in our attempts to analyze the effects of the War on the country's economy.

In refutation of these claims, it was urged by President Coolidge himself that we could not possibly have made a profit out of a war the cost of which to the Federal Government had been officially estimated as thirty-six and one-half billion dollars to November, 1928, with a sequel of continuing burdens which he considered likely to raise the total to nearly one hundred billions before the last war bond should be redeemed and the last veteran or dependent compensated.[1] This contention may seem self-evident, but it must in turn be subjected to scrutiny. Social-economic costs may be greater, or less, than is indicated by governmental fiscal outlays. For the present, and for illustrative purposes only, we may note that the fiscal estimates include both principal and interest on the war debt. This is legitimate in the sense that the principal was not, in the main, spent for lucrative properties like railroads or factories, which could themselves sustain the interest charges; on the contrary both principal and interest must ultimately be paid out of the Government's general sources of revenue. Both appear in the volume of fiscal transfers of funds which the Government must carry out.

But such fiscal transfers are not the whole story. If they were, why should not the principal appear twice: once when the loans were made and the money spent, and once when the bonds are redeemed? Socially speaking, the outlay was made when the principal of the loans was spent for goods and services to be devoted to the uses of war. The immediate funds were furnished by lenders, while the ultimate burden rests on taxpayers, in the form of an obligation to pay

---

[1] See his armistice-day speech, reported in the daily press of November 12, 1928. The estimate of cost to date was based on the Treasury Department's published allocation to June 30, 1927 (contained in the Secretary's *Annual Report*, pp. 89, 642–647), amounting to $35,119,622,144, with additions for the subsequent period.

principal and interest in the future. And the discounted worth of this obligation at the time of raising the loan was approximately equal to the amount advanced and spent. Either the actual amount borrowed, or the discounted worth of repayments, may be taken to represent the social outlay made at the time of the War, but hardly both. The subsequent transfer of funds from taxpayers to bond-holders is not in itself a social outlay. The country as a whole is not made poorer by the full amount of these transfers. They involve bur-dens beyond the costs of collection and fiscal administration, and the ultimate incidence of the whole process of transfer is a matter for some conjecture; but the social costs of the outlays made from loans do not include the full amount of interest or anything approaching it.

This is but an instance of the type of problem met in undertaking to probe beneath the financial outlays to the goods and services they represent; and beneath these in turn to the efforts and sacrifices in which the ultimate incidence is to be found. And there is another dif-ficulty even more baffling. The effects of our own belligerency cannot be fully separated from the effects resulting from the existence of a war in Europe, whether we entered it or not. We profited greatly as a neutral country, and after the War we profited by serving the needs of Europe's reconstruction. But Europe would have needed reconstruction whether we entered the War or not; and we must try, at least, to distinguish gains due to other people's wars from the costs of our own. How much of our post-war prosperity was due to Europe's needs and how much to the impetus of our own reconstruc-tion demands and activities? No one can say. The profits of neu-trality were swallowed up in the costs of belligerency. As for our average state of post-war prosperity, including the two major de-pressions of 1921 and 1930, it has been above the pre-war level, but not above a prolongation of the pre-war upward trend. The best that can be said is that, if the efforts and sacrifices of the actual war period are forgotten, our subsequent state may not have been demon-strably worse than it would have been if the War had never occurred. Even this is doubtful, but if it should be true, the United States is the only one among the belligerents seriously engaged which could make even such a qualifiedly favorable showing.

But the returns are not all in. Death and disability involve continuing burdens, the total amounts of which are uncertain; and the effects of the legacy of international debt settlements are much more conjectural. But greater than both these, we are now, over twelve years after the signing of the armistice, in the depths of a major depression which is almost certainly, to some unmeasurable extent, not only a sequel of the War but a result of the chain of consequences which trace their origin back to it. Moreover, this depression involves a shrinkage of income, measured from the peak reached in 1929, which is quite certain to bulk larger, before recovery is fully achieved, than the whole immediate cost of the War itself to the national economy. If the previous post-war prosperity had canceled the cost of the War, the present depression may more than cancel the cancellation. This can, of course, never be definitely known, since the normal level with which to compare our actual post-war record must remain in the conjectural realm of what might have been had the world remained at peace. This is an uncertainty which cannot be fully resolved.

Similarly as to Europe; its economic recovery had proceeded to a point at which something like a reasonably healthy post-war normal seemed to be in process of emerging, when the world-wide depression arrived, not only to set back the development, but to cast doubt on the soundness of the basis on which it was built. Has the attempt to rebuild industrial structures, in which each nation sought to develop similar basic industries, resulted in duplications and an excess of facilities which must fail to find full outlets and thus partially defeat the end in view? Must the basis of development be revised before stability can be reached?

In this country, will a revival quickly bring us to a resumption of the upward trend which marked the years 1922–29, or was that degree of prosperity based on temporary conditions which will not return? Did our recovery acquire a cumulative momentum that carried it to an abnormal height? Was this effect strengthened by distress-buying and borrowing from Europe which could not permanently continue? Has our post-war economy been built upon a basis which will have to be revised downward before we can resume development on a sound and normal basis? The overwhelming probability seems to be that this is the case. If so, will the ultimate development be slower than that of the past decade, and what are the adjustments that must be made to absorb our unemployed population?

Evidently, the balance sheet of the War cannot be drawn up with confident accuracy. Nevertheless, a reasonable approximation may be made to the more obvious and direct burdens.

CHAPTER I

THE UNITED STATES IN 1913–14

To measure exactly the economic effects of the War on this country, it would be necessary to know what the course of its economic life would have been if the War had not occurred. This can, of course, be only conjectured, or at best roughly approximated; but a fair basis may be furnished by a picture of conditions as they were at the outbreak of hostilities, and of the main trends then prevailing.

This country was, as is well known, the richest in the world, both in aggregate and *per capita* wealth and production. Our higher scale of money prices exaggerated this difference, and the differing content of national budgets of production and consumption makes it impossible to measure with scientific precision, but of its existence there can be no doubt. We were also the world's greatest debtor nation. It was estimated by Sir George Paish that in 1910 Europe held approximately six billion dollars of American securities, on which the annual return due from us amounted to $225,000,000.[1] A much smaller estimate, of $2,400,000,000 at market values, was made by L. F. Loree as of July, 1914.[2] While we also had some investments in other countries, Professor H. L. Bogart estimated our yearly net debit on this score, in the years immediately preceding the War, at $175,000,000.[3] This would seem to indicate not quite four billions of net debt. He also estimated our total debit on the "invisible items" in the international balance at some $600,000,000 in good years and some $500,000,000 in poor years.[4] As this was very nearly the amount of our "favorable balance" of commodity trade for these years (as may be seen from the accompanying table) the conclusion is that we were holding our own, and neither increasing nor decreasing our net debt to foreign countries.

[1] *Report of National Monetary Commission*, XX, 169.

[2] *See* Noyes, *The War Period of American Finance*, p. 60, also *Commercial and Financial Chronicle*, July 3, 1915.

[3] *War Costs and Their Financing*, 1921, p. 72.

[4] *Ibid.*, also p. 14.

Merchandise Exports and Imports, 1910 to 1914 (in millions).[5]

	1910	1911	1912	1913	1914
Total exports	$1,744.9	$2,049.3	$2,204.3	$2,465.8	$2,364.5
Total imports	1,556.9	1,527.2	1,653.2	1,813.0	1,893.9
Excess of exports	188.0	522.1	551.1	652.8	470.6

Our national wealth was estimated by the Census Bureau as 188 billions for 1912, and was growing at a rate which would indicate 205 to 210 billions for 1914. The national income has been estimated by the National Bureau of Economic Research by two methods: by sources and by personal receipts. For 1913 the first method showed 35½ billions, or $367 *per capita*, while the second method showed 33½ billions, or $344 *per capita*. The two methods of estimate happened to show their largest discrepancy for this particular year.[6] One result of this fact is that the former estimate shows a definite upward trend of income *per capita* for the pre-war years (in dollars of 1913) while the latter estimate shows none. The following table shows the figures for the entire period covered by the Bureau's study.[7]

	Estimate by sources of income		Estimate by incomes received	
Year	Total income, 1913 dollars (billions)	Per capita income, 1913 dollars	Total income, 1913 dollars (billions)	Per capita income, 1913 dollars
1909	$30.1	$333	...	...
1910	32.5	357	$31.8	$345
1911	31.7	338	31.7	338
1912	33.7	354	32.7	343
1913	35.6	367	33.5	344
1914	33.6	339	32.5	328
1915	35.3	352	35.1	349
1916	41.3	406	40.2	395
1917	41.9	407	39.7	385
1918	39.1	375	38.6	371
1919	...	...	37.6	359

These figures, together with a later study from the same source, afford perhaps the best available testimony as to the total income out of which the costs of the War had to be paid, though they will be

[5] From Bogart, *War Costs and Their Financing*, p. 72.

[6] *Income in the United States*, II, 16, 234, 338. The year 1917 shows a slightly larger absolute discrepancy (measured in dollars of 1913) but a smaller one in percentage terms, as the absolute totals are larger.

[7] Adapted from tables in *Income in the United States*, II, 16, 234, 337, 338.

subject to certain adjustments in bringing them to include the precise materials relevant to this particular purpose. As they stand, they show a large increase in income during the war period, sufficient on its face to neutralize a major part of the costs of the War to the United States, if the period of our neutrality is included and the advances to our Allies deducted. The necessary adjustments will affect the amount of this war surplus, but will not falsify the preliminary conclusion just indicated. Further testimony is afforded by indexes of physical production, which for various reasons fluctuate more than the figures of income, but show very similar general trends. It appears that an appreciable part of the cost of the War to the country as a whole was borne out of increased production and real income during the war period. Including the profitable period of our neutrality, this compensation might amount to more than one-third of the immediate war costs. Omitting the profits of neutrality, not more than one-fourth of the immediate war costs would be offset.

Of the national income a very considerable part is saved, and a corresponding part of production devoted to increase in productive equipment. Data on consumption and savings are scant, and conclusions must needs be tentative, but an approximation can be made. The Census Bureau figures show an increase in national wealth, exclusive of land, of about forty-eight billions for the eight years from 1904 to 1912,[8] or about six billions per year, including increases in items of "consumers' wealth" and increases due to the upward course of prices. Allowance for this last factor is uncertain, owing to varying methods of accounting. But we may take $4\frac{1}{2}$ billions per year at 1912 prices, as the lowest possible estimate of the increase in physical wealth other than land. The highest possible estimate would be close to the uncorrected figure of six billions.

Another estimate, by David Friday, places the excess of production over consumption for 1913 at 6.5 billions.[9] His estimate of agricultural savings, however, is half a billion in excess of that of the National Bureau of Economic Research. And the item of securities issued is probably in need of scaling down on account of the practice of issuing both stocks and bonds at a discount. Furthermore,

[8] *Wealth, Debt, and Taxation*, V, I, 21. The deduction for land is made by Bogart, *op. cit.*, p. 77.

[9] "War and the Supply of Capital," *Amer. Econ. Rev. Sup.*, March, 1919, p. 80.

as corporate surplus is partly invested in securities, there is some probable duplication involved in adding these two items together. The National Bureau's estimate of total business savings (including agricultural) is 2.4 billions, or 1.5 billions less than Friday's estimate of corresponding items.[10] This would indicate a reduction of Friday's total figure to 5 billions, which seems a more probable amount. Corroborative evidence is found in the fact that Friday's figures for the whole period 1913–18 are very much higher than those of the National Bureau for corresponding items, reaching in 1918 the seemingly incredible total of 22 billions.[11]

Of the total income of 35,580 millions in 1913, 15,778 millions was estimated as the share of "entrepreneurs, investors and other owners of property used in industry," of which 5,101 millions was in agriculture. A major part of these 5,101 millions, and a substantial portion of the remaining 10,677 millions, is, of course, to be classed as "labor income." Total disbursements to employees (including pensions, compensation for injuries, and payment for contract work) amounted to 19,801 millions.[12] Of the income of entrepreneurs and property owners we may roughly estimate that one-fourth or more was saved, and of other income one-tenth or less; though such an allocation is necessarily arbitrary for persons receiving both labor and property income. In manufacturing, employees received 74.5 per cent of net value product: the percentage showing a slight upward tendency for the five pre-war years. Average compensation per employee was $705: this amount showing a very strong upward tendency for the same five years, even after making allowance for increased prices.[13]

In agriculture, employees as such received only 13.4 per cent of net value product, or $328 per employee. At a 5 per cent interest rate, 38.4 per cent was assignable to property, while the remainder constituted a "reward for management and labor" of $444 per farmer.[14] The proper rate of property return to charge against farm production is probably less than 5 per cent, since the present

---

[10] *Income in the United States,* Table 20H, p. 246.

[11] Friday, *op. cit.* The figure includes five billions of war taxes paid or reserved.

[12] *Income in the United States,* p. 243, also Table 20D, p. 240.

[13] *Ibid.,* pp. 91, 98. Does not include hand trades.

[14] *Ibid.,* pp. 58, 63.

worth of farm land capitalizes expected future increases in value as well as current yield from production. Land is often bought at prices which capitalize the current yield at more nearly 3 per cent than 5 per cent. And current yield and "unearned increment" together have, over a period of fairly consistent upward trends of values, typically grouped around 6 per cent.[15] The substitution of 4 per cent for 5 per cent in calculating the reward chargeable to property would raise the farmer's income from labor and management to $515 per farmer. We must also remember that the farmer's dollar will buy somewhat more goods than that of the average townsman engaged in manufactures, on account of the lower average prices prevailing in rural districts. But no allowances can make agriculture seem as well rewarded as other typical branches of industry.

In mines, quarries, and oil wells, employees received 73.4 per cent of net value product, with an average compensation of $649 per employee. Coal mining accounted for nearly two-thirds of the employees in this group.[16] In railroad transportation, employees received 65 per cent of net value product, or $781 per employee.[17] In street and electric railways, employees received 52.7 per cent of value product, or $731 per employee.[18] In private electric light and power companies, employees received 35.7 per cent of value product, or $751 per employee.[19] This includes hydroelectric properties, where capital per employee is greater than in any other important branch of industry.

All in all, 27,391,000 employees received 19,801 million dollars, or $723 per employee; 6,400 farm entrepreneurs received 5,101 million dollars, or $797 per entrepreneur; and 3,310 other entrepreneurs (persons or organizations) received 10,677 million dollars, or $3,226 per entrepreneur.[20] This was in a year of business "prosperity." And compensation per employee was trending definitely upward, both in money and in purchasing power.[21]

[15] *See* Chambers, "The Relation of Farm Land Income to Farm Land Value," *Amer. Econ. Rev.*, XIV, 673–698, December, 1924.

[16] *Income in the United States*, pp. 74–75.

[17] *Ibid.*, pp. 129, 131.   [18] *Ibid.*, pp. 151, 153.   [19] *Ibid.*, pp. 165, 166.

[20] Calculated from tables in *ibid.*, pp. 33, 38, 240, 243.

[21] Two indications of this trend are given in the accompanying table. One is total compensation (including pensions, etc.) per employee attached to industries (including those not currently employed), calculated from King's

The reader will, of course, remember that these figures are in dollars of far greater purchasing power than the war-time dollar possessed, and appreciably greater than the present dollar possesses. In making allowance for the war-time revolution in the value of the money unit, it has become customary to translate later values into dollars having the purchasing power of these pre-war, 1913 dollars. It would, of course, be equally logical to translate into post-war dollars, and for some purposes this is the significant or necessary procedure. For instance, in estimating the fiscal effects of war borrowing, it will be necessary to compare the sums borrowed with the sums to be repaid in dollars of equal purchasing power: that is, to measure the purchasing power of the war loans in terms of *post-war* dollars.

Another major feature of any economy consists of the movements going on within it. This includes regional shiftings, and the movement as between urban and rural occupations. More especially, perhaps, it includes the relative growth or decline of different branches of production; and of the surpluses available for export or the shortages that have to be made good by imports. As is well known, the pre-war United States was becoming more and more urban, and the War greatly increased this tendency. The center of population was still moving westward, though at a decreasing rate, and in this respect the War had a reverse influence, bringing many people to work in the centers of production near the Atlantic seaboard. It also greatly stimulated the northern migration of the negro. Our greatest expansion was in manufacturing and mercantile pursuits, while in agriculture physical product was barely more than keeping pace

figures. The other is Douglas' index of real earnings of employees, from a manuscript revision of the table published in *Amer. Econ. Rev. Sup.*, March, 1926, p. 33.

	1909	1910	1911	1912	1913	1914	1915	1916	1917	1918
Compensation per employee in 1913 dollars	657	672	658	697	723	667	678	642.5	744	682
Real earnings of employees (1890–99 = 100)		103	104	100	102	104	104	106	109	105	108

with population.[22] The War vastly stimulated the growth of manufactures, while physical product in agriculture fell below its trend-
line in 1916–19.[23] We were a country, in general, of declining ex-
portable surpluses of agricultural products, with the outstanding
exception of cotton, which furnished the largest single item of agricultural exports.

In the twenty years preceding 1913, the production of pig iron
had more than quadrupled, that of steel had grown nearly eightfold,
and that of tin plates, fifteen-fold. Production of copper had increased 270 per cent, of lead 150 per cent, of cement 1000 per cent,
of coal 212 per cent, of petroleum 400 per cent. During the same
period, production of wheat had fluctuated about an upward trend
representing an increase of nearly 53 per cent in twenty years,
most of which, however, came in the middle decade of the period.[24]
Corn increased about 50 per cent; wool remained stationary. Swine
on farms increased 32 per cent, cattle increased 8 per cent, but were
actually decreasing at the end of the period. Sugar production increased between three and fourfold, and rice even more, while cotton
increased 71 per cent from the period 1890–94 to 1910–14.

In terms of value of products, farming and manufactures grew
about equally during the period from 1899 or 1900 to 1913; gross
value of farm products being almost equal to value of manufactured
products less materials, and both increasing something more than
75 per cent, with the qualification that the successive census reports
for farming are not strictly comparable. The more discriminating
analysis of the National Bureau of Economic Research shows, for
1909–13, an increase in net value product for all industries of 24
per cent; for factory manufactures 31 per cent, for agriculture 25
per cent, for mining 32 per cent, for railways 18 per cent, for construction a decrease of 18 per cent, and for unclassified industries an
increase of 28 per cent.[25] However, prices of agricultural products

[22] *See* E. E. Day's index of physical production, *Rev. of Econ. Statistics,*
September–January, 1921, p. 11.

[23] *Ibid.*

[24] Average annual production by successive five-year periods, 1890–1914,
inclusive, in millions of bushels, was as follows: 477, 529, 626, 693, 728.
The increases from each five-year period to the next were: 53, 97, 67, 35.
The data on all these articles are taken from the *Statistical Abstract of the
United States, 1918,* Table 474.

[25] *Income in the United States,* p. 244. In net value product as estimated

had risen more than those of manufactures, and Day's index of physical production shows for these same years an increase of 14.5 per cent for manufactures, and 3.4 per cent for agriculture. From 1899 to 1913, Day's trend-line for agriculture rose about 30 per cent, while manufacturing (for which no trend-line is constructed) rose 87 per cent, mining 127 per cent, and the combined index (weighted in terms of values), 63 per cent.[26] Our increase in physical products *per capita* was occurring entirely in other branches than agriculture.

In the field of export trade, agricultural products had averaged more than 75 per cent of our domestic exports from before the Civil War down to 1892. From then on they declined to 46.3 per cent in 1913. Foodstuffs accounted for 20.72 per cent of our exports, as

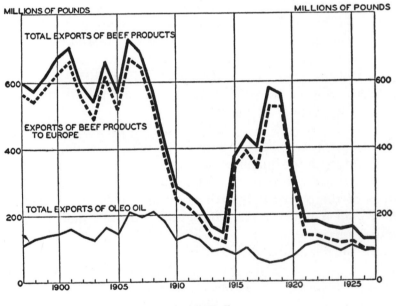

CHART I.

Exports of Beef Products from the United States, 1897–1927.

by the National Bureau, agriculture ranged from 72 per cent to 85 per cent of factory manufactures during this period.

[26] See *Rev. of Econ. Statistics,* September–January, 1921. W. F. Maxwell's revision of this index tells a similar general story, with differences of detail. *See* later volumes of same journal.

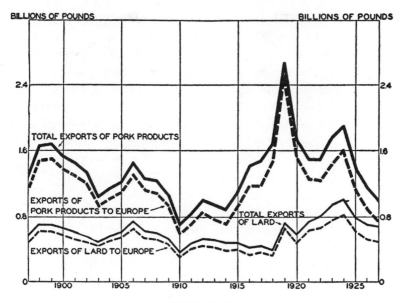

CHART II.

Exports of Pork Products from the United States, 1897–1927.

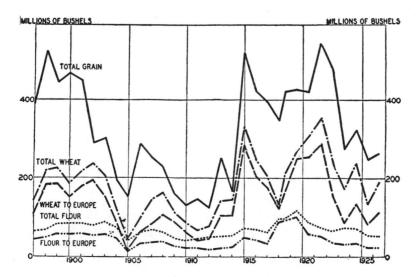

CHART III.

*Exports of Grain, Wheat (Including Flour), and Flour
from the United States, 1897–1927.*

against more than twice that percentage twenty years earlier. Manufactures accounted for 48.8 per cent of our exports (two-thirds of which was classed as ready for consumption) as against 21.57 per cent in 1893. The course of exports of beef, pork, and grain products is indicated in the accompanying charts.[27] Exports of cotton had long maintained a rate of about two-thirds of our total crop.

One further feature of major importance to American economic life is immigration. This had grown enormously during the fifteen years preceding the World War; and had also been changing radically in racial character. From 230,000 in 1897 and 229,000 in 1898, total immigration had grown to 1,198,000 in 1913 and 1,218,000 in 1914.[28] Net arrivals as estimated by Jerome grew from 308,000 in 1900 to 815,000 in 1913 and 769,000 in 1914.[29] Aside from Oriental exclusion, restriction still remained on a basis of personal fitness which was not calculated to exclude large numbers. The tightening of regulations and of their enforcement had resulted in a great increase in debarments and deportations, yet these amounted to only 23,391 in 1913. While the number prevented from coming was undoubtedly greater than this, our policy clearly had no great effect in reducing numbers of arrivals from Europe, and was limited to the exclusion of Asiatics and of certain obvious classes of undesirables.

The much-discussed change in the racial composition of this stream had for some time been a source of serious anxiety, though not all students admitted that it was an evil. Prior to 1880 almost the entire European immigration came from the United Kingdom, Germany, France, Belgium, Holland, Switzerland, Denmark, Sweden, and Norway; and in the decade 1880–90, more than four-fifths still came from these countries. Since 1900, more than three-fourths of the Europeans have come from Austria-Hungary, Russia, Balkan and Mediterranean countries, and Portugal. This situation might have led to some action, even without the War, but the discussion would probably have dragged its tedious way through much

[27] Reproduced by permission from E. G. Nourse, "The Trend of Agricultural Exports," *Journal of Pol. Econ.*, XXXVI, 333, 334, 337. June, 1928.

[28] Year ending June 30, in each case. 1914 is thus wholly a pre-war year. From *Statistical Abstract, 1918*.

[29] See *Migration and Business Cycles*, Nat. Bur. of Econ. Research, 1926, p. 50.

iteration of the old formulas to some half-hearted compromise. Instead, we were precipitated into drastic action by a sudden emergency. While the country was still wondering whether it could successfully reabsorb between three and four million service men and remobilize its entire economic life, it was threatened with an added flood of unknown and probably unheard-of size from an impoverished Europe. The result was the introduction of the quota system.

The bare bones of statistical tables, necessary as they are to a survey of the present sort, tell only part of the story of a nation's economic condition. Some mention at least must be made of financial conditions and institutions, of education, of the state of the labor movement and of economic radicalism, of business organization and the relation of government to business, and of prevalent attitudes and issues bearing on international economics.

In the last-named field, American attention had been largely focused on immigration and the tariff. Our most active issues in 1913 were those growing out of our economic penetration of Latin America: chiefly Mexico. The Wilson administration had taken the position that American dollars invested in turbulent countries must take the chances inseparable from such conditions; but was ultimately driven to the occupation of Vera Cruz and, after Villa's invasion of American soil, to General Pershing's abortive pursuit-expedition. The situation well illustrated the virtual impossibility of avoiding governmental entanglements consequent on the outward movement of capital and enterprise; and the feelings it awakens in those who, rightly or wrongly, feel themselves exploited and economically subjugated.

In this situation, conscious rivalry with Europe had, on the whole, played a minor part. Our economic penetration had not gone to the extent of seriously cramping the scope of investors and traders from across the Atlantic. And the complications arising from the export of capital to Europe itself, and economic penetration there on a large scale—these were still in the future.

Relations of government to business were marked, in the railroad field, by the passage of the Federal Valuation Act in 1913, and by the first real setback in the long upward climb of the rate of return on railroad capital. At the same time regulation was for the first time having a material effect in limiting the general level of railroad earnings, using as an instrument the power to suspend advances in rates which was granted in the Mann-Elkins Act of 1910. The Northern Securities case and the Union Pacific–Southern Pacific dissolution emphasized the fact that the Government stood firmly against combinations of competing systems. This policy has been reversed since the War, but there is no proof that the War was responsible for the reversal.

In the trust field, the Standard Oil and Tobacco Trust dissolutions had placed the more obvious emphasis on the breaking up of combinations, while at the same time the enunciation of the "rule of reason" prepared the way for a shift of emphasis. The real significance of these decisions lay not only in the plans for dissolution, but quite as much in the rules laid down or implied for the control of subsequent competitive behavior. The Clayton Act and Federal Trade Commission Act, both of 1914, greatly strengthened this phase of regulation, which was thus destined to live through its formative period under the disturbed conditions of foreign war. In the period of profitable neutrality, hostility to combinations was certainly not relaxed, and the feeling of the futility of dissolution proceedings led numbers to the conclusion that we had best permit combination and secure the economies it makes possible, while regulating prices and quality of product as those of railroads and public utilities were already being regulated. This proposal rested on two illusions: first, that we had demonstrated our ability to control the level of rates satisfactorily in the railroad and public utility fields, and, second, that similar regulation in the field of general industry and commerce would present no greater difficulties. The post-war crisis in public utility regulation dissipated the first of these illusions, and the war-time experience of general price-regulation may fairly be said to have dissipated the second. At any rate, the movement based on them has apparently spent its force and the "rule of reason," with administrative formulation and codification, is the keynote of the present trust policy. The War has perhaps contributed to a growingly tolerant attitude toward big business.

Our system made cartels impossible, and also made it unsafe for combinations in any form to control more than about half of the domestic market in any branch of production. It thus had substantially the effect of Bryan's proposed 50 per cent limit on size, but without the rigidity of a statutory formula. While this prevented trades from being so organized that they could be mobilized as units in case of war, a fairly effective organ of common action in certain directions was growing up in the trade association, which was becoming more and more nearly universal.

In the techniques of industry, "scientific management," as it was then called, was a young and vigorous movement with some remarkable achievements to its credit. Engineers and technically trained men were becoming more and more important in the guidance of policies of production; and one of their characteristic policies—standardization—had received a considerable amount of attention in certain fields, and was ready for the enormous development which the War brought with it. Psychologists had made beginnings with the techniques of testing vocational aptitudes, and the more academic "intelligence tests" had been developed to a point where their usefulness was readily conceded, despite shortcomings.

The American business executive, viewed as an asset toward the conduct of a war, had strongly marked characteristics. Infinite as are the varieties of type in any such group, there stand out as prevalent qualities energy, initiative, willingness to assume responsibility, and a readiness to demand results from himself and others with relatively little regard to obstacles. One prevalent phase of the ideal executive is hit off in the phrase: "go-getter." This expresses aptly the strong and weak points of the individualistic type of executive from the standpoint of mobilizing a nation's economic resources for the common task of war. He will drive, but will he coördinate? He will see that his unit produces results. The task consists of two parts: getting materials, workers, and other means of achievement, and organizing them after they are secured. In the latter task the insistence on results is clearly a force for efficiency. But in the realm of struggle to acquire the means of achievement, it may lead one unit to lock up for its own use more than its present needs, thus assuring its future; while more important needs may thereby be deprived of things urgently necessary through coming into the market a trifle later or having a slightly less efficient go-getter to represent them. Where collective efficiency required coördination, the go-getter had to be kept in check. Fortunately, the American executive is genuinely adaptable under recognized necessity, and he has also developed a deal of the spirit of team-work, even though this may be a recent affair and less ingrained than some of his older qualities.

Organized labor in the United States was strong in many fields, though only a trifle over 10 per cent of all employees were members of unions.[30] The dominant organization, the American Federation of Labor under the long-continued leadership of Samuel Gompers, was maintaining, as it still does, its traditional policy of reliance on collective bargaining, and the seeking of political reforms through pressure on the existing parties rather than through the formation of a separate party of labor. Being organized on a craft basis, and strongest in the highly skilled fields, this organization appeared aristocratic to the masses of unskilled labor. This feeling found expression in the I.W.W., with its emphasis on inclusiveness, on units taking in all the employees in a given industry, and on the tactics of revolutionary syndicalism. This was regarded as the danger spot in the labor movement, from the standpoint of loyal support of public needs in case of war.

"Socialism" in this country was mainly of the political type which would work through the ballot and the existing frame of government. It was strong in its denunciations of war as a capitalistic enterprise, and in its assertions that the workers on both sides were the natural allies against the capitalists of both sides, rather than workers and capitalists of any nation against workers and capitalists of any other. On this basis it was proposed that the workers refuse to support any war. Yet much as the Socialist hated democratic-individualistic industrialism, there were grounds for suspecting that he hated dynastic militarism more. And his temper was not prevailingly marked by that recklessness in action (as distinct from doctrine) necessary to oppose such a *fait accompli* as war always presents by the time the public is asked to support it. He might have been provoked beyond endurance by any serious evidence that his own country was being steered by its capitalists along paths of profit-seeking aggrandizement. But he would not condemn without a hearing and his mind was open to assurances of reasonable good faith.

Before the War, this country was already marked by an enormous quantitative growth of higher education. The period of our actual belligerency naturally brought heavy reductions in enrolment; but

[30] *See* Wolman, *Growth of American Trade Unions,* Nat. Bur. of Econ. Research, 1924, p. 33 and Tables 14–19, 25–27. Cf. *Income in the United States,* p. 38, for total number of employees.

this was a temporary setback and the growth has since gone on, to figures which dwarf all pre-war records.

In the field of finance, two of our greatest measures of preparedness were the Federal Income Tax and the Federal Reserve System. The former furnished the nucleus of our greatest single source of war revenue; while without the latter, our banking system could hardly have withstood the strains put upon it. Ever since the panic of 1907 taught us that a change was imperative, systematic studies had been going on, which culminated in the passage of the Federal Reserve Act and the organization of the system, just too late to meet the first shock of August, 1914. This was tided over with the help of emergency notes issued under the stop-gap Aldrich-Vreeland Act, and of a hundred-million-dollar gold pool formed among the New York bankers. Thus the system had to "find itself" under thoroughly abnormal conditions, but whether this was a bane or a blessing in disguise would not be easy to say. At least there was a respite during 1915 and 1916, in which a background of policies could be worked out—or at least of operating habits—before the supreme strain that came with 1917.

Such, in broad outlines, was the United States at the outbreak of the World War—rich, strong, heterogeneous, and unorganized in a national sense. A country preoccupied with internal conflicts of interest, internationally unsophisticated and inclined to make a merit of that isolation for which sole credit belongs to the Designer of the Atlantic Ocean. A country with enormous energy at command and little disposition to submit to discipline or central control in the use of it. A country whose best leaders were in business and had the business stamp upon them, rather despising the morale of the public official, yet destined to play that rôle themselves through nearly three years of conflict. A country which did not know how it would act in the unthinkable contingency of finding itself actually engaged in sending all the armed force at its command to fight in a European war on European soil. And a country with no sure willingness to bear the enormous economic sacrifices which such a war seemed certain to entail.

CHAPTER II

THE PERIOD OF NEUTRALITY

THE outbreak of hostilities found the United States in a condition of mildly depressed business, following the fairly prosperous year of 1913. The immediate effect was a violent deepening of the depression, continuing through the remaining five months of the year. This was due mainly to the cutting off of normal European markets for our goods, and to the fact that the special war demands of belligerent Europe did not at once materialize nor rapidly grow to sufficient proportions to compensate for the loss of peace-time markets. The War also opened to us some markets formerly held by belligerents who could not now supply them; but this compensation also failed to take effect at once. The most immediate effect of all was a violent financial crisis caused by the rush of European creditors to realize on notes, bills, and securities: in short, to turn all possible assets into cash.

The second and more important effect was an enormous increase in American exports, bringing about a boom which was intense, though far from universal in its effects on different branches of production. These exports were paid for by the return of American securities held abroad, by new loans to the belligerent countries from private American sources, and by large imports of gold. The net result was that the United States entered the War no longer a debtor nation—its net indebtedness having been approximately wiped out during the period of neutrality[1]—in possession of an abnormally large supply of specie, and with many industries serving the needs of war already equipped with largely increased productive capacity.

The details of the financial crisis are hardly essential to the present study. It is a commonplace of our credit economy that a sudden insistence of all creditors on realizing their claims must defeat itself and force the whole system into temporary insolvency. While Europe did not hold sufficient quick claims against American business in general to inflict this fate on us directly, the danger was hardly less serious. The volume of quick claims threatened to force suspen-

[1] *See* estimate, pp. 24, 25–26 footnote, below.

sion of specie payment by the New York banks (not yet organized under the Federal Reserve Act), while the wholesale throwing overboard of American securities by European holders bade fair to create price quotations so low as to render technically unsound the collateral on which a vast structure of loans was based. The closing of the New York stock exchange, following similar action abroad, prevented the official quoting of such prices, though it did not wholly stop the sale of securities.

The threat to maintenance of domestic specie payment (or rather currency payment) was met with the help of the issue of Aldrich-Vreeland emergency currency to a maximum amount of 364 millions. There remained the fact that this country, having sent abroad 117 millions of gold in the first seven months of 1914, was faced with immediately maturing foreign obligations estimated at more than half the entire gold reserve of the reporting banks.[2] Obligations maturing January 1 amounted to some 530 millions, including an 80-million-dollar loan of the city of New York. This crisis was met by a show of willingness to export gold, and an actual exportation of nearly 105 millions, most of which went to Canada, where the Bank of England had established a branch. The net loss of gold in the last five months of the year was $81,720,000, a small return flow having begun before the end of the year. The exchanges, which had gone strongly against this country in the first rush of liquidation, had come back to normal before the end of the year, and subsequently ran in our favor. The remainder of the period of neutrality brought the United States a net gain in gold of approximately one billion dollars. The avoidance of an actual default in the critical first period no doubt helped New York greatly toward assuming its indicated rôle of center to which foreign countries looked for loans; though the permanent enabling circumstance was the enormous export trade balance which soon set in and continued throughout the War.

In the general business field, the first effects of the War were no less disturbing than in the realm of finance. A record crop of wheat had just begun to move, and the cutting off of normal markets produced a fall in the price, instead of the rise which war regularly brings with it. The state of cotton was worse, as the 1914 crop was also the largest we had ever raised, and the countries which had

[2] See Noyes, *The War Period of American Finance*, pp. 82–85, also *Statements of Comptroller of the Currency*, Treasury Report, 1914, p. 539.

taken three-fourths of our previous exports were now at war.[3] The price fell from $62.50 per bale at the end of July to $36.25 in December, and the Government was driven to special measures of treasury credit relief, while citizens at large were urged to "buy a bale of cotton" as a public-spirited measure of support. Prices of other commodities fell—steel and steel manufactures, copper, meats, and oil. Steel production fell to 30 per cent of capacity, and stood at 50 per cent in January, 1915, while the United States Steel Corporation was not earning the interest on its bonds. Unemployment continued a problem through the first half of 1915. First expectations of war profits were apparently disappointed, and few observers at the end of 1914 could have confidently predicted the prosperity which was on the point of materializing.

The effect of this prosperity on domestic production and income is seen in the figures of the National Bureau of Economic Research, already cited.[4] The effect on our international balance of commodity trade is seen in the following table.[5] This must be interpreted in the light of the fact that our normal debit balance in the "invisible items" was probably cut in half after the outbreak of the War, with the result that there is probably not much more than three-quarters of a billion of invisible debits to be deducted from the export credit shown for the whole three-year period, 1915–17. It seems probable that the period of neutrality yielded a net gain in foreign trade of between 4½ and 5 billions, and that this substantially canceled our previous net debt.

Year ending June 30	Excess of commodity exports
1914	$ 470,653,000
1915	1,094,419,000
1916	2,135,600,000
1917	3,630,481,000

A comparison of these two tables yields plausible ground for a conclusion of great interest and significance. It is a fair assumption that the main precipitating cause of our general prosperity in the neutrality period was the increase of our exports, as shown in the

[3] *See* Noyes, *op. cit.*, pp. 64–65, also 67, 68, 94, 96, for data on other commodities mentioned below.

[4] *See* p. 8 above.

[5] Bogart, *War Costs and Their Financing*, p. 59.

trade balance. But the resulting increase in national income was several times as large as the excess of exports. Valuing this excess in 1913 dollars would reduce it to approximately 4 billions. But the excess of national income for the same period above the 1914 rate was 11½ billions (averaging the results of the two methods of estimate). Allowing for increased population by figuring the excess income above the 1914 rate *per capita* gives smaller results, averaging 9.9 billions by the two methods of estimate. Other adjustments might be made, but are hardly justified by the nature of the problem. It appears that the additional goods we sent to Europe were not a subtraction from home production, but added to it so much that they left a remainder larger than before, by more than the amount taken away. It is not orthodox arithmetic to take one from ten and leave eleven and one-half, but it seems to be possible economics, if the ten represents income at the worst point of a depression, and the one is a new "effective demand" for goods. The great elasticity of a nation's productive system is one of the basic facts in the economics of war.

The corresponding elasticity of the credit system is, of course, an essential enabling cause. Without it, extra sales of goods abroad, made on a credit basis as most of these were, would reduce the immediate dollar buying power of those from whom the credit came, by the same amount that they added to the buying power of the producers and exporters of the goods; and the increased effective demand for some things would be balanced by decreased effective demand for others. But an elastic credit system works differently. Our excess of exports in this period was paid for by net gold imports of something over 900 millions, by loans of about 2.9 billions, and by imports of securities amounting apparently to about 1.5 billions at par.[6] With-

---

[6] *Ibid.*, p. 143, gives a table of net gold movements, as follows:

August 1–December 31, 1914	$ 81,719,000 loss
January 1–December 31, 1915	429,529,000 gain
January 1–December 31, 1916	529,952,000 gain
January 1–December 31, 1917	181,542,000 gain
January 1–December 31, 1918	21,102,000 gain
January 1–December 31, 1919	46,543,000 loss

He also gives a table of loans floated in the United States, pp. 67–68; and estimates of American securities held abroad at various dates, made by L. F. Loree, with his own conclusion as to the amount remaining on July 31, 1917. If Loree's earlier estimate of American securities held abroad is correct, we

out presuming absolute accuracy in these estimates, it is evident that our excess of exports was financed largely by credit extended by our financial institutions, tending to expand our credit structure.

Another essential feature in the cumulative piling-up of prosperity was the fact that demand was created for extraordinary additions to productive equipment. Steel was needed, not only for munitions to be exported, but even more for buildings and plant with which to make them, and for increased capacity in the steel-making industry itself, with which to make both the goods for export and the plants to make them, also the increased amounts of goods which prosperity enabled home consumers to buy, and the increases in plant capacity which these demands called forth. Thus the effects of the war demand were cumulative in multiple fashion, virtually up to the limits set by capacity to expand in those industries on which the resultant increase in demand was most sharply concentrated.

The first impetus came from orders placed by the belligerent countries for shrapnel and bars for their manufacture, for machine tools and wire; and the ultimate result of these and other orders was a striking increase in the capacity of American steel plants in 1915 and 1916. Pig iron production in 1916 was 27 per cent above the level of 1913, and 70 per cent above 1914. In 1917 and 1918 it actually declined slightly. Output of steel ingots and castings in 1916 was 36⅔ per cent above 1913, while 1917 showed a slightly larger output and 1918 a slightly smaller one. In tin production, the American Smelting and Refining Company stepped into the gap left by the cutting off of the German product, and in 1915 built a large plant at Perth Amboy, which in 1918 made 16,800,000 lbs. of tin, other American production being negligible. The duPont Company increased its facilities for making military powder from half a million pounds per month to nearly thirty million pounds, during the period of neutrality. In coal-tar dyes and optical glass, formerly imported from Germany, virtually new industries were created.[7] In

were already a creditor nation on a considerable scale at the moment of our entry into the War. If Paish's earlier estimate (cited above) is correct, there is some doubt whether we had fully canceled our net debt. In any case, our net debt was substantially wiped out.

[7] See Bernard M. Baruch, *American Industry in the War*, pp. 6, 11–13, 42.

short, it appears that in steel, tin, and probably other basic industries, the neutrality-boom furnished the country, in advance of its own belligerency, with the bulk of the increased plant capacity of which actual use was made in fighting the War.

Figures are not available to measure the total amount of this type of investment. In general, if our advances to Europe, which were used to buy war materials from us, are counted as savings, our total savings increased during the neutrality period by considerably more than the amount of these advances to belligerents, while still leaving an enlarged margin for consumption. Some of this increased war-service plant was, of course, actually paid for out of the profits of the export trade in war supplies during this period—how much, there are again no figures available to determine. But what seems clear is that this added plant came out of the increased national productivity, largely traceable to the stimulus afforded by this export trade, and not out of national abstinence in the sense of decreased consumption.

If we take as our point of departure, not the depressed condition of 1914, but an assumed normal representing an estimated average of 1913 and the first seven months of 1914, and if we deflate savings by a price index of costs of construction, a rough estimate indicates that savings during the neutrality period were in excess of the assumed normal by approximately the amount of our (deflated) excess of international credits during this period.[8] If Friday's estimate of savings is correct, the excess during neutrality was much greater than this. In other words we were able to lend Europe our products (in effect), to restore our flow of home investments to a satisfactory normal level (or possibly more) and in any case to a level far above that of 1914, and to have more left for consumption than ever before, even on a *per capita* basis.[9]

[8] Estimates of savings are based on the National Bureau of Economic Research estimate of business savings, plus Friday's estimate of personal savings. Savings are credited to the first seven months of 1914 at a rate 20 per cent greater than the last five months. Such an estimate is of the most uncertain sort, hinging as it does on the margin of difference between two quantities, each of which is an estimate liable to a large degree of error.

[9] Based on total expenditures (other than for war purposes) as estimated in *Income in the United States,* p. 336, deflated and reduced to a *per capita* basis.

Shipping losses during neutrality were not heavy enough to have a material effect on the total picture of prosperity—twenty-one ships totaling 79,562 gross tons.[10] Against these losses the system of government war-risk insurance was inaugurated, which was successfully carried through the period of our active belligerency, on a self-sustaining basis.

As to how this prosperity was divided among different groups of the population, testimony is not clear on all points. Over half the gain came in factory industries, which received twice their *pro rata* share, while mining received just short of its *pro rata* share, and agriculture a little less than two-thirds. Unclassified industries—the largest aggregate—received just less than half their *pro rata* share of the increase.[11] Real wages increased moderately, but the share going to entrepreneurs and property owners showed an increase about 2½ times as great in absolute terms, and of course more in relative terms, increasing from 44 per cent to 48 per cent of the total (this includes the labor income of entrepreneurs, which forms a large part of the total in the case of agriculture, where "entrepreneurs" furnish the bulk of the labor). But the bulk of the increase in entrepreneur and property income was absorbed by increases in business savings; so that the remainder available for personal savings and consumption increased less than wages.

Prices rose during this period, but by only a small fraction of the ultimate war inflation. In 1916, wholesale prices had risen 27 per cent above the 1913 level, and retail prices of goods entering into the cost of living, apparently about 10 per cent. Unlike other booms, this one was marked by the loss of most of our annual net gain from immigration: a fact which may plausibly claim some part of the credit for the increase in real wages. While the resulting slackening of the rate of growth of the total population was not large, the immigrant quotas contribute disproportionately to the ranks of wage-earners; and the shrinkage in new arrivals may be responsible for a slight observed decrease in the percentage of gainfully employed in the total population. It also reduced the element of unadjusted aliens whose wages are naturally below the average.

[10] United States Shipping Board, *Annual Report,* 1919, p. 37.

[11] Based on estimates of net value product in 1913 dollars, converted into percentage increases of 1916 above 1913. See *Income in the United States,* p. 245.

In estimating the service of economic preparedness which the period of our neutrality rendered to the subsequent period of our participation, not the least important element was the mental preparedness: the lessons learned from the European experience. We acquired a respect for the power of the Teutonic military machine, a sense of the seriousness of the effort to be required of us, and a chance to train our troops in the methods of trench warfare rather than solely from our obsolete pre-war manuals, based mainly on open-order fighting. We also learned that modern war is the organized mobilization of all the economic resources of a nation; and were ready to apply what were for us unprecedented measures of control; while leaders of industry, in turn, were ready to submit and to coöperate to an extent well-nigh incredible in the light of our individualistic prepossessions. The successful resort to compulsory military service, the control of prices, restriction of consumption and of industrial uses of essential materials: all gained immeasurably from this period of preparation. Clumsy as were our efforts in some of these fields, there was vastly less waste, futility, and confusion than we must otherwise have suffered.

CHAPTER III

THE PERIOD OF AMERICAN BELLIGERENCY

No adequate and ordered picture of America's greatest economic effort has yet been drawn, and it may be that none is possible of such a many-sided and chaotic series of happenings. This preliminary survey will deal with the main outlines only, leaving details for later chapters.

The actual war expenditures of our Federal Government have been officially estimated by the method of subtracting from the total budget an amount assumed to represent normal peace-time expenses. This introduces an element of somewhat arbitrary estimate at the start, but is probably the best that can be done. The earliest estimate, that of Col. Leonard Ayres, is $21,850,000,000 through April, 1919, after deducting $1,650,000,000 as normal expenses for this period.[1] The first official treasury estimate is approximately 24 billions to June 30, 1920, deducting $3,750,000,000 as normal expenses during the 3¼ fiscal years covered.[2] To this is to be added loans to our Allies, amounting to about 9½ billions, making a grand total of 33½ billion dollars. This includes, be it noted, $1,768,000,-000 of interest on our domestic debt, which is not a clear outlay from the standpoint of the nation as an economic unit, though a proper part of the picture of government finances. Expenses representing social outlays of goods and services are estimated below at something over 31 billions, while State, local, and private outlays bring the total up to 32 billions.[3]

Of the fiscal outlays, $10,703,000,000 was raised by taxes in excess of the estimated normal budget of revenues and expenses, and the remainder, or some 23 billions,[4] by loans. The war debt reached

---

[1] *The War with Germany,* Washington, Government Printing Office, 1919.

[2] Secretary of the Treasury, *Annual Report for 1920,* pp. 104–106.

[3] *See* Chapter VII, pp. 112–113, below, also Chapter VIII.

[4] A later summary would place the actual increase of net debt above June 30, 1916, at 22,957 millions to June 30, 1920, or 23,248 millions to June 30, 1919, approximately its highest point. Based on table, annual report of the Secretary of the Treasury for 1927, p. 616. The actual peak came August 30, 1919, at 24½ billions, but this was reduced some 400 millions the next month by the help of the quarterly income-tax receipts.

its peak in August, 1919, at a figure of approximately 24½ billions, but this was materially reduced during 1920.[5]

If the loans to our Allies be deducted from the borrowings at home, net borrowings to June 30, 1920, would be reduced to some 13½ billions, while total taxes, without deducting "normal" peace-time revenues, would amount to $14,453,000,000, or more than net borrowings. This estimate of net borrowings is, however, unduly low, as the debt settlements involve a material reduction of the "present worth" of our claims on a compound interest basis. But even allowing for this, the United States bore a remarkably large part of its war outlays out of taxes. The showing in this respect was not nearly so good for the earlier years, owing to inevitable delays in bringing taxes to the point of actual revenue yield: nevertheless our policy showed a commendable appreciation of the virtue of laying as much of the war burden as reasonably possible on the taxpayer at once.

These expenditures were made, of course, on a rapidly rising scale of prices, making the dollar values an exaggerated measure of the real outlays of economic resources. This inflation was in itself one of the heavy costs of the War; and much administrative effort was spent in the attempt to minimize the resulting injustices, though nothing could completely remove them. One of the more specific fiscal effects of inflation is frequently a disproportion between the real values borrowed and those ultimately repaid. A government which borrows at war prices and repays at much-reduced peace prices is the loser in a fiscal sense by paying back a larger purchasing power than it borrowed; while a government which allows the maximum war-time depreciation of the currency to persist or even to increase, may escape part of its debt burden in this way. The burden, of course, is not one that rests finally on the government as such, but is passed on to the taxpayers.

In the case of the United States, the peak of prices came in 1920, the year in which the first reductions of the debt were made. Prices remained approximately stable from 1922 to 1928 at levels interme-

[5] The condition at the end of the fiscal year 1919 was approximately: net war borrowings, 23¼ billions; net pre-war debt, 1 billion; "general fund balance," 1¼ billions; gross debt, 25½ billions. This "general fund balance" is more than 1 billion in excess of the levels of 1916 and of 1924–27. In other words, of the maximum gross debt, over 1 billion was painlessly retired by the mere shrinkage of the war-swollen "general fund balance."

diate between the pre-war level of 1913 and the highest point reached during the War.[6] This period of qualified stability was followed by a heavy fall in 1929–31, for which final indexes are not yet available.

Thus future "normal" levels are peculiarly uncertain, making it impossible to estimate closely the gain or loss on war borrowings resulting from changes in the value of the dollar. The difficulty is increased by the fact that wholesale prices and consumers' costs of living have been radically different in their movements. Wholesale prices rose higher and far more promptly, and then declined faster and farther. A rough calculation, taking 1913 price levels as 100, indicates that in terms of wholesale prices we borrowed, on the average, a 52-cent dollar and have been repaying a 63-cent dollar; while in terms of costs of living we borrowed a 66⅔-cent dollar and have been repaying a 59-cent dollar. The first figure would indicate a loss to taxpayers of about one billion dollars of 1913 value, the second, a gain of about three-fourths of a billion. The recent fall in prices has apparently widened this discrepancy, but that is likely to be temporary. It has not so far affected the relation between the values of dollars borrowed and dollars repaid, for the simple reason that we have stopped reducing our debt.

Which type of index is more pertinent to this problem? From the standpoint of the burden on the ultimate taxpayer, the argument is in favor of the cost-of-living type, though the burden of business taxes might seem to depend more on wholesale prices. The safest verdict is that no definite gain or loss is proved, to either taxpayers or bondholders as a whole. The ultimate outcome depends on the future course of prices, which can hardly be predicted, though the drop in the past two years argues a lower level for the future, which would cause future taxpayers to pay, and bondholders to receive, more valuable dollars. But in either case, what the bondholder gains, the taxpayer will lose, and *vice versa*. The burden which can be increased or diminished by price movements is a burden of fiscal transfer. The basic cost to the national economy as a whole remains the same: funds advanced and spent at the time of the conflict, calling forth goods and efforts for the uses of war instead of for the uses of peace.

That the production of goods rather than the raising of dollars

[6] There was in fact a moderate rise from 1921 to 1925 and a similar decline thereafter, prior to the heavy drop of 1929–30.

was the more significant fact was soon indicated, for it proved easier to expand the raising of funds than the effective spending of them. And if it had not been for the running start, so to speak, which the period of neutrality had afforded, this difficulty would have been many times worse. Airplanes, ships, heavy cannon, and many other things would have been bought willingly at almost any price; but they were not to be had for the expenditure of mere money. They had to be made, and the price included making shipyards and other mechanical equipment, training workers, building houses for them, discovering how existing plants could most readily be converted to the production of needed articles or auxiliary parts, and seeing to it that the work was not blocked by the preëmpting of limited supplies of basic materials to less urgent uses. The mobilization of funds was only a means to the mobilization of economic resources, and, as such, it was far from being all-sufficient.

What part of our national income was spent for war? A "conjectural" estimate by the National Bureau of Economic Research places the maximum war expenditure in the calendar year 1918 at 14.6 billions out of a total national income of 62 billions or 23½ per cent.[7] The gross treasury figures include large amounts of supplies never used for war and ultimately sold at a salvage price. In estimating the ultimate cost of the War, some deduction must be made for these supplies; but for the purpose of gauging the immediate economic effort they should certainly be included. Incidental receipts of other sorts, however, should probably be deducted, as well as interest on the war debt. A calculation on this basis gives war expenses representing actual national economic effort at approximately 16 billions for the calendar year 1918, out of a total national income of 62 billions, or somewhat over 25 per cent.[8] While these are

[7] See *Income in the United States*, II, 336. This estimate, being in terms of calendar years, does not correspond to the treasury reports for fiscal years.

[8] Figures from annual report of the Secretary of the Treasury for 1927, pp. 646 ff. These tables lump the receipts for the whole period of the War, and allocation was made by the present writer on the basis of yearly expenses. Figure for national income taken from *Income in the United States*, II, 336. For purposes of converting from fiscal to calendar years, monthly statements of total outlays are available, but not of outlays due to war, nor of interest or other items deducted. Hence the approximate character of the result. The later figure, in *The National Income and Its Purchasing Power*, is only 60.4

only rough approximations, we may provisionally conclude that the year of our greatest war effort saw more than one-quarter of our total economic resources diverted to war uses.

The total diversion of man-power to war efforts can only be roughly estimated. American practice differed from European in that work ordinarily handled by civilians was kept almost wholly on a civilian basis, rather than putting men in uniform and giving them civilian work to do. Those who were in the army and navy and subject to military discipline were performing only such industrial or economic functions as are regularly included in military or naval duties (though these, be it noted in passing, are far from negligible). Perhaps the chief exception to this rule was the manning of some 2½ million deadweight tons of shipping by navy crews, representing a probable personnel in the neighborhood of 20,000.[9]

The maximum number in the armed forces, at about the time of the armistice, appears to have been between 4.1 and 4.2 millions, to which may be added those who had already lost their lives—probably not far short of 100,000. Some 2 million soldiers and marines were in the expeditionary force, of whom nearly 1.4 millions saw actual front-line service at one time or another. Combat divisions to the number of 29 served an average of 46 days each in quiet and 31 in active sectors.[10]

A War Department estimate shows 9.4 millions in war work, including 7,150,000 men and 2,250,000 women.[11] This may be compared with a probable 37 millions gainfully employed in 1918 outside the armed forces, indicating a maximum of about one in four engaged in war work. War workers and armed forces together accounted, on this basis, for almost exactly one in three of the total gainfully employed. The average diversion throughout the war period was, of course, much smaller. Reckoning demobilization as complete at the end of the calendar year 1919, after two and three-quarters years of war, the armed forces had absorbed in that time 5

billions, but this is subject to some upward adjustments for the present purpose. (*See* Chapter IX, below.)

[9] Hurley, *The Bridge to France,* p. 209.

[10] Leonard P. Ayres, *The War with Germany,* p. 114.

[11] From *Annual Report of Secretary of War,* 1919; also cited in *Statistical Abstract, 1921,* pp. 808–809.

to 5½ million man-years of service.[12] The corresponding figure for civilian work destined to war uses may be conjecturally placed somewhere in the general neighborhood of 15 to 16 million person-years for the same period, or between 40 per cent and 45 per cent of one year's total economic effort.[13]

Including the armed forces, the War absorbed probably over 20 million person-years, or more than half of one year's normal gain-fully employed man-power for the country as a whole. In other words, it was as if war work of one sort or another had claimed every "gainfully employed" person for six months, with perhaps two weeks or more thrown in for good measure. This to maintain a "spear-point" representing a number of days in actual front-line service equivalent to not more than ¼ million man-years—though that is obviously not a fair way of representing time spent in the trenches.[14] In our greatest effort—the Meuse-Argonne offensive—1,200,000 men were engaged, though probably not more than 400,000 were in action at any one time. They were backed up by 3 million others in uniform and by the 9 million civilian war workers. One must remember also that these figures of time in active combat service end with the armistice, though that was far from seeing the end of the War's absorption of man-power.

[12] Figure of 5 million computed from monthly figures published by War and Navy Departments, and reprinted in the *Statistical Abstract,* modified in the light of later revised estimates indicating lower totals for certain dates, and in the light of surgeon-generals' figures of average numbers in service, used as basis for computing sickness rates. King's estimate indicates 5½ million, possibly based on the earlier and larger figures; *The National Income and Its Purchasing Power,* p. 361.

[13] Figures obtained by estimating federal war expenses representing real diversion of goods and industrial services, dividing by average employee's compensation plus average margin for other shares per employee, as indicated in studies of the National Bureau of Economic Research, and adding allowance for entrepreneurs actually engaged in such work.

[14] Based on Ayres's figures for division-days, cited above, and reckoning 40,000 men per division. The standard strength of an American division was 28,000, but the total was swollen by troops not organized in divisions and probably by replacements, to such an extent that the number engaged in the Meuse-Argonne offensive is given as 1,200,000 though only twenty-nine divisions saw service at any time. Ayres also gives figures by months (p. 33), in which divisions are credited with continuous service from the time they first entered the lines. These figures are naturally larger. These estimates do not count naval service, and are to that extent inadequate.

Those from whom the War took a final toll of all their power of productive effort included probably at least 170,000 dead and some 34,600 permanently and totally disabled. The entire roll of disabled receiving compensation at any one time has amounted to 262,000, and the average loss of earning power, as officially estimated, is about 44 per cent. The resultant loss of man-power may be reckoned as equivalent to that of over 285,000 persons out of about 40 million gainfully employed at the time of the War. (Virtually all the service men were either gainfully employed or soon to become so.)[15] To the actual loss of man-power must be added the cost of hospital care, vocational rehabilitation, and other activities necessary to preventing the loss of man-power from being even greater. These burdens are mainly represented by the expenditures of the Veterans' Bureau, which, with "allied expenses," now total over half a billion annually.[16] This outlay represents approximately .6 of 1 per cent of our total national income, against a loss of man-power representing some .7 of 1 per cent of the total gainfully employed at the time of the War. Figured in this way, the burden is not heavy; and we should be thankful that as a nation we are rich enough, at so light a total sacrifice, to give the sufferers from these losses something approaching compensation for the purely economic dimensions of their loss.

The Government offered the service men term life insurance at rates based on regular life tables, urging the men to take the full amount of $10,000, which most of them did. It also took charge of allotments of pay for the benefit of dependents. Later came compensation (independent of insurance) for dependents of those who had lost their lives, compensation for disabilities related to war service, hospital and other medical care, and vocational rehabilitation. There have been shortcomings, abuses, and sore spots; but it seems only fair to say that the care of the World War veterans has been more intelligent and equitable than that received by the veterans of any of our previous wars; and more adequate than any other nation

[15] For detailed estimates of loss of life and disability *see* Chapters XIII and XIV, below.

[16] President Coolidge, in his armistice-day speech, reported in the public press of November 12, 1928. The actual budget of the Veterans' Bureau for 1927 was 492 millions (*Report of Secretary of the Treasury for 1927*, p. 647).

could afford to make it. It will at least bear successfully the test of comparison with an estimate of the actual financial loss which the veterans and their dependents can be shown to have suffered.[17]

In the meantime, what happened to the national output of economic goods and services: the real income out of which the costs of war had to be defrayed? The testimony is not altogether clear; but one fact stands out unmistakably. Economists and others had predicted that the withdrawal of millions of men from production would necessarily cause something like a proportionate shrinkage in national output; but in fact, nothing of the sort occurred. Indexes of physical production show for the most part an actual increase for the period of the War, as compared to 1916; though one shows a decrease for 1919. Of the two estimates of national income compiled by the National Bureau of Economic Research, one shows a slight increase in 1917 and a slightly greater decrease in 1918 as compared to 1916; while the other shows a steady decrease, but less than in proportion to the numbers of persons taken into war service.[18]

As between these two types of measure, figures of national income are probably entitled to the greater weight, as indexes of physical production emphasize those forms of product which were regarded as essential, and omit just those varieties of services on which the War made the greatest inroads.[19] The most probable conclusion seems to be that the national output of goods and services showed no very significant change in 1917 and 1918, and declined moderately in 1919; the whole amount for the war period standing slightly below the 1916 level, but decidedly above that of any previous year, even on a *per capita* basis. The war economy seems to have been slightly less productive than the peak year of the neutrality economy, a fact which may be discounted by the likelihood that the 1916 pace could not have been maintained in the face of the unrestricted submarine warfare. And the war economy was decidedly

[17] *See* Chapter XIV, below.

[18] Data taken from *Income in the United States,* II, 234, 338. Production indexes are those of Day (*Review of Economic Statistics,* 1921), and that used by M. A. Copeland (*Recent Economic Changes,* Chapter XII).

[19] On the other hand, the treatment of taxes and public expenditures in the studies of the National Bureau seems to give ground for a slight adjustment upward for the war years, for the purposes of the present analysis. This matter will be gone into in more detail in a later chapter (Chapter IX).

more productive than the average of the whole neutrality period; and more than any previous peace-time economy.

In the first place, the men taken into war service were not a clear loss, since new workers entered the ranks of industry in numbers sufficient to neutralize well over half the withdrawals.[20] Unemployment shrank to a minimum and work in essential industries went on at high pressure and with long hours. On the other hand, workers were unskilled in the new processes; and war-time conversion left much idle capital adapted to peace-time work only; while strikes, transportation congestion, "heatless Mondays," and shortages of essential materials, parts, and equipment introduced many vexatious delays. War-time production (except perhaps in agriculture) was abnormally costly in labor and capital per unit of goods turned out; and still more so in terms of goods actually delivered in time to be of service at the fighting front.

Many of these wastes were inseparable from the character of a sudden need lasting only a short time; or from the uncertainty as to the size of the army that must be raised, transported, and supplied; and the time when the War would end. Shipways must be built, even though each might turn out only a single ship before the firing of the last gun. Ammunition must be ready to ensure a decisive superiority in the 1919 campaign, even though the 1919 campaign might never need to be fought. Plants which could not produce entire guns, mounts, and shells were assigned to the production of parts, but the failure to synchronize these meant that the number of complete gun units at the time of the armistice was far short of a fair result for the amount of construction actually accomplished. Of 3,499 guns received by our forces in France, up to the armistice, only 477 were of

[20] On this point the latest estimate of Professor King is as follows (*The National Income and Its Purchasing Power,* p. 50). His earlier estimate (*Income in the United States,* II, 38) differs very little from this, showing slightly smaller figures throughout, and a decline in private business, from 1916 to 1917, of 74,000 instead of the increase of 76,000 shown below.

	Total gainfully employed	*Employed by government*	*Employed by private business*
1916	38,638,000	2,085,000	36,553,000
1917	39,373,000	2,744,000	36,629,000
1918	40,383,000	5,210,000	35,173,000
1919	40,282,000	4,042,000	36,240,000
1920	40,008,000	2,719,000	37,289,000

American manufacture. However, in this matter the reliance on allied production for 1918 was inevitable. If there was an error, it lay probably in treating this as a temporary and somewhat discreditable emergency necessity, to be removed as soon as possible by building up our own productive capacity; instead of recognizing it as a natural and economical division of labor to be made use of for the duration of the War. For the Allies possessed the plant capacity which had been necessary to the quick expansion of their own equipment of guns, and this was far greater than was necessary to maintain it once it had been built up. This excess represented a resource not needing to be duplicated by the United States, which could furnish instead supplies of materials and other things needed by the Allies. But in such a situation, failures of perfect coördination are only to be expected.

Other wastes and delays were due to failures—natural but no less maddening—of the human factor of management when faced with a novel emergency. Building shipyards takes time necessarily, but five months of 1917 were lost before the construction of the Hog Island yard was begun, and precious months were spent in disputes over the proper types of ships to build, while resulting shifts in the personnel at the head of the Shipping Board caused other delays while the work of scrutinizing contracts was done over again by new officials. Ships lay idle in harbors awaiting orders—or permission—to load cargoes, while ports were congested with goods for export and the Government was slowly being forced to the necessity of centralized and coördinated supervision of such matters, from rail shipments to ship routings. And we are told of baffling conditions at our French ports of debarkation, such as "knockdown houses among a thousand parts of which there was not a complete house."[21] Evidently, with all the aid we received by way of "mental preparedness" during the period of neutrality, the uncertainty and novelty of our task still imposed a heavy toll.

The opinion sometimes expressed, that consumption was fully maintained or even increased during the War, finds no adequate support in the figures.[22] Consumption certainly declined as com-

---

[21] See J. Russell Smith, "Influence of the Great War upon Shipping," *Carnegie Endowment Series*, No. 9, 1919, p. 203. For other conditions described, see pp. 200–216, 227–228, 275–307.

[22] See detailed analysis in Chapter IX, below.

pared to 1916, and probably as compared to the average of the neutrality period; 1918 being a year of genuine restriction in numerous directions. The most that can be said is that it may not have been materially below the level of the whole neutrality period. There was enough buying of silk shirts by war workers to create an impression of extravagance out of proportion to the importance of such things in the national budget. Not everyone could be a shipyard worker; and retrenchment is proverbially less conspicuous than unusual lavishness.

The aggregate increase in national income was not sufficient to pay the whole cost of the War, or half of it, even after deducting items constituting transfers rather than outlays for the nation's economy as a whole, such as interest on the war debt, and allowing for the subsistence of those in the army and navy. The War was not self-supporting even if we count in the income of the neutrality period, especially if we reckon the private advances made to the allied countries during our neutrality as a form of war outlay on a par with the later public loans. Both must be reckoned as part of the immediate diversion of resources to war uses, though the prospect of repayment may remove them from the category of ultimate net costs.

Farmers actually gained during the War enough to pay their contributions of taxes and loans and still increase their consumption. While all the other major classes suffered some decline in consumption, they did not therefore all fare alike in respect of their whole wealth, for some were receiving increased income and turning it into savings on a large scale. Wage-earners apparently gained ground slightly in total earnings, but their contributions to war loans and taxes probably canceled their gains and brought some shrinkage of consumption. In wage rates per hour or per piece they lost ground; and made it up largely by lessened unemployment; also by working longer hours or turning out more pieces. In that connection it is worth remembering that the incredible and hitherto unheard-of earnings of shipyard riveters were matched by an equally incredible multiplication of the number of rivets driven in a day's work, many times beyond the best previous performances.[23]

[23] *See* Hurley, *The Bridge to France,* pp. 153–154. In the early days of the shipbuilding drive 658 rivets in eight hours was a record. Later the record was raised to 5,620! But this meant resting several days afterward, so

Business profits leaped upward, even above the 1916 level, but the greater part was stopped before reaching the individual recipients. Despite a slight gain in 1917, they received less real purchasing power during the War than during neutrality.[24] Corporate net incomes reached unheard-of heights in 1917, standing at nearly three times their pre-war level (without allowance for rising prices). Then they receded under the impact of war-taxation, and for the next two years maintained a level possibly 30 per cent higher in real purchasing power than that of 1913.[25] Increasing proportions were retained as surplus, interest-disbursements shrank in buying power, while dividends on common stocks in 1916 and 1917 were about 60 per cent above their pre-war real value. For the whole period, 1916–19, common stock dividends ran about 43 per cent above their pre-war level in real buying power.[26] For the security-holding class as a whole, the war-time personal-income taxes more than absorbed these gains.

In agriculture, a declining number of workers managed to maintain a normal rate of physical output relative to the total population of the country; and sold it at prices which gave them a substantial increase in real purchasing power.[27] While in other industries the bulk of the war profits were kept in the business as corporate surplus or other forms of business savings; in agriculture such savings appear to have suffered an actual decline.

The greatest flow of added workers was into manufactures, where numbers increased greatly in 1916 and moderately in the following years. Physical output, however, did not increase after 1916, and actually declined from 1917 to 1919, rising in 1920 for the first time

exhausting was the effort. Earnings of $50 to $100 per day per "team" were recorded, but were not common.

[24] Based on table in King's *The National Income and Its Purchasing Power*, p. 112. Income from agriculture, government, and miscellaneous sources was deducted from the total to find business income proper. The result is: for the three years 1914–16, 28,398 millions of 1913 dollars; for the three years 1917–19, 26,777 millions of 1913 dollars. There seems little possibility that errors in the estimates would falsify the conclusion drawn above.

[25] See *ibid.*, p. 278, for income figures. The choice of a deflating index is capable of making the result vary almost anywhere from 22 per cent to 36 per cent because wholesale prices rose so much faster than costs of living.

[26] *Ibid.*, p. 193.

[27] *Cf.* Chapters IX–XI, below, for fuller analysis.

to a figure above that of 1916. Output per worker increased in 1916, but declined quite materially in 1917 and 1918—an evidence that war-time production was more than ordinarily costly in terms of economic effort.

One reason for this may be found in a list of war-time conversions of industries to the production of unfamiliar things, in which both workers and employers would naturally have much to learn, and many delays would naturally be experienced. Automobile plants were turned to making airplanes, "Eagle" boats, and tanks. Even such a conversion as the development of the "liberty motor" involved delays and readjustments. Parts for these motors were made by vacuum-cleaner plants and many others. Piano-makers made airplane wings; printing-machine makers turned to making fuses, and computing-machine makers to assembling them. Makers of carpets made blankets and duck; makers of refrigerators made field hospital tables; makers of horseshoes made trench picks; makers of toys made packing boxes; makers of radiators made big guns; makers of bottle caps made machine-gun mounts. Makers of fish rods found their war-opportunity in flagstaffs, portable wireless masts, and other varieties of jointed poles; makers of stoves, in grenades and trench bombs; makers of corsets, in medical corps belts and fencing masks; makers of gears, in gunsights; makers of rubber and canvas, in gas-masks, makers of ladies' waists, in signal flags. Even makers of pipe organs found their niche.[28]

These conversions were not wholly voluntary, as many of the original products were classed as "nonessential" and suffered curtailment of essential supplies such as steel and coal. The result was that such producers besieged the Washington authorities to know what they might do to be saved: what essential product they could find to keep their plants and workers occupied. Many of the conversions are far from obvious and show considerable ingenuity; serving to reduce one of the natural wastes of war—the letting of contracts to persons having no plants or knowledge suitable to filling them. Conversion was, however, far from complete, and many industries suffered heavy curtailment. Lumber production and road-making

[28] *See* Baruch, *American Industry in the War,* United States War Industries Board, pp. 41–42, and Crowell and Wilson, *The Giant Hand,* pp. 59–64.

were reduced; and the building of cantonments and houses for ship-builders fell far short of making good the decline in general building construction. The war demands in the field of construction and construction materials were urgent but irregular, creating alternate pressure and curtailment and making for relatively low output per worker attached to the industry.[29]

Much of the war production could not be supplied by existing plants and required the creation of new ones, some of which hardly delivered any finished products before the armistice. The building of shipyards was still not fully completed at the time of the armistice. At our entry into the War this country was already actively expanding its fleet. It had 61 yards with 142 ways for steel vessels and 73 ways for wood; about 100 of the steel-vessel ways having navy hulls on them, and the rest being occupied by vessels later requisitioned by the United States Shipbuilding Corporation. At the armistice we had 341 yards "practically completed," with 1,284 ways. E. E. Day reckons the number of ways then available for the program of the Shipbuilding Corporation at 398 for steel ships and 418 for wood.[30] Shipyard workers were raised from 50,000 to 350,000; Congress appropriated $75,000,000 for a housing program to take care of 28,863 workers, and millions more for facilities to transport workers to and from their work. As Mr. Hurley says: "It cost the nation at least three hundred million dollars to teach 350,000 men and 130 new managements to build ships."[31] To the date of the armistice these

[29] See Clarkson, *Industrial America and the World War*, pp. 422, 431.

[30] "The American Merchant Fleet," *Quar. Jour. of Econ.*, XXXIV, 583, August, 1920.

[31] The above facts taken from Hurley, *The Bridge to France*, pp. 60, 174, 180, 184–186. *See* also pp. 77, 80. Total appropriations for the shipbuilding program to December 31, 1918, were as follows (given in Day's article, cited above):

Requisitioned ships	$ 415,000,000
Contract ships	1,823,788,500
Plant and property	177,000,000
Housing	75,000,000
Transportation	20,000,000
Dry docks and marine railways	59,662,500
Foreign shipyard construction .	55,000,000
Total	$2,625,451,000

facilities had delivered to the Emergency Fleet Corporation some 480 ships totaling 2,750,000 deadweight tons, two-thirds of which was requisitioned tonnage.[32] The steel ways, of which some 42 were available at the start and 398 at the armistice, had turned out approximately 390 vessels, two-thirds of them requisitioned. Of these, 150 were in various stages of construction at the time of the August requisition order, leaving 240 as the number begun and finished under the Shipbuilding Corporation. Wooden construction was slower, only about 90 ships being turned out, all on contract. Four times as much tonnage was finished after the armistice as before, and half the expeditionary force had still to be moved in British vessels.[33] This last fact is, to be sure, somewhat misleading, as our army's cargo fleet, which was several times as large as the transport fleet, was mostly American.

This disappointing outcome was in part inevitable and in part due to delays which seem unnecessary and even blameworthy if blame can be attached to the efforts and cross-purposes of conscientious men trying earnestly to perform an unfamiliar duty.[34] It is in part, no doubt, to be written down as an instance of inefficiency on the part of popular government in meeting an emergency of this character. This effort is not therefore to be judged a failure: it was a success, and without it the War could almost certainly not have been won in 1918, if at all. Even the ships still unbuilt played their part in making it possible to dare to place in France an army larger than we could fully equip and supply with the vessels then on the water. And yet there could hardly be a more forceful example of the lavishness and inevitable waste—if such a term is permissible—which are almost inseparable from meeting a national emergency which is inexorably sudden, and short, especially in a country of democratic individualism. Other examples include huge explosive plants and electric power establishments, which did not reach effective production by the time of the armistice.

The industrial mobilization carried with it considerable geographical movements, chiefly to the industrial sections of the north

---

[32] See *Statistical Abstract of the United States, 1920*, p. 372, for figures of numbers of vessels. For tonnage, *see* E. E. Day's article, "The American Merchant Fleet," *Quar. Jour. of Econ.*, XXXIV, 583.

[33] *See* Ayres, *The War with Germany*, pp. 41–43, *cf.* also pp. 146–147.

[34] *See* J. Russell Smith, *op. cit.*, pp. 275–307.

and east. Cities like Bridgeport, Connecticut—a center of munitions manufacture—and towns near the new shipyards, grew rapidly in population, while the curtailment of new residential construction created a heavy housing shortage. Negroes moved to northern cities in large numbers, creating difficult problems in the field of social and political relations as well as in real estate values. Unlike many of the war movements, this one appears to have been permanent. Women entered war work in manufactures in numbers estimated at 1½ millions; while the War Department has estimated 2¼ millions as engaged in all forms of war work. But, in manufactures at least, by far the greater part—some estimates place it as high as 95 per cent— came from other gainful occupations, so that it is doubtful if the percentage of women employed outside the home rose materially above normal, except possibly at the height of the war effort.[35] Thus, while there were problems of adjustment resulting from women living in new communities, and problems of health and fatigue resulting from engaging in unfamiliar work, there was no problem of millions taken from the home, as in some of the European belligerents.

Our export trade balance, in dollar values, increased during our belligerency beyond even the neutrality level, averaging well over 3 billions per year. The true balance of exchange, however, was complicated by unprecedented elements. Our purchases abroad for the army and our bill for services rendered by French railways and other agencies constituted a new form of "invisible imports" of huge dimensions: 2,375 millions in 1919. We further shipped vast amounts of supplies abroad for the expeditionary force which were not counted in the trade figures; but large quantities of which were sold after the armistice and thus became a form of deferred exports, roughly canceling the claims then outstanding against us on account of the expeditionary force abroad.[36] In the aggregate, our 9½ billions of war loans to our Allies probably constitutes a moderate overstatement of the extent to which we became a creditor nation during this period, even without writing down the value of these loans to the discounted worth of the payments called for by the present debt settlements. This sum represents, not a literal "profit" made

[35] See "War-time Industrial Employment of Women in the United States," *Jour. of Pol. Econ.,* XXVII, 639 ff., October, 1919.

[36] See *Annual Report,* War Department, 1920, p. 69.

out of the War, but a residue of realizable assets, paid for by effort and abstinence during hostilities and remaining as a credit to future generations, if they can collect it in a form which really makes them richer—a matter about which there is some doubt. In any case it is a fiscal asset to the Government. The original loans represented a surplus of production over consumption but not of gains above social costs or sacrifices. And, of course, for the economy of the world as a whole, the result is not a surplus of any sort; but a debt of other nations to us for goods consumed in a process which, unlike investment of capital in productive assets, left them poorer than before and not richer.

In the meantime, many things were happening which did not enter directly into the statistics of production and consumption, but which bore on them directly or indirectly, or affected the background of public opinion, social attitudes, and human relations which go so far toward determining the quality of living. In the first place, the public interest in methods of production brought something new into American economic life, making what bids fair to be a permanent contribution to technical methods, and to the industrial organization and the social-political arrangements by which they are influenced. The War gave an enormous impetus to the movement toward standardization and "simplified practice," and to the interchange of information between producers whereby each may become aware of his weak points and strengthen them, thus raising the efficiency of the whole. The reduction of the number of sizes, shapes, and types of all sorts of products and parts resulted in economizing essential materials when the worth of such economy was more than could be measured in money.[37]

The movement thus brought into the limelight has continued, ably furthered by Mr. Hoover in his term as Secretary of Commerce, and seems to have approved itself by the more ordinary and permanent standards of economy appropriate to times of peace. Fewer sizes in larger lots are both cheaper to produce and save the idle inventory which results from the necessity of keeping many sizes in stock. Secretary McAdoo's standardized locomotives, judged as a war measure, probably were not worth the delay involved in developing the plans, and the system has not subsequently made its way against the demand of different roads for engines more precisely suited to their

[37] *See* Baruch, *American Industry in the War,* especially pp. 61–69, 99.

various individual conditions of traffic and grades; but other forms of the practice have proved of permanent worth.

In the realm of consumption the War gave us the short skirt—originally a measure to economize dress goods—and a deal of semi-voluntary food-saving, coupled with a very valuable course of education in the science of food values. No very substantial percentage reduction was brought about in our consumption of food, but such savings as were made were of importance to Europe. In most branches of consumption, however, the most effective control was *via* production; through rationing supplies of coal and essential materials.

Labor had its part in the whole task of economic mobilization, constituting a story the parts of which have not yet been brought together, and which is too large to be even outlined here. From the standpoint of the nation one of the chief problems was to keep labor at work, avoiding strikes, and substituting for them a controlled labor market with systems of adjudication to give labor the increased money wages which simple justice required, as an offset to increased costs of living. Another problem was to fill the gaps made by military service, increasing the supply of qualified workers where increases were needed and as rapidly as possible, and removing all working rules and restrictions which might limit output.

Labor, as represented by the American Federation, loyally supported the War and would do nothing to obstruct the necessities of the war program. Government, in turn, was eager to see labor as completely organized as possible, so long as the unions were loyal, since organized labor could be so much more easily dealt with. Union membership thus enjoyed a mushroom growth, with the active support of the Government. In the west, the Loyal Legion of Loggers and Lumbermen was formed as a war-supporting organization in a field where the strength of the I.W.W. element had led to fears of serious trouble if not of systematic sabotage. Labor made some gains, but there was no general or concerted labor "profiteering." Labor was not unaware of what it was asked to give up, especially the use of that standard weapon—the strike—which would in all ordinary likelihood prove necessary to keep real wages from shrinking disastrously as prices rose. Labor was also asked to abandon restrictions on output and to see highly skilled fields invaded by large numbers of new workers who had attempted to condense into a few weeks of intensive schooling the training formerly gained by a full-length apprenticeship. In the ultimate outcome, this does not seem to have weakened materially the position of skilled labor.

Strikes did not disappear, though they were less serious than in Great Britain's early war effort. Labor adjustment boards were kept busy in efforts to compose differences, and with fair success. There was fairly widespread adoption of the principle of adjusting money wages to changing money costs of living; implying a sublime faith that industry would be productive enough to make such a standard possible by producing all the war supplies and the customary consumption of labor in addition! Or perhaps it was merely a refusal to see or to admit that the maintenance of real wages depended on the maintenance of such an exacting standard of physical output. In shipbuilding the effort was to set wages high enough to afford amply strong attractions, and to attempt to make the same wages standard in all plants, and prevent further competitive bidding for men. One object of this was that labor might have no reason for spending time in drifting from plant to plant looking for the highest wages the market afforded; but could be assured that it was getting as much wherever it might be as it could get anywhere else. This was not the only instance during the War of the principle that more pay was likely to call forth less work rather than more. Patriotic appeals had also to be made to war workers not to lay off to spend their unaccustomed surplus at the "movies" or other amusements.

As we have seen, there was a large growth in the membership of labor organizations, and part of this has since been maintained. Total membership of unions had remained virtually stationary from 1904 to 1909 at about 2 million, had grown to 2.7 million in 1914, to 2.8 million in 1916, and reached its peak in 1920 at over 5 million. By 1923 it had fallen to 3,780,000.[38]

The general course of wages has been mentioned. As between different groups, unskilled labor appears to have gained on skilled labor; possibly under the influence of the cost-of-living figures which were used in wage adjustments to such a large extent, or possibly on account of the "dilution" of skilled labor with the products of a

[38] Figures from Wolman: *Growth of American Trade Unions, 1880–1923*, p. 33. This is perhaps the best study in a field where the official membership figures are notoriously unreliable.

hasty trade-school training.[39] One instance of this shift in relative adjustment may be of significance. Under the Federal Railroad Administration, revisions of wages and salaries were definitely on the principle of reducing differentials between highest and lowest rewards. The higher salary scales suffered an absolute decline in dollars, and of course a still greater decline in purchasing power; while the lowest-paid workers received the greatest increases. One index of this movement is the relative earnings of trainmen and of other railway wageworkers. In 1909 trainmen's earnings were 81 per cent above those of other railway workers, and for the period 1909–17 they averaged 86 per cent above. In 1918 trainmen's earnings, in dollars of constant purchasing power, rose very slightly, but real wages of other railway workers rose 30 per cent, and the trainmen now earned only 42 per cent more than the others. That this differential was abnormally low is attested by the fact that since then it has increased in every year but one, and by 1927 it was back above 82 per cent, the preliminary figure for 1928 showing 82.8 per cent.

Another gauge of the same bit of wage-history is as follows. From 1909 to 1917, inclusive, earnings of "other railway workers" followed those of factory operatives with surprising closeness, averaging a trifle over 1 per cent higher. In 1918 they were nearly 24 per cent higher; from 1918 to 1922, inclusive, they averaged 14⅔ per cent higher; and from 1924 on they have gone back to the old equality, though the real earnings of both groups have risen over 25 per cent.[40]

What does this prove? It may perhaps be taken to illustrate the force of supply and demand tending to restore a normal wage-relationship after it has been arbitrarily disturbed. But it is worth noting that the readjustment took place mainly through a rise in the real earnings of the groups which had been left behind, and only to a slight extent by a fall in the real earnings of the group which received the special increase. A readjustment which had to be wholly downward might have encountered greater resistance.

Other developments having a bearing on labor included the army trade tests and intelligence tests, which were undoubtedly significant steps in the development of these two types of testing. Beyond this

---

[39] Cf. *Recent Economic Changes*, p. 438.

[40] For figures affording material for this analysis, *see* news-bulletin, National Bureau of Economic Research, February 10, 1929.

very general fact, the effect of these developments can hardly be appraised at present. The revelation that the average drafted man was not mentally adult (after the preconceived standards of the test-makers) has not yet led to the overt abandonment of democracy; but has it had no effect? The relation between occupations and intelligence-quotients is not only of much general interest, but seems to have some bearing on the fact that this is the "age of the expert" as well as on the type of radicalism which looks to placing the control of industry in the hands of manual workers. May one refer also to the reported fact that the highest group of all in intelligence-quotients were the "conscientious objectors" in Leavenworth Prison?

The War also played its part in the progress of studies of workers' budgets for purposes of determining reasonable compensation. The Department of Labor, in seeking standards of compensation for federal employees, developed budgets which, naturally, broke all previous records for dollar magnitude. The result was to direct increased attention to the fact, which such studies have always brought out, that it seemed hopeless to expect to fix wages which would give everyone as much as the indicated standard of fair subsistence. One immediate result was an agitation for a "family allowance" system of paying wages, such as has been tried in France. It seems at least possible that another result was to strengthen the resistance of wages to post-war deflation and thus to bring about an increase in their purchasing power which might have been impossible by any other method.

One of the costs of war consists in the interruption of education, and the World War in America was no exception. Yet there was no general depopulation of our institutions of higher learning, but rather, so far as numbers are concerned, only a slight setback in the midst of an amazingly rapid growth. From 1916 to 1918, male college students fell off from 152,860 to 134,271, or 18,589, while female students increased 15,255, leaving a net decline of only 3,334. Male graduate students fell off by 2,718. The real effect of the War is more than these figures indicate, however, as the normal growth in male students during these two years may be estimated at about 18,000. The War probably interrupted or postponed the education of over 40,000 male students in all divisions of the higher institutions. Many of these returned; the college enrolments showing the effects in 1920, the graduate schools not till 1922 (the figures being published biennially).[41] The more serious effect was probably qualitative, consisting in interrupted habits of study; the delay costing many students a very real reduction in the benefits they were able to get from their postponed education. Possibly these men needed a special and different type of training: one which the colleges and universities were not in a position, at a moment's notice, to furnish. The decline in numbers of graduate students stood for a temporary but very real deterioration in the quality of university-trained instructors which the colleges were able to secure in the post-war years in response to their rapidly increasing demands.

Not least among the War's incidental contributions to our economic life is its contribution to the coming-in of nation-wide prohibition. This was introduced as a war measure and perpetuated by the Eighteenth Amendment. It might, of course, have come ultimately in any case; but the War at least hastened its coming. Needless to say, its ultimate effects are too contradictory and uncertain to be even estimated in a study which attempts to deal with reasonably well-demonstrated facts. During the war and immediate post-war period, it was working at its best, as shown in a notable decrease in deaths from alcoholism and in other related statistics. During this period, it was undoubtedly an economic success. As to the subsequent balance sheet, no attempt will be made here to draw it up. Ultimate success or failure rests with the future.

Such, in the broadest outlines, was the story of our participation in the World War: a story of great efforts, great wastes, and great achievements. The costs did not end with the signing of the armistice, nor with the completion of military demobilization; some of them are still far in the future. Indeed, the true nature and weight of many of the accounts are only to be seen by a study of the period of post-war readjustment; to which, therefore, we may next turn.

[41] Figures taken from *Statistical Abstract of the United States.*

CHAPTER IV

THE AFTERMATH OF WAR

THE demobilization of the armed forces was substantially complete before the end of 1919, but industry was still in a disturbed state which lasted through the post-war boom of 1920 and the crisis and major depression of 1921. All this may be thought of as the period of immediate post-war disturbance and readjustment. With 1922 begins a totally different period: one of unprecedented and sustained prosperity, all the more outstanding in contrast to the impoverished state of the rest of the world. This came to a violent end in the depression of 1929–30, a recession as deep as that of 1921 and one which bids fair to be more prolonged. To what extent, if at all, were this prosperity and this subsequent depression due to the War or to forces which the War set in motion? To this question, of course, no exact and certain answer can be given; and therefore no exact and certain balance sheet of the ultimate economic effects of the War can be drawn up. Many features of such a balance sheet can, however, be set down; and with regard to others, the chief question is often not so much the size of the items as the degree of responsibility which should be assigned to the War as a cause. In these matters we must be content to go merely as far as the means at hand permit.

So far as government was concerned, getting back to normal consisted mainly of disbanding the armed forces, closing up war contracts, and disposing of surplus supplies or—in the case of permanent productive assets which could best be kept in public hands—providing for their future administration. There was also the war-time system of economic controls to be disbanded, and the revenue system to be put on its post-war basis. But these were only the governmental side of the much larger process of remobilizing industry into the ways of peace. Men disbanded must be reabsorbed; and the canceling of war contracts meant the dismissal from civilian war service of many more workers than had ever borne arms, and corresponding amounts of capital. Most of these workers must also be reabsorbed—if possible under their existing employers. Thus the employers faced a task of serious magnitude, even apart from the reëmploying of disbanded soldiers. The dropping of war-time controls was a part of the process of allowing prices and production to find their levels; while business faced the task of adjusting itself to these new levels when they should be found, and meanwhile dealt as best it could with the large element of uncertainty as to what these levels would be. Productive capital remaining in public hands may be exemplified by Muscle Shoals and the new ships and shipyards; both representing problems in economic utilization which are not yet fully and successfully solved.

The general policy of the Government was to demobilize as rapidly as possible without obvious waste or injustice, and to leave to private enterprise the task of reabsorbing workers and re-forming the lines of industry. The boom of 1919–20 proved that private industry had great powers of reabsorption and revival, while the depression of 1921 showed that such a great and rapid remobilization was attended by grave economic dangers. It remains a doubtful question whether the retention of a larger amount of public supervision would have brought about a more desirable result. It might have been possible to prevent the great increase in prices which attended the removal of war-time controls, and which undoubtedly intensified the post-war boom. This might have made the revival both slower and smoother; at the price of postponing the time when industry would stand fully on its own feet.

In demobilizing the armed forces no attempt was made, as in England, to release first those of whose services industry had the greatest need; and who by reason of this fact could count on immediate reabsorption. Demobilization proceeded by whole military units; and the only concession to the problems of readjustment was to afford individuals whose units had been disbanded the privilege of continuing in service with other units if they so desired. This privilege was taken advantage of by only a few. As was natural, army demobilization began at home, with those not yet sent overseas; and over 600,000 of them were discharged in December, 1918, before any substantial number of the expeditionary force had been returned. For the next seven months an average of 337,000 per month was discharged, making a total of nearly 3 millions in eight months. In one year after the armistice, demobilization in this sense was almost complete, with some 3¼ millions discharged. During the same period the navy was reduced by some 400,000 men and the marine corps by some 50,000, making a total of approximately 3.7 millions.

The army was now reduced to some 220,000 men, the navy to something over 125,000, and the marine corps to about 22,000.

War contracts were generally canceled, with payment for work already done and, in some cases at least, allowances for capital invested which was to have been amortized by the payments from the Government. Some contracts had cancellation clauses; others required negotiation and adjustment. Unfinished portions of War Department contracts suspended at the time of the armistice amounted to $3,834,010,000; and by October 2, 1920, $3,300,853,000 of this had been liquidated at a settlement cost of $437,819,000, or something over 13 per cent of the full amount of the contracts so settled.[1] The navy canceled without liability contracts to the amount of $26,392,000, and adjusted others in which the canceled portions amounted to $46,397,000, at a cost to the Government of $10,780,-700. This cost covered materials and stores taken over by the Government, plant taken over or amortized, and no-profit prices allowed on work in process.[2] Our settlements with our Allies for supplies, obligations on account of railroad transport, etc., called for payments to them of $893,716,000, which was largely canceled by sales of our property abroad, amounting to $822,923,000.[3]

The full story of the disposal of surplus materials is difficult to decipher, in view of the different bases on which successive statements are made. To June 30, 1922, a total of supplies costing 2¼ billions was reported by the War Department as sold, transferred or withdrawn, with an additional ¼ billion (at cost) remaining on hand. Goods costing $1,957,607,000 had been sold, the receipts amounting to $874,131,000. This apparently does not include the goods disposed of abroad for credit. In addition, the navy had, from the armistice to June 30, 1920, received about $106,000,000 from sales, including $6,000,000 or more from the sale of miscellaneous small vessels and airplanes. In the fiscal year 1920, the navy sold goods costing 66½ millions at a profit of 3½ millions.

Besides the supplies sold, large amounts were held for future use, and were realized upon in this way. The exact amounts can only be estimated, but there is at least one purpose for which such an estimate is needed: namely, the scrutiny of post-war military and naval

---

[1] War Department, *Annual Report for 1920,* p. 19.
[2] Navy Department, *Annual Report for 1919,* pp. 100–101.
[3] War Department, *Annual Report for 1920,* p. 69.

expenditures to see what effect the War has had on them. To the extent that they were using up a left-over surplus of war supplies, the fiscal expenses of these post-war activities understate the real consumption of assets chargeable against them, and correspondingly overstate the amounts chargeable against the actual conduct of the World War. Of course, if the problem is to ascertain the total cost chargeable to war as an institution, this is merely a matter of shifting from one heading to another within the main account without affecting the total result. And the same is true even from the standpoint of finding the costs specifically traceable to the World War, in case it turns out that there is an increase in post-war military and naval expenses which is properly chargeable as an after-effect of this particular conflict. Such after-effects are sometimes among the most serious costs of a war.

Besides current supplies carried over, there are the army cantonments and other permanent equipment retained by the Government for military uses. These may, to some extent, reduce the expenses which would otherwise be incurred for summer training camps and other military activities; but of this there may be some doubt. And on the whole, it does not seem unfair to charge the whole cost of these items to the World War itself.

The largest single item of property carried over consisted of the ships and shipbuilding plant of the Shipping Board and Emergency Fleet Corporation. These organizations had expended, to June 30, 1921, $3,316,100,000; most of it for ships, shipyards, houses, transportation facilities, and other durable productive assets. The real economic value of these assets carried over is a doubtful quantity; certainly only a very small portion of their cost, and in many cases a minus quantity. Some have simply lain idle, some have been sold, and some have been operated at a loss. In the treasury's estimate of war costs, made in 1927, credit is given for Shipping Board property sold and for the estimated value of property remaining in 1927, and operating deficits are deducted. The deficits wipe out all but $280,504,000 of the credits, leaving the net war costs on account of these items over 3 billions, or over nine-tenths of the total expenses of the Shipping Board and its shipbuilding company.[4] The full story of these operations must be reserved for a later chapter.

[4] *Report of Secretary of the Treasury for 1927,* p. 643. *Cf.* more detailed analysis below, Chapter VII, pp. 111–112.

To sum up, it appears that not less than 6 billions of the Government's expenditures, and very likely considerably more, went into surplus supplies, or permanent equipment which remained after the end of hostilities; and that the salvage on these outlays, while large absolutely, was only a small fraction of what had been spent. Thus the greater part of these outlays must be charged as war costs. To this should be added private capital invested for war purposes, so far as it was not amortized out of the prices of the goods produced. Salvage on these private investments has been a matter of converting plants to peace-time uses where possible, or making the best of a difficult situation, as in the case of ships and shipyards, which cannot be converted into anything else. The DuPont interests appear to have met remarkable success in converting a part of their huge munitions plants to post-war usefulness. The shipbuilding industry, on the other hand, is, naturally enough, seriously depressed.

The actual reabsorption of the armed forces appears to have taken place with no very serious stagnation and unemployment; despite the fact that government assistance in this matter was far from commensurate with the magnitude of the problem. The United States Employment Service in the Department of Labor took over general responsibility, coöperating with local organizations; but was hampered by lack of funds, and was virtually discontinued by October, 1919.[5] Some further work was done under the War Department, by the Service and Information Branch of the War Plans Division, formed in September of the same year. The War Department also directly placed some 20,000 technicians.

The problem was that of turning from war production as rapidly as possible and replacing it with a larger volume of peace-time production; so as to absorb as much as possible of the net increase in the army of private industry resulting from the disbanding of the army of war. It was not necessary, however, to increase the volume of private employment by anything like the full number of service men discharged. Many of these came from nonindustrial pursuits and went back to them again; chiefly to resume their interrupted educations. And many temporary war workers left industry when the emergency was over. While this did not leave empty places to be filled (since the war work was itself disbanded), it still reduced by

[5] War Department, *Annual Report for 1920,* pp. 166–167.

that much the aggregate increase in the number for whom places were to be found in private business.

The remainder—and this is a sobering fact—could all have joined the army of the unemployed without raising that army to the proportions customary in a major business depression. According to the best figures available, the shrinkage of employment from the third quarter of 1920 to the first quarter of 1922 amounted to five million workers, or probably nearly twice the net increase which industry was called on to absorb in 1919, as a result of the discharge of men from army and navy.[6] In other words, the majority of the ex-service men found employment in the post-war boom, after which a still larger number were thrown out of work in the subsequent depression.

As to the causes of this economic upheaval, or rather the special causes peculiar to it and marking it off from other cycles; one of the foremost is probably the great rise in prices following the termination of government controls. Such a rise regularly induces a super-structure of secondary or speculative demand on top of the primary demand for goods for use. And by creating profits which are, in a sense, fictitious, it is likely to induce producers to expand operations excessively, creating a sudden and concentrated demand for equipment and materials, as well as labor.

Underlying this, the primary demand itself was affected by the fact that output of "nonessentials" had been sharply restricted, leaving a gap which consumers would naturally rush to fill at the earliest opportunity. Furthermore, just as the equipping of millions of men for military life caused a sudden increased demand for clothing and other consumables, in some cases far in excess of the previous annual consumption of the entire country; so the sudden re-equipping of the same men for civil life created, to a less extent, a similar concentrated demand for civilian goods, which the surplus army stocks were not suited to supply, except in small part.

Factories reconverted from war production must modernize their former peace-time equipment, while industries partially suspended must, in addition, make up as rapidly as possible for lost growth. The construction industry had declined until in 1918 it employed only

---

[6] W. I. King, *Employment, Hours and Earnings in Prosperity and Depression* (Nat. Bur. of Econ. Research, 1923), p. 30. This decline is partly seasonal, perhaps to the extent of nearly a million.

47 per cent as many workers as in 1913, and there was a heavy housing shortage to be made up.[7] Reconstruction brought a building
boom which carried employment in the construction industries, in
the third quarter of 1920, virtually back to the 1913 level or possibly even above it.[8] But this did not last, even long enough to make
good the initial shortage. The continued control of rentals, which
lasted longer than other forms of war control, made it difficult to secure an adequate return on the costs of post-war construction; and
the making good of the housing shortage had to await the deflation
of the 1920 cost levels and the relaxation or disappearance of the
post-war control of rents; coming about finally by a slower process,
less exposed to quick reversal.

One contributing cause of the reconstruction boom was undoubtedly the fact that civilian production revived while work was still
going on on some of the war contracts, chiefly the shipbuilding program, which continued through 1920. Europe also continued an urgent customer, unable to make full payment in goods, and therefore
buying on credit. So far as the credit is furnished out of the elasticity of the credit system rather than out of ultimate personal savings and so far as the credit system remains safe, such sales undoubtedly afford more aggregate stimulus to home production than
if paid for by imports. The home producer has the home demand as
well as the foreign demand to fill. Any expansion of purchasing
financed by expansion of credit has this stimulating effect.

The effectiveness of these reconstruction demands for goods rested
on one condition: namely, that the needs which have been mentioned
should be coupled with command of dollars with which to buy the
means of satisfaction—especially in the case of the returned service
men. The outcome seems to indicate that purchasing power was
forthcoming: that a major part of the service men were taken upon
the pay rolls of industry before their funds or their credit were
exhausted.

The end of the boom can be traced to a number of causes. The rise
in prices could not go on forever, and the unstable profits due to this

[7] See *Income in the United States*, II, 38.

[8] Compare figures cited above with King, *Employment, Hours and Earnings in Prosperity and Depression*, p. 30. The latter figures are for persons
actually on the pay rolls, by quarters; the former are for persons attached to
the industry, by years. Hence the comparison is not exact.

rise were destined to evaporate, and to be replaced by losses as deflation set in. The reëquipping of plants was a movement inherently likely to start off at a pace it could not maintain; as was also the initial reëquipping of consumers. Congestion of railways and other means of transportation in 1920 set limits beyond which production could not rise and this, so far as expectations had been capitalized, was calculated to give rise to losses tending to cause a reaction. The end of the construction boom and of the government shipbuilding program tended in the same direction. Furthermore the railroads, returned to private hands, were faced with the need of sharp retrenchment if they were to reëstablish normal net earnings, even at increased rates. As a result, they carried out economies which reduced their working force from over 2 millions to about 1.7 millions; this representing a permanent change in their operating methods. The extreme decline in railroad employment from the third quarter of 1920 to the first quarter of 1922 was over 600,000 workers.[9] This did not mean a net reduction of this amount in the nation's demand for labor, as it carried with it a demand for larger and more efficient equipment: nevertheless, it was an element in the immediate situation. While the added equipment was being produced, and before the resulting economies were realized, employment received the benefit on both accounts, and was for the moment abnormally high: afterward a reaction was inevitable.

The depression of 1921—the worst since that of 1907–8—carried with it the deflation of prices and costs from the post-war peak to a level which proved to be fairly stable up to 1929; and ushered in the period of post-war prosperity. This, despite depression in agriculture, coal mining, shipbuilding, and other industries, and a considerable amount of continued unemployment, has been the greatest prosperity any country has ever known. While the causes of it are to a considerable degree conjectural, and may to some extent always remain so, certain features are plain and others may be traced with reasonable confidence.

Wages were not deflated in the same proportion as costs of living, leaving a slight increase in real earnings per worker. The causes of this are undoubtedly complex, but the fact seems hardly open to question. Employers took advantage of the bargaining position

[9] See *ibid.*, p. 30.

which depression afforded to attack the power of organized labor, with large measure of success. The expansion in numbers of organized workers during the War had been artificially stimulated and not well consolidated; and yielded to the first serious pressure. The movement for the open shop made headway, and the establishment of company unions varied from a genuine attempt to give the workers representation in industry to a movement to undermine the power of the more formidable national organizations.

But with all this went apparently an unwillingness to give labor cause to fear an attack on its standard of living. The very real fear of "bolshevism" which was a part of the post-war psychology of the return to "normalcy" may well have been one of the causes of this; in which case it may be said to have had its redeeming features to offset its grimmer manifestations in the shape of excessive repression.

Along with this has come the development of a new philosophy of high wages—new, that is, as a thing generally accepted by organized labor and to some extent even by employers. This is the theory that wages must be high to provide industry with the demand for its products which is essential to the prosperity of large-scale mass production. This theory in its defensible form must be distinguished from the fallacy which results from ignoring the fact that money distributed as profits is spent for goods, and spent just as much even if it is saved and invested. This is true, and yet the distribution of the income does have an effect on the kinds of goods for which the money is spent, as well as on the promptness of the expenditures. And the modern mass production must be able to market its products to the many and not solely or chiefly to the few, or the whole basis of its large and cheap production is undermined.

Whatever the cause, money earnings of wage-earners did not decline as fast as prices, and rates of real earnings increased. And this seems to have been a favorable condition for the growth of an industrial prosperity which depended in part on marketing automobiles and radio equipment in quantities which would not have been possible unless wage-earners had afforded a material part of the market. Another facilitating cause of the expansion of these industries was the much-discussed development of instalment selling, without which these expensive forms of durable consumer's equipment could not have been popularized among the more numerous consuming classes: those with small or moderate incomes.

An interesting question, however, arises: namely, just how is the beneficence of the principle of high wages affected when they are accompanied by large amounts of unemployment, such as we have experienced in the past seven years? Such a condition may be more favorable to the sale of automobiles, radios, and possibly rayon, than a condition of lower wages paid to more people; but it is not easy to show that it is better for industry in the aggregate, on the score of wider demand. Whether it is favorable to general business "prosperity" depends on other factors; chief of which are probably the effect of sustained wages on productivity, and the ultimate incidence of unemployment. And in any case, the effect of the War on these elements in the situation, beyond the revival of 1922, is a matter of sheer conjecture.

To the extent that existing conditions depend on prohibition and on the drastic restriction of immigration, it seems fair to rank the War as the precipitating cause of movements which would otherwise have been feeling their way slowly for at most a very small fraction of the distance we have covered at a single leap. Prohibition is credited by its advocates with an increase in the output of labor variously estimated at 5 per cent to 10 per cent. Needless to say, no method of proving the truth of such blanket estimates has been forthcoming, though in some cases it is possible to measure a decline in certain specific losses and wastes fairly definitely traced to previous habits of alcoholic consumption. The restriction of immigration must be looked on as a cause helping to sustain wages; if "economic laws" have any meaning. And the two facts together have undoubtedly acted as a stimulant to the movement toward increasing capital equipment per worker with a resulting increase in *per capita* output.[10] This movement is as old as the industrial revolution and would in any case have continued to make headway throughout this period, so that only a part of the recent shifts can be attributed to changes brought about by the War. To isolate this part with any exactness is a hopeless task.

[10] Some controversy exists among economists as to whether high wages are truly a cause of increased employment of capital. *See* H. G. Hayes, *Amer. Econ. Rev.*, September, 1923, p. 461; also C. O. Fisher and H. G. Hayes in the same journal, December, 1923, pp. 564, 665. A partial answer to Hayes's argument is indicated by the present writer in the same journal, September, 1928, p. 452, footnote.

One feature of the post-war situation, however, is distinctly a war legacy: namely, the balance of international trade and indebtedness. Neutrality had wiped out our previous debt to Europe; participation saw us lending far larger sums to our Allies; and at the end we were for the first time a creditor nation—creditor to about the amount of these government war loans. At this time Europe was in no condition to pay interest on these borrowings, let alone any instalments of principal. Financially, she was in need of further advances; commercially and industrially she was still in need of American goods and not in a position to export her own in payment to anything like the same amount. Hence our credit balance has piled up to undreamed-of heights, making us the second greatest creditor nation in the world: a creditor to at least double the sum that we were in debt in 1913, after allowing for the shrinkage in purchasing power of monetary units. To the 9½ billions of war advances we have apparently added a net export of capital, for 1919–29 inclusive, amounting to over 6 billions, as estimated from the yearly statements of our foreign balance of payments issued by the Department of Commerce. That this may be an underestimate is indicated by the fact that our credit balance on account of interest on private investments of all sorts amounted in 1929 to 562 millions, in addition to over 200 millions of interest on government loans. Half a billion of interest indicates far more than 6 billions of principal, even at very high rates of interest. Some of this, of course, may have been accumulated during the period of neutrality. One estimate places our foreign lendings at 26 billions and their annual increase at 2 billions.[11] This seems clearly a heavy overestimate, even if it refers to the gross movement without deducting foreign investments in this country. It is not impossible that the world's net debt to us amounts to some 15 billions even after scaling down the principal of the governmental debt (as the Treasury Department has done in its estimate of war costs), to a present worth of some 7 billions, reached by capitalizing the annuities at a higher interest rate than the foreign governments are being required to pay.[12]

[11] Dr. Max Winkler, reported in *New York Times,* December 21, 1928.

[12] *See* United States Department of Commerce, *The Balance of International Payments of the United States in 1929.* Figures are given from 1919 on, but the various years are not comparable with each other, nor with the

The balance of trade is itself becoming more complicated. Perhaps the outstanding fact is that with the growth of interest payments due us from abroad, and of freights earned by American vessels, our customary debit balance in the "invisible items" has virtually disappeared, leaving the balance of commodity exports as almost a clear net credit. This balance was 4 billions in 1919 and nearly 3 billions in 1920; while government loans were still being made in large amounts. It fell below 2 billions in 1921, and since then has averaged something under 600 millions. Allowing for changed price levels, our merchandise export balance is smaller than it was immediately before the outbreak of the War, but it has a changed significance. Now, instead of approximately canceling our debit balance in the "invisible items," it represents a progressive accumulation of credits.

It is, of course, hardly thinkable that exports of capital should forever exceed the returns in interest. Some day, barring some great catastrophe, this country must adjust its economy to the reverse situation, accompanied by an excess of merchandise imports. The ultimate effects may be desirable or undesirable; in any case, they are apparently inevitable. Even if we should make a downward revision of our foreign war-debt claims, it could only delay the ultimate outcome.

This export of American capital, from the foreign standpoint, takes on the aspect of an American invasion which is already causing serious disquietude. Foreigners who accept the inevitable prospect of a continued flow of capital are nevertheless attempting to draw distinctions between types of industry, marking off some as being of such key importance that American control is, from their standpoint, a definite evil. Public utilities and the companies supplying them appear to be the chief items in this list at present. Investments in such companies in South America are felt to carry with them a hold on an export market of special significance. And the proposal to limit American holdings in the British General Electric Company aroused some feeling on both sides of the water; as has also the British Ford Company's voluntary limitation on American holdings of voting stock.[13] This is a problem of which we have not heard the last.

treasury's statements on government foreign loans, as given in *Annual Report* for 1927, p. 647. Hence the above is only a rough estimate.

[13] Cf. *New York Times*, December 17, 1928. Other companies mentioned

It is perhaps significant that the discussion of the post-war period
has gone so far without mentioning the fiscal facts of continued governmental expenditures on account of the War. These have not been
light; but they are far from having dominated the post-war picture.
The treasury's official estimate shows, for the fiscal year 1920, expenses for the War of over 5 billions, less sales of surplus property
and other receipts. During the first half of this fiscal year demobilization was still going on at a heavy rate, mustering out the last
800,000. Continuing foreign loans and interest on our own war debt
accounted for 1,424 million dollars. In the fiscal year 1921 the expenditures were 3.8 billions, including over 1 billion for interest on
our war debt and for foreign loans—the latter being less than 75
millions. For subsequent years, no departmental expenses are
charged to the War, for the reason that it is considered officially
ended by the President's proclamation of July 2, 1921; and the only
continuing items carried further are the interest on our debt and
the expenses of the Veterans' Bureau, plus a small item under the
head of hospital construction. In effect, however, the Shipping
Board's deficits are also charged, as they are deducted from the estimated value of its remaining assets in figuring net costs. Calculated
in this way, the total net costs of the War to the end of the fiscal
year 1927 are 35 billions, after deducting 7,470 millions as the net
worth of our foreign obligations as of June 30, 1921. The continuing costs since 1921 have been going on at a rate of about 1.3 billions per year, the expense for care of veterans increasing as the interest on the war debt diminished. The interest on the debt, as
already noted, is not a social cost in the same sense as expenditures
representing services currently performed or goods currently consumed. The social cost involved consists mainly of the net burdens
involved in transferring funds from taxpayers to bondholders as
compensation for "abstinence" undergone during the War; and the
whole constitutes a difficult problem in social incidence.

Of course, the date of the official proclamation of peace has no
necessary connection with the termination of the expenses caused by
the War. But it did in fact coincide with the subsiding of ordinary
governmental expenses to very nearly the level they have since main-

as taking measures of defense are the Imperial Airways and the Canadian
Marconi. Department stores are mentioned as a field in which American investments are welcomed.

tained, which may be taken as the post-war "normal." These expenses, other than debt-retirement items, were approximately 3⅓ billions in the fiscal year 1922, and from 1924 on have remained close to 3 billions. Continuing departmental outlays for 1922–23, in excess of the post-war normal, amount to a trifle over ½ billion. This amount may be regarded as due to the War, combined with the inertia with which public expenses oppose any process of paring down.

The question still remains whether this post-war normal is itself higher than it would otherwise have been, as an after-effect of the War. The gross amounts in dollars are obviously much increased. Deducting the 1.3 billions already noted, there remains 1.7 billions as compared to approximately ¾ of one billion in 1916. To judge whether this is an abnormal increase it is necessary, first, to deflate for the shrunken value of the post-war dollar. Next the figures should be reduced to a *per capita* basis. These two adjustments eliminate most of the apparent post-war excess. Next a study should be made of the pre-war trend of *per capita* expenses in dollars of constant purchasing power, to see if an upward trend in real outlays *per capita* is to be regarded as normal; and if such a trend is found, it should be projected forward to the post-war years. Finally, if possible, a study should be made of such real increases as may be found, to determine whether they are of a productive character and not to be regarded as a burden on our national economy. It is quite conceivable that the War may have stimulated the undertaking of some activities which should have been initiated sooner; in which case the outlays, though caused by the War, should hardly be charged as part of its costs. Some of the services of the Department of Commerce may well fall in this category. On the other hand, post-war economy may in other cases have cramped the desirable development of valuable peace-time functions.

The chief place to look for increased real outlays of an unproductive character is, naturally, in the War and Navy Departments. A survey of the type outlined above is made in a later chapter, and seems to indicate that the real outlays in these departments are very little above the pre-war normal amounts *per capita* (not including the increased outlays carried by the recent cruiser bill).[14] The War brought a great development in aviation, chemical warfare, tanks,

[14] *See* Chapter VII, below.

submarines, and other new devices, all tending to make an armed force more expensive; but some part of this would have come in any case through the ordinary course of technical advance. It is at least possible that expenses for armed forces are now no heavier than they would have been if the War had not occurred. The Washington Conference did not reduce these expenses below their pre-war level, even on a basis of real expense *per capita;* but it did cut off the greater part of the increase which would otherwise have come as the aftermath of the conflict. Whether or not the War is ultimately to be credited with a genuine decrease in warlike expenses, for us or for the rest of the world, rests with the future developments of the standing peace machinery it has set in motion.

War revenues overtook expenses in 1920, reaching their peak in that year at 6,694 millions and showing a small surplus. Two years later they had declined to about 4 billions, and remained thereafter near that level. Expenses declined still more, leaving a surplus in every year, which was duly applied to reduce the war debt.[15] The surplus, however, is over and above a liberal sinking fund and other funds required by statute to be applied to debt retirements, including payments received from foreign governments on the debts due from them. Thus the treasury was able to reduce the net debt 8 billions in ten years, while the aggregate "surplus" contributed less than 3¼ billions.[16] While surpluses have fluctuated, retirements from sinking fund have increased progressively, owing to the cumulative feature of the fund. These ten years cleared away over one-third of the total debt and reduced interest charges from 1,016 millions to 606 millions. The latest treasury estimate, made at the end of the fiscal year 1930, placed the probable date of extinguishment of the war debt at 1949. The unexpectedly large deficit recorded in

[15] For a more detailed treatment of debt retirement, *see* below, Chapter VII, pp. 105–108.

[16] Figures from address by Under-Secretary Mills, covering results to June 30, 1930. For earlier figures *see* tables, *Report of Secretary of the Treasury for 1927,* pp. 445, 602–604. Where there are discrepancies between the tables, the figures compiled on the basis of daily statements are to be preferred for our purpose to those compiled on the basis of warrants issued. Gross debt was reduced 9 billions, the extra billion coming from the reduction of the war-swollen "general fund balance" in 1919, before substantial retirements from income had begun. For details of debt retirements, *see* below, Chapter VII.

1931—$903,000,000—represents a setback of about two years in this program, causing the net debt to increase by $463,000,000 instead of decreasing by that amount or more. This increase does not fully wipe out the decrease recorded in 1930. And it is worth noting that the tax burdens which have sustained this program of debt reduction have not crippled industry—on the contrary, they have coincided with our greatest period of prosperity, and cannot apparently be charged with any major share of responsibility for the subsequent depression.

The economic effects of paying off a public debt at a rate of nearly a billion a year afford in themselves an interesting field for study. The funds naturally seek reinvestment, constituting a weighty reinforcement to the ordinary flow of savings. And while the taxes laid to raise the money may to some extent have the effect of repressing savings that would otherwise have been made by the taxpayers, this is only a partial offset and very likely a minor one. Our continued lendings to foreign countries have been large enough to absorb at least the larger part of the released funds, and probably the whole, if they had all chosen this outlet. On the other hand, our own State and local governments have also been increasing their borrowings almost as fast as the federal debt has decreased, with the result that the total volume of governmental debts has declined little more than one billion in all.[17] But however one may look at it, the moral certainty remains that the supply of loanable funds was made billions larger than it would have been if the federal debt had not been paid off to the extent that it was. This was a time of prosperity when large savings could easily be made and a large flow might be expected in any case. Federal debt redemptions made it still larger. And the runaway stock market of 1929 might logically be taken as a symptom (among other things) of a supply of investable funds larger than we well knew what to do with. Thus the retirement of the war debt may have had some connection with the stock market crash which ushered in the present depression.

But we must not fall into the fallacy of charging all unpleasant experiences of the after-war time as consequences of the War, even though a causal connection can be traced. The War was one of the forces helping to set the stage for all the troubles we have since experienced—also for all the turns of good fortune, since nothing has

[17] From statement issued by Professor Irving Fisher, in leaflet form.

escaped its influence. But we may be sure that if there had been no war there would still have been troubles of some sort and, let us hope, turns of good fortune as well. The aftermath of the War is an important story, but we must beware of taking its details too seriously when we come to the task of drawing up the table of social costs for which the War is responsible.

For that is the task to which this very much abbreviated narrative serves as an introduction. And the story will have served one of its chief purposes if it has brought into view a rather bewildering number of items whose exact place and weight in the debit-and-credit account of the War is far from clear at first glance. For this reason, having at least indicated the main facts, the next step is to turn our attention to the principles which may guide us in the attempt to turn these facts into a systematic appraisal. In other words, we must examine the theory of war costs. We shall not learn from it whether the treasury's figure of 35 billions is an accurate sum in accounting, but we may learn something of the significance of the various items that go to make up this sum. Can they be taken over without adjustment into an account which purports to show the net effect of war on our whole economic organism? Possibly we may also get some light on the outstanding paradox which this narrative has only served to sharpen: namely, how can a nation, after pouring 35 billions into the maw of war, emerge richer than ever before? Did this wealth come in spite of the war nightmare; or can it have been, in part at least, because of it? And if the War had any compensating effects in stimulating the production of wealth in this country, was this due at all to our own warlike activities, or solely to the demands for our goods arising from the warlike activities of Europe?

CHAPTER V

THE NATURE OF WAR COSTS

AFTER what has gone before, no time need be wasted in convincing the reader that the analysis of war costs is not a simple and self-evident affair. These costs form a tangled pattern of interrelated facts, whose bearings on the ultimate social profit-and-loss account are often far from clear. First, there are the governmental expenditures for goods and services; the goods including food and clothes for soldiers as well as ships, guns, and explosives, and the services including the cooking of meals in company kitchens as well as the storming of hostile machine-gun nests and, for the armed forces, a virtual socialistic substitute for our whole mercantile distributive system. The government disbursements also include loans to our Allies, interest on our own government borrowings, and items of financial adjustment such as the making good of the "deficits" of the railroads below the income guaranteed them under federal operation. In the post-war period the main fiscal items are debt charges, and care of veterans and their dependents; consisting of payments of money and services from our Government to its own citizens, in reimbursement for very varied kinds of sacrifices.

Then there are the taxes, the loans, and the inflation involved in furnishing these funds to the government, with all the difficult questions of the ultimate incidence of this financing. There are also the actual goods and services used to fight the war, toward the securing of which all these fiscal measures were directed as means to an end. There is also the effect of the war on the volume of industrial production, and the after-effects in the post-war period. There are the extra efforts needed to replace those taken from industry into war service, the extra consumption of limited natural materials like coal and oil, and the privations of decreased consumption. And there is the actual loss of life and health: the real cost for which the expenses of the Veterans' Bureau constitute the more or less inaccurate money measure and compensation. There are the effects of the war on the distribution of prosperity between different industries and different classes of the population; and the question whether these are, in the aggregate, a national gain or loss, and of what importance. And there are the effects of immigration restriction and of prohibition, and the changes in our international economic position and dealings. And there are the still more intangible effects of war on the status of labor, on liberalism and social progress, and on the spirit of the people in general. All these matters have their place in the picture, and each one has a different bearing on the ultimate appraisal. Clearly, some way is needed of simplifying this maze of relationships, so far as may be done without sacrificing completeness and accuracy.

If we start with the spending of funds by government and follow the incidence of this act in one direction, we come to the raising of the revenues by taxes or by loans. Indeed, we may look at the government as an intermediary agent by means of which the resources of the people are diverted to the uses of war, the whole diversion being one fact which may be observed at various points in the chain of fiscal operations involved without destroying its essential unity. Taxes and simple loans from individuals are alike in their proximate effect, of transferring purchasing power to the government, increasing by so much the goods government can buy, and decreasing by so much the goods the individuals can buy. They are unlike in that the lender receives compensation in the form of claims to future reimbursement against the taxpayers in general, including himself.

If taxes were laid in the same proportions in which bonds are subscribed for, this reimbursement might seem to be wholly illusory; though even so the whole process would undoubtedly have some effect on the proportion of wealth remaining as capital at the end of the transaction. But as it is, the single bondholder suffers no appreciable loss in his total wealth from his individual act of lending, since if he had not done so, he would still have borne substantially the same burden of taxes for the reimbursement of the other bondholders. Thus from his private standpoint the reimbursement is real, even though he may pay in taxes as much as he receives in interest on his bonds. Moreover, his act is voluntary, or quasi-voluntary. Nevertheless, to repeat, the immediate effect is the same as that of taxes in that the government receives present command over more of society's goods and the individual less. This present command over goods is what the individual gives up.

Where loans come out of the elasticity of the credit system and result in inflation the effect is shifted, though its ultimate character is not fundamentally transformed. If the inflation has no effect on the supply of goods, then whatever the government is able to buy with its borrowed funds means that others can buy that much less, though they have as much nominal purchasing power as before. The result is naturally brought about by an increase in prices, diluting the purchasing power of all funds, including those the government has just borrowed, along with those which businesses or individuals still hold. One way of looking at it is that the government has obtained, for instance, 10 per cent of the purchasing power of the country, by borrowing $11\frac{1}{9}$ per cent of the *previous* purchasing power, and can command 10 per cent of the goods (ignoring for the moment the problem of unequal price movements in different groups of commodities and services). If the amount of goods available is unaffected by the inflation, the immediate effect is precisely as if every holder of funds had been taxed 10 per cent of his holdings. The same amount of goods is transferred from private to public use. Ultimate effects, of course, are far-reaching, and constitute a story by themselves; but they also, when traced, take the same basic form. Those whose incomes fail to increase as fast as prices can command less goods; and those whose incomes increase faster can command more.

The simplest method of approximating the effects of inflation goes on the assumption, already indicated, that it has no effect on the volume of goods turned out. But that it should have no effect at all is well-nigh impossible. The effect due to government borrowings alone can only be conjectured, as it is hopelessly merged in the effect of the credit expansion which would have resulted in any case from the demands of private industry, and the effect the emergency needs would have produced, even if no credit expansion of any sort had been permitted. The probability is overwhelming that in a great emergency calling with suddenly increased insistence for the utmost output of productive effort, much of it directed into altered channels, the strict avoidance of any "inflation," or the rigid maintenance of an unchanged average price level, would seriously hamper the needed mobilization. If credit could not be extended in one direction without being first, or simultaneously, contracted in other quarters: if prices of essentials could rise only to the extent that prices of nonessentials fell, expansion of essential production would be limited to a fraction of what is industrially possible, while disorganization of nonessential industry might be more than is industrially necessary or useful.

The situation is best handled if credit can be expanded in some directions without suffering simultaneous and equal contraction in others; even if the total is allowed to expand somewhat more than physical production. Such expansion, even with rising prices and some dilution of purchasing power, seems the most effective way of meeting the needs of the case. On the other hand, if there were no curtailment at all in nonessential quarters, and the expansion in essential directions were a clear increase, the result would be a definite obstacle to the most economical mobilization. This would be true especially if the resulting increase in prices were followed by corresponding further inflation all around in essential and nonessential goods alike. This would be an evil if only by reason of the uncertainties it would introduce and the undue support it would afford to the policy of "business as usual," and without regard to the injustices inflicted on bondholders and the salaried classes.

Credit expansion, then, may result in increasing the government's command over goods more, or less, than it decreases that of private buyers; with a corresponding enlargement or shrinkage of total production as compared to what it would otherwise have been. If we take for granted the expansion naturally brought about by private demands, the further expansion resulting from government borrowings seems virtually certain to be in excess of the amount that could serve any industrially useful purpose, if there were any other way in which government could secure its needed share of the total purchasing power of the country. But however that may be, the immediate effect of expansion as a means of war mobilization is to be sought in its effect on volumes of goods: the volume going to government and the volume remaining for private use; the two together making up the national economic income.

The incidence of inflation, then, includes whatever effect it may have on total production. And while the incidence of taxes is often analyzed as if it could be separated from this larger fact, it is not so separate in practice. And the fuller picture must include the incidence of the whole process of which taxation is but a part: the process of taxing, spending, and thereby mobilizing industry, with the greatest possible increase, or the smallest possible decrease, in the aggregate productive effort put forth. Diversion of goods, with a credit or debit for increase or decrease in aggregate production, is the crucial fact for the purpose in hand.

If we follow the incidence of governmental expenses in the other direction, through the spending of the funds, we come back at once to the same fact: the spending of money has its primary effect in calling forth goods, and any expenditures which do not do this—such as interest on the public debt—are only in a secondary and fiscal sense war expenditures at all. They are transfers of purchasing power from private taxpayers to private bondholders (or from subscribers to new loans to those holding older issues) and it is only the incidence of the process of transfer that can be figured as a cost to the economy of the nation.

Thus, from the maze of interrelated facts, one group seems to be emerging in a central position: one group on which the effects of the financial transactions converge and from which diverge the more intangible questions of the seriousness of the sacrifices involved. This group of facts consists of the amount of goods and services produced and the amount taken for war uses. The more ultimate costs which we may trace from this central fact take the shape mainly of added efforts put forth in maintaining production and filling the gaps left by taking producers into war service; and privations of decreased consumption. And there perhaps our inquiry should properly end.

But there are further questions which will not be wholly ignored; questions as to the ultimate human importance of these things. Are these efforts and privations more or less serious than those commonly represented by the same dollar measures or the same physical quantities in an ordinary peace-time economy? Are these personal sacrifices and privations less seriously felt by reason of the very fact that they are due to a national emergency and not to personal inefficiency, failure, or misfortune? Are they less serious because all bear them more or less in common, and large classes in more or less the same measure, and they therefore (in most cases) do not dislodge individuals from the position they have gained relative to others in the economic class structure? Or are some of these sacrifices sharpened by their unequal and unjust incidence: by the helplessness of those dependent on fixed incomes to escape undeserved losses, or by the fact that business profits and losses are distributed not so much according to merit as by the accident of strategic location as between industries of equal peace-time standing and importance, some of which are essential for war and some not? These are real, if difficult, problems in the theory of war costs. In general, it seems that the mental suffering that comes with the purely economic privations of war is mitigated by their community character, but this is probably a poor compensation for the other stresses and sufferings that war brings with it.

But to return to the fact which seems the most available focus on which to center our study. On this basic conception of present goods and services as central facts in the picture of war costs hinge two questions, well worn by controversy but possibly not yet quite worn out. First: can domestic loans shift the burden of war to future generations, or is it true, as economists have so often claimed, that the cost is borne when the war is fought and can in no such way be shifted? With this is involved the question whether domestic borrowing as a means of financing a war is necessarily a mistake, failing to lighten the immediate load and adding to it a useless aftermath of fiscal burdens. Second: can disaster such as fire, flood, or war, be good for business by creating demand for its products, making work for it to do or "putting money in circulation," and so perhaps actually making for prosperity? Or is the economist right when he insists that there is no magic whereby the destruction of wealth can be anything but an economic loss? These two cases will serve very well as tools with which to study the strong and weak points of the "basic conception" of diversion of goods and services as the real costs of the war.

Can loans "postpone the burden of war to future generations"? Loans are simply one way by which government secures purchasing power, and it secures it simply as a means to securing goods and services—men and munitions. By taking these goods and services out of the common fund, it either leaves that much less for individuals, or compels them to do more work to make up the deficiency, or has a mixture of the two effects. This effect is the basic burden for the nation as a whole; and it cannot be postponed without postponing the government's supply of men and munitions until it is too late to help win the war. As has been often said: one cannot win a battle today with shells to be made tomorrow, nor man the trenches with children yet unborn.

The work of making munitions is not postponed, nor any curtailment of private consumption or of private industrial investment which is thereby necessitated. The spending of money by government is not postponed, nor the raising of that money from private parties. What is postponed is simply the final allocation of this fiscal burden to the people in their capacity as taxpayers, and this is done by getting the immediate funds instead from some of the same people as quasi-voluntary loans. This leaves to future generations simply the task of making the final distribution by collecting money from taxpayers and paying it out to bondholders: a mere fiscal transfer to pay for shells long ago fired, or for "abstinence" long ago incurred. And this "abstinence" was a final cost at the time it was incurred, in the sense that it left behind no productive capital out of which the payments of interest and principal might come. The contention has been made that this remaining task of fiscal transfer and settlement is simply a useless burden due to our lacking the moral courage to make our fiscal measures as definitive as the social expenditures they are used to finance: to make the raising of revenues as final as the burning of the explosives which they serve to procure. In other words, the claim is that our task would be simplified and our real burdens made no greater, at the time of the war or any other time, if the borrowed funds had instead been raised by taxes.

Or, to look at it another way, the subscribers to war loans supply funds by sacrificing that much private purchasing power (if there is no inflation). They make this sacrifice on behalf of the nation at the time the loan is subscribed and, for the nation as a whole, this sacrifice is final and there is no reimbursement. Why is it not better, then, to take the same amount of money from more or less the same people in the form of taxes, which leave behind no obligation to pay for dead horses and burnt powder? If there is inflation, still—the argument goes—government gets only as much effective purchasing power as private interests lose, but the money of both is diluted, and the dilution is itself the source of many injustices between economic groups, while the taxpayers will ultimately have to pay for these diluted dollars, perhaps in dollars of full value and in any case in dollars which are almost sure to have a different value from those borrowed. If bondholders do not profiteer at the expense of taxpayers, taxpayers will profiteer at the expense of bondholders, and either is equally an evil.

Another point raised is that the effect of loans is to shift part of the ultimate tax financing from war-time, when the war-spirit makes it possible to exact great sacrifices from the rich, to peace-time, when this can no longer be done. As a result, it is argued, the burden falls more heavily on the poor and on those with moderate incomes. This point was made during the War, and can now be reviewed in the light of the war and post-war experience. And in the light of such experience this argument is shown to be valid only against a policy which relies on loans much more heavily than we actually did during the past war. Our actual policy, it will be remembered, was roughly described as one of two-thirds loans and one-third taxes, though the reader will also recall that if our borrowings to lend to our Allies are canceled out, taxes made a substantially larger showing. As things actually were, any attempt to raise more by taxes and less by loans would have resulted in laying a larger part of the burden on small and moderate incomes and a smaller portion on the very rich.

War-time taxes are almost of necessity steeply progressive, and our income tax set a new record for the severity of the rates on the highest incomes. It took more than half of the largest incomes, and in 1918 reached 77 per cent of increments above $2,000,000. It is true that present rates on large incomes are much less than this, but it is also true that the combination of lower rates and increased exemptions has resulted in an even greater proportional lowering of the total burden on incomes of moderate size, especially "earned incomes." Thus the income tax has grown more progressive since the War, and not less, in terms of the relative number of dollars exacted from small and large incomes. The effect of the whole tax system is a different matter, but there is at least no proof that it has become less progressive. The personal and corporate income taxes, which are progressive in their effects, have almost held their own as compared to other elements in the tax system, and between them account for about half of total ordinary receipts.[1]

But this is not, after all, the decisive point. The crucial question is whether, if we had financed the War, let us say, two-thirds out of taxes instead of one-third, the *additional* burdens would have fallen more heavily on the rich than the subsequent peace-time taxes which the borrowing has made necessary. As to this, the answer is absolutely certain. A heavy increase in war taxes could not have fallen on the very rich, for the simple reason that our system had already gone as far as possible in this direction, and the very rich were paying the majority of their incomes to the Government. Any heavy in-

---

[1] *See* reports of the Commissioner of Internal Revenue.

crease in tax revenues must have come mainly from moderate and small incomes.

The distribution of the resulting benefits is a matter of more doubt: but it is hardly conceivable that the small and moderate incomes should benefit more in the post-war period than they had suffered during the War. On the score of progressive taxation as a desirable thing, then, not much can be said for a program of exclusive tax financing as a means of placing the burden more heavily on the rich. The argument would possibly be valid as against a policy of laying no war taxes at all until the War was over, but hardly against the policy which this country actually followed.

This point bears on another argument which criticizes the post-war legacy of taxes to repay bondholders as a bad distribution of wealth, since the taxpayers are, on the average, poorer than the bondholders and the funds are therefore transferred from those to whom they are more important to those to whom they are less.[2] This is strictly true, but it does not dispose of the obstinate difficulty already raised. It would be a valid criticism if there had been any practicable way of levying additional taxes so that the *added* burden would have fallen on the rich in the same proportion as the subscriptions they actually made to the war loans. But this, as we have seen, was out of the question.

This knot can, of course, be cut by the process of borrowing and then repudiating, either directly or indirectly through a depreciated currency. But neither policy commends itself except as it may be forced upon a country by a choice of evils far more serious than the one we are now discussing. Repudiation may be regarded as turning the loan into a tax retroactively, in which case it would be a tax of such unequal, unjust, and haphazard incidence as no government could deliberately levy. What such an outcome would really mean may perhaps be seen in clearer perspective if we look for a moment at the reasons why money can be extracted from the people by loans which could not be extracted by any practicable or desirable system

[2] Strictly speaking, the pertinent comparison is not between taxpayers and present bondholders, but between taxpayers and original subscribers, who included more persons in the low income groups. But even original bond subscriptions came more heavily from the rich than do present taxes, so that the point does not invalidate the general argument of the criticism.

of taxation. This fact, indeed, is the decisive justification for relying on bonds as one considerable source of war revenues. While taxes may be laid on the principle of "ability to pay," this ability has to be gauged by general indexes, such as income; and such indexes cannot differentiate between persons to whom the same income may represent, for the moment at least, very different degrees of taxpaying ability. One man has many dependents, another none. One man has business commitments which call for all the present income he can spare from family needs; another has just received the principal of an expired bond or mortgage and is in a position to furnish present purchasing power in excess of his present income, though it would be neither fair nor practicable to take this in the form of taxes. A business may have surplus or reserves of various sorts to invest, and so be in a position to furnish present purchasing power in the form of bond subscriptions, where to take the same amount in taxes would either cut down its net income, perhaps to the vanishing point, or make necessary higher prices which would cut down demand and seriously hamper normal productive activity.

Thus, while bonds do not postpone the immediate sacrifice of purchasing power and of private control over goods, they may prevent it from being aggravated by the effects of exorbitant taxes in stifling production. And they also distribute it in ways making possible the gathering in of a larger percentage of the nation's economic power than would otherwise be practicable. This is a matter of methods of securing present goods and services to spend for war, after which the nation does not have to furnish these goods and services over again: that has been done once for all. The nation is left with a series of assets and liabilities which offset each other. The bondholders hold assets which they themselves, together with all the other taxpayers or bearers of ultimate tax burdens, must liquidate. To the nonexistent average individual who is both an average bondholder and an average tax bearer, the liability exactly equals the asset: what is collected as taxes on this account precisely equals what is paid in interest and principal on bonds (plus costs of collection and administration). The repayments may be more or less than fair compensation for the value originally loaned, according as the money unit may have been stabilized at a higher purchasing power than prevailed during the war, or at a depreciated level which may rob the bondholder of most of the value of his claims. That, however, does not affect the balance between post-war collections and post-war disbursements, both measured in post-war money units.

One further point, however, has been made. In this post-war obligation to transfer wealth, the asset side is capitalized in a definite funded obligation in the hands of individuals constituting private wealth which may be bought, sold, or pledged as security for loans. The liability side, as it affects individuals, does not take the corresponding form of a contractual claim constituting a lien for a definite amount on their personal wealth or income, but merely an untraceable share in the additional general tax burdens which the debt charges necessitate. The burden to individuals is not capitalized, but is felt only as the taxes are laid and collected; and even then is not earmarked so as to make it possible to distinguish the part due to war borrowing. On this basis Professor Seligman has taken the position that the "subjective cost" of the war is postponed by national borrowing. This is, in substance, a true expression of the way individuals feel about the transaction, and also of the more tangible way in which it affects their immediate financial standing. This last is of very substantial importance, as we have seen in the case of loans subscribed by business organizations.

Nor is the matter entirely one of warped perspective which capitalizes contractual assets and fails to capitalize the corresponding noncontractual liabilities. The individual would have the same burden of post-war taxes to bear whether he personally subscribed to a loan or not. His financial prospects are made worse by the issuance of the loan, but not (perceptibly) by his own subscription thereto. This act, while reducing his margin available for personal expenditure, does not affect materially his total private wealth, even if his liability to future taxes were to be capitalized and deducted.

For the purposes of this study, we may best make our way out of this dilemma by treating the costs of the war primarily as social aggregates of goods and services. From this standpoint they are not postponed as a result of war borrowing: merely raised in a provisional way requiring a later final settlement. This settlement may best be treated as a matter of the distribution and incidence of the burden. This ultimate distribution and incidence are postponed. The social cost, then, includes the goods and services bought with the proceeds of loans, at the time the funds are so spent by government. It further includes the costs of war-tax collections and fiscal administration of war taxes and loans through the whole life of the war debt, and also any effect the fiscal transactions may have in reducing the aggregate social dividend turned out by industry or otherwise affecting the nation's economic welfare.

The costs of fiscal administration are presumably increased by loans, through being spread over a longer period. The depressing effects of post-war taxes on aggregate economic output are very real, especially if the taxes are as heavy as they have been in Europe; but they are presumably mitigated, as compared to a policy of financing exclusively by taxes, for reasons already indicated. An exclusive tax policy would undoubtedly involve a serious shrinkage in war-time industrial output; though a more serious result would be a heavy limitation in the volume of social income the government could thus acquire. Whether the United States employed taxes and loans in optimum proportions is a question impossible of anything like exact solution, and may well be regarded as outside the scope of the present study. But at any rate its policy does not stand obviously condemned.

So far as loans are made in ways which bring about inflation, an added problem is raised, which may be approached by a simple illustration. If the government raises a billion dollars without inflation, it has the billion dollars and other purchasers have that much less to spend. If it raises the billion dollars wholly through inflation, it has an added billion of nominal purchasing power while other purchasers have no less nominal purchasing power than before. But the result is to raise prices and so to dilute the purchasing power of: (1) the dollars remaining in the hands of private purchasers, (2) the billion the government has raised through inflation, and (3) all other billions which the government may have raised in ways not involving inflation. The result is to give government a larger proportion of the total purchasing power of the country than before, but far less than the full value of the billion dollars, even at its post-inflation buying power. In practice, the results are less simple than this, since the raising of prices tends to induce further inflation in the shape of increased dollar loans to private business, which still further neutralizes the government's acquisitions of buying power. It is even theoretically possible that, if the government has already secured most of its war revenues by methods not involving inflation, further inflationary borrowings might actually decrease its total percentage of the buying power of the nation. This, however, is not likely.

The immediate effect of inflationary borrowing, then, is to be found in the increased flow of goods and services it enables the government to command through diversion from private uses, compounded with any effects it may have on the total flow of such things in the national economy. The incidence of the burden on individuals is quite as complex as that of taxes, and even more disturbing in its effects. These effects last as long as the combined duration of the inflation and of bonds issued in the preinflation period. If deflation ensues, then further disturbances occur in the opposite direction, lasting as long as the life of bonds issued while the inflation was in effect. Inflationary borrowing, then, does not postpone the sacrifice of goods and services, but distributes the burden more unjustly than any other method of financing, and leaves more disturbing consequences in the way of subsequent financial adjustments. It may be justified if the immediate command of goods and services cannot be secured in any other way, but it is a deplorably expensive method of securing such command. As we have already seen, moderate inflation may have its uses in developing latent productive power, but there is practically certain to be all that can serve such a useful purpose, and more, without any stimulus from governmental borrowing.

This discussion brings out one point worthy of every possible emphasis. The fact that costs in the social sense cannot be postponed, if by that is meant relieving the nation of the immediate burden, does not mean that there are not also continuing social burdens to be borne. These may take the shape of direct outlays of goods and services, as in the care of veterans, or of maldistribution of the national dividend, as in the results of inflation and subsequent deflation, or of a hampering of industrial activity such as may result from wastage of capital or from the effects of post-war deflation or the incidence of post-war taxes. These effects are in addition to the direct and non-postponable material costs of the war.

We come next to the question whether disasters which consume or destroy wealth can be, after all, advantageous to the social economy because the demand they create is "good for business" and leads to increased production and circulation of wealth. Traditional economics says: "No. The breaking of windows, for example, can never be anything but destruction of wealth; it cannot be metamorphosed into the creation of wealth, no matter how far its effects may be traced as they ramify through the economic system." It is admitted that breaking windows may help glaziers for the moment, but only at the expense of other producers; those who would otherwise have received the money the glaziers got for replacing the panes, and in exchange would have satisfied some additional want beyond the need for windows that will keep the weather out. That extra satisfaction is lost when the pane is broken. And for the rest, glaziers work more and receive more, while others work less and receive less. This view is certainly sound, on traditional economic assumptions; but is it all-sufficient and equally applicable to all cases? The experience of the War seems to afford ground for giving the question some fresh examination.

The crux of the question lies here: is the effective demand for other things, and the consequent production of other things, necessarily cut down by exactly the amount that is spent on replacing the broken panes? Or, to put it the other way around, if the panes had not been broken, would other things have been demanded, produced, and consumed to an exactly equal amount? As a matter of long-run adjustment, the establishment of a permanent habit of breaking some thousands or millions of panes every year might be expected to have substantially this effect. But we are not dealing with the long-run results of permanent habits, but with single events which break into the customary spending and producing habits of the people; and we must examine the case at issue on that basis.

Such evidence as the war experience offers is suggestive, but not by itself conclusive. For the record of a complex historical episode seldom carries within itself the proof of the precise effect of each one of a multitude of collaborating causes. America prospered in the period of neutrality, when it was in the position of the glaziers in our illustration. Prosperity in such a situation proves nothing that is not admitted at the start. But the suggestive thing about this prosperity is the fact that we prospered by making goods *without getting paid for them*. The glazier who lets his customer's bill run may be doing well by himself, if the customer is "good pay" in the end, but we should hardly expect him to live high in the meantime from his work for that particular customer. From the fact that we improved our living moderately as well as expanded our glassworks very substantially over and above the credits we were accumulating for unbalanced exports, one may conclude that the actual situation contains elements which the simplified illustration does not indicate.

The general nature of these elements of productive expansion has already been indicated: namely, the new demand not balanced by an equal falling off in other demands, the additional derived demand for capital equipment, the increase in employment and volume of work done, and the further resultant demand for goods by more prosperous workers and other participants in the earnings of industry. The net increase in aggregate money demand was seen to be made readily possible by the elasticity of the credit system, the stimulus to production intensified by the well-known effects of rising prices, and the increased money demand, representing an increase in the world's economic necessities, was enabled to take effect as an increased total of "effective demand" for actual goods by reason of the elasticity of our productive powers, which were then, as at most times, working short of full capacity.

It may be remarked in passing that the "elasticity of the credit system" is no matter of inscrutable necromancy conjuring something from nothing, magical as its effects may appear. Banks can multiply purchasing power because depositors are willing to accept the position of lenders without interest. Depositors do this to the extent of most of their reserves for current spendings, in exchange for the privilege of calling these deposits at any moment by the process of drawing a check. This is a painless and largely unconscious form of lending, involving no increase of abstinence. Expansion of deposits through expansion of loans finds its main base (aside from adequate cash reserves) in a quasi-automatic increase in this painless and unconscious furnishing of credit.

Turning to the experience of our actual participation in the War, the evidence it affords on the question at issue is less conclusive in one way than the experience of neutrality, and stronger in another. It is less conclusive in that consumption of wealth did not actually increase; and it is stronger in that whatever compensating effects were secured, were secured in the face of the fact that it was now our own windows that were being broken, as well as those of our European neighbors; so that we were no longer in the position of glaziers who might expect to profit for quite obvious reasons. The work and materials absorbed by our window-smashings were clearly not a net subtraction from our previous or our normal activities but involved an increase in the gross total. Production increased to a limit apparently set largely by congestion of rail facilities under an abnormal concentration of traffic at the Atlantic seaboard, rather than by any more general and abstract law of economic equilibrium. Economic effort, it must be noted, increased more than results; since war production was abnormally wasteful and lavishly expensive.

Other nations fared far worse, in this respect, than the United States. In France, for instance, the calling of the army to the colors resulted in throwing a still larger army of unemployed on the streets: a condition which was only very gradually remedied. Instead of calling the existing unemployed into the workshops to take the places of those who had gone to the front, many shops were closed because the employer had gone to the front, and his employees not liable to service were left to find new work if possible. Thus French production fell off on account of this element of disorganization, as well as on account of the more obvious and unavoidable fact that the first invasion had snatched from her an area in which a large section of her heavy industries and mines was located. In this case the smashing of windows was emphatically not "good for business."

Further evidence might be sought in the general testimony of studies of the business cycle, to the effect that reviving demand acts cumulatively, at least within fairly liberal limits. This does not prove that an economic disaster brings an increase in effective demand for goods; but it indicates that such an increase is not impossible.

To sum up: the effect seems to depend on the character and extent of the disaster, on the attitude with which it is met, and on the state of the credit system and of business activity in general. A disaster which does not cripple the machinery of production, of an extent which spurs people to increased efforts rather than reducing them to helpless despair, coupled with a credit system and an industrial system each of which has some unused capacity for expansion—these conditions enable a disaster to be self-repairing in part at least, through stimulus to productive activity.

One of the penalties of increasing economic power is the need to find new forms of consumption in which to embody it. This process is tentative, risky, and wasteful. We are limited in our imagination as consumers as to the best ways to use increasing spending power: still more as producers in devising economically practicable goods which will capture the consumers' unformulated buying potentialities. Nowadays producers must, perforce, try to meet the consumers' latent desires more than halfway—to form them, indeed, in ways capable of successful and profitable gratification. But this attempt is inherently uncertain. And there is, as a consequence perhaps in part of this uncertainty and of these limits on our economic imagination, a tendency to waste capital in unimaginative duplication of existing types of facilities, to produce familiar goods. This being the case, production by these facilities is limited by the limited demand for these familiar things; the more nearly unlimited potential demand for new goods being no help to those who have not diagnosed the potentialities aright. In such a situation, anything which increases the need for familiar types of goods may be a blessed relief from the very perplexities of progress, enabling industry to go ahead with certainty and confidence rather than undertaking the more difficult task of diagnosing the consumers' unknown potentialities and devising or selecting goods to call them forth. With a known wastage to make good, industry can count on what it has to do and on the necessary instruments; and it may move forward far more rapidly and easily in repairing the known wastage than if it were doing pioneering work in developing new and untested demands.

Will the new demands therefore remain just so much longer undeveloped and unsatisfied? Perhaps that question may remain for omniscience to answer.

CHAPTER VI

THE NATURE OF WAR COSTS (Continued)

ONE matter which should not long detain us is the question whether war is or is not in itself a "productive act." Our task is to find what this act cost rather than to dispute over its proper classification. Certainly no time will be wasted over the question whether war is a rational profit-making enterprise for a modern nation. So far as concerns the United States and the World War, this study should furnish some basis for a conclusion as to whether we gained or lost by our participation. During our neutrality, as distinct from our participation, there can be little doubt that we gained; and there is equally little doubt that some other neutral nations suffered heavy losses. But this is a separate question.

Another form of the question is the claim that the gratification of all desires is equally productive; and that if a nation wants a war fought, and spends its resources in this way, this is no less "productive" than shooting off peaceful fireworks or hiring moving-picture actors to risk their lives in perilous "stunts." Another view likens war to the policeman or the vigilance committee; or rather, to the still cruder and more wasteful means that would have to be followed to settle disputes and protect life and property if there were no policemen or vigilance committees. With this view no issue will be taken here. It cannot erase the obstinate fact that war is an affair of mutual defeat as the raising of wheat is not. Activities of mutual defeat will repay all the scrutiny we can give them, both within and without the bounds of "normal" business. But all this is beside the point of what the War actually cost: and the only reason for bringing up the question is that it enters into one of the estimates of national income made by the National Bureau of Economic Research, which constitute one of the most valuable sources of material for gauging the effect of the War on the nation's economy. Here the "value product of government" is reckoned as equal to the wages and salaries it pays to all its servants, including the army and navy. As a result, this "value product" was enormously increased by our entry into the War. If private industry exactly filled the gaps left in its ranks by the enlistment of millions of soldiers and sailors, and turned out as much output as before, then the nation's total "value product" would have increased by the whole pay of army, navy, and additional civil servants made necessary by the War.

As an evidence of increased economic welfare this is, of course, meaningless. But as an evidence of economic *effort* it is quite correct in principle. It gives the total from which we must deduct the war outlay in order to measure the effect of the War on the flow of ordinary "economic goods and service" to our individual citizens. There are complications of detail, but any other method of computation would have created greater ones.

If pay of army and navy had not been counted as "value product," there would still have been the munitions and war supplies representing a diversion of man-power from peace to war uses just as definitely as the armed forces. These amounts would have had to be segregated from the total war expenses and then deducted to find what was left for peace-time goods and services. It is far simpler to have a total from which the entire war budget can be deducted as it stands; and the total given by the National Bureau serves this purpose, with some adjustments which can be fairly easily made.[1]

Two items in the "value product of government" raise somewhat puzzling questions: namely, interest paid to individuals and the subsistence of soldiers and sailors. The item of interest can hardly be accepted for our purpose, while the item of subsistence is acceptable, in spite of apparent difficulties.[2] The "value product of government" is estimated at cost, for lack of any direct estimate of value. On this basis, interest might theoretically be computed on the Government's whole investment in buildings, public works, and supplies; save that data for the purpose are not available. Interest actually paid on government debt, viewed as an index of the cost-value of gov-

[1] This statement applies equally to the totals appearing in the National Bureau's later study, in which the estimate by sources of production is abandoned, and along with it the assigning of a "value product" to government.

[2] One of the purposes governing the National Bureau was to adopt a definition under which the estimate of income by sources ("value products") should harmonize with the estimate by incomes received by individuals. Interest paid to individuals, and subsistence of service men belong naturally in the second estimate (provided the estimate of private incomes has deducted the corresponding *taxes*); and this fact probably explains their inclusion in the first.

ernment services, is open to the criticism that it varies independently of the actual capital investment used by the Government. The War left us an enormous increase in interest charges and no commensurate increase in "used and useful" public investment—to apply the test familiar in the field of public utilities, where cost is actually a principal governor of value.

The payment of the interest can hardly be regarded as in itself a service of government constituting a "value product" rendered to the recipient, except in a sense hardly defensible in this connection. For it is being used as an index of the cost-value of the *other* services of government. So far as the gain to the recipient is concerned, we are justified in falling back on the obvious character of the payment as a simple transfer of funds, creating no value.

Whether its inclusion in the national income involves double-counting or not depends on the treatment of the other side of the transfer; namely, the taxes out of which the interest is paid. If the taxes are deducted before figuring private incomes, then the inclusion of these interest payments is not double-counting. If the taxes are not deducted, then the money would be counted twice. As some taxes are treated in one way and some in the other, and neither is earmarked as destined for any particular class of disbursements, the question cannot be literally answered as it was put. It becomes a question whether the total of taxes deducted is in excess of the total of interest payments (and of any other items which may have a similar purport in respect to double-counting). And for our present purpose we may further limit the question to the changes in these classes of items produced by the War. This inquiry will be made in a later chapter, in which the statistics of national income are analyzed.

Another item which calls for some scrutiny is the subsistence of the army and navy, especially in so far as it consists of goods produced by private industry and already represented in its "value product." It is a settled principle of such national aggregates that each industry is credited only with the value it adds to the materials it uses, the value of the materials being the product of previous processes in the economic series. In harmony with this, the food fed to soldiers, and the lumber going into their cantonment barracks, is the product of private industry and not of government. As to whether its inclusion involves double-counting, the answer is the same as with interest on the public debt. If the taxes that paid for these materials are deducted from the "value product" of private industry, then the equivalent should be counted when the government spends the money. If the taxes were not deducted, then to count also the spending of the money by government would be to count it twice.

But while the food itself—or other materials—is certainly not a "value product of government," it belongs here for a totally different reason. Being part of the compensation of government employees, it is part of the *cost-value of their services,* which have nothing to do with raising food or cutting lumber. Viewed in this light, the amount may appear twice without real double-counting. If government let the soldiers buy their own food from private dealers and paid them enough additional money for the purpose, then the amount would appear twice; as "value product" of private food dealers and as pay of soldiers; but there would be no suspicion of double-counting. Incidentally, in that case the amount would be considerably larger than it is.

The actual allowance for subsistence in the estimates of the National Bureau of Economic Research is not based on a segregation of the costs of furnishing that subsistence, delivered, under war conditions, but on pre-war allowances inflated by an index of prices of food and clothing. It amounts, for all ranks, to about $220 per year in dollars of 1913 buying power. What it cost, above this amount, is represented largely by work done by service men themselves and is merged in their pay and subsistence, taken as a measure of the cost of their services. The final conclusion will be that this combined figure is a rather scant measure of the cost involved to the country as a whole in taking these persons from their peace-time pursuits. But whatever figure we may take, we must keep always in mind that it is a figure representing cost, not "utility." Its great increase during the War represents an increase of economic effort, not of economic welfare in any accepted sense. For it is effort directed to war, not to peace-time production.

There is, however, a true credit to be allowed for the subsistence of men in service. Regardless of all questions of double-counting for supplies, the whole worth of the service men's subsistence is a proper credit. This covers not merely the supplies themselves but the services rendered by men in the service in putting the goods where they were wanted, when they were wanted, in the shape they were wanted. The large total amount of the effort of army and navy personnel spent on these economic services ministering to subsistence is one of the surprising things in a service supposedly devoted to fighting.

It is reflected in the size of the commissary and a portion of the quartermaster's departments and in the huge "army behind the front." It includes its quota of the cost of transporting supplies across the Atlantic and up to the front.[3] It includes part of the cost of docks, cranes, motor trucks, roads, and railroads, built or used or repaired in this service. It includes the work of army cooks, the care and transportation of army kitchens, and any work done by the service men themselves in furnishing living quarters. Even the casualties incident to these services might be charged against them; but it is not necessary for our purposes to go that far. One of the regular offsets to low army pay is the furnishing of goods through "post exchanges" at prices which cover the cost of the bare goods but not of the services involved—services of transportation, handling, and merchandising for which the private purchaser often pays more than half of each dollar he pays the retailer. The army may be able to perform these services (in peace-time) at lower real cost than our private commercial agencies; but they are still far from costless. And in time of war the cost of some of these services becomes very great indeed.

For that very reason there is no need of estimating the amount of effort and outlay absorbed in this way. We may simply accept the fact that war-time subsistence of service men represents more cost and less comfort than typical peace-time subsistence. The increase of cost due to war is a charge to cost of war, not a credit to subsistence; hence we do not need to segregate it from other war costs. Soldiers eat more (when they can), wear out clothes faster, and live in quarters whose temporary character makes them expensive per unit of service out of proportion to their quality. They betake themselves to places where it is extraordinarily difficult and costly to get supplies to them. The mere fact of separating the soldiers from their families makes the maintenance of both a more expensive matter.

The cost-value of these services, then, if we could find it, would be merely a curiosity, vastly more than any proper credit for value received by the service men. The comfort-value, on the other hand, can be covered by a very modest estimate and is certainly below, and not above, the worth of corresponding peace-time subsistence.

[3] So far as done by men in government service.

The bearing of some of these points may perhaps be best seen in a simplified example. We may suppose a nation with a national dividend of 100 units of goods, produced by 100 workers who receive 60 per cent of the product as wages. To carry on a war, the government takes 10 workers into the army, and buys 20 units of goods as war supplies. If the workers taken into the army are not replaced, and product is reduced proportionately, then the social cost of their army service is 10 goods-units, though their former earnings were only 6 and their army pay is, let us say, only 3. There are now only 70 workers making goods for peace-time uses and turning out 70 units of goods; 20 working on army supplies and turning out 20 units of such goods, and 10 in army service producing whatever national values the fighting of a war can be said to produce. The total cost of this operation is 30 goods-units lost to the ends of peace.

But there are credits, as has been noted. The army uses 4 goods-units directly or indirectly, in feeding, clothing, and housing the soldiers, so that 4 out of the 20 units of army supplies may be charged to peace-time uses. And the 10 soldiers use two man-units of time in furnishing themselves and each other their meals and other subsistence. Thus 2 out of 10 man-units of army service are devoted to peace-time purposes. Shall we, then, allow a credit of 6 goods-units for soldiers' subsistence, reducing the cost of the war from 30 to 24? This credit of 6 would represent the *cost* of the soldiers' subsistence, but hardly its service-value. The total of army pay and subsistence can certainly not be taken as giving a better living than was afforded by wages before, presumably not so good. Perhaps a fair credit for army subsistence would be 2 goods-units, reducing the total war cost to 28.

The financial cost to the government would be a different matter. Instead of 10 goods-units representing lost product, there would be the money equivalent of 3 units representing wages and 4 representing subsistence supplies. The subsistence service, being communistically organized, would not appear in a financial estimate. The total "cost" of the War would then be simply 20 for supplies and 3 for army pay. This 3 not only falls materially short of fully representing the social costs of taking men for the army, but also fails to agree with the "value product of government" as reported by the National Bureau of Economic Research; since the latter includes an allowance for subsistence. To that extent the work of men in the army and navy is the basis of an item of national income in the National Bureau's figures larger than the corresponding charge to cost of war in the treasury figures. This fact must be kept in mind in making our final adjustments.

But none of these estimates is an adequate basis for gauging the social cost of taking men into the army. Let us suppose that the 10 soldiers are replaced by 10 other workers, that work becomes less efficient but more working-time is expended so that industrial output is restored to 100. The places of the workers are filled, but at a cost of 13 added work-units to replace 10. Let us assume that the ultimate human cost of this replacement-labor is no less than that formerly measured by .6 goods-unit per worker: and let us accept that as its economic measure. (Whether war-time real wages-rates go up or down is not essential for the present purpose.) Then the cost of filling the places of the soldiers in industry is measured by 13 × .6 or 7.8 goods-units; or .78 unit per man taken into service.

Thus we have numerous ways of rating the cost to the national economy of taking 10 men into the army. One is their army pay, 3, or their pay and subsistence supplies, 7. One is their pay plus the use-worth of their subsistence, both together being reckoned here at 5. This figure corresponds in principle with the "value product" of the soldiers in the National Bureau figures. Another figure, based on cost of replacement in industry, is 7.8. Another, based on the provisional assumption that the labor was not replaced, was 10, representing the full product of these workers. Strictly speaking, it is the product of these workers and the capital equipment they worked with: but the whole would be lost if the workers stopped working suddenly and were not replaced, leaving the capital equipment to that extent unmanned.

In the United States, the places of the soldiers were, in general, filled, though at a disproportionately high expenditure of effort. Thus the $30-a-month private who had been earning $100 may have cost $120 worth of effort to replace. In this respect we were fortunate. In France, as already noted, industry's first reaction to mobilization was not to fill the places of the soldiers, but to throw many more into involuntary idleness and shrink the national output much more than in proportion to the number of men taken.

In principle, then, the costs of war may be analyzed into (1) additional economic efforts put forth, and (2) goods taken out of the channels of normal private use; with a credit for any private consumption that may be sustained by these diverted goods. There is implied also a debit or credit for any decrease or increase in total output which may be turned out with the help of the additional efforts. The "goods-units" are represented in the statistical records by the familiar "dollars of constant purchasing power." The meaning of such units may become somewhat controversial when war supplies leap from negligible amounts to enormous fractions of the total output, while relative costs and values are quite unstable.

This difficulty could be avoided if statistics were available in the necessary form, and the whole process could be simplified still further by confining the goods-account to goods devoted to the "uses of peace." This would mean private consumption, private investment, and—in principle—the peace-time functions of government. Army consumption would be estimated at "use-value" rather than at cost. Any reduction in this account of goods-income would measure the cost of war in goods, whether brought about by taxes, loans, or rising prices, and regardless of the large or small amount of war supplies for which this sacrifice may be made or their high or low prices or costs of production. Any extra efforts expended would constitute a further cost. These extra efforts would include not merely those needed to replace men taken out of industry, but some allowance for those taken from other pursuits, chiefly education. Since there is no good way of measuring directly the amount of real income remaining for peaceful uses after war has taken its share, we must needs estimate the amount taken by war and subtract it from the available totals.

A large part of the goods actually spent by this country represented loans to our Allies, and the question arises of deduction for the value of the expected repayments. This appears obvious, yet it involves two questions of great difficulty: namely, the appropriateness of applying compound-interest discounting in social surveys of this character, and the relation between an international financial payment and the real income of the nation to which the payment is made.

One difficulty of the discounting process is that the funds loaned are not industrial capital destined to be put to uses increasing the measurable flow of economic goods and so furnishing a tangible basis for the allowance of interest, as distinct from the more intangible

basis afforded by speculations on the matter of psychic time-per-
spective. In lending, the United States did not reduce by just that
much the industrial capital it would otherwise have employed at
home; and the discounting process does not mean that if we had kept
the funds we loaned, our production of economic values would have
been, for all future time, increased by the amount of such interest;
nor that a delay in repayment involves a loss of such added productivity which we should otherwise enjoy.

When the Treasury deducts approximately 7½ billions from its
estimate of war costs for the worth of foreign obligations, it is putting a present value on continuing future payments reaching many
years in the future and involving more than a little uncertainty.
Now it so happens that there are continuing war costs also of long
duration and considerable uncertainty. These consist mainly of the
costs of disability and the losses suffered by the dependents of those
who died—or who will die in the future as a result of war injuries of
various sorts. There are also continuing deficits on government
properties and operations; chiefly shipping. Surely the most rational course is to separate these continuing items from the costs
borne during the War, and to offset them against each other so far
as may be done.

Whether the credits would offset the debits cannot in the nature
of the quantities be absolutely proved, but such estimates as are possible seem to indicate that the amounts may approximately cancel
each other. This is a favorable conjecture, as the credits are far more
likely to shrink, and the debits to expand. Up to the present, the
debits have far exceeded the credits, in the actual fiscal transactions.
The Veterans' Bureau alone is spending over half a billion a year,
while receipts on account of foreign war loans are about 200 millions. If present agreements are carried out to the end, the receipts
may continue large after the expenses have dwindled; but at no one
knows what cost in the undermining of world economic stability,
our own included. In any case, there seems not the least possibility
that the sum of post-war credits will exceed that of post-war debits.
Later, we shall attempt some calculation of these debits. For the
present it seems clear that the loans to the Allies are best treated as
war costs as of the time the loans were made, without deduction for
the worth of future repayments. This corresponds to the actual in-

cidence on our economic system. And as post-war repayments are not likely to outweigh continuing war costs, this treatment will in all probability stand without need of future reduction.

A further question must be raised, however: namely, can these debts be paid in a way that will enrich the American producing-and-consuming economy, as distinct from filling the federal Treasury and relieving taxpayers of some monetary burdens? Real repayment, it is generally understood, must be in goods. And to accomplish its end, the goods must be a clear addition to what we should otherwise have produced and enjoyed. They must not, for instance, displace our home products and reduce our domestic output and domestic employment by that much. The fear of this is seen in our present policy of increased tariff protection. Rightly or wrongly, American industry does not regard an increase of imports as an asset. And if this evil be avoided and increased imports confined to noncompetitive goods, there is still another danger, equivalent to the first but less direct. If imports are not increased sufficiently to pay the whole debt, and if foreign power to buy our goods is limited to something less than the imports (by the amount of debt repayments), will this decrease the amount of American production for export, and so have the same ultimate effect of displacing home production and canceling just that much of the gain our national economy is supposed to receive from the debt settlements?

This question cannot be answered *a priori*, nor can the processes of statistics probably ever afford ironclad proof. Traditional theory might assume that imports are a gain and that if producers are displaced, they will turn to something else. This "turning to something else," however, is doubtful, especially when rapid advances in productive power are already freeing men and resources so fast that the search for "something else" to produce is a crowded field of activity, taxing our best ingenuity. At such a time, as we have seen, the productiveness of industry may be limited by demands of the traditional sorts, plus the not unlimited rate at which new demands can be developed and exploited. This being the case, the claim that repayment of war debts may to some extent displace American production seems to represent, not a proved fact, but at least a possibility. It is the writer's conviction that these debts are not fully collectible assets: that if we receive fiscal payment in full, our national economy will not gain that much real wealth, and might conceivably even lose rather than gain.[4]

This is bound up with another question: namely, is the impoverishment of Europe a gain or a loss to us, or a matter of indifference? Here again, *a priori* reasoning is not final. In general it is true that the rich customer is the more profitable; possibly also the rich competitor is likely to be the less formidable. It is to our selfish interest that Europe should be prosperous and not impoverished. In its extreme form, this proposition is vividly borne out by the present world-wide depression. The modern industrial world is organically interrelated and no major part can prosper wholly without regard to what is happening to the other parts. A completely prostrate and bankrupt Europe would be a calamity to the United States which must at almost any cost be avoided or prevented.

Nevertheless, short of disastrous collapse, the immediate effects may be different from the ultimate outcome; and either may depend on particular conditions; on the kind and degree of impoverishment and the way it is met. The poor man may not be a good customer, but the man in great temporary need, who has credit or goods to pledge, may be the most profitable of customers, if not the safest. A strong nation, needing capital to get back on its feet, has buying power as well as buying need. This process of distress-buying on credit is, of course, inherently temporary, but it may last for a considerable term of years, as witness our continued post-war selling and lending abroad, which has apparently now come to an end.

During this period we have gained from this trade—what? Not goods, but a creditor position representing claims to goods in the future—claims at present postponed and therefore mounting cumulatively—claims to goods we do not want to receive. This cannot go on forever. If Europe is economically unsound, the credits we hold are worthless. The present depression has shaken them, especially at their real source, the German reparations payments, and has led

---

[4] This view receives some confirmation from the one-year moratorium on the international debts which has just been negotiated as these pages go to press. This may not involve a recognition of the above proposition in full, but it recognizes at least that in the present depression the economic welfare of all the nations is so bound together that those which can make concessions have an interest in doing so.

to a qualified one-year moratorium which seems merely the prelude
to further necessary concessions.

If the settlements are resumed and continued, the interest payments due us must sometime outgrow the further lendings of principal, unless we are to hold a mortgage on all the wealth of Europe.
This condition is new to our experience and we cannot be sure if the
outcome will be good. We know it has bred much ill feeling already.
And whatever it may ultimately bring, it is the result of the impoverishment of Europe. It has given us a form of wealth on which
we do not know how to realize, and a creditor position fraught with
possibilities of danger.

This condition is a joint result of the profits of our neutrality, of
loans to our Allies during our belligerency, and of the post-war
prostration and rebuilding of Europe. And exact allocation of it to
these various sources is not possible—if indeed it could serve any
useful purpose to distinguish between our war and Europe's war
after the day when we made Europe's war ours. It is clear, however,
that the seriously unbalanced state of our international indebtedness occurred after we entered the War. What had happened before
that was the wiping out of our former debtor balance and the (approximate) squaring of our accounts with Europe. This change in
our previous condition would have occasioned some readjustments,
but they could hardly have been of a very serious nature. The serious features of the situation are due to transactions following our
entry into the War; and beyond that allocation can hardly go.

One last question, and then the rest must be postponed until they
have to be faced in dealing with particular sections of our material.
Are we dealing merely with the costs specifically traceable to this
war, or with any and all costs of a warlike nature occurring within
the period? The difference is illustrated by the Treasury's method
of estimating the cost of this war, by deducting assumed normal
peace-time expenses; so that only the increase occasioned by the
War is charged against it. On this basis the "cost of the War" does
not include the whole cost of the army and navy that fought it;
merely the excess above the normal peace-time cost which would still
have been borne if there had been no war.

This is logical, if we are attempting to measure the effects precipitated by the assassination at Sarajevo; yet if the cost of every war
be reckoned in this way, the sum would fail to include the cost of de-

fense and preparedness for which these same wars as a whole are responsible. More correctly, perhaps, responsibility rests on the likelihood of war as distinct from its actual occurrence; but the two are
so inseparable in fact that a sharp distinction between them seems
like a metaphysical subtlety. Expense for national defense is a form
of "overhead cost" for which allocation is difficult if not impossible.
Certainly the peace-time military and naval establishment provides
indispensable means for the prosecution of war when war comes. And
if war were a commercial product the accounts would include as its
cost at least the whole cost of military and naval establishments
while the war was going on. One method of accounting would require them also to include the whole cost of peace-time preparedness,
while another method would treat that as a "cost of idleness" rather
than a cost of productive operation. But war is not a commercial
product, and civilization will not admit that it is a desired and desirable end of policies of "national defense." One is reminded of the
old question whether it is logical to pay the doctor when one is sick or
only so long as he keeps one well. Whichever we do, his pay is both
cost of sickness and cost of health maintenance. Neither aspect ex-
cludes the other.

For our purposes, the proper course is to take note of the peace-
time costs of preparedness, of the added burden of the late conflict,
and of the sum of the two. This done, the reader may do what he
likes with the logical problems of allocation.

CHAPTER VII

THE EVIDENCE OF FISCAL OUTLAYS

THE economic resources devoted to war are for the most part paid for by government, and thus are represented in its fiscal budgets, either directly or indirectly. But the budgets include some fiscal transfers that do not represent the use of man-power or materials in the actual performance of functions, or which misrepresent them for one or another reason—as by paying soldiers $30 a month who are worth a great deal more in private employments. A nation devotes one-fourth of its economic resources to war. To do this it will normally have to transfer something like one-fourth of its annual purchasing power to government to spend. If it can accomplish the miracle of raising this amount by taxation, that is an end of the matter. If it relies on loans, then subsequent budgets must carry an additional sum for interest which will increase the budget, even though the government is putting forth precisely the same material effort as it did the previous year. If it follows the path of currency inflation, directly or indirectly, then the dollar magnitudes of public and private economic efforts alike are distorted, and the government may borrow cheapened dollars which it may have to pay back later when their value has increased. All these are important facts, and affect the amount, character, and incidence of the ultimate fiscal burdens on government and taxpayers, but beneath them all is still the fact that the nation has been devoting one-fourth of its resources to war. The figures of financial expenses must be searched, then, partly for their own sake but still more for evidence of the use of man-power and goods for the actual work of war.

As shown in Chart IV, the expenses of the Federal Government mounted from less than ¾ of a billion in 1916 to over 2 billions in 1917, to about 13⅔ billions in 1918 and between 18 and 19 billions in 1919. In 1920 they had fallen to a trifle over 6 billions, in 1921 to a little less than 5 billions, and in 1922 they reached approximate stability at about 3½ billions. These figures include the loans to our Allies, which represented immediate economic effort in the shape of goods produced and shipped abroad. Chart V, by quarters, gives the

story in more detail, showing how the expenses mounted to a peak in
the last quarter of the calendar year 1918. For that quarter, the
Government was spending at the rate of about 22½ billions a year
or about half the entire national income of 1916! Even allowing for
the shrunken dollar in which these war expenses are measured, this
represents about 35 per cent of the national income of 1916, which
was a year of unusual prosperity. Whether or not this is an accurate
measure of economic effort, it clearly represents an economic effort
of surprising magnitude and intensity.

Revenues did not keep pace with expenses, leaving deficits (see
Chart VI) which aggregated over 23 billions before the budget was
balanced in 1920. These, of course, had to be met by borrowings. In
fact, the borrowings were somewhat larger, because the enormous
scale of financial operations called for much larger sums of ready
cash than the Government had been in the habit of carrying, and the

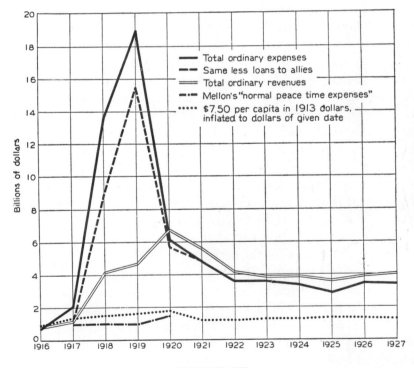

CHART IV.

Ordinary Revenues and Expenses, Compared to Pre-War Levels.

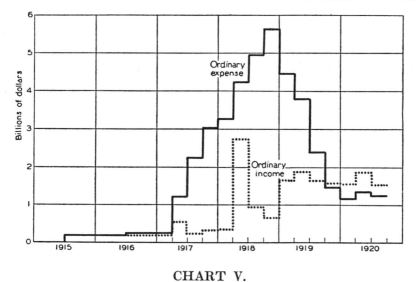

CHART V.

*Ordinary Income and Expenses, by Quarters.**

borrowings had to be large enough to cover the necessary increase in the "general fund balance." With the end of the War, most of this increase in ready cash was no longer needed, and was applied at once to reducing the debt. Some of the increase, however, was permanent, as the budget remained at more than four times its pre-war level.

This fact raises an interesting question which may well be disposed of before we pass on to the attempt to interpret the war outlays themselves. The whole post-war budget is so completely out of touch with pre-war magnitudes that, on the surface, no comparison seems possible, and the question arises whether any of our major divisions of expenditure will ever return to anything like a pre-war normal. Are we not paying for the results of the War throughout our entire federal budget? Are we not permanently spending more on our army and navy as an aftermath of the War, and more on the civil functions of government?

This question calls for an analysis of post-war expenses to show the sources of the vast increase. First, the expenses clearly due to the World War must be segregated from those which can fairly

* The fiscal year 1915–16, and the first three quarters of the following fiscal year, are shown as units but at *quarterly rates,* for purposes of comparison.

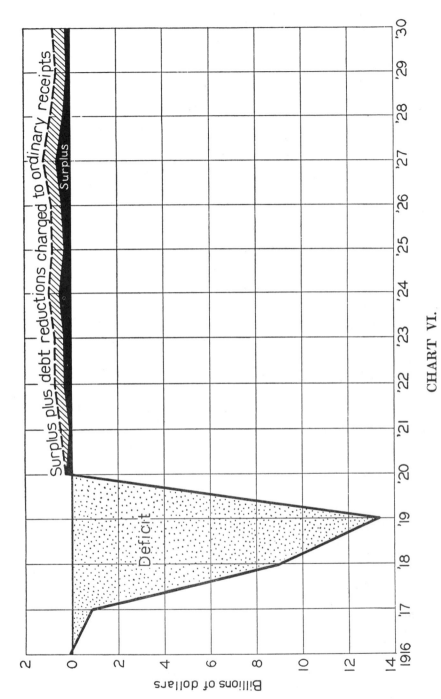

CHART VI.

Federal Deficits and Surpluses.

claim to represent normal peace-time activities of government, including peace-time outlays on army and navy. These latter must
then be compared with some standard of normal growth, first eliminating the increase due to the shrunken dollar, which affects government income equally with government outgo. And the best standard
of normal growth consists of outlays *per capita* of the population, in
dollars of constant purchasing power. There is probably a slight
tendency for both military and civil expenses to increase faster than
population, but this is a doubtful quantity, and we shall be on the
conservative side if we first compare post-war expenses with the pre-
war rate *per capita*, and then ask whether the increase seems more
than would probably have occurred if there had been no war. This
analysis is attempted in Charts VII and VIII.

Chart VII shows the pre-war and post-war outlays of the War
and Navy Departments, *per capita*, in 1913 dollars. The price index
used is the Bureau of Labor index of wholesale prices; which, while
not ideal for the particular purpose in hand, is probably as good
as any index available for the period. The average outlay for the
ten years preceding the World War is very close to $3.50 *per capita*.
There is also evidence of a long-run upward trend which would bring
the post-war normal closer to $4.00. And the post-war expenses, up
to 1929, average less than $4.00 *per capita*. A price index of the

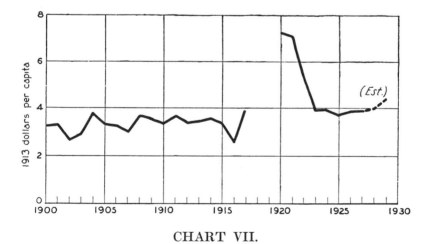

CHART VII.

*Pre-War and Post-War Outlays of War and Navy Depart-
ments in 1913 Dollars per Capita of Total Population.*

"cost of living" type would show a substantially lower level of post-war expenses. Thus there is no positive evidence that post-war military and naval expenses, at least up to 1929, were increased at all by the World War.

The actual outcome has undoubtedly been the resultant of forces working in opposite directions. Aviation and other technical developments would have made military and naval establishments more expensive in any case. The War stimulated these developments, adding chemical warfare and tanks and stimulating the general motorization of land forces. On the other hand, it left the army with much surplus equipment and the navy with large forces of secondary craft, especially destroyers, thus reducing the need for replacements and new construction until the existing equipment should become ob-

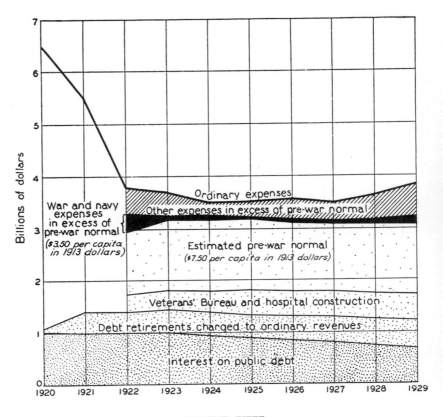

CHART VIII.

Post-War Outlays Analyzed.

solete. Thus the full effect of the War on post-war armaments may be only now on the verge of showing itself, and it remains to be seen whether conferences on limitation of armaments will be able to keep it within bounds. At any rate, up to the present there has been no definite and substantial increase clearly traceable to the War.

Chart VIII shows the analysis of the entire post-war budget. Slightly over half of it is definitely chargeable to the World War and not to normal peace-time activities, civil or military. This half consists of interest on the public debt, sinking fund, and other debt retirements charged to "ordinary revenues," and expenses for the care of the World War veterans. It is the remainder, representing civil and military functions, which has to be compared with the pre-war "normal," which is here taken as $7.50 *per capita* in dollars of 1913. The result depends so much on the type of price index used that only the most general conclusions should be drawn. The most conservative index, that of wholesale prices, already used, shows post-war expenses about 25 per cent in excess of the pre-war normal, most of the excess being accounted for by civil and not military expenses. A more representative price index would show a very much smaller excess, practically all due to civil functions. As these "civil" functions still include the deficits of the Shipping Board and some other items definitely left behind by the War, we may fairly conclude that the general civil activities of government are not suffering from any very material post-war inflation.

The progress of retirement of the war debt is exhibited in Charts IX and X. As soon as the Government achieved a surplus, in 1920, a sinking fund was set up, with a basic annual credit of $253,404,864 and with the provision that as it was used to retire outstanding debt, the interest on the debt so retired should continue to go into the fund.[1] Retirements from this source were about $260,000,000 in 1921 (par amount) and have steadily increased to nearly $370,000,-000 in 1929. In addition certain sources of income were earmarked for the reduction of the debt: chiefly debt payments from foreign countries. These debt retirements "charged to ordinary revenues" have averaged approximately half a billion for the years 1924–29

---

[1] The basic credit consists of $2\frac{1}{2}$ per cent on the excess of Liberty bonds and Victory notes outstanding July 1, 1920, above obligations of foreign governments (at par) held at that time. See *Report of the Secretary of the Treasury*, 1929, p. 16.

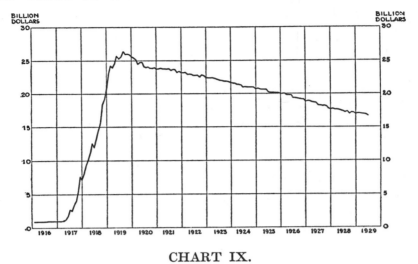

CHART IX.

*Interest-Bearing Debt of the United States Government.**

inclusive, amounting to nearly $550,000,000 in the latter year. This is really surplus revenue earmarked for debt reduction, but does not appear in the technical "surplus" as reported by the Treasury. The fiscal year 1930 showed a surplus of $184,000,000, in addition to these statutory debt retirements. The year 1931 showed the full effects of the depression in a deficit of $903,000,000, which more than offset the statutory debt retirements and caused an increase in net debt of $463,000,000. Thus, for the first time since the War, there has been not only a technical "deficit," but an actual setback in the process of debt reduction. This illustrates the basic principle that a sinking fund will not reduce a debt unless there are revenues sufficient to bring about the reduction. The sinking fund is not therefore useless, since it sets a dead-line below which a government with the financial power of ours will not permanently allow its revenues to be reduced. Barring further wars, the setback to the process of debt reduction must be regarded as temporary.

Even if there is no substantial help from future surpluses, the sinking fund with its cumulative increase, and the other statutory debt retirements, will wipe out the actual war borrowings by 1950 or soon after. A reduction of debt payments from foreign countries would postpone this date somewhat. Nevertheless the recent estimate

* From *Annual Report of the Secretary of the Treasury,* 1929, p. 12.

of Under-Secretary Mills (made in December, 1930) that the debt
might be retired by 1949, appears to have been reasonable and not
unduly optimistic, relying very little on the doubtful factor of surpluses. If he were to make this estimate again in the light of the final
results of the fiscal year 1931, he would presumably advance the date
one year on account of the unexpected size of the deficit of that year,
and possibly more on account of the foreign debt situation, with its
likelihood of the necessity of further concessions beyond the moratorium granted in July, 1931; and also on account of the probability of a lean season in our own budget in the years just ahead.
There certainly seems little likelihood that the Government will in
the future achieve any such surpluses as were recorded in the period
of post-war prosperity, just closed. And hence there is little likelihood of extinguishing the debt before 1950. To date, including the
setback of 1931, approximately one-third of the net war borrowing

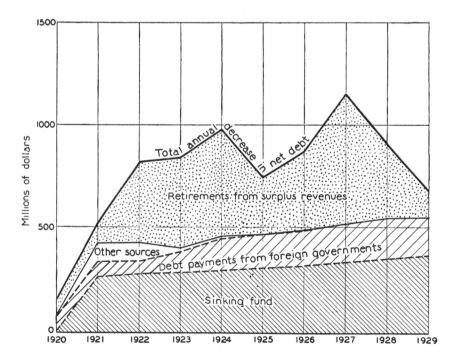

CHART X.

Reduction of National Debt by Sources.

has been wiped out, leaving the total interest-bearing debt something over 16½ billions, the net debt being some 15½ billions more than when we entered the War.

When the debt is finally extinguished, the budget will be freed of debt charges for interest, sinking fund, and kindred items, which in 1929 totaled 1,200 millions, as well as of the pressure to maintain a surplus to be used for debt retirement beyond what the sinking fund provides. And at about the same time the war-time term insurance annuities will have expired, and the adjusted service compensation fund will have been completed, thus removing about 250 millions annually of further war charges. Other veterans' items may have increased, but the net relief to the budget can hardly be less than 1⅓ billions. By this time, if no further wars intervene, government expenses will be back upon what may fairly be called a peace-time basis. Until then, taxation will be bearing a large continuing burden of war financing.

There remains one central problem: the cost of the War as indicated in the fiscal outlays of government. This has been officially estimated by the Secretary of the Treasury at about 37 billions to June 30, 1929, including 27 billions to the end of the fiscal year 1921 (the official termination of hostilities having been on July 2 of that year) and about 10 billions since that time, in the form of interest on the public debt and expenses of the Veterans' Bureau. This is an estimate of the added cost of the War above normal peace-time outlays, which are deducted.

If total costs for war purposes are sought, the answer is much larger. These had been absorbing, before the War, close to 70 per cent of the federal budget, and the War increased this total to 81.7 per cent in 1917, to 97.4 per cent in 1918, and to 98.4 per cent in 1919. The percentage then declined to 93.7 per cent in 1920 and to 87.7 per cent in 1921, after which it fluctuated about 87 per cent.[2] This would bring total outlays for war purposes from 1917 through 1921 to the huge total of over 43 billions, with about 3 billions a year during the post-war period. These percentages include large items of a purely fiscal character, and it seems probable that expenditures on the actual performance of war functions, on a normal peace-time basis but at actually prevailing price levels, would have

[2] Estimate of Mr. Edward B. Rosa of the Bureau of Standards. See *Annual Report of the Secretary of the Treasury*, 1927, pp. 19–20.

amounted to about 4 billions from our entry into the War to the close of the fiscal year 1921, or something over 3 billions to the close of the fiscal year 1920. These amounts may be added to the further costs of similar character chargeable to the World War itself, to get an estimate of the total expenditure of economic resources for war purposes of all sorts, while the War was going on.

In interpreting the treasury statements of fiscal costs, it is impossible to make all the adjustments necessary to eliminate purely fiscal items and leave only those which represent expenditure of social resources for the nation as an economic whole. Even the major adjustments can only be approximated, and the margin of error in these estimates is so large as to make the minor items of little importance. These major adjustments include interest on the public debt, loans to foreign countries, the social cost represented by persons taken into the government service, the "deficits" of the Federal Railroad Administration and the net outlays of the Shipping Board and Emergency Fleet Corporation. The adjustments on these accounts include both additions and subtractions.

Interest on the war debt through 1921 amounted to about 2¾ billions—a fiscal transfer as a sequel to an expenditure in men and goods already represented in full by the original spending of the principal of the loans. This, then, may be subtracted from the present estimate, though not from the sum of the fiscal task imposed on the machinery of taxation.

Under loans to foreign countries the treasury estimates deduct the estimated worth of the resulting claims, reckoned at 7,470 millions. For the present purpose the amount thus deducted should be restored, since the loans represented goods exported, and the subsequent repayments are more appropriately treated as an offset against our own continuing war costs. A minor matter is the fact that this 7,470 millions includes amounts resulting from sales of surplus war material and relief supplies on credit. The result is to reduce the apparent net fiscal loss on loans to our Allies, and to increase the apparent costs of the War Department and of European relief by taking away a credit due them on surplus supplies. If this is the case, however, it is merely a matter of departmental allocation and does not affect the totals.

The fiscal cost of persons in the government service is represented by pay, and actual goods consumed as subsistence. The social cost is better represented by the real earnings these persons could have made in private employments if there had not been a war:—in other words, by real wages at pre-war rates. This is a fairer gauge of the economic worth of the man-power taken.

Army and navy pay per year, with the commodity cost of subsistence, as reported by the National Bureau of Economic Research, average $1,015 for the three years 1917–19.[3] If these men had been otherwise employed at average rates of employees' compensation for these same years, their average reward would have been $1,055. At 1915 rates of pay they would have earned about the same real purchasing power, so that their value may be set at $1,055 war-time dollars. Diverting their efforts to war, then, may be judged to have cost the national dividend about $40 more than their pay and subsistence. For the whole amount of service-time represented, this amounts to from 200 to 230 millions. No attempt will be made to make similar adjustments for government employees not in the armed services; their pay may be taken as more nearly representing the worth of their services, at least for the general run of employees. As for the "dollar-a-year men," no fiscal figures can measure their worth or the cost of withdrawing them from private industry. Their absence may have been in some small part responsible for the fact that war-time production in private industry was unusually costly: and to that extent the cost of diverting these men to government service will be taken account of when we come to consider the general reaction of the War on national production and the national dividend. But there is no way of isolating it.

The "deficits" of the Federal Railroad Administration raise another difficult question. Railroad rates did not increase as much as wages and costs of materials and equipment, and the Government made good the shortage, on private and government traffic alike. The result is a subsidy to an industry serving nonwar purposes far more than those of war; where the question now at issue is the extent to which these facilities and services were diverted from peace to war uses, and the extent to which government payments for war freight and troop movements failed to cover the costs properly chargeable to them.

[3] King, *The National Income and Its Purchasing Power,* p. 365. Data used in the computation that follows from pp. 56, 60, 122, 130, of the same volume.

In the absence of an extended survey, these amounts can only be roughly estimated. The government business was responsible for its *pro rata* share of the general shortage of net earnings, and something more. First, government was a favored shipper on the "land-grant" roads, receiving a variety of concessions in rates, the aggregate amount of which is not recorded in available form. Second, the war business was responsible for the congestion which increased the cost of transportation in general, and so is properly chargeable with substantially more than its *pro rata* share of costs. But so far as the payments made under the government guaranty of pre-war rates of earnings merely meant that government was paying the cost of private business which the rates paid by private shippers did not cover, to that extent the "deficits" are fiscal transfers and not measures of economic resources devoted to war uses. Out of the total fiscal cost of public control of transportation systems—1,565 millions— one may roughly estimate that not over 400 millions is properly chargeable to war business either directly or indirectly *via* its effect in increasing the cost of business in general.[4] This leaves 1,165 millions to be deducted from the fiscal estimates.

There remains the cost on account of the Shipping Board and Emergency Fleet Corporation. These organizations spent 3,316 millions and were left with ships, plants, structures, and materials which were worth only a small fraction of their cost. The corporation continued to operate shipping after the War, at a substantial loss, but it has been curtailing the scale of its operations until the operating loss in 1929 was only $13\frac{2}{3}$ millions. Nearly two-thirds of the original fleet (in terms of deadweight tons) has been disposed of, mostly by sale, and the remainder is carried on the books at a valuation of $78,600,940, together with three millions in surplus materials for sale.

In the Treasury's statement of war costs, the post-war deficits on shipping operation are deducted from the value of assets remaining June 30, 1921. So far as these assets have been sold since 1921, the valuation is based on the result of these subsequent sales and so is removed from the realm of speculation, except so far as obligations representing credit sales may not prove fully collectible. The total credit for remaining assets is $280\frac{1}{2}$ millions, leaving a net war cost of $3,035\frac{1}{2}$ millions, or $91\frac{1}{2}$ per cent of the total outlay. If, in the

[4] *See* more detailed analysis in Chapter XVI, below, pp. 238, 241–244.

ultimate outcome, it should be necessary to add something like 100 millions to this total, the adjustment would not be material, compared to the probable error of the total figures.

Some further adjustments should perhaps be made. The Sugar Equalization Board and the War Finance Corporation show net earnings of nearly 82 millions which are deducted from the financial cost of the War, while the Grain Corporation shows a loss of 25 millions which is added, though the appropriateness of these deductions and additions is doubtful from a social standpoint.

Summing up these adjustments, we have the following result.

Additions to Estimate of Fiscal Cost.

Worth of foreign obligations	$ 7,470,000,000
Adjustment, cost of persons in government service . .	230,000,000
Other adjustments, approximately	200,000,000
Total additions	$ 7,900,000,000

Deductions from Estimate of Fiscal Cost.

Interest on war debt	$ 2,746,640,992
"Deficits" of Federal Railroad Administration . . .	1,165,000,000
Total deductions	$ 3,911,640,992
Net addition	$ 3,988,359,008
Treasury estimate, war cost to June 30, 1921	27,183,989,752
Total	$31,172,348,760

Even if these adjustments were all correctly made, we should still not have a gauge of the immediate war effort of the nation. On the one hand, deduction is still made for surplus supplies sold or salable at the end of the War, whereas the salvage value of these supplies was no deduction from the economic effort of producing them at the time they were being produced. On the other hand, many supplies were bought from abroad, on which the ultimate economic effort of repayment, in goods and services, was probably in part postponed. These two quantities tend to offset each other, and data are not at hand to determine the precise balance between them. In any case they do not affect the ultimate real cost of the War, merely the estimate of the economic effort made at the time.

To sum up, the immediate economic cost of the War to the nation, mainly in goods and services devoted to war uses, so far as represented in the federal budgets, may be estimated at something over 31 billions. That is, it consisted of goods and services whose dollar value at the varying price levels prevailing during the period of war effort adds up to that amount. In pre-war dollars, the amount would of course be far less. Whether it would be worth more or less in dollars of present purchasing power is a question that may be answered in more than one way. In general the average purchasing power of war-time dollars probably does not differ very greatly from the general run of purchasing power in the period from 1922 to 1929. In terms of wholesale prices, the purchasing power of the war-time dollar was less than that of the post-war dollar; in terms of an index of cost of living it was greater.[5]

A price index of expenditures for war, from 1913 to 1919, in Dr. Knauth's study of national income, follows fairly closely the course of the Bureau of Labor index of wholesale prices, as far as it extends.[6] The Government's dollar, then, shrank in buying power more than did the general consumer's dollar, in terms of actual goods. But the Government apparently suffered no more than other *wholesale* buyers. For this and for other reasons there is still doubt whether, all things considered, the public dollar did not command as much of ultimate economic resources, efforts, and sacrifices as the private dollar. This is a question incapable of exact answer, beside which the uncertainties of measurement of the actual dollar quantities involved are of relatively minor importance.

To make an extreme case, if the high prices of war goods, beyond the general rise of goods for common consumption, merely meant doubled real wages for shipyard workers, doubled real profits to war contractors, in short, doubled real rewards to all concerned, then the diversion of one-tenth of our dollar income to war goods would have succeeded in diverting only one-twentieth of our productive resources in that direction, and another twentieth to serving the ordi-

[5] The heavy decline in prices accompanying the depression of 1929–31 has brought wholesale prices down to some 10 per cent to 15 per cent above the 1913 level, while cost of living has lagged greatly on the downward movement. Thus the present state of prices is unsettled and the future uncertain.

[6] See *Income in the United States*, National Bureau of Economic Research, 1922, p. 336.

nary private ends of the producers of the war goods. This second twentieth is an undesired diversion, to persons whom the nation has no special desire to reward in this way, and in that sense it is a cost of the war-mobilization of the country's economic forces. But it has not been lost like powder burned and ships sunk. It has made private persons richer. It is a social cost, not because it is a reduction of the total income serving private ends, but because it is a maldistribution of that income. That is, provided we could agree that it *was* a maldistribution; certainly we could never agree as to just which gains and which losses deserved this term and just how serious the matter was. How many dollars transferred from A to B are equal as "social costs" to one dollar sunk in the sea or burned up in the Argonne offensive? Only an arbitrary answer could be given: the two are not commensurable quantities.

There were, of course, large profits made out of the War. But they were made out of the private consumer as well as out of government, and it is not possible from available records to disentangle the two, or even to say for certain that the Government's dollar bore a heavier load of such profits on its back than the dollar of the private consumer. About the only course open is to consider the government dollar on a par with the private dollar, each being taken to represent the same share of the national income. The question of warped distribution would then remain for separate consideration.

In diverting to war the economic resources represented by our estimate of 31 billions, the Government incurred fiscal responsibilities that bulked larger, especially in their after-effects. Against some 9½ billions loaned abroad we are scheduled to receive 22 billions through some 65 years, and against 23 billions of net war borrowing at home we shall probably pay back over 36 billions, principal and interest, through a period of some thirty years. And we shall probably spend in the long run as much on the Veterans' Bureau as we are due to receive from foreign debt settlements, and we shall certainly spend it faster in the first twenty-five years from the official end of the War. To date we have spent some 2 billion more on the Veterans' Bureau than we have received on foreign debt settlements and this amount is likely to be trebled before the two annual sums come into balance—if they ever do.

Speaking in fiscal terms, the largest estimate of war outlays is about 34½ billions to June 30, 1921, including all foreign loans. To this are to be added subsequent outlays of over 13 billions of interest on our own public debt up to its probable retirement, some ½ billion of abnormal general expenses through 1923, and any possible excess of Veterans' Bureau expenses above the amounts we receive on the foreign debt settlements. If the Veterans' Bureau expenses are kept within what seem reasonable bounds, and if the foreign debt settlements are fully carried out, there will be little or no excess of cost in the ultimate balance of these two items. This makes a probable net total of 48 billions to be found out of taxes. What is less uncertain is that we must first spend considerably more than this, and then collect a rebate from Europe—if we can. Within a period of something over thirty years, from 1917 to 1950, the total burden on taxes will be over 52 billions and probably in the neighborhood of 54 billions, by which time our own war debt will be wiped out or nearly so, and the payments on foreign debt settlements will be reaching their full magnitude. These payments, when no longer subject to the claims of our own debt retirement program, should produce an actual net income to the Government above the Veterans' Bureau expenses, unless these have in the meantime been swollen by grants out of proportion to the burdens reasonably traceable to war service.[7] This excess of income might amount in forty years to 5 billions or more.

Perhaps when this time is reached, if not before, the matter of further revision of the terms of the war debts may look differently to our statesmen. It is one thing to place the interest of the domestic taxpayer first when he still has twenty-odd billions of war debt to pay off; it may be somewhat different when that debt is fully paid and when further receipts from abroad would go to defray the ordinary expenses of operating our Government. The Government, as a government, certainly made no profit out of the War, but faces a minimum net fiscal outlay of 45 billions under the most favorable conditions. This fact has been urged in refutation of the charge that we were unduly grasping in our claims for debt settlements. This being the case, would it not be strange for us to begin to make a profit a generation after the end of the War? The Government may find even a belated profit a positive source of embarrassment. The chief force which might be capable of bringing about a revision ear-

[7] For fuller discussion of this whole matter, see Chapters IX and X, and Appendix A.

lier is a conviction that this country's economy stands to lose more by full collection than by revision.

The three contingencies which are capable of having a major effect on the fiscal aftermath of the War are: large fresh burdens for veterans' relief; a failure to collect from abroad the full amount called for in the present debt settlements; and a failure of our own Government to balance its budget and maintain its sinking fund, resulting in prolonging the life of our own war debt and so increasing the total burden of interest. If all these should do their worst, our total fiscal burdens might mount up to the 100 billions which President Coolidge mentioned in his armistice-day speech of 1928.[8] With ordinary good management and good fortune, a little over half that amount should see the end of them, even if some further scaling down of foreign debts should be found advisable. An average of 2 billions a year in added taxes for thirty years, starting with the fiscal year 1918, when the war revenues began to be effective, should see us through, even if the war debts were canceled tomorrow.

This, be it noted, is the fiscal burden: the task of collecting money from taxpayers and handing it over to others—to businesses furnishing goods, to bondholders, to veterans or their dependents, etc. To what extent does this process of fiscal transfer constitute an addition to the social costs estimated on the basis of goods and services diverted to war purposes? To the extent of the added administrative costs of collection and disbursement (if these are not already reckoned in) and to the further extent of any cutting down of productive activity which may result from the business incidence of the taxes laid, and from the other effects of the War on business both immediate and postponed. In some foreign countries, where the post-war tax burdens are far heavier than ours, it seems probable that productive activity is definitely hampered thereby. But in our case no such effect is evident. In fact, our great post-war prosperity tends on its face toward the conclusion that the net effect of all the forces set in motion by the War has been to stimulate production rather than to depress it, at least up to the beginning of the depression of

[8] His statement was in general terms: "It is probable that the final cost will run well toward 100 billions." (*New York Times,* November 12, 1928.) President Coolidge was apparently contemplating a growth in the Veterans' Bureau outlays comparable to the course of Civil War pensions. This it seems reasonable to hope we can escape (*see* Chapter XIII, below).

1929–30. This optimistic view should not be accepted without critical examination, but at any rate the opposite is not proved.

The Government clearly did not make a profit out of the War, but this does not dispose of the question whether the nation as a whole made one. Did the War, and its after-effects, increase our national productiveness? If the evidence is not conclusive, that lies in the nature of the problem, since no one can tell exactly what would have happened if there had been no war.

CHAPTER VIII

STATE, LOCAL, AND PRIVATE EXPENSES

BESIDES the Federal Government, traceable fiscal outlays for war purposes were made by State and local governments and by private organizations. We may take up first the State governments, whose principal war outlay consisted of bonuses to discharged service men. The complete total of outlays made and obligations incurred for this purpose has not been compiled, but compilations have been made of States passing bonuses through the year 1926, the amount of the bond issues or other fiscal provisions made for financing them, the total of "funds allotted," and, for a majority of the States in question, the major amounts actually spent.[1] Twenty-one States are reported as having passed some form of veterans' compensation. The original enactments were mostly made in the years 1919–21, inclusive, though Vermont passed an act in 1917, and Kansas in 1923. There has, naturally, been a train of supplementary legislation.

The total amount of bond issues authorized for this purpose amounted to $324,000,000, not including North Dakota and Oregon, which made provisions out of taxes. The total amount of "funds allotted" up to 1926 amounted to nearly $358,000,000, while the amounts actually spent, so far as reported, fall not far short of the total allotted, indicating that very nearly $350,000,000 has been spent. The probable total of interest charges would bring the fiscal burden up to at least $500,000,000.

This $350,000,000 is an addition to the federal "soldiers' bonus," by which the Government undertook liabilities worth about 2 billions at the time they were undertaken. It is thus a substantial addition to service compensation, but does not make much impression on the total budget of veterans' care and relief, which will probably mount up to at least 20 billions.[2]

[1] Compilations made by the Legislative Reference Service of the Library of Congress, which has kindly furnished copies to the writer. The States reported are California, Illinois, Iowa, Kansas, Maine, Massachusetts, Michigan, Minnesota, Missouri, Montana, New Hampshire, New Jersey, New York, North Dakota, Ohio, Oregon, Rhode Island, South Dakota, Vermont, Washington, and Wisconsin.

[2] *See* Chapter XIII, below.

The total number of soldiers furnished by these twenty-one States (not including other service persons) was over 2 million, indicating, with sailors, marines, and others, a total of about 2½ million service persons of all classes potentially eligible for compensation.[3] This makes the average compensation per person potentially eligible amount to about $140. The average for those actually receiving compensation would, of course, be higher.

It is of interest to note that of the fourteen States furnishing the largest numbers of soldiers eleven are included in the list. The list includes all the New England States except Connecticut, and all the Pacific Coast States. It includes most of the northernmost States, while the South, including the tier of States from Texas to Arizona, is not represented. The amounts of individual compensation vary from $10 per month of service, or a flat maximum of $100, to $1.00 per day of service in the case of Kansas. In two cases the compensation takes the form of aid in acquiring a farm or home, and in two cases educational expenses are especially provided for.

In addition to direct compensation, other privileges have been granted to veterans by the States, chiefly in the form of preference in civil service appointments. Whether this involves any financial burden cannot be determined. Certainly, if it does, the amount cannot be estimated.

Besides the compensation of veterans, the States incurred some expenses for care of veterans in institutions, and for various war activities while the War was going on. These latter are partially reported in *Financial Statistics of States*, by the Bureau of the Census, while its *Financial Statistics of Cities* adds something to the totals. These reports cover thirty-one States, and the largest cities. There is, however, no uniformity in the accounting methods of allocation, and therefore the totals simply mean the amounts which the accounting officials in each governing body have found it practicable to allocate to the War. The amounts so reported amounted to $20,411,432 in 1918 and $15,821,637 in 1919. In view of the partial nature of these reports, it seems fair to place a minimum figure of $50,000,000 on these expenses, while the actual total may well run above $100,000,000.

This figure does not include the outlays for militia and armories, which are not strictly war expenses in the special sense of being de-

[3] *See* Leonard Ayres, *The War with Germany*, pp. 22, 23.

voted directly to the fighting of this particular war. The training afforded in the years before the War to members of the National Guard who subsequently served in our National Army is, of course, an expense which could quite properly be charged to the World War in a more general sense. But this expense cannot be segregated. The expenses for militia and armories do not seem to have been increased during the War; rather reduced, if the shrinkage of the dollar is taken into account. In 1915 they amounted to $7,507,000, in 1918 to $9,193,000, in 1919 to $7,358,000, and in 1923 to $10,836,000. This does not reveal any excess amount strictly chargeable to the World War.

In addition to States and cities, much war work was done by private organizations. The chief ones of these, officially endorsed by the United States Government, were the Red Cross, the Y.M.C.A., the Y.W.C.A., the War Camp Community Service, the Knights of Columbus, the Jewish Welfare Board, the American Library Service, and the Salvation Army. The total amount subscribed by the public to these various organizations has been estimated at approximately $560,000,000. It is also estimated that several hundred millions were spent on war relief work by allied organizations which found their chief support in the United States.[4] It is interesting to note that the Red Cross had a surplus of funds left over from war contributions, and has devoted these funds to the relief of veterans. This surplus is only now on the point of exhaustion.[5]

To sum up, it appears that the fiscal expenditures by States, localities, and private organizations have amounted to more than one billion dollars at the lowest estimate, and probably several hundred million more. The outlays of money and services made by individuals directly constitute another large total, but one which it is hopeless to attempt to reduce to figures.

The amounts representing social outlays of goods and services during the War include nearly all of the $560,000,000 spent by private agencies, the $50,000,000 or more of State and local expenditures, and most of the undetermined amount estimated at "several hundred millions" spent by allied organizations relying largely on American support. The total may be put roughly at $800,000,000

[4] Letter from Mr. Pierce Williams, executive of the National Bureau of Economic Research.

[5] *New York Times,* October 12, 1930.

to $900,000,000. The $350,000,000 of State veterans' compensation, with subsequent interest charges, comes in the class of post-war fiscal transfers and does not materially affect the underlying aggregate cost of the War to the national economy as a whole.

Adding these to the totals obtained from the federal figures, the immediate social cost of the World War may be estimated at 32 billions. Fiscal outlays for the World War during the period 1917–21, inclusive, came to perhaps 35½ billions, with some 4 billions more spent for general war purposes not traceable to this particular war. And ultimate probable fiscal outlays traceable to the World War, on the assumption of full payment of foreign debt settlements, may amount to nearly 48 billions; while they are fairly certain to exceed 53 billions by 1947 or 1950, before the foreign debt settlements begin to exceed our own post-war outlays and afford a postponed rebate. The ultimate net social cost may be estimated at anything from the original 32 billions up to 50 billions or more, according as one does or does not believe that the foreign debt settlements will constitute a real net addition to our available national income of ultimate goods and services.

For purposes of comparing the war costs with the estimates of national income, they need to be allocated to calendar years instead of the fiscal years in which the fiscal statements appear. For this purpose the quarterly statements furnish a serviceable basis. The deductions for fiscal transfers which do not represent national outlays of goods and services are heavier for the later years. Interest on the war debt alone mounts from nothing at the beginning of 1917 to approximately one billion dollars for 1920. By calendar years, then, the real social outlays for prosecuting the War may be roughly estimated as follows: for 1917, 6 billions; for 1918, 16 billions; for 1919, 9 billions, and for 1920, 1 billion.

CHAPTER IX

HOW THE BURDEN WAS BORNE: EVIDENCE FROM STATISTICS OF NATIONAL INCOME AND PRODUCTION

IT is an undoubted fact that this country bore the burden of the War without any marked or serious privations for the people as a whole. Superficial observation of the lavish spendings of a considerable number of war workers has led some to conclude that labor "profiteered" largely, while similar general impressions of huge war profits sustained the belief that "capital" gained also; and that the cost of the War was substantially met out of increased production, without any inroads on consumption. It is true that, by certain methods of comparison, both wage-earners and "capital" made some gains; but by equally justifiable standards they could be shown to have lost. And by no stretch of the methods of statistical comparison is it possible to sustain the claim that the War paid for itself while it was being fought. The only possible basis for such a conclusion, in the face of the sober evidence of statistics, is the extremely dubious assumption that the War caused the whole of our post-war "prosperity" but did not cause the present depression. It was probably in some measure responsible for both, but to what extent can never be proved.

Aside from this possibility, the idea that the War was self-sustaining is clearly out of the question, in the nature of the case. At the height of our war effort, during the calendar year 1918, we devoted to the War some 16 billions' worth of goods and services out of a total national income of something over 60 billions, or over one-fourth of our total income. To have done this out of added output would have required an increase of one-third above normal peace-time productivity; and no such increase took place. Our whole war expenditure during something like three years from our entry into the struggle amounted to materially more than one-half-year's total national dividend, or one-sixth of our total economic effort during the three years. To be self-sustaining, this would require an increase of 20 per cent in national product above a peace-time normal for the whole three-year period, and something more to make up for the post-war depression. And there was clearly no such increase as this.

In fact, the figures leave no real doubt that our production for the whole war period was below the normal upward trend of peace-time output and not above it, even though such a "normal trend" can never be accurately determined. Some increases there were, to be sure. The demands of war unleashed great amounts of productive effort. But they also imposed handicaps and wastes, and in manufactures at least the yield of the war effort was definitely below normal in proportion to effort expended.[1] War production was expensive production, aside from the confusing effects of the inflation of dollar values. Output increased greatly in 1916, and again somewhat in 1917, but fell off again in 1919; and the average for 1917–19 was apparently not very different from the high level already reached in 1916.

In one sense it may be true that the cost of war came out of increased output. Taking the least prosperous pre-war year as a starting point, the increases in "realized income" during the whole war period, including that of our neutrality, may have equaled that part of the cost of the War which was met from increased taxation. Thus the rest of the war cost, which was met by borrowing, corresponded to decreased consumption but was largely balanced, for the country as a whole, by private "savings," personal and corporate, and thus did not figure as a net loss of private income. But, of course, these "savings" represented no national productive assets and the amounts so contributed represented national costs as definitely as taxes. There is, however, one mitigation. There are indications that something like 5¾ billions of the war borrowing came from corporations: that is, from sources which do not appear in the "realized income" of King's estimates. Business taxes and other adjustments (to be discussed later) might add 2 or 3 billions more. This leaves only about 24 billions to come out of "realized income," and brings the remainder probably little more than 13 billions below the 1914 level, indicating that much retrenchment beyond that of 1914.

This 1914 level is, of course, well below normal, and any normal or secular upward trend is forgotten when we simply ask how the war years compared with 1914. This does not tell us how much, if at all,

---

[1] The author has developed this point in "Inductive Evidence on Marginal Productivity," *Amer. Econ. Rev.*, September, 1928, pp. 449 ff.

the national income was increased as a result of the War, beyond what it would otherwise have been. It is chiefly of interest as a way of comparing war-retrenchment with that of what passed for hard times before we entered the War. The war retrenchment was far greater.

One way of approaching this problem is to take the 1913 rate of income *per capita* as a point of departure, and see how great was the total margin of income in subsequent years above the amount needed to furnish this 1913 standard to the population of the later years. The result is shown in the accompanying table.[2]

Year	Total realized income, current dollars (millions)	Current dollars needed to furnish 1913 purchasing power per capita	Difference	Approximate war cost
1913	35,723	35,723		
1914	35,647	36,800	—1,153	
1915	37,205	37,560	— 355	
1916	43,288	41,000	+2,288	
1917	51,331	48,500	+2,831	6,000
1918	60,408	57,800	+2,608	16,000
1919	65,959	66,200	— 251[3]	9,000
1920	73,999	77,250	—3,249[3]	1,000

No reliance should be placed on the precise figures of difference between the actual income and the amount needed to maintain the 1913 standard, as these are comparatively narrow margins of difference between large totals which are themselves subject to considerable error. Indeed the same is true throughout the calculations made in this chapter. Wherever fractions of billions appear, they do so rather for convenience in expressing the outcome of a particular computation than because the precision of the data justifies them. Usually it does not. But the general character of the story the figures tell is probably fairly reliable.

[2] Data from King, *The National Income and Its Purchasing Power,* National Bureau of Economic Research, 1930. Column 3 computed on the assumption of the same percentage of price inflation as found by King for the national income as a whole, resulting from a composite of different index numbers for different groups of incomes. Computations were made by slide-rule and are therefore only approximately accurate.

[3] These two figures appear decidedly doubtful, for reasons which will appear as the discussion proceeds.

It appears that the country could have devoted well over 5 billions to war in 1917–18—the true figure is likely to be even larger—and still have had left for peace-time uses as much income *per capita* as in 1913. This amounts to approximately one-fourth of the actual war outlay for these years. Or it could have devoted some $6\frac{1}{4}$ billions in the three years 1917–19 and still have had as much left as in 1915. This is about one-fifth of the war outlay for these three years. At least this much of the war cost we may assume was defrayed out of increased national income. The true amount of increased production is undoubtedly considerably larger, as has been indicated. On the other hand, this favorable showing is largely canceled if account is taken of the shortages of income in 1920–21.

There was, then, increased income, but it was not costless; far from it. It had to be produced by men and women, some of whom would not normally have been working in industry, some of whom worked at unfamiliar tasks, and subject to unfamiliar dangers, often for long hours and under heavy pressure, frequently in congested housing conditions or unable to find housing reasonably near their places of work. In all these ways this excess war income represented more than normal human sacrifices of production. At this price we were saved from having to meet the whole cost of the War out of retrenchment from our pre-war level of expenditures.

Not all this retrenchment was in actual current consumption of goods, and therefore it does not accurately represent the real tightening of the consumer's belt. Much of it represents a decrease in expenditures on what may be called the consumer's capital account: on the maintenance, replacement, and increase of our national stock of durable consumption goods. The decline in private building construction is only one leading example. As for industrial capital, we have seen how the boom of 1915–16 provided us with a considerable part of the productive capacity with which we fought the War. The war years saw a continued building up of capital at more than normal rates, except perhaps for 1918. Corporate savings in 1917–19 were large enough to absorb billions of Liberty bonds and still have more than a normal amount left over in dollars of 1913 buying power, and new capital invested in corporations by individuals was also above normal for these same years, in dollars of 1913 buying power.[4]

[4] Based on tables in King, *op. cit.*, pp. 216, 280.

However, these corporate savings are very doubtful quantities in view of the uncertainties of accounting practices in a time of radical price inflation. The new funds invested are a more reliable evidence of what was happening to capital. It may also be that even genuine investments made in war-time were in types of equipment which had little permanent peace-time value. But they afford fair evidence that the war burden was not shifted on to the capital account by allowing the national plant to run down—except to some slight extent in agriculture. What did not come out of increased production had to come out of decreased private spending by consumers.

A word as to the appropriateness of the figures of "national income" we have been using for this particular purpose. They are based on "realized income" received by individuals, and thus corporate savings and taxes paid by businesses directly are not included. Physical production, if we had adequate measures of it, might be a more appropriate figure. The "total realized income" of King's latest study agrees remarkably closely with Day's index of physical production (which goes through 1919), but the index of physical production computed by Professor Copeland and appearing in *Recent Economic Changes* shows a stronger upward trend for the war years, and even more so for 1920.[5] In Copeland's index, 1917, 1918, and 1919 are all above 1916, and 1920 is highest of all. Even this index, however, shows a downward trend from 1917 to 1919. This production index fluctuates far more violently than does the "realized income" figure in the activity of 1920, the depression of 1921, and the subsequent recovery. This is natural, when one remembers that corporate savings and surplus act as a buffer between business earnings and personal incomes derived therefrom. In 1921, indeed, corporations disbursed to security holders some 2½ billions more than they earned in that year.[6] But the matter lends point to the query whether the figure of "national realized income" is of such a character that its movements during the war period are faithful indications of the movements of that fund out of which the costs of the War had to come.

For one thing, the omission of corporate savings leaves out one of the material sources of the funds that went into Liberty bonds and so helped directly to pay for the War. The figures of interest on such

[5] See *Recent Economic Changes,* p. 761.
[6] King, *op. cit.,* p. 280.

bonds paid to corporations indicate that about one-fourth of the Government's war borrowing came from corporations. How much their payments to security holders were diminished by this lending can only be conjectured. It would be desirable, if it were possible, to include business savings so far as they represent things actually produced and not mere value-inflations. This, however, seems impossible.

Another question has to do with the treatment of taxes and government expenditures. Taxes paid by businesses do not appear in the figures of national income, though they represent a division of the income of the business in which the Government gets funds which might otherwise have been divided to stockholders. If the Government pays this money out again to businesses for supplies, and then repeats the process, there is a whole stream of production and consumption that never appears as "realized income" at all. On the other hand any amounts the Government disburses to individuals do appear as income paid to these individuals. These sums include interest on war debt, pay of army and navy, and the like, as distinct from payment to businesses for supplies bought. It appears, then, that if the increase in government revenues collected from businesses is balanced by the increase in disbursements to individuals, there is no distortion in the figure of national income. But if the increase in revenues collected from businesses is greater than the increase in disbursements to individuals, then some of the national income has escaped counting. And if the increase in disbursements to persons is greater than the increase in revenues from businesses, then some of the national income is counted twice.[7]

A man, let us say, works in a textile factory and receives, as his share of the yield of that factory, a salary of $5,000. He pays $100 as income tax to the Government, which pays the $100 to a soldier, and the result is $5,100 of reported income. In one sense this is quite appropriate, since the soldier has rendered a valuable service, and the $100 may be an inadequate measure of it. But this service is not economically self-sustaining. It is not part of the economic income out of which the war services have to be paid for. Income in that

---

[7] This is on the assumption that the work of the extra government personnel is unproductive. This seems justified, for the present purpose, as their work constituted part of the war cost and not part of the national income out of which that cost was met.

sense is only $5,000, no matter how much of it is shared with soldiers, sailors, and holders of Liberty bonds.

On the other hand, if the Government takes the $100 tax from the business, so that it has only $4,900 to divide instead of $5,000, and pays the $100 as salary to a soldier, then "realized income" stands at $5,000. If the Government takes the $100 tax from the individual and spends it for cloth, then again "realized income" shows $5,000. But if government takes the tax from the business and spends it for cloth, then "realized income" shows only $4,900, for the same production and consumption of wealth.

It seems that in 1917 and 1918, the Government expanded its spending to persons faster than its revenues from businesses; while in 1920 and 1921 the war revenues were at their height and the war army was disbanded, with the result that more was being collected from businesses than was disbursed to persons.[8] This would mean (if not neutralized by other adjustments) that "total realized income" would give too large a figure for our present purpose in 1917–18, and too small in 1920–21. It seems possible, however, that the element of business savings would more than neutralize the discrepancies in 1917–18 and in 1921.

Another doubtful element, which cannot be measured, is concerned with the effects of credit inflation. When credit institutions lend the government funds to prosecute a war, by expanding the total volume of credit, they give the government command over part of the social income which has not previously appeared in the incomes of individuals and did not come out of taxes of any kind. This affords another reason for supposing that the true social income may have been somewhat larger during the period of credit expansion than the reported figures show. While the amount of these adjustments can never be exactly ascertained, we can estimate roughly that the actual income exceeded "realized income" by possibly more than 1 billion in 1919, and by possibly 2 billions in 1920, over and above loans made by corporations to the Government. For purposes of tracing the incidence of the burden, since the figures of "realized income" for various groups furnish the best working material, the necessary allowances can best be made, not by changing our estimates of the national income, but by changing instead the estimates of the war

[8] In each case it is the amount in excess of the pre-war level that is significant as bearing on the *change* in the national income.

costs which are to be regarded as having been borne out of "realized income" as reported in King's figures. The largest adjustment is that for corporate lendings, which we may put at 5¾ billions. On this basis the costs of the War which have to be regarded as subtractions from "realized income" are approximately as follows: in the calendar year 1917, 5 billions; in 1918, 13 billions; and in 1919, 6 billions: a total for the three crucial years of about 24 billions. This is far less than the total of 31 billions of national resources actually devoted to war purposes during those three years, but it is still an enormous sum.

On what groups or classes did this burden fall? Here the statistics are decidedly helpful, showing as they do the "realized income" of different classes in dollars of constant purchasing power. The chief difficulty is the choice of a normal standard with which to compare the war years in order to judge their effect. Conditions in 1913 were prosperous, so that that year must be reckoned as above normal, yet normal progress in the next six years might have more than made up for this. Of the three years of our neutrality, 1914 was decidedly depressed, and was made somewhat more so by the effects of the conflict abroad. The next year was probably, on the average, fairly normal, while 1916 was a year of booming business, due to the War, but representing a rate of prosperity which we could probably not have maintained even if we had remained neutral. The average of these three years was probably fairly normal, but not for all classes. Real salaries remained virtually stable from 1912 through 1915, but fell in 1916 with the first substantial rise of American prices resulting from the War, and continued falling through 1919. Real wages slumped in 1914, partially recovered in the following year, and rose in 1916 to new high levels. Profits rose throughout the neutrality period, reaching an abnormally high level in 1916.

Profits, however, are not reckoned on a basis comparable to that used for "real wages" and "real salaries" and cannot be. Wages and salaries for this purpose mean annual earnings per person attached to some branch of industry. "Profits" means merely the "total realized income" from property and enterprise. Thus profits grow with the expansion of population and industry and the investment of added capital, without necessarily signifying that industry is more profitable in the sense of a higher percentage return on investment. Data for such a figure are not available, but the tremendous increases of earnings in the neutrality and war periods are only to a small extent balanced by increased investment.

Since normal levels of the national dividend and its several parts can only be conjectured, it follows that the true effect of the War on these incomes lies also in the realms of conjecture. What can be done is to select some definite year as a point of departure and trace the changes in these various incomes. Thus we may conclude whether the cost of the War came out of increased income as compared to the base year, or out of decreased consumption as compared to that year, knowing that this does not tell us whether the War caused increased income beyond what would have been realized without it, or how much it curtailed consumption below what would have been possible without it.

For this purpose the year 1915 is here used. Real salaries were so stable from 1912 through 1915 that the choice of a standard year makes little difference. Real wages, however, fluctuated so much that the choice of a standard year makes all the difference between a showing of gain and of loss for wage-earners during the War. Real wages in 1915 were almost certainly subnormal; still more is the 1915 level of real wages a subnormal standard when applied to the years 1917 and after. The result of choosing this year is to show a gain in real wages during the War, whereas by other equally plausible standards a loss would be shown. This does no harm if we remember always that the "gain" is merely a gain above the 1915 level. In the same way this analysis will show part of the cost of our participation in the War coming from increased income—above the 1915 level. Later, we may enter more speculative realms and conclude that the War made both real wages and total production during the war years smaller than they would otherwise have been. This reduction is an additional cost of the War, over and above the visible diversion of economic resources. Whether it is balanced by favorable after-effects—whether the War is to be credited with a share in our post-war prosperity—this is a still more speculative matter. But to return to our more definite comparisons.

We have already estimated that pay and subsistence in the armed services represented a loss of some 230 millions as compared to earnings in other employments. Counting only the war-time increase in these services we should have something over 200 millions as the loss suffered on this score by those whom the War brought into armed service. In making our estimate of the social cost of the War we have reckoned their services at a value representing average general earning power and not government pay. The difference may be thought of as a contribution to the cost of the War, made by this class but never appearing either in the government budgets or in the statistics of "realized income" in the country as a whole. For this contribution, handsome recompense in the form of "bonuses" has been arranged for.

There were others who suffered loss but got no recompense. Government employees, other than those entering the service on account of the War, contributed by way of a loss in the purchasing power of their salaries an amount that may be reckoned as at least 2 billions. In 1916 there were 2,085,000 persons employed by all branches of government in the United States, and the upward trend from 1909 indicates a probable number in 1921 of some 2,400,000, aside from the effects of the War.[9] Their average pay, in dollars of 1913 purchasing power, reached a peak in 1914 at $836 and then declined, and did not again pass the 1914 level until 1922. From 1915 to 1916 their salaries lost over 100 millions in purchasing power. For the years 1916–21, inclusive, the total shortage in purchasing power, measured from the 1915 level, was 2 billions for the original number of employees. Allowing for normal increase in numbers would bring this shortage up nearly to 2.2 billions. For the three years 1917–19, inclusive, their loss in terms of current dollars would be more than 1.9 billions. Including the estimated loss of the service men the total would be over 2.1 billions. Thus this class made a large contribution to the War and were forced to restrict their consumption very largely, aside from their subscriptions to Liberty loans or other direct contributions. The burden of inflation fell on them in very tangible form.

Salaries in industries followed a similar course, and show a similar loss in purchasing power. For the whole salaried class in both public and private employments there was an uninterrupted decline from

[9] This computation is based on tables in King, *op. cit.*, pp. 140, 361, 366. The more obvious war-time increases in armed forces and civil departments were deducted, and their *pro rata* share of the pay of their particular groups was similarly deducted from total pay and the average per employee recomputed as a basis for estimating the losses in purchasing power of those who would have been in government service if the War had not occurred.

1914 to 1919 amounting to about 25 per cent, or over 22 per cent from 1916 to 1919. A calculation of the same sort as the one already made, for the entire salaried class, indicates a total loss in purchasing power of well over 4 billions from 1916 to 1922, inclusive, or nearly 3½ billions for 1917 to 1920, inclusive.[10] These amounts are in "1913 dollars." Converted into dollars of current purchasing power, they would amount to between 5½ and 6 billions for the years 1917 to 1920, inclusive, or some 7 billions through 1922. Thus the salaried class bore, *via* the losses from inflation, between one-fifth and one-sixth of the total cost of the War, aside from whatever direct contribution they made through taxes or subscriptions to Liberty loans. For the crucial years 1917–19, their loss may be estimated at some 4 billions in current dollars. The total shrinkage in their consumption would be materially more than the figures given. Taxes and war loans might well add two billions to the war-time abstinence of this group, though any such estimate is purely conjectural. Here is a class to which the War did not bring prosperity. They had to tighten their belts under a sterner compulsion than the mandates of food conservation committees.

Wage-earners, on the other hand, secured an actual gain in real earnings per worker as compared to the level of 1915, though they did not maintain the high level reached in 1916, and were almost certainly well below a fair peace-time normal for the war years. As nearly as can be estimated, the total gain, during the years 1917–20, inclusive, was about 2.6 billions in "1913 dollars," and may have been 3 billions or more if pensions, accident compensation, etc., are included.[11] For the years 1917–19, the gain was over 2 billions in current dollars. This gain, however, was undoubtedly secured at the cost of longer hours and greater intensity of work. There were fewer wage-earners at work for private employers, but more persons gainfully employed, including those in government service. Furthermore, wage-earners as a class undoubtedly invested a considerable part of their gains in Liberty bonds leaving at best only a very moderate in-

[10] This calculation is based on tables in King, *op. cit.*, pp. 61, 140, 361, 366. The "loss" is loss in real earnings per worker, multiplied by an estimated normal number of workers. Increased aggregate income due to increased numbers working is not counted a gain.

[11] Based on tables in *ibid.*, pp. 56, 152.

crease in actual consumption and probably an actual decrease during 1917–19.

The gains of wage-earners cancel over half the losses of salaried workers, and leave a net loss in the compensation of wage and salaried workers together of something less than 2 billions of current dollars. There are some further gains from a slight shifting of wage-workers into salaried positions, and from increased numbers working beyond a normal quota of the whole population, which probably wipe out most of the remainder, leaving little or no loss in aggregate consuming power; or possibly a fraction of a billion. This, be it repeated, is a loss before counting the contributions made in taxes and loans to the Government which may be conjecturally estimated at 5 or 6 billions more.[12] The resultant therefore represents almost certainly a very material shrinkage of consumption, for the two groups, amounting to possibly nearly one-fifth of the total cost of the War.

Entrepreneurs and property owners gained as a class by comparison with 1915, though, like wage-earners, they failed to maintain the prosperity of 1916 throughout the war period. In 1917 and 1918, however, they received more real income than even in 1916.[13] In the years 1917–19 entrepreneur and property income received by individuals made gains amounting to about 6½ billions in current dollars, nearly 5¼ billions of which went to farmers. Thus farmers were the one class which scored substantial economic gains during the War. They could have contributed 3 billions in loans and taxes —a liberal estimate—and still have increased their consumption over 2 billions.

All the rest of entrepreneur and property income, including the whole of "business income" in the usual sense, showed a gain for the years 1917–19—always compared to 1915—of about 1¼ billions in current dollars. It is well to remember that this group is dominated by corporations, and that corporate income as such is not shown in the figures; merely amounts distributed to holders of stocks and bonds. Corporate net income increased enormously, but the greater part of the increase was kept as "corporate savings," and the extent

---

[12] Knauth estimates that 30 per cent of the Liberty loans, or about 7 billions, went to persons with incomes of $2,000 or less. The portion of these that went to farmers and small traders may be partially offset by those that went to salaried persons receiving over $2,000.

[13] King, op. cit., p. 112.

to which these increases represented increased physical production or increased real wealth is highly questionable. A great deal undoubtedly represented mere appreciation of goods on hand, and the greater part of this was wiped out in the deflation of 1921. On the other hand, the heavy rates of taxation gave an incentive to the concealment of income by overmaintenance or other methods. The most talked-of diversion of income, however, was of a sort that probably yielded little of real capital value to business as a whole, namely, building up good will by liberal advertising.

At any rate, a large part of the reported surpluses were undoubtedly real: indeed, they might all be real, though that would be in the nature of a coincidence. In the present estimate, after reckoning decreased consumption and increased "realized income" there remains unaccounted for some 8 or 9 billions of the total social cost of the War. It may be inferred, with serious reservations, that this amount represented increased national output of wealth not reckoned in "realized income," and the greater part of this took the form of undivided corporate profits, or of business taxes.

The income realized by persons, then, out of business profits, increased only some 1¼ billions. Out of this "realized income" came probably some seven-eighths of the taxes on personal incomes and three-fifths of the personal subscriptions to government loans, the total amounting probably to fully 14 billions. This class, then, diminished their personal outlays by something like 12½ to 13 billions. The shrinkage in their consumption was even greater, as they invested new money in corporations to an amount well over a billion in excess of normal. Thus they bore the largest burden of war costs, though the salaried class bore the burden which was felt most heavily.

These statements are so important that it will be well to look into some of the details of the evidence on which they rest. First come the returns on corporate securities. Interest payments suffered only a slight slackening in their steady rate of growth, but their purchasing power fell off by virtually the full amount of the price inflation. Dividends on preferred stocks proved more elastic, rising in 1916 and again in 1917, declining in 1918 and again in 1919, rising to a new high level in 1920 and then declining again. Their war-time increase was not nearly enough to counteract the effect of inflation and their purchasing power declined only less than that of interest payments.

Dividends on common stocks doubled from 1915 to 1917, and then declined steadily till 1922, when they stood at barely over two-thirds of the 1917 peak. It was of course these dividends which felt the chief effect of war taxation of business incomes in the years after 1917. In terms of purchasing power, they reached their peak in 1916 and their lowest point in 1922, at almost exactly half of the 1916 level. There was actually a slight increase in 1921, the fall in prices more than counteracting the decline of money disbursements. In this year "corporate savings" were a minus quantity larger than the whole sum of dividend disbursements on common stock.[14] These dividends, then, were not earned in that year. The trend here can best be summarized in a table showing corporate payments of interest, dividends on preferred stock, dividends on common stock, and the sum of the three, all in dollars of 1913 purchasing power.[15]

Returns on Securities, in Millions of 1913 Dollars.

Year	Interest	Preferred dividends	Common dividends	Total
1915	1,208	569	1,505	3,282
1916	1,160	591	2,544	4,295
1917	1,044	631	2,509	4,184
1918	918	540	2,020	3,478
1919	836	440	1,600	2,876
1920	770	429	1,294	2,493
1921	873	443	1,324	2,640
1922	942	391	1,271	2,604

This shows an increase of total security holders' income, during the years 1917–19, of about three-quarters of a billion. For the whole period covered it shows a decline. It also shows that holders of common stock gained while holders of bonds and preferred stocks lost.

Security holders as a class gained, in the purchasing power of the income distributed to them, over a billion of 1913 dollars in 1916, as compared to 1915. For the next four years their real receipts shrank

[14] King, *op. cit.*, p. 280, gives this figure in current dollars.

[15] From *ibid.*, p. 193. The last column is inserted by the present writer. Cf. *ibid.*, p. 278 for total corporate net income.

steadily, and these four years as a whole show a slight average loss as compared to 1915. Even without allowing for price inflation the actual number of dollars distributed declined steadily from over 5 billions in 1917 to 4,151 millions in 1922. The net incomes of corporations fluctuated even more strikingly, from 10,101 millions in 1917 to 458 millions in 1921.[16] They showed a huge gain for the war period, even after allowing for the shrinking dollar. Thus, while the security holders received slightly less value in cash distributions during the whole 5-year war period than in 1915, income was being "plowed back into the business" in unusually large amounts, from which they should ultimately have received the benefit. Including this element they gained during the War, but they cannot be said to have begun to realize their gains until 1923 to 1924.

It must be remembered that these corporate and business incomes are reckoned after paying the corporation income and excess profits taxes, and various war excises and other business taxes. And it must be further remembered that out of these incomes, after they reached the individual recipients, came the heaviest burden of personal income-taxation, and also the largest volume of subscriptions to Liberty bonds. On these matters the following indications are available.

For all income-groups above $5,000, wages and salaries furnish a minor part of the income, and these are the income-groups which furnish the great preponderance of personal income taxes—from 84.57 per cent in 1920 to 98.11 per cent in 1925.[17] For the years 1917–20, inclusive, wages and salaries furnished about 45 per cent of the income reported in personal income tax schedules, but probably between 10 per cent and 15 per cent of the taxes. Let us say, roughly, that wages and salaries furnished about half a billion out of about 4 billions of personal income taxes paid in these four years. This amount, of course, came in the main from salaries. The contribution of agriculture to the personal income tax was probably almost negligible in comparison to the large amounts with which we are deal-

[16] King, *op. cit.,* p. 278. These figures omit certain classes of corporations which are included in the figures for disbursements of interest and dividends. Hence the true aggregate would be materially larger.

[17] In 1919 wages and salaries constituted 36.6 per cent of the income in the $5,000–$10,000 group, and much less for all higher groups. This percentage varied from 1918 to 1921, between about 33 per cent and about 40 per cent. Figures from *Statistics of Income,* issued by United States Office of Internal Revenue, for the various years.

ing. The distribution of Liberty bond issues can only be surmised, the chief evidence being the denominations in which they were issued. While the number of small denomination bonds was large, the bulk of the funds came from bonds in denominations too large to be taken by persons of small or moderate incomes. Knauth estimates that about 30 per cent (or about 7 billions) came from incomes of $2,000 or less. Deducting nearly 6 billions taken by corporations, this leaves over 10 billions to come out of personal incomes of substantial size: chiefly business incomes.

To sum up: it appears that wage-earners lived nearly as well during the War as before the 1916 boom, and farmers lived markedly better. Salaried workers, on the other hand, lost during 1917–19 the equivalent of some 4 billions in the purchasing power of their salaries, and some 2 billions to 3 billions more in later years, before their salaries caught up with prices. In addition they contributed some half a billion in taxation and a materially larger amount in subscriptions to Liberty bonds—possibly in the neighborhood of 2 billions. Allowing for the fact that part of these war-loan subscriptions represented merely a diversion into government securities of savings that would otherwise have taken some other form, it still seems fair to estimate that the salaried class were forced to curtail their consumption by the equivalent of some 6 billions as their part in the nation's retrenchment in consumption during the three crucial years. And their real incomes continued below the 1915 level for three years more.

This leaves the class of business incomes as furnishing some $3\frac{1}{2}$ billions of personal income taxes, much of the luxury taxation, and probably 10 billions of loans (not counting bonds taken by business organizations directly). Nearly all of this came out of reduced personal outlays, and as private investments increased, consumption would seem to have declined some 13 to 14 billions.

For a grand summary, we may return to an earlier and simpler estimate, noting that it is at least not inconsistent with the very approximate figures given for the various classes. Out of some 31 billions of national resources devoted to war, in the three years 1917–19, possibly 18 billions came out of decreased consumption as compared to the 1915 rate *per capita*, some $5\frac{3}{4}$ billions came out of increased personal real income beyond the 1915 *per capita* level, which leaves $7\frac{1}{4}$ billions to come out of increased productive effort represented in undivided corporate income, either borrowed or taken as taxes. Of the 1 billion of war costs we have charged against 1920, all may be considered to have come out of decreased consumption.

As to the $7\frac{1}{4}$ billions we are tracing to undivided corporate income, this does not mean that the consumer did not pay it in increased prices of goods; it merely means that when his "real income" is computed, discounting his money income by the increase in prices, these indirect contributions are already automatically deducted. The corporation has performed a service of "stoppage at the source." Actually, in addition to what we have reckoned above, there was somewhat more contributed as taxes and received back as interest by bondholders or in other fiscal payments, but we are here limiting ourselves to the estimated 32 billions of actual social outlay represented by these transactions.

Of this we are estimating that some 13 billions came out of increased productive effort, and some 19 billions out of decreased consumption. The true net change in capital is too uncertain to be taken account of in this extremely rough estimate. Looked at from another angle, of the 32 billions, some 6 billions or more represented personal services rendered directly, and the rest represented goods devoted to war uses.

No class was ruined by the War, as was the case in some European countries. The worst years for the salaried class were 1919 and 1920 and in those years the loss in the purchasing power of their incomes amounted to some 20 per cent of the 1915 level. From 1915 to 1920, income from bonds as a whole had shrunk about 36 per cent in buying power. And anyone whose whole income came from bonds of fixed money yield, and who made no new investments during the period, lost about 49 per cent of his real income in 1920 and over 40 per cent during the era of post-war prosperity. Fortunately, such persons in this country constitute a relatively small class.

These, then, are the main outlines of the incidence of the war burden, so far as the available statistics present them. It would of course be interesting and valuable to trace the incidence of particular taxes, though such tracing is necessarily very uncertain. But for an understanding of the whole effect of the War, such particular problems are of less importance than the ultimate resultant of them all. Business taxes during the War may not have been literally shifted in their entirety, but as a whole they were paid out of increased business income collected from consumers.

At the risk of tedium let us repeat that these increases and decreases of income are merely changes as compared to the level of 1915, which was too low to represent a fair normal for the war years. So when we say, for instance, that "production increased 13 billions," we do *not* mean that the War brought about such an increase, making the national dividend that much larger than it would otherwise have been. More than half of this went into business assets of one sort or another, but there is no evidence that these had any effect in increasing the market value of the properties to their owners.[18] Thus they constitute a very doubtful element of "national income." In fact, there is every reason to believe that the War had the opposite effect and made the national dividend smaller than it would otherwise have been, allowing for normal peace-time growth. This means that there is a loss of income to be added to the costs of the War which have been already reckoned. But how much? The attempt to set a figure on this national income which "might have been" is beset with insurmountable difficulties and hence the true cost of the War in this fullest sense cannot be appraised. We may, however, at least face the problem and ask in a later chapter: what was the probable effect of the War on the national dividend?

[18] *Cf.* King, *op. cit.*, p. 281.

CHAPTER X

THE DISPLACEMENT OF MAN-POWER

To what extent did the demands of war divert personnel from industry and to what extent did it draw them from nonindustrial pursuits? It is clear that most of the increase in government pay rolls came from private occupations, though the exact numbers depend on the figures taken to represent the normal volume of private employment. The best standard is in the form of a normal percentage of the total population. The percentage "gainfully employed" fluctuates very little. The extreme variation outside of the actual war years was from 38.38 per cent in 1914 to 37.65 in 1922, while the highest percentage during the war period was 38.70 per cent in 1918 and the lowest was 37.60 per cent in 1920.[1] A fair normal for these war years would seem to be approximately 38 per cent, or possibly 37.9 per cent. On the latter basis the excess above normal in 1918 amounted to 835,000 persons, on the former basis, to 731,000. In 1920, when the gainfully employed fell to 37.6 per cent of the total population, there were actually 320,000 to 425,000 less than a "normal" number gainfully employed. This represents some totally disabled service men, some taking "vocational rehabilitation" training, some resuming interrupted educations in school and college, and presumably some who had simply not yet found positions. An unemployed person would ordinarily be counted as attached to the industry in which he regularly worked when work was available, but some discharged soldiers in similar plight might not be counted in the 1920 Census of Occupations, from which the data were taken.

All in all, the four years 1917 to 1920 saw an excess above normal of approximately 1 million person-years; while the corresponding excess of persons on the government pay rolls was something over 5 million person-years in army and navy and something under 1 million in civilian departments, the total coming very close to 6 mil-

---

[1] *See* King, *op. cit.,* pp. 50–53, for the basic data utilized in this discussion.

lion person-years.[2] This indicates a shortage in private industry amounting to 5 million person-years, as compared to assumed normal numbers, relative to the growing population. In terms of absolute numbers, compared to the 1916 level, there was even a slight excess in 1917, a shortage of about 1,300,000 in 1918, a shortage of about 140,000 in 1919, and an excess of nearly 1 million in 1920, the total shortage for the four years being a little over 350,000 person-years, or less than one-fourth of 1 per cent of the total number attached to peace-time pursuits during that period. For the years 1917–19 the total shortage would be over 1,300,000, or about .86 of 1 per cent.

In other words, the growth of population neutralized most of the diversion of man-power to direct government service and left peace-time pursuits with so nearly their former numbers that the absorption of most of the pre-war quota of unemployed could easily bring about an actual increase in the numbers effectively at work. This serves to explain why our productive power was not crippled, but even showed some slight increases. In fact, it raises the question why the increase was not greater; and points to the conclusion that our war-time man-power was, after all, somewhat wastefully utilized—as in the nature of the case was inevitable. The wastes could easily have been much greater.

The movements of man-power as between different industrial groups are also interesting and significant.[3] The War found American agriculture a stationary industry in terms of absolute numbers engaged, though physical product still showed a strong upward trend. In terms of the percentage of our total working population engaged, agriculture shows an uninterrupted decline for the whole period 1909 to 1927, with the exception of the years 1919 and 1920, when there was a very slight reversal of this downward movement. Absolute numbers were virtually stationary from 1909 through 1915; then there was a slight increase until in 1919 there were 146,000 more than in 1916. In 1920 there were 70,000 more than in 1916, and in 1921, 59,000 more. After this there was a definite

[2] See *ibid.*, p. 50. These excess numbers are figured from a basis involving an assumed normal rate of increase, and hence are only approximate.

[3] The figures on which the following discussion is based are found in *ibid.*, pp. 50–51, 53, also in Day's index of physical production, *Rev. of Econ. Statistics,* September–January, 1921.

downward trend which is apparently still going on.[4] The maximum increase in 1920 amounts to only 1⅔ per cent of the 1916 numbers and consists almost entirely of wage-earners. The number of "entrepreneurs" increased only 13,000 from 1916 to 1919, and 22,000 from 1916 to 1921, when it reached its maximum. Apparently, the post-war difficulties of agriculture were very slightly accentuated by the return of some service men to the calling of farmers, but most of the war-time increase consisted of persons on a wage-earning status who did not take deep root in the occupation.

The greatest war-time concentration in man-power was in manufacturing. For the whole war period it was greater than in army and navy and all other departments of government put together, though it probably did not reach as high a peak at the time of the armistice. Except for the war years, the percentage of the total population engaged in manufactures has been quite steady from 1909 to 1927, and 9 per cent may be taken as a fair normal for the war period. (The figure for 1927 is only a trifle over 9.1 per cent.) On this basis the neutrality boom of 1916 called in an excess of about 850,000 workers, and this excess rose to over 1½ millions in 1917 and to 2 millions in 1919, declining to 1.8 millions in 1920. After this, numbers declined steadily until 1925, by which time they amounted to 9¼ per cent of the total population.

This war-time increase in personnel brought about a large increase in physical product, but not a proportionate increase. According to Day's index, the increase of physical product from 1915 to 1916 was more than proportionate to increased man-power, but after that output actually declined until 1919. In the subsequent revision of Day's figures, the average output of 1917 and 1918 is the same as that of 1916, while 1920 shows a substantial increase.

In comparison with 1915, in 1916 an 11 per cent excess of workers (in absolute numbers) produced a 19 per cent increase in output. In 1917, a 20 per cent excess of workers above 1915 turned out a 20 per cent excess of product. In 1918, a 25 per cent excess of workers created a 15¼ per cent excess of product and in 1920 a 26¼ per cent excess of workers was responsible for a 22 per cent excess of product. After the collapse of 1921, output more than recovered; 1922 exceeded 1920, and later years showed further large increases, while the number of workers was actually declining. In

[4] *See* King, *op. cit.,* p. 50. The latest estimates are for 1927.

1925 there were some 18 per cent more workers than in 1915, and over 53 per cent more output.

These figures give only part of the picture of changes in man-power, but unfortunately data for some of the missing elements are quite unsatisfactory. These missing elements include changes in unemployment, in the length of the standard working week, and in actual hours worked so far as they differed from standard.

Unemployment was large in 1914 and continued large through a considerable part of 1915. From 1916 through 1920 it was below normal, then rose far above the 1914 level and continued high through 1922, after which it fluctuated about a fairly normal percentage. This means that man-power actually at work, relative to 1914–15, was higher than shown by the figures of workers attached to the industry throughout the war effort and also from 1923 on. And it was lower in 1921–22.[5]

In the meantime the length of the standard working week was trending quite steadily downward, and the years from 1917 to 1920 showed a sharp increase in this trend.[6] However, indications point to the conclusion that during the period of the war effort this was considerably more than offset by increases in actual hours worked, relative to the standard week.[7] Not until 1921 and after is there much assurance that the shortening of the standard week took effect in decreased hours of actual work.

The general indication is that output per hour worked by wage-earners remained about constant in 1914–16, fell definitely in 1917–18, returned to its former level in 1919–20, and then began the strong upward climb that marked the period of post-war prosperity. These figures are, of course, estimates subject to error, but the gen-

[5] Professor Paul Douglas has constructed an index of unemployment in manufacturing, railways, and street railways; see his *Real Wages in the United States*, 1930, especially pp. 443, 445, 455, 457. The above statement is based on his figures.

[6] See *ibid.*, p. 116.

[7] This conclusion rests on a comparison of earnings per worker employed (earnings and number of workers from King and percentage of unemployment from Douglas) with full-time weekly earnings (from Douglas). Actual earnings relative to 1914 fell short of full-time earnings only in 1921. Nineteen fourteen, the base year, was presumably a year when actual hours fell well below the standard week. Such indirect evidence as this should, of course, not be relied on as accurate but is entitled to some weight.

eral character of the story they tell is unmistakable and convincing, as is the story told by the accompanying chart.[8] While in agriculture yield per worker was fully maintained during the War or even increased slightly, in manufactures it decreased until the emergency was over, and then soared upward to the highest levels ever known. The War was a definitely disorganizing influence on American manufactures. It reduced their productive efficiency.

There are, of course, many reasons for this. The character of agricultural products and processes and of the equipment needed did not change as did the corresponding requirements of war-time manufacturing. The shrinkage in production of "nonessential" things left much equipment idle and rendered the special skill of many workers valueless. Other plants were being pushed beyond normal capacity with overtime work and night shifts, entailing inevitable losses in efficiency.[9] The adaptations of plants and working forces which took place were not costless. Supplies of coal, materials, and essential parts were not to be counted on; time was lost in putting new articles under quantity production. And the fact that many of the best executives were serving in Washington at a dollar a year can hardly have failed to have some unfavorable effect on the efficiency with which these difficulties were met, though there is no way to isolate this element in war cost. All in all, the performance was creditable, though unavoidably wasteful.

In all, the excess man-power in manufactures above a normal percentage of the total population—the increase presumably due to the War—amounted to 7¼ million person-years for the four years 1917–20, or over 8 million if 1916 is included. This is greater even than the corresponding excess of 6 billion in government service. The total man-power actually devoted to manufacturing for war purposes was still greater, as war production made heavy inroads on production for normal private consumption. The release of restric-

[8] Reproduced by permission from *Recent Economic Changes*, Chapter VI, by Leo Wolman, p. 455. Report of the Committee on Recent Economic Changes of the President's Conference on Unemployment, Herbert Hoover, Chairman, including the reports of a special staff of the National Bureau of Economic Research, New York, McGraw-Hill Book Co., Inc., 1929.

[9] Overtime work would not naturally reduce output per worker, though it might reduce output per hour. Night shifts, on the other hand, are proverbially less productive than day shifts.

tions on such "nonessential" production is no doubt responsible, jointly with the absorption of discharged service men, for the fact that the peak of manufacturing man-power came in 1919 and not in 1918. In 1918 there were nearly 3.1 million persons more than normal in government service and about 1,880,000 more than normal in manufacturing. In 1919 the excess number in government service decreased to about 1.9 millions and the excess number in manufactures *increased* to over 2 millions.

Very different was the effect of the War on the man-power engaged in the construction industries. Here the number of workers declined from 1,795,000 in 1914 to 1,037,000 in 1918. After a recovery in 1919 it stood at 1,092,000 in 1920 and 1921. The postwar recovery brought the numbers back to 1,799,000 in 1925, with slight declines in the next two years. Private housing construction

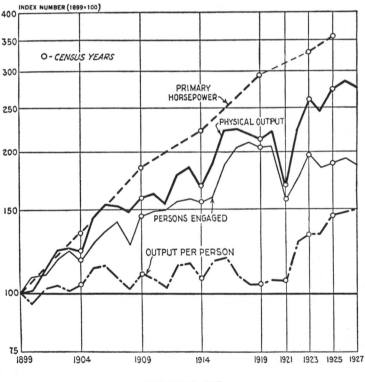

CHART XI.

Growth of Manufactures in the United States, 1899–1927.

was largely cut off as being, from the standpoint of the war-emergency, nonessential; and the construction of cantonments, war plants and houses for war workers did not fill the gap. As already pointed out, the war-time demand in this field was strong at times, but irregular. It is difficult to say, however, how much of the decline in numbers was due to the War, as the shrinkage went on through 1915 and 1916, and was only moderately accentuated in 1918. Possibly a quarter of a million workers were drawn off from construction work to other forms of war effort, beyond the shrinkage which was apparently going on for other reasons.

In mercantile pursuits there was a decline of something over 100,000 in 1918, and curiously enough the decline was mostly in entrepreneurs rather than in wage and salary workers. This may represent small tradesmen directly drafted into the army, and constitutes an exception to the general rule that heads of enterprises who could not be replaced were left in their private occupations. Aside from this one year there was no interruption in the steady increase of numbers engaged in mercantile pursuits, this increase being slightly faster than the general increase in population or in those gainfully employed.

In mines, quarries, and oil wells there was no marked change in numbers, merely a falling off of a few thousand in 1918. In banking there was a steady increase, especially marked between 1919 and 1920. In the transportation group also there was a steady increase continuing through 1920.[10] From then on, numbers declined gradually, the movement being dominated by a shrinkage of over 300,000 in railroad employees from 1920 to 1927. Transport did not begin to absorb notably more than its usual percentage of the total population until 1918, and the greatest excess came in 1919 and 1920. In the latter year perhaps half a million persons beyond a "normal" quota were engaged in this group of industries.

There are two other features of the story of economic mobilization in this industry which stand out strongly in the figures. One is the discrepancy between average numbers actually employed, as reported by the Interstate Commerce Commission, and numbers "attached to the industry," as reported by the National Bureau of Economic Research. This discrepancy presumably reflects the National Bureau's estimate of the amount of unemployment among those at-

[10] This does not include motor transport.

tached to the industry. The other matter is the change in hours worked per worker.

Numbers actually at work fluctuated decidedly more than numbers attached to the industry. Our entrance into the War brought the number at work up closer to the total number attached to the industry, diminishing the margin of unemployment indicated. The movement can probably best be seen in the percentage relation between the two figures, as shown in the accompanying table. The "average number employed" is for Class I carriers only, and they employ approximately 95 per cent of the total for all carriers. Hence the percentage figure is an indication of unemployment only as it falls materially below 95 per cent. If the data are to be relied on, the great and lasting falling off in working force employed by railroads which took place in 1921 produced only a very slow decline in numbers attached to the industry until *four years later,* when at

Year	Estimated number attached to the industry in thousands	Average number employed	Percentage	Hours worked per worker employed
1916	1,844	1,647,097	89.3	3,150.9
1917	1,852	1,732,876	94.6	3,138.1
1918	1,969	1,841,575	93.5	3,095.9
1919	2,075	1,913,422	92.2	2,630.1
1920	2,163	2,022,832	93.6	2,692.6
1921	2,122	1,659,513	78.2	2,499.1
1922	2,097	1,626,834	77.6	2,650.0
1923	2,080	1,857,674	89.3	2,653.1
1924	2,040	1,751,362	85.9	2,589.3
1925	1,891	1,744,311	92.2	2,597.8
1926	1,902	1,779,275	93.6	2,625.6

last the numbers attached to the industry shrank sufficiently to bring the percentage employed back above 90. The declines in these successive years were in thousands, 41, 25, 17, 40, 149.

This four-year lag may be taken (subject to possible improvement in the estimates) as an interesting example of slow mobility of labor in leaving an industry where volume of employment is declining, as distinct from the more rapid flow toward industries which are booming. The slowness is perhaps to be understood in the light of the fact that there were no large industrial groups in which employment was expanding spectacularly, while despite the shrinkage in volume of labor employed, average annual earnings of wageworkers remained high and increasing, almost catching up, in fact, with the highest-paid group of all; namely, construction workers.[11] Another factor helping to retard the decline in number of workers was the large and lasting drop in number of hours worked per worker, which took place from 1918 to 1919.

The decline in real annual earnings of workers attached to railroads in 1919, and the heavier decline in 1921, represented in the main, not a decline in wage rates, but for the most part a shrinkage in employment. The average real compensation of workers actually employed declined in 1919, but was higher in 1921 than in 1918. This despite the fact that the total purchasing power distributed to employees was less in 1921 than in 1918 and the total number "attached to the industry" was greater. In water transportation, on the contrary, real earnings not only fell after the War, but failed to recover with the return of prosperity and remained permanently below the level of the war years.

The part played by the War in this whole movement consisted partly in temporarily bringing more workers into an industry where economic forces were destined soon to produce a decline, thus accentuating the difficulty of the ultimate adjustment. It also left the railroads, as a result of inflation superimposed on the culmination of their pre-war difficulties, in an impoverished condition which undoubtedly made their retrenchment in 1921 and 1922 more severe than it would otherwise have been. Thus it must be held responsible for the extreme character of the shrinkage of railroad employment in these years. To sum up, the War brought an abnormally large labor force into the transportation industry, with a sequel of at least two years of quite abnormally heavy unemployment before the labor supply contracted sufficiently to restore the balance. Wages, being protected from the full effects of competition, did not fall as they otherwise would have done as a result of the large oversupply of labor.

The industrial group which showed the heaviest decline in manpower, and which furnished the largest number of workers to the other groups, was the group of "unclassified" industries and occupations. This includes the professions, domestic and personal service, and numerous miscellaneous trades and callings. This group

[11] *See* King, *op. cit.*, pp. 152–153. For 1923, railroad wages (annual earnings) actually exceeded those in construction.

showed a decline in absolute numbers, from 1915, of over 2.7 millions in 1918. If we add the decline in the construction industry (the only other group showing a significant shrinkage) the total comes to more than 3¼ millions, or slightly more than the increase in all branches of government service. If we allow for normal increase the shrinkages become greater and the expansion less, so that these two groups may be said to have set free for other war work more persons than the Government absorbed, by over three-fifths of a million.

Thus the sources of increased man-power for war work outside the "construction" and "unclassified" groups included, first, some 3¼ millions shifted from these two groups from 1915 to 1918, second, the whole normal increase in the working population, or something over 1½ millions, and third, about 800,000 beyond the normal increase, representing persons drawn into service of one sort or another from outside the ranks of industry. The total is over 5,550,000. From these sources came the man-power which was able to furnish an increase of nearly 3.2 millions in government service and of over 2¼ millions in manufactures. These figures are averages for entire years, and so do not show the condition at the time of the armistice, when the armed forces alone numbered between 4.1 and 4¼ millions, or nearly 4 millions above the pre-war level.

This picture of mobilization does not, of course, count shifts within the groups. A large part of the remaining construction work was for war uses, directly or indirectly. Nonessential manufactures were ruthlessly curtailed and plants converted to war uses, as we have seen. The farmer raising his regular crop, the miner, lumberman, and steel worker at their regular jobs, all became war workers to the extent that their products were diverted to war uses from the regular uses of peace.

Of the total diversion of man-power only a rough estimate can be made. The chief evidence is the bare fact that the nation spent, in 1918, approximately 25 per cent of its total income on the War, of which slightly over 5 per cent went for pay of government war-personnel and slightly less than 20 per cent went for industrial products and services. As the total personnel of private occupations was 35,173,000, it seems a fair first approximation to conclude that labor power equivalent to 7 million private workers for a full year was absorbed by the War in 1918. This does not include production of goods to be consumed by persons in government service for their ordinary subsistence. Credit is also allowed for the subsequent salvage value of surplus stocks of war supplies. The figure, then, is an estimate of man-power devoted to what may fairly be called economic waste or destruction. As an estimate of the peak of the gross effort without these deductions, the War Department's figure of 9.4 millions seems not impossibly high.

Of course, funds expended are not an accurate gauge of labor absorbed, but the war effort was probably fairly representative in that respect, including agriculture, where value produced per worker is low, and manufacturing and construction where it is high. It also appears that the dollar spent by the Government shrank in purchasing power by about the same amount as the average dollar spent in the wholesale markets.[12]

A similar calculation for the other war years reveals a diversion of about 4½ millions in 1917, over 3¾ millions in 1919 and a small amount less than 200,000 in 1920. The total for the four years, on this basis of approximation, would be about 15¼ million person-years. This is in addition to the war increase of persons in government service, amounting to over 6 million person-years in all, approximately 665,000 in 1917, 3,100,000 in 1918, 1,820,000 in 1919 and 440,000 in 1920. At the time of the armistice there were over 4,100,000 in army, navy, and marines (normal peace strength being possibly 170,000) and probably about 350,000 in civil departments of the Federal Government beyond what peace-time functions would have required, or a war increase of practically 4,300,000. The total diversion of man-power in the four years, then, may be roughly reckoned at from 21 to 21½ million person-years, or well over half a normal year's economic effort for the entire country.

[12] Based on comparison of the price index of war expenses in King with the United States Bureau of Labor wholesale price index.

CHAPTER XI

SHIFTS IN MAN-POWER VS. SHIFTS IN INCOME

WE have already discussed the effects of the War on the incomes of different classes: wage-earners, salaried workers, security holders, and others. No less important are the effects on the different groups engaged in different industries. Did the demand which caused millions of workers to flow out of certain industries and into others cause a correspondingly great increase in rewards in the directions in which demand was concentrated, and decrease elsewhere? It would undoubtedly have done so in the absence of governmental control to an extent that would have greatly increased the burdens of the War and actually hampered the war effort.

Writers have pointed out that war demands were virtually unlimited. Mobilization of usable funds outstripped the possible mobilization of products, with the result that prices of essential goods would have risen beyond the levels that were necessary or effective in stimulating the utmost increase of output. Incompetent producers bidding for materials would have stood in the way of adequate supplies for those who could make more effective use of them. Workers in receipt of high wages would have used them to bid against the Government, diverting priceless man-power to producing the unaccustomed luxuries which the War placed within their reach. And they would have spent time moving from place to place, hunting the employer who would pay the highest wages, instead of working for some employer in the industries where their services were obviously needed. All these things happened as it was, but they would have happened on a far more disastrous scale in the absence of governmental control.

The actual outcome was a resultant of the forces of supply and demand, modified by taxation and by governmental control and modified further by the control exercised by industrial groups themselves, especially organized labor. In general terms, the groups whose products were most in demand showed the greatest prosperity, and those which were least in demand suffered most, but each industrial group exhibited special characteristics and had its own individual story.

Manufacturing was, as we have seen, the group in which the greatest expansion took place. And as was to be expected, profits were high.[1] But in terms of purchasing power, and deducting taxes paid by business as such, profits reached their peak in 1916. They had gained about 50 per cent in a single year, but by 1918 they had lost more than half of this gain. Even without deducting business taxes paid to the Federal Government, it seems fairly certain that the peak came in 1917, and that later years were materially lower. The total amount of compensation paid to employees, in terms of constant purchasing power, increased more slowly but did not decline. In 1916 it was 24½ per cent above the 1915 level and in 1918 it was 38 per cent above. It lagged behind profits at first, and then passed them. From 1917 to 1918, employees gained just about what entrepreneurs lost. This represented, however, an increase in numbers of employees and not in compensation per worker. Real wages per worker in 1916 were over 14 per cent above the 1915 level, and in 1917 and 1918 were 12½ per cent above. Salaries, on the same basis, were in 1916 a little over 1 per cent below the 1915 level, and in 1918, 5 per cent below. Real salaries in manufacturing fell hardly at all, while the average for all industries showed a decline of 23.6 per cent. And wages in manufacturing gained 38 per cent, compared to an average gain for all industries of 6.4 per cent.

In the post-war readjustment the story was different. Entrepreneur income had shrunk in 1922 to two-thirds of its 1918 level, while total compensation to workers shrank only 8 per cent. Wages (annual earnings) per worker shrank 6½ per cent and salaries per worker shrank 3.7 per cent.

This refers only to income actually divided. Income earned was larger, and corporate savings were abnormally large from 1916 through 1919. This may be regarded as having had the effect of accumulating reserves against post-war deflation; and any abnormal amount so accumulated was undoubtedly dissipated in the disastrous year 1921, when corporate savings of factories were drawn down by $1,647,000 to maintain interest and dividend payments.[2] Uncertainties as to the precise effect of corporate bookkeeping in the face of enormous price changes make any exact statement impossible.

[1] The basic data used in this discussion are the tables in King, *op. cit.*, pp. 112–113, 130–131, 136–137, 152–153, 164–165.

[2] *Ibid.*, p. 280.

Agriculture was emphatically an "essential industry," but one in which man-power increased hardly at all. Physical product was well maintained, showing a very slight increase for 1917–19 over the average of 1913–16. The increase of workers was still smaller. The value of the product, on the other hand, rose very materially. The purchasing power realized by all those drawing incomes from agriculture went up in 1916 to 8 per cent above the 1915 level, and in 1918 to 25 per cent above. This means that agricultural prices had increased about that much more than the cost of living.

The greater part of this income goes to farmers and farm owners, and the real income of entrepreneurs and other property owners in agriculture increased 29 per cent from 1915 to 1918. The real earnings of wage-earners increased only a trifle over 2 per cent, while the few salaried workers lost 9.6 per cent of their real income. This condition is perhaps natural. Here is an industry in which little increase in personnel is brought about, and wages rise only slightly more than enough to balance the rising cost of living. It is also an industry in which wage-labor is not organized. Did it fail to attract more personnel because real wages did not rise appreciably, or did wages fail to rise because the industry needed, or could use, only a slight increase in hired labor? A little of both, perhaps. The industry could certainly not have made effective use of any such flood of man-power as went into manufacturing. And in view of the competing needs, there was no apparent expectation of largely increasing farming personnel: despite the fact that the country was most earnestly longing for more foodstuffs. Actual effort concentrated largely on such increased acreage as could be secured with little increase in personnel, and on the turning out of the products best suited to the war needs. The general inelasticity of the industry may have prevented both a large flow of workers into it, and a corresponding increase in wages, while the lack of labor organization no doubt contributed to the result. The gains here went mainly to the farmers themselves. Needless to say, they were not maintained after 1920.

The general story of railroads during the War is well known. Here rates were not raised proportionately to increases in expenses, and net earnings shrank until for a time they were actually less than zero. The "realized income" of the owners did not suffer, in terms of actual dollars, because of the federal guaranty, but while it remained very nearly constant in money terms, it naturally suffered the full effect of the shrinkage in purchasing power of the dollar. Thus, even with the help of the guaranty, the real incomes of railroad owners were heavily reduced. Wage-earners attached to this industry gained nearly 33 per cent in real earnings from 1915 to 1918, partly through an increase in the proportion of workers employed to those attached to the industry (a reduction of unemployment), but mainly through increased wages. They thus fared materially better than wage-earners in general, who gained on the average about 6.4 per cent. Salaried workers on railroads lost something over 3 per cent, as compared to the average loss of 23.6 per cent for all salaried workers; thus they also fared better than the general average. The war-time wage scales in this industry were marked by two outstanding characteristics: a leveling out of sectional differences in wages, which resulted in the greatest gains for southern employees, and a deliberate narrowing of the spread between the lowest and the highest rates of pay. The lowest-paid workers made the largest gains.

Water transportation affords another special case. The numbers engaged show no growth until 1918 and remarkably little growth then, but this is largely due to the manning of our new ships with navy crews to the number of probably about 20,000. By 1920 numbers had reached their peak, at 408,000 or 63 per cent above the numbers of 1915. This reflects the fact that some four-fifths of our shipbuilding program was completed after the armistice. Meanwhile the income realized from this service was growing by leaps and bounds even before our entry into the War, and in 1920 it was 76 per cent above its 1914 level, in terms of constant purchasing power. Wages and salaries both shared in this increase, real wages rising over 24 per cent from 1914 to 1918, and real salaries nearly 31 per cent. This is unique in that salaries not only gained more than enough to offset the rising price-level, but gained more than wages. And wages in this group of industries gained far more than the general average. Risk was of course a large element in bringing about these large increases.

The course of business profits in this industry has little or no significance, owing to the taking over of ocean shipping by the Government. Profits, under these conditions, show a sharp increase until 1917, and then a decrease.

In street railways, numbers engaged show no effect traceable to the War, but merely a gradual and normal increase. Income, on the other hand, failed to keep pace with the general rise of prices and hence showed a heavy decrease in terms of purchasing power; the result of the rigidity of the five-cent fare as dictated by custom or fixed by the terms of franchises. Even as late as 1925, the "total realized income" in this field was still slightly below the level of 1914–15.[3] Physical performance, in terms of revenue car-miles per employee attached to the industry, showed no very significant changes. It rose to a maximum of over 7,000 in 1916 and 1917 and then fell off slightly. The total number of car-miles increased very slowly from 1913 on, increasing about 10 per cent in ten years and remaining virtually stationary thereafter, with the result that the volume of service *per capita* of the total population declined nearly 10 per cent from 1914 to 1927. This is a relatively declining industry.

Salaries declined some 15 per cent from 1915 to 1918 in purchasing power, but recovered fully by 1921, after which they neither rose nor fell materially. Wages on the same basis fell some 9 per cent, and by 1923 were approximately stabilized at a level about 20 per cent above that of 1915. Thus salaried employees fared somewhat better than in other industries, losing somewhat less than the average, but wage-earners fared markedly worse than the average, both in the war and post-war periods. Yet even a relatively declining industry, with a virtually stationary personnel, had to raise money wages in the war period so that in 1918 they fell only 9 per cent short of the inflation of living costs, and by 1920, when costs of living were at their peak, money wages had definitely outstripped them. And during the post-war period, despite a desperate financial crisis in the industry, with every motive to retrenchment, money wages were still maintained at very nearly the peak levels of 1919–20, with the result that real wages rose with the post-war deflation to new high levels.

As compared to the average course of wages, street railway workers had made most of their post-war gain by 1921 or 1922, while workers in general made most of theirs afterward. Another way of describing the movement is to note that before the War street railway wages were higher than the general average by about 20 per cent, that by 1918 they had lost most of this advantage, in 1921 they had leaped into a lead of nearly 50 per cent, after which gen-

[3] King, *op. cit.*, p. 101.

eral wages rose rapidly and street railway real wages very little, with the final result that in 1927 their advantage was 20 per cent or only a little less than in 1915. This is an example of something of which many more instances could be cited—a disturbance of pre-war relationships followed by an approximate or partial restoration during the post-war period.

Profits in this industry are the share at the expense of which wages and salaries have been maintained or increased. In terms of total purchasing power divided, they began to shrink in 1916, reached a minimum in 1920 at barely over half their 1915 level, recovered in 1923 to slightly more than two-thirds of the 1915 level, and then declined somewhat to 1925. Even in terms of actual dollars, divided profits shrank during the War, and for the four years 1918–21 stood at an average of 177 millions as against 189 millions in 1914 and 196 millions in 1916. In 1925 they were again 196 millions. This is in spite of any increases in investment made during the period. These increases, from 1917 on, were very small, probably not more than an average of 1 per cent per year.[4]

The other two great public utility groups, telephones and electric light and power, unlike street railways, are expanding industries, especially the latter, yet the rewards of their employees do not accurately reflect their relative condition of growth. Real wages in the telephone industry rose more than the general average, while in the electric light and power industry, which was expanding much faster, real wages rose less than the general average. The personnel of the telephone industry rose from 226,000 in 1914 to 385,000 in 1927, while that of the electric utilities rose from 82,000 to 221,000 in the same period. The War had no clear effect on this growth, except perhaps to retard it somewhat during the period of actual hostilities and immediate post-war readjustment.

Total income, in terms of constant purchasing power, grew faster than personnel in the case of telephones, and not quite as fast in the case of electric current—another slight anomaly, since the latter industry was expanding more rapidly.

Real wages in electric utilities suffered even more than in street

---

[4] Data bearing on this question are found in King, *op. cit.*, pp. 206, 208, 240–242, 280. These tables give total market values of securities, new money invested by individual security holders, and corporate savings (the last only at five-year intervals).

railways in 1918, and recovered more slowly. In 1927 they stood in almost the same relative position to street railway wages which they had held in 1914–15, being 2 per cent lower, though from 1909 to 1913 they had been from 3 per cent to 4 per cent higher. Telephone wages also fell during the War about as much as those in the electric industry, but subsequently rose much more. Salaries in the electric industry had fallen 36 per cent in 1919, in purchasing power, while telephone salaries fell 16 per cent. By 1927, salaries in electric utilities had recovered to slightly more than their 1915 level, while telephone salaries showed a gain of nearly 32 per cent above this level. From a pre-war range of 9 per cent to 17 per cent below those in electric utilities they had risen to a level 5 per cent above them.

Profits in the telephone industry, in terms of purchasing power, increased somewhat less than personnel, while in electric utilities they increased materially faster. This whole situation possibly reflects the fact that in electric utilities greater strides were made in increasing the capacity of mechanical equipment per employee, and so substituting large increases in investment for the services of manual workers. The automatic telephone, on the other hand, was just beginning to be introduced, under the impulse of an incipient shortage in the rather restricted market from which telephone operators are drawn.

In the mercantile field no spectacular changes seem to have occurred. Total personnel showed less than normal increase during the War, and a small decline, of something over 2½ per cent, from 1917 to 1918. Realized profits remained remarkably stable about a level of approximately 2¾ billions, rising ¼ billion above this level in 1917 and falling below it by about 300 millions in 1920 and 200 millions in 1921. From 1923 on, there was a sudden rise to new high levels. Real wages and salaries declined. Annual real earnings of wage-earners fell nearly 11 per cent from 1915 to 1918, while salaries did not reach bottom until 1920, when they had lost nearly 27 per cent as compared to the 1915 level. In this industrial group, profits were better protected than either wages or salaries.

The construction industry was one of the heavy losers by the War. Personnel declined steadily from 1914 to 1918, the total decline being 42 per cent. But the very fact that the decline began so soon suggests that other forces than the War were at work. The total realized income of the industry did not decline materially until

1917; in current dollars it even increased in 1916. In 1918 it had shrunk, in terms of constant purchasing power, 43 per cent of its 1915 level (or 44 per cent of the level of 1914). Profits followed a corresponding course, remaining almost undiminished in terms of purchasing power through 1916, and then dropping to 27.6 per cent of their 1915 level. Wages meanwhile rose substantially (in terms of real annual earnings) although a large part of the rise must be attributed to a lessening of unemployment going along with the shrinkage of the personnel attached to the industry. The year 1917, when profits shrank enormously, brought only a small and temporary setback to real wages; and this was more than made good in the following year. The real earnings of salaried workers declined, but very slightly. Money salaries almost kept pace with rising costs of living, and left salaried workers far better off here than on the average. In this industry workers' incomes were better protected than profits. As to explanations, aside from the strength of the building-trades unions, we have in this industry a somewhat exceptional situation in that, while much construction was "nonessential," the remainder was not only highly essential but highly irregular and highly urgent. When construction workers were wanted, they were wanted very badly indeed.

In "mines, quarries, and oil wells," on the contrary, profits rose enormously, real wages rose 32 per cent and even real salaries showed a slight gain. Here the demand was increasing insistently, while personnel remained substantially unchanged. In coal mining (which largely dominates this group) physical output per worker increased very materially; though not in as large proportion as the rise in wages.[5] This reflects largely the effect of steadier employment, as the war-time coal industry was able to give its workers considerably more days' work per year than had been customary. The especially large increase in profits presumably reflects the necessity (real or supposed) of permitting prices that would afford a profit to inferior workings, in order to make up the supply needed by the country.

There remain the unclassified occupations. That these contained a disproportionately large amount of "nonessential" production is witnessed by their enormously heavy decline in personnel, far larger

[5] *See* King, *op. cit.,* p. 319.

than in any other group and beginning as early as 1916. In terms of earnings, the war-time history of this group is possibly more peculiar and instructive than that of any other. Total realized earnings declined, in terms of constant purchasing power, slightly more than the decline of personnel, indicating that prices charged for these goods and services—largely "nonessential"—probably rose less than the general average. Profits, on the other hand, shrank far less than total earnings, after allowing for the inflated dollar. Real profits shrank 17 per cent from 1915 to 1918, while total earnings, in 1913 dollars, shrank 37.7 per cent. Nineteen nineteen showed shrinkages of 28.7 per cent in profits and 43.5 per cent in total earnings. Total wages and salaries naturally showed a heavy shrinkage, total wages declining 52¾ per cent in purchasing power from 1915 to 1919. In terms of average annual real earnings per worker, wages fell over 18 per cent from 1915 to 1919, but more than recovered in 1922. Salaries, on the same basis, fell nearly 34 per cent (reaching their low point in 1920) and never recovered their 1915 level.

The "unclassified" group may perhaps be taken as reflecting, in a blurred way as any such heterogeneous group must do, the story of nonessential production. The decline of output was brought about not merely by declining demand, but also by public policy acting on supply, through rationing of coal and any other materials which might be essential in nonmanufacturing productions; also by railroad priorities and other means. Prices of nonessentials were not regulated, with the result that they rose nearly as much as prices of essentials. Moreover, the natural lag of wages when prices rise was not, in nonessential industries, so strenuously combated by public policy acting through wage-adjustment boards and aiming to make wages keep pace with rising costs of living. Some differential to the disadvantage of wage levels in nonessential production was actually in the public interest. Thus a heavy fall in real wages was natural. And between these two movements, of wages and of prices, it was natural that profits should have been amply protected, despite declining production.

In connection with the matter of shifts in income as between groups, the question naturally arises: what effect did the War have on the relative prosperity of rich and poor? Did it tend to make the rich relatively richer or relatively poorer? On this question the best evidence is probably that contained in King's study.[6] Here incomes are grouped, not according to the deceptive criterion of actual dollars, but according to purchasing power. Thus the lowest income-group consists of those receiving less than $5,000 in 1913, or less than $8,309 in 1926. Otherwise the fictitious swelling of the mere dollar magnitude of incomes would have produced a very great apparent shift to higher income-groups, due merely to war-time inflation. Even so, the figures must be construed in the light of the fact that a general increase in prosperity, increasing real incomes, and affecting all alike, would increase the percentages in the higher income-groups.

In summary, the years 1916 and 1917 showed an increase in the percentage of incomes above what we may call the $5,000 class, 1918 and 1919 showed a return to the 1914 level, 1920 and 1921 showed a slight decrease, and 1922 to 1926 showed a steady increase, bringing these larger incomes to what is undoubtedly a new high percentage. The boom of 1916 affected chiefly the percentage of incomes above $25,000, more than trebling the percentage in the highest group, from $150,000 of 1913 upward. In 1917 there was a recession of the proportion of incomes in these two highest classes, which was more than made up by an increase in the percentage falling in the third group, $5,000 to $25,000. In 1918 all percentages returned approximately to the 1914 level and remained near it in 1919, except that some of the highest group fell into the group next below. Thus, during the actual participation of the United States in the War, there was no marked shift of these income-groups from their pre-war relationships, whatever may have happened within the groups or whatever may have been the shifts of individuals from one group to another. If some individuals sank into lower groups, others rose into higher groups in approximately equal numbers.

In 1920–21, all the higher income-groups suffered, the smallest group of highest incomes showing the greatest relative shrinkage. This group fell to about one-fourth to one-fifth of its 1914 magnitude. By 1926 the percentage in this highest income-group had returned to slightly above its pre-war magnitude, while the two intermediate groups, covering the range from $5,000 to $150,000 in 1913 dollars, had increased greatly. The second group had risen from

[6] See *The National Income and Its Purchasing Power,* Chapter VII, especially pp. 177–179.

.064 per cent to .106 per cent and the third from .599 per cent to .961 per cent. This bears out the general impression that post-war prosperity has brought about an unprecedented increase in the numbers of the well-to-do and substantially wealthy.

These figures, however, tell nothing of shifts within the great group of incomes under $5,000, which still includes nearly 99 per cent of the total, and within which the most pressing problems of inequality are to be found. Within this group, there were tendencies during the War making for greater equality, and some making in the other direction, but those making for equality appear to predominate. One such tendency was the rise of wages and the fall of salaries, tending to bring the averages of these two groups closer together. Another tendency, resulting from the use of cost-of-living figures in wage adjustments, was the granting of greater relative increases to the lowest-paid workers whose need was the greatest. Both these tendencies are seen most markedly in the adjustments of railway wages and salaries. Sectional differences were also ironed out in the railway wage scales, though this may have produced as much real inequality as it eliminated, or more, due to sectional differences in the cost of living. In general, the war period showed a reduction of the previous differentials between skilled and unskilled labor.[7] These differentials have since been restored nearly, but apparently not quite, to the pre-war average. Perhaps one of the greatest forces making for greater equality was the reduction of unemployment, since it is the chronically unemployed who make up the lowest income-group.

Inequality was also affected by the differences in the course of wages and salaries as between different industries; for example, if a low-paid industry improved its relative position, or lost ground. On the whole, these shifts during the war period seem to have tended in the main toward greater equality in salaries, and possibly slightly greater inequality in wages. The course of salaries as shown by King[8] indicates less dispersion between different industries from 1917 on, especially if the course of government salaries be eliminated as distorted by the millions of service persons who would normally be in the wage-earning rather than in the salaried class. For wage-earners, these figures show reduced dispersion from 1916 to

[7] *Recent Economic Changes,* p. 438.
[8] King, *op. cit.,* pp. 167–169.

1920, with the exception of public utilities and transportation.[9] Even the transportation group shows reduced dispersion within itself in 1919–20, but in 1918 railway real earnings were conspicuously high and street railways conspicuously low. Wages in water transport were abnormally high through the whole war period, rising from a position below the average to one near the top. Street railway wages fell from a position above the average to one below. When all the groups except agriculture are combined, the extreme spread in 1918 between railroad wages, at $897 in 1913 dollars, and telephone wages at $384 certainly represents a large increase in the extreme dispersion, chargeable to the War. Whether mean dispersion increased or diminished is not so clear, but it probably increased, and there were large shifts in the relative position of different industries which represented disturbance in the *status quo*, whether they made for greater or less inequality in particular cases.

To sum up, there can be little doubt that the immediate effect of the War was in the direction of greater equality in the distribution of personal incomes. This may, of course, be simply the effect of the holding back by corporations of an increased proportion of their net earnings. It is true even before taking account of the progressive character of direct war-taxation. The regressive character of indirect taxes is already taken account of in the figures of real income themselves, since this income is figured after deduction of taxes paid by businesses, and the effect of taxes in raising the prices of products is largely included in the indexes of the shrinking purchasing power of the dollar. Some things, of course, such as taxes on amusements and club dues, are not covered by these price indexes, but these omissions are not sufficiently important to change the general character of the result. The chief exception to this tendency toward greater equality consists of a limited number of very large incomes in 1916, representing the profits of the neutrality boom in business. In the post-war period there has been a general rise of all classes of incomes, and the chief source of increased inequality has been the fact that while wages have been high for those who had jobs, unemployment has increased, and there has been a great increase in the number of incomes representing the levels intermediate between the moderately well-to-do and the very rich.

[9] King, *op. cit.*, pp. 154–156.

CHAPTER XII

EFFECTS OF THE WAR ON THE
NATIONAL DIVIDEND

WE have seen that the national dividend was larger during our participation in the War than in the years immediately preceding, except possibly for the abnormally prosperous year 1916, when we were acting as supply-merchants for a war that had not yet become our own. And we have also seen that this fact tells us little or nothing of the true effect of the War on our national output of wealth. It remains to attack this latter question and to try to shed some light on it, even if it cannot be definitely answered.

One method is the study of trends of production and income. By way of an index of production, the writer has combined Day's well-known combined index of agriculture, mining, and manufacturing, which runs from 1899 to 1919, with Copeland's index of physical production from 1913 to 1927, the resulting combined index covering a span of twenty-eight years.[1] This should be sufficient to establish a secular trend, and indeed the trend is clear enough and could well be represented by a straight line, especially if the war years are excluded. If this is done, the clear showing is that 1914, 1919, 1921, and 1922 are well below the trend, while the years 1915–18 and 1923–27 are so close to the trend that they would be classed on this basis as normal—almost abnormally so, since the usual cyclical ups and downs hardly appear in these two periods. Our great post-war prosperity appears to lie exactly in the prolongation of the trend for 1899–1913.

Figures for "realized income" go back only to 1909, and hence a normal pre-war trend is harder to establish. The secular trend for the whole period agrees quite closely with that of the production index, but the shorter fluctuations are markedly different. A straight line drawn from 1909 to 1923 affords an excellent fit to the pre-war years. Nineteen fourteen and 1915 lie below it, 1916 and 1917

---

[1] For Copeland's index, see *Recent Economic Changes,* pp. 761, 763. The indexes were combined by applying a conversion-factor which would make their average values equal for the seven years common to both.

above, and the entire four-year period 1919–22, inclusive, lies far below the line. The total excess area below the line from 1914 to 1922, inclusive, represents the sum of 17.7 billions of 1913 dollars by which "realized income" in these years fell below this rough-and-ready trend-line. Translated into current dollars, this would be very nearly equal to the whole immediate cost of the War. The period 1924–29 lies above this projected line, but 1930 will, of course, fall below it.

As we have seen in an earlier chapter,[2] there is reason to think that adjustments for business savings, taxes on businesses, and other matters would show the true national dividend to have been somewhat larger in the war period than these figures of "realized income" indicate, with the qualification that the business savings had no discernible effect in increasing the market values of the properties to their owners. A conjectural estimate of the effect of all these adjustments tends toward the conclusion that the national dividend for the four years 1917–20 was equal to this tentative "normal," or possibly some 2 billions in excess of it, leaving the violent post-war depression of 1921–22 as the period when the great deficit occurred. This adjusted result agrees more closely with the index of physical production than do the unadjusted figures, and seems to harmonize better with general observation. On this basis the shortage of national income, as compared to "normal," would be only about 12 to 14 billions of 1913 dollars, or a little less than two-thirds of the immediate cost of the War.[3] Even this is sufficiently large.

To sum up, it appears that the pre-war trend, prolonged, would agree as closely as may be with the post-war trend (1923–29) and leave the period between showing a shortage, chiefly in the years 1921–22. This is an interesting fact, but it is far from safe to conclude that such a rough-and-ready "normal" can be used to measure the effects of the War or to represent what the national income would have been if the War had not happened.

This "normal" really rests on the period 1909–13 almost entirely. The fact that the trend continued much the same through 1916

[2] Chapter IX.

[3] The 33 billions which we have set as the cost of the war are equivalent to 20.98 billions of 1913 dollars, using the type of composite cost-of-living index which results from an aggregative average of the separate group indexes used by King.

lends only partial support, as these three added years were themselves made abnormal by the effects of the War. And the fact that the prolongation of this trend agrees closely with the trend of our post-war prosperity and subsequent depression can hardly be used to support the correctness of this trend-line, because one of the questions we are raising is whether the post-war prosperity, or the depression, or both, were themselves results of the War. To use the post-war trend as part of the "normal" trend-line from which to measure the effects of the War would be assuming a negative answer to part of the main question we are raising.

Not only is the period 1909–13 too short to establish a trend with confidence, and the prolongation far too long: there is a possibility that this period may contain some upward movement of a cyclical character. Nineteen nine may not have represented full recovery from the depression of 1907–8, and 1913 saw the peak and downward turn of a much milder cycle. This possibility is discounted by the fact that the trend we are using agrees closely with the trend of Day's index of physical production, running ten years farther back; nevertheless there remains some probability that the post-war trend to 1929 was slightly above the trend prevailing from the opening of the century through 1913.

Hence our conclusions can be most safely put in the negative form: the figures afford no evidence that the national dividend in the period of active hostilities was either raised or lowered as a result of the War, and no sure evidence that our post-war prosperity was either greater or less than it would otherwise have been. They do afford convincing evidence that the national dividend in 1921–22 was far below normal, and that this depression was not offset to any material extent by supernormal productivity in the years just preceding. And this depression was a direct sequel and result of war conditions. Thus the evidence points to a net shortage of many billions of dollars, caused by the War but occurring a year or more after the disbanding of the armed forces was substantially accomplished.[4]

For further light we must fall back on other evidence, examining

[4] These figures might gain something in validity by being reduced to a *per capita* basis, but the trend of growth of population is itself so close to a straight line that this would make little difference in the result. The years 1919 and 1920 would appear very slightly more prosperous by this method.

especially the known effects of the War on the conditions which make
for increased or decreased productiveness. What are these conditions? Those most pertinent to the present discussion may be grouped
under the following heads: technical methods and equipment, economic organization and the coördination of the many essentials such
as materials and transportation, the adequacy of management and
of management methods, the competence and coöperativeness of labor, the correspondence between productive power and demand for
products, and the development on an efficient scale of the production
of new and desired varieties of product into which to put increases of
productive power.

The last two items may call for some comment. The attitude of
economists toward the problem of overproduction has changed radically since the days when it was dismissed with the statement that
supply of one thing constitutes demand for something else, and
therefore general overproduction is an impossibility. The economist
no longer endangers his professional standing if he expresses doubt
as to the finality and all-sufficiency of this dogma of the older school,
or even if he admits that under certain conditions demand rather
than technical power to produce goods may be the strategic factor
limiting the amount of goods that is actually produced.

Increased productive power may be taken out in working less or
in producing and consuming more. Working less may contribute to
economic welfare, though not to a larger national dividend. If it takes
the shape of shorter hours for all, of leisure well distributed and
wisely used, it will contribute to welfare. The steady shortening of the
standard full-time working week is evidence that part of our productive power is going into distributed leisure. But our increased masses
of unemployed workers are evidence that we have not mastered the
adjustments necessary to put in the form of well-distributed leisure
all the productive power which is not wanted in the shape of increased goods. The more conspicuous result is full employment for
some and none at all for others. This waste productive power could
be set to work if we could match it with demand for goods. To do
this requires the development of new goods. But this has already
been going on at a pace that taxes the capacity of the consumer to
assimilate new ideas and new ways of living. It has also been taxing
the capacity and ingenuity of our demand-stimulating institutions
and calling into them an ever increasing percentage of our working

population. Automobiles, household machinery, airplanes, radios, rayon, and other goods have absorbed enormous amounts of productive power, and it is hard to imagine this process going on much faster.

But if it could have gone on faster, we could have produced and consumed even more goods than we did in the past eight years. Demand, then, is worth considering as a factor of prosperity. It cannot exist without productive power—the man with no income cannot "demand" anything in the economic sense, and income must spring from someone's production—but with a modern credit system current demand may for a time exceed current "realized income" by anticipating the future. It is chiefly in this way that an increase in "effective demand" can actually precede an increase in production and stimulate it.[5]

In the period of neutrality, demand for American goods was first sharply curtailed and then still more sharply increased, largely on a credit basis. This is the main cause of the heavy fluctuations of 1914–16. If the War had not broken out, the depression which we had already entered in 1914 would probably have continued for a time but would presumably have been milder, and the recovery which was to be expected would also have been milder, but the average might not have been very different.

The other conditions of efficiency during the neutrality period are worth noting largely for the hints they afford of what might have happened later if peace had continued.[6] The basic conditions of progress were all present. Technical invention and the devising of new goods had become an integral part of the institution of organized business, systematically pursued by specialized departments. The "science of industrial management" was shaking free of the encumbrance of quack efficiency experts and ill-digested attempts to apply "scientific management"; and was attaining a healthy growth with promise of more to come.

Less favorable conditions appeared in some directions; chiefly perhaps the reaction of business to the antitrust laws, and the atti-

---

[5] This is true of credit *expansion,* not, of course, of a mere *transference* of credit which would otherwise have been used to purchase something different.

[6] It seems hardly worth while speculating on what would have happened if the war in Europe had continued and the United States had remained neutral. We should not have continued to prosper as we did in 1916!

tude of labor. Industrial combinations, and the development of the activities of trade associations, were neither of them stopped by the antitrust laws, but they were retarded; forced to proceed cautiously. Without questioning the justification of this, in view of the dangers of monopoly to a country which has not yet learned how to control it, it probably prevented or postponed numerous developments which would have made for economy and efficiency in production.

With regard to labor, the situation was far from happy, and contained many possibilities of trouble. Real wages did not appear to be rising as they should—possibly not rising at all—until the boom of 1916. Radicalism was growing in the labor movement, with possibilities destructive to continued increase of production. In the American Federation of Labor, the hold of the Gompers policies was apparently growing more insecure; and in place of his methods of getting as much as possible by the bargaining route, the feeling was growing that the future belonged to more radical courses of action. Industrial unionism, as distinct from the craft unionism typical of the American Federation, was growing among unskilled workers and was permeated by the philosophy of revolutionary direct action and sabotage. The situation contained much dynamite. The spirit of harmony and willing coöperation with management in promoting output and economy were, in general, conspicuous by their absence; and equally conspicuous was the lack of any general policy or attitude on the part of management promising to restore this harmony and coöperation.

America's entrance into the War submerged these retarding or disquieting influences in a flood of patriotic feeling and a sense of the necessity of making concessions and coöperating toward the winning of the War. More perhaps than ever before did labor consciously undertake concession and coöperation in the interest of increased output for the sake of increased output, giving up limitations on output and on eligibility to enter skilled and unionized trades, and adopting a policy of refraining from using the national emergency to strike for all the gains their temporary economic power would yield them. In return they received the promise of corresponding checks on price-profiteering by management, and of the adjustment of wages to rising money costs of living. These they received from government, while from the nature of the economic situation itself they received the more certain and perhaps more important assurance that they were in no danger of working themselves out of their jobs, no matter how much output they might achieve in the realms of essential war commodities.

So far, the effect of the War on labor conditions was wholly favorable. On the other hand, the taking up of many unfamiliar types of production was an unfavorable factor, and the dilution of skilled workers with the products of hasty trade-school education may also have been unfavorable.

In the realm of management and organization, combination and coöperative action were vastly promoted by the War, as was standardization and simplified practice. Many technical and trade secrets were pooled, revealing the fact that no producer had the best methods in all parts of the work, and that by combining the best methods actually in practice an attainable standard could be set up considerably higher than that of the most efficient management. On the other hand, coördination in the large was sadly imperfect. Transportation was congested, half crippled, supplies of coal were inadequate, processes were held up for lack of some essential part or material or for lack of synchronization of all the essential elements, and wasteful expedients were used to overcome these obstacles, while capital equipment was inadequate for many war supplies and had to be installed under emergency pressure. On the whole, the unfavorable conditions seem to bulk at least as large as the favorable.

Limitations due to limited demand were removed, for all producers who could adapt themselves to the production of "essentials." It is true that the new consumption goods into which our increased productive power was already being poured, became nonessentials, and their development was set back or retarded as well as that of some other goods, especially housing. But the war demands more than offset this and it may have acted as a favorable force later on, leaving us after the War with an unusually large area of unsatisfied demands or of potential demands marked out for development but not exploited. Much of the private consumption cut off by the War, together with the production to serve it, may have been merely postponed.

As a resultant of all these forces, the national dividend during the War was neither plainly above normal nor plainly below. What would it have been if peace had continued? All that can be said is that the elements of continued progress were there and would presumably have brought about an increase of production not very different in amount from what actually took place (though very different in kind) with one proviso. That is, that the explosive forces latent in the labor situation had not developed into serious trouble. No one can be sure whether they would have done so or not. That was a real threat, which the War and its after-effects served to remove for a decade and a half. That the present depression has not more definitely revived it, is a testimonial to labor's tolerance and willingness to accept well-intentioned efforts in default of effective remedies. This tolerance may not survive another depression; in which case an intangible economic asset of the first magnitude will evaporate. But we are moving ahead of our story.

The depression of 1921 was definitely a result of the War. After the release of war-time controls over prices and of restrictions on nonessential production, prices rose even higher than during the War, and this helped stimulate a boom which was destined to collapse. Prices were too high, the boom could not survive the inevitable deflation, and conditions of efficient production had not yet been restored. Continued regulation of rentals made it difficult or impossible to build houses at a profit to fill up the shortage left by the War. Railroads were still not in a condition to handle a boom-volume of traffic, and uncertainties as to their financial prospects tended to retard the process of enlarging their facilities. Agriculture was overexpanded, and its artificial support was removed. Hence agricultural prices fell farther than other prices while the farmers were in a peculiarly exposed and defenseless position against such a catastrophe, unable to limit output currently in support of a price policy, as manufacturers are to a certain extent able to do.

But there is probably no need of rehearsing the history of all industries in this period in order to establish the general fact that the post-war depression was the direct outcome of war conditions. This is perhaps not a very revealing truth, and the fact remains that if there had been no war a depression might well have come at about the same time, due to different specific causes. Indeed, the War very probably prevented the occurrence of one depression which might otherwise have taken place in 1917 or 1918. But if we are to reason in this way, we must also recognize the strong evidence that war conditions prevented production from rising as high as it would presumably have risen in the subsequent revival. Thus, even if a depression might have come in 1921 or 1922 without any war to bring it on, the probability is that it would have started from a higher level of prosperity, and would have been nowhere near so violent.

There remains. the question whether the War prepared the conditions which were responsible for the remarkable burst of prosperity which followed 1922. Leaving out of account the immediate recovery from the depression of 1921, some combination of forces carried our national dividend upward from 1923 to 1929 in a rise which reached new heights and was steadier than for any recent period of similar length. How shall we diagnose the relation of the War to this great movement? Here again certainty is beyond our reach; all that can be found are probabilities. These probabilities seem to point to the conclusion that the War did play some part in setting up the conditions which carried our national dividend to heights it might not otherwise have reached in the same time, and that it thus made partial amends for its depressing effect on our total national income from 1917 to 1922. On the other hand, these conjectural gains seem destined to be more than neutralized by the results of the present depression, which also has claims to being in large part a war sequel.

With respect to technical methods and equipment, the effects of the War were mixed, not to say confused. Most of our inventive talent went into war production, and the results had frequently only a limited usefulness for subsequent peace-time production. Yet war production ramified so widely that it had many peace-time applications. And the War gave a large stimulus to standardization and to the practice of interchange of information among separate concerns, both of which have been continuing forces in the post-war period, making for greater efficiency and economy.

As to equipment, the War stopped or retarded the expansion of productive facilities for many peace-time products, though for others it actually stimulated overequipment. But it left undamaged the basic facilities needed for making good the lost growth, with the result that the shortage may have afforded, after a brief interval, more of stimulus than of handicap to industrial activity. Furthermore, the fact that equipment had not had its normal growth during the war period had its compensation in that there was less loss in scrapping existing machinery for the sake of reëquipping with more modern plant units. Once the extremely high equipment costs of 1920 had been deflated—painful as the process was—modernization became practicable. And this modernization was one of the major factors in the post-war prosperity, introducing labor-saving methods involving new and more automatic equipment with a large increase in the amount of capital investment per worker. This was, of course, a movement which had been going on since the Industrial Revolution, but it appears to have been making unusually rapid and effective headway since the War.

One thing which seems to have contributed strongly to this post-war increase was the rise of real wages resulting from the fact that money wages were not so heavily deflated as prices in 1921. There was some talk at this time of a determined movement to "deflate labor," the consequences of which might have been serious in more ways than one. As it was, the fact that money wages did not fall as much as prices afforded a stimulus to avoid rising labor costs by the use of improved equipment and more of it. The success of this movement undoubtedly afforded opportunity for the spread of the "new economy of high wages," both as a theory and as a policy. This theory holds that industry should, in its own interest, pay high wages as the only means of establishing that kind of market in which the products of mass production can be sold in the large volume on which the great success of mass production depends.

Is this all a result of the War? Or of the enlightenment of progressive employers, or of an exaggerated fear of Bolshevism which helped to stay the hands of the more extreme labor deflationists for fear of provoking revolutionary outbreaks? It is, of course, a joint resultant of many forces. But without the War there would in all probability not have occurred any such large shift in values as actually occurred, bringing about as it did an involuntary increase in real wages and almost forcing on the business community a more thoroughgoing test of the "economy of high wages" than would have been at all likely without some such impulse from without.

Another contributing factor has been the attitude of labor itself, and in this the War must be credited with a large influence. We have seen how it swung the balance away from limitation of output and sabotage, and in the direction of conscious coöperation by labor in the promotion of output. This shift to a more coöperative attitude has managed to survive the crisis of reconstruction, and the gradual growth of unemployment—sometimes called "technological unemployment"—through the years of the post-war expansion. If it manages further to survive the present depression it will have shown really surprising vitality.

Can it survive permanently? One may hazard the guess that the thing most likely to decide this question is the amount and effectiveness of the responsibility assumed by employers or the State for the evils of unemployment. A wise and succeessful unemployment program may make it possible to consolidate the very real gains which have been made, and to credit the War with a share in bringing about one of the greatest possible advances in the essential conditions of national prosperity. Without a successful unemployment policy, and with increasing chronic unemployment and recurring crises, it is too much to expect that increased coöperativeness of labor will survive as a permanent contribution to our economic life.

Aside from the things already mentioned, it seems quite impossible to say whether the effect of the War on the general efficiency of management was on the whole favorable or unfavorable. There was undoubtedly much nervous strain and wear and tear which cannot be measured. And the eagerness with which the business class sought the discarding of all public controls and a return to private enterprise contained more than a suggestion that they had learned nothing and forgotten nothing from the war episode.

However, no such far-reaching experience could be wholly without results, for good or for ill. Managers had proved their ability to make radical transformations and meet seemingly insuperable difficulties, on the whole successfully. With this background they faced the necessity of adapting themselves to the further difficulties and new conditions of reconstruction. In the typical case, a settling back into old ruts was hardly possible. Many of them at least were caught in one of those obvious and compelling necessities which are recognized as having the capacity to take hold of men who are doing their supposed best under the ordinary spur of profits, and make them do something still better. The benefits of standardization, coöperation, and interchange of information were not forgotten, while government continued to promote such activities or leave increased scope for them by a more liberal handling of the antitrust laws. In short, the balance of results on these various counts seems not to have been unfavorable.

In the realm of demand and potential demand, the conditions left by the War were surprisingly favorable. There had been slackened production of durable goods not essential to war, and this had left gaps to be filled. The most conspicuous of these gaps—the housing shortage—did not at once take full effect in stimulating production, on account of the continued legal limitations on rentals. Ultimately, however, the gap was filled; post-war production made up for the slowing-down of the War. More important, perhaps, the demand for automobiles developed capacity for expansion beyond what anyone would have thought possible, while there were ample new goods ready to seek markets, to match the increased purchasing power that came with increased real wages and reviving industrial activity.

And credit, in various forms, stood ready to do its part in making potential demands active, whether by the large development of in- stalment selling which followed the War, or by the continued lending to foreign countries which enabled them to remain strong purchasers of goods while still not in a position to send goods to us in payment. As we have seen, such a credit demand from abroad may, tempo- rarily at least, furnish a stronger stimulus to home production than if payment were being made in goods. These elements of credit ex- pansion could not last indefinitely. While they continued, they un- doubtedly made for larger production and a larger national divi- dend in this country,[7] which may mean that the post-war prosperity was based on temporary stimuli, some of which will not return.

To sum up, then, it seems fair to conclude that the conditions left by the War were at least partly responsible for the burst of pros- perity that followed. As to whether it made any lasting contribution to national productiveness, that is a more doubtful question and hinges too much on the outcome of the present depression to permit

[7] James Harvey Rogers sums up the results of an extended examination into the relation between our post-war export of capital and our excess of commodity exports as follows: "The close correspondence in the movements of the two series from year to year seems to leave little doubt that our favor- able trade balances are dependent on a continuation of increasing net foreign lendings." (*Recent Economic Changes*, pp. 748–749.) The evidence inclines him to the view that the movement of goods is the more active or independent variable, taking the lead while the adjustments of credit appear to lag some- what, but he holds that the export of capital is a necessary enabling condi- tion. Indeed, this proposition seems self-evident. The excess of commodity exports is greater than the export of capital, as a portion is neutralized by our debit balance in the "invisible items." This debit balance is much smaller than before the War, and would be turned into a credit balance were it not for the post-war increase of American tourist expenditures abroad.

even a plausible surmise at the present, if ever. On the face of the returns up to 1929 the post-war prosperity may be taken as an offset to the immediate post-war depression, the conclusion being that it is not possible to say with confidence that the total national dividend for the whole period was made either larger or smaller because of the War.

Were it not for the "post-war prosperity," we should have to reckon a considerable part of the losses from the depression of 1921 as social war costs, in addition to the portion of our national dividend actually taken for war uses. For some of the foreign participants, this element of reduced productive power constitutes an enormous addition to their actual war outlays. As it is, the United States showed no clearly demonstrable excess or shortage of production due to the War, over the entire period to 1929, so that our estimate of war costs might fairly be confined to the goods and services actually diverted to war uses, if the story had ended there.

There is no need of emphasizing the fact that the showing of the United States is incomparably better than that of the other main belligerents in respect to maintaining their volume of production through the shocks of war and the stresses of reconstruction. Mr. Carl Snyder has constructed index numbers of world production from 1875 to the present, showing the effect of the War as vastly worse than the worst industrial crises—possibly worse than all of them put together.[8] His chart shows an amazingly steady upward trend through 1913, followed by the first and only serious and sustained decline. This continues to the low levels of 1919 and 1921, with a slight rise intervening in 1920. The absolute decline is less than five years' normal growth; but if the loss is measured from the level which would presumably have been reached if the War had not intervened, it appears that the world was set back by ten years' normal increase of production. And this loss can presumably never be made good. The upward trend has been resumed at a faster rate than before, but still at a rate which would require some fifty years to catch up with the prolongation of the pre-war trend, to say nothing of showing any excess to make up for the loss suffered by reason of the War.

Mr. Snyder roughly estimates the total loss to date, measured

[8] See *Proceedings, Amer. Academy of Pol. Science,* June, 1931, p. 20; *cf.* also pp. 23, 27.

from the prolongation of the pre-war trend, at 400 billions, which he speaks of as the real cost of the War, as distinct from the fiscal outlays of the various governments. Strictly speaking, both are to be counted. The cost of the War includes the shortage in production plus the absorption of goods and services which the fiscal outlays reflect. Of this burden of decreased production, little or none fell on the United States—or had done so up to the middle of 1929.

Our post-war period of expanding production came to a full stop with the present depression: one of the most widespread, deep, and sustained which the world has witnessed. Is this also a result of the War, a belated instalment of war's economic burdens? It would certainly be rash to conclude that if there had been no war there would have been no depressions—these would surely have come, and unless history ceased to repeat itself, an occasional major one among them. Nevertheless, the peculiar qualities of this crisis—its combination of universality, severity, and persistence—join together to give it rank among the worst in history, and just at the time when optimists were predicting that modern business methods were placing this evil under control. And the special circumstances which are, in all human probability, accountable for that bad eminence, are, in one way or another, sequels of the war experience.

We have been turned back a long way in our economic progress, losing a large part of the advances we had made since 1913. Hope of a quick recovery, such as that of 1922, has long since vanished; and the question now is whether, when revival comes, business activity can be expected to resume its course at anything like the rate of 1923-29, or whether we must begin to build up from a considerably lower level. If the latter gloomy forecast materializes, it will almost certainly be due to elements of weakness left over from the War and the post-war period of reconstruction.

One of the outstanding features of this depression is its universal character, and the fact that the crisis in Europe is a peculiarly large element in our own difficulties. Back of that lies the weakened condition of Europe's convalescent economy, which is struggling with so many difficulties that any major disturbance threatens complete prostration, and menaces the solvency of governments and the stability of currencies, with possible revolution in the background. This condition is part of the aftermath of the War.

Undoubtedly one of the foremost factors increasing the severity and duration of the depression is the world-wide fall in prices which began in 1929, and which has wiped out by far the greater part of what then remained of the war-time increase in the wholesale price level. This it is only fair to charge as a part of the post-war deflation. Another noteworthy feature, from the American standpoint, is the fact that the decline of our exports was one of the leading factors, in point of time, starting in November, 1928, seven months before the downward turn of general business conditions, and six months before the decline in imports. This decline in exports is associated with the decline of our lendings to foreign countries. It is not easy to say whether one is the cause of the other; but it seems probable that both are the result of the reduced economic activity of Europe; reducing at once the demand for goods and for credit, and at the same time reducing this country's favorable balance of commodity trade, which constituted the most available source of credits for lending abroad. The balance has been partially restored by the shrinkage of our imports. This behavior of American exports is a special feature of this depression, and an especially unfavorable feature, and it is apparently traceable to roots in the post-war conditions of Europe.

In general, the story of a cycle of prosperity and depression typically includes a period in which is concentrated more than its share of expansion of capital equipment and of general building construction. The concentrated activity in the industries serving these demands is reflected in increased buying power on the part of those engaged in them; and this takes effect in increased demand for general consumers' goods. But this increased demand rests on a temporary basis. It is not in excess of the permanent needs of the people, or their permanent power to produce; and given sufficient time, these needs and this producing power would presumably articulate together and keep all the producing power at work. But one business cycle does not afford the time necessary for this adjustment. Productive equipment and construction cannot keep on piling up indefinitely at the rate characteristic of a boom, and in existing forms. And when the pace slackens, there is a decrease in the purchasing power of the workers in these industries and a corresponding decrease in the effective demand for consumers' goods in general. The post-war situation, both here and in Europe, obviously afforded an unusually great potential demand for capital equipment and construction; and after 1921 this demand was better sustained than such waves of activity usually are. This fact may naturally be held responsible for a heavier reaction than usual when the boom had gone as far as it could go.

The most conspicuous precipitating cause of the present depression was the reckless boom in the New York stock market and the ensuing crash. This was not the original cause responsible for the coming of a depression at that time; for the beginnings of a reaction were already apparent; but it was undoubtedly one of the causes of its peculiar severity. This phenomenon does not stand by itself as the result of a single cause; and it has its parallel in previous major crises marking it as a characteristic occurrence; but it may be interpreted as having at least a large part of its basis in the other conditions which have already been discussed, and which were sequels of the War.

The seriousness of the crisis was increased by the fact that our system included numerous handicapped industries which had constituted weak spots in the post-war prosperity, but which had been outweighed by strength in other quarters. Agriculture had been depressed since the War; and while it would have experienced some of these difficulties in any case, the abnormal expansion of the war period made necessary a much sharper contraction than would otherwise have occurred, and increased the seriousness of the condition. Much the same is true of coal and textiles, to name two others among our "sick industries."

To sum up, to charge the War with the whole responsibility for the existing depression would be to imply that without the War there would have been continuous prosperity with no setbacks, and this is negatived by the whole history of modern industrialism. But the particular form of the depression and the special conditions accountable for its peculiar severity, are all conditioned by the forces which the War set in motion.

As for the prospects for the future, they must be assessed largely in the light of international conditions. Here, in addition to the weakened condition of Europe, a conspicuous part is played by the high tariff policy of the United States and the reprisals which it has produced on the part of other countries. Our foreign trade faces increased handicaps in the near future. This gives added force to the conclusion, which seems inevitable in any case, that capital exports cannot be expected indefinitely to sustain the large balance of commodity exports which has characterized the post-war period through 1929. It is possible that from now on we shall begin to bear for the first time one of the serious after-effects of the War from which we have hitherto been protected: namely, the diminished buying power of our customers in other countries. How long this remains a serious burden depends on the speed and completeness of the economic recovery these other nations make. To facilitate this recovery, even at some present sacrifice, is one of the wisest things this country could do, in its own selfish interest. To cripple it or allow it to be crippled through failure to coöperate, would be the most calamitous of policies for the United States.

And this must end our present inquiry into the more general after-effects of the War—an inquiry which raises more questions than it answers. Some further light may be shed by a brief survey of the post-war history of a few of the particular industries or industrial groups on which the War had especially direct effects.

CHAPTER XIII

THE TOLL OF DEATH AND DISABILITY:
RELIEF AND COMPENSATION

THE greatest continuing cost of the War to the national economy is the burden resulting from death and disability, represented in the national budget since 1921 by the expenses of the Veterans' Bureau. Interest on the public debt, plus retirement of the principal, is a much larger fiscal item, but it will not last as long, and it is not a social burden in the same sense. It has been suggested here that this continuing burden on account of veterans be offset against the continuing income from the foreign war debts, if only to segregate these difficult and speculative post-war items. Ultimate collections from foreign countries are still matters of some uncertainty, and the resulting economic gains to our national economy are still more so. And the uncertainty of the burdens of future disability is obvious.

Under the present debt settlements the United States is due to receive a total of 22 billions in payments continuing through 1987. Through most of that time we shall have material expenses to meet for the care of the World War veterans. The writer's best estimate of these expenses, based on a reasonable continuance and development of present policies,[1] falls between the limits of 20 and 25 billions for the whole post-war period. This does not allow for life pensions for young widows who in the future marry aging veterans, but the larger sum does allow something for the care of all veterans during the disabilities of old age, regardless of whether or not the disability was the result of war service. Roughly, the care of veterans is likely to cost us something like as much as the war debts bring in.

The two sums are very different, however, in their distribution through the years. The economic burden of death and disability (as distinct from government payments to veterans, which may become the plaything of politics) will probably go on growing until 1940 or

[1] The above was written in 1929 and revised to include figures as of June 30, 1930. Therefore it does not take account of broadened rights to compensation under the amendment of July 3, 1930. For the effect of future possible changes in policy, *see* pp. 199, 201 below. The consolidation of veterans' aid activities also is not taken account of.

1945, after which it will taper off, and will have reached vanishing proportions by 1975–80, through decreasing numbers and termination of the survivors' normal earning period.[2] The debt settlements, on the other hand, begin with moderate payments and increase to a maximum which continues after the burden of death and disability (and also, let us hope, the payments on account of it) will have shrunk to little or nothing. If the two gross fiscal sums were equal, the debt settlements would represent a materially smaller discounted present worth. At present, the Veterans' Bureau outlays are much the larger amount; and they will remain larger at least until after 1946. They are now over half a billion a year, while the debt settlements in 1928 amounted to 210 millions. After 1946, the veterans' budget will be relieved of war-insurance annuities and of payments into the Adjusted Service Certificate fund, and from then on it will be smaller than the debt settlements, unless swollen by unexpectedly large increases in disability or by fresh additions to our scheme of compensation.

All of which suggests many thoughts. If the American debt settlements, absorbing the major portion of the German reparations, are at present far short of the burdens arising from our relatively small casualties, how great is the burden from death and disability borne by our former Allies with relatively little aid from the balance of international payments? It is well for us to remember that in studying the American losses we are dealing with about 1 per cent of the total war casualties. And while foreign losses register on a lower scale of money values, and of real wealth-producing capacity per person, nevertheless the human burden is made heavier abroad by the very poverty which prevents adequate compensation. Compensation lightens the load by distributing it, and avoiding those crushing hardships that result when the loss is left wherever shell and gas and disease have placed it.

We shall attempt to estimate both the fiscal outlays and the underlying social burdens they imperfectly reflect. But the best preliminary to both estimates is a concrete picture of the principal facts. There were some 5 million persons who, at one time or another during the War, were in the armed forces of the United States, and

---

[2] The economic burden of death is figured as a continuing loss of income, depending on the normal working period the deceased service man might have expected, had he lived. *See* below, Chapter XIV and Appendix B.

most of them were liable to war injuries of one sort or another. The total amount of service-time was about 5 million man-years. "Battle casualties" accounted for over 50,000 dead and over 224,000 wounded in the expeditionary force.[3] Total deaths in army and navy were estimated at 125,500 to July 1, 1919, and later estimates have continued to swell the numbers.[4] A recent statement from the Adjutant General's office gives 119,956 deaths for the army alone, indicating a probable total of about 130,000 for army and navy.[5] And men died after leaving the service, and are still dying, from injuries and illnesses traceable to the War in some degree or other, though the degree of responsibility in such cases is necessarily a matter of doubtful estimate.

One thing to remember is that out of the millions of men in service, normal mortality would in any case have accounted for something like 20,000 deaths, leaving some 110,000 as the actual excess of deaths above normal, caused by the War to men actually in service.[6]

The attempt to estimate the aftermath of war-caused deaths is beset with difficulties. One of the most definite indications is the fact that 48 per cent of the death awards are for deaths occurring after June 20, 1921.[7] If this refers to all awards that have ever been made and not merely to those now active, it indicates not less than 55,500 post-war deaths, nor more than about 120,000. The minimum figure is based on the assumption that all the post-war deaths were represented in the awards, which is clearly too conservative. The maximum figure is based on the assumption that there were about 130,000 deaths before June 30, 1921, and that this is 52 per cent of the total; in other words, assuming that the post-war deaths are no more fully represented in the awards than the deaths occurring during the War. This is too liberal, as the post-war deaths are sure to have left

[3] *Reports of War Department* (Surgeon-general), 1925, XV, 1017. Also Ayres, *The War with Germany*, p. 122. Ayres's figures for wounded are 205,690, but are of earlier date. Of the dead, 35,560 were "killed in battle" and 14,720 "died of wounds," according to Ayres's figures.

[4] Ayres, *op. cit.*, p. 123.   [5] Given in a letter of July 10, 1929.

[6] Normal mortality for males of the age-groups in question would be in the neighborhood of 24,000, on the basis of 1924 life-tables used by Louis I. Dublin in computations referred to below (Appendix A). The service men, being a selected group, presumably had a lower normal mortality; hence the round figure of 20,000.

[7] U. S. Veterans' Bureau, *Annual Report*, 1930, p. 26.

more dependents, and therefore to be more fully represented in the awards. In deciding on our estimate, we may be helped by canvassing the other available indications.

One is the fact that slightly more than 31,000 disability awards have been changed to death awards through 1930. This represents post-war deaths recognized as due to the War and leaving behind dependents entitled to compensation. In addition to these, there are the deaths of men on the disability compensation rolls who left no compensable dependents and whose awards were therefore merely terminated. And there are further some war-caused deaths among men who were never on the disability compensation rolls. The indications are that these last virtually all occurred before the end of 1922, or 1923 at the latest.

Disability awards terminated by death can only be estimated, as they are merged with death awards terminated by death of beneficiary, for the years when they were presumably most numerous. Those separately reported number 8,354, and the total may be estimated at from 15,000 to 20,000.[8] Normal deaths for the numbers involved would be in the neighborhood of 9,500 to 10,000, leaving 5,000 to 10,000 probable war deaths from the disability rolls in addition to the 31,000 converted to death awards.

For deaths among veterans who were never on the disability rolls there is no really reliable basis of estimate, the only available material being the insurance records. About one-eighth of the veterans kept up their policies, but this is a biased sample, as indicated by the fact that about one-third of those drawing compensation for permanent total disability were also receiving insurance. The disabled veterans were more prone to keep up their policies. Insurance disability awards changed to death awards total 18,263, most of which are probably already in the compensation figures, though a few thousand might need to be added. Outside of this group, the death rates shown in the insurance figures are below normal rather than above, except for the earliest years. They thus afford no indication of war-caused deaths except for the years up to and including 1922, or possibly 1923. One may estimate, very roughly, 10,000 deaths above

[8] Disability awards terminated by death number 8,354 for 1926–30, inclusive. For 1922–25, inclusive, the figure is not separately reported, but terminations of disability *and death* awards through death of beneficiary number well over 20,000 for these four years.

normal mortality for this group of insured during these early years. How many deaths do these figures indicate for the veterans as a whole? Not a proportionate number since those suffering from ailments likely to cause death were those who most typically kept up their insurance policies. A conservative estimate of the total of deaths in excess of normal mortality would be under 20,000, a liberal one might exceed 35,000. This total overlaps the deaths of veterans receiving disability compensation, but not by more than 40 per cent in all probability.[9] These deaths occurred in the years before the enrolment of disability compensation cases was anything like complete. We are, however, probably justified in adding at least 10,000 to the totals already indicated, and possibly 20,000 or even more. Our total estimate of war-caused deaths occurring after the War would be, then, from 48,000 to 70,000. Such deaths are still occurring among the disabled at a heavy but diminishing rate, at present about 3,000 annually.[10]

This estimate points toward the minimum limit of the previous estimate. And of course it is true that the Veterans' Bureau, not being in a position to deduct normal mortality rates, but having to decide in each case whether the War had some material connection with the fatality, might quite properly report more awards than the number of deaths statistically attributable to the War during the same period. On the whole, 60,000 to 65,000 post-war deaths, caused by the War, seems a conservative estimate. Added to the 110,000 service deaths in excess of normal mortality, this would make 170,000 to 175,000 deaths caused by the War to those who were in service. If we count the whole 130,000 service deaths, without deduction for normal death rates, the total would be 190,000 to 195,000.[11] This is

[9] Disability awards changed to death awards through 1922 are just under 4,000; those terminated can only be estimated, and might raise the total to 8,000 or to 12,000.

[10] Disability awards changed to death awards in 1929 were 3,004, a decline from 4,913 in 1926. Disability awards terminated by death in 1929 were 956, not far below normal mortality.

[11] Since writing the above, I am informed by the Veterans' Administration that their estimate is 200,000, with a possibility of as many as 236,000. This is based largely on the total of 113,388 death awards of all classes, together with the estimate that only 48 per cent of the veterans had dependents. The later deaths, however, probably have a higher percentage with dependents. More important is the fact that deaths only partly due to service causes are

a large figure, but the after-effects of the war of trenches, high explosives, and chemicals are something new in war experience.

For those who escaped battle casualties, the War was still from three to four times as dangerous as staying at home and earning one's bread and butter in the usual way. Charging the aftermath of war-caused deaths against the period of service, it was probably six or seven times as dangerous.

It may seem strange that there is so much doubt as to the number of war deaths among those who were in the federal service. But this uncertainty becomes insignificant beside the utter lack of knowledge as to the effect of the War on civilian mortality. If the influenza epidemic of 1918, and the sequel of 1919, were caused by the War, then it caused something like 400,000 civilian deaths, or some $2\frac{3}{4}$ times the number of deaths due to armed service. If these epidemics would have come without the War just the same, then the War's toll of civilian lives in this country was negligible. It seems probable that an unusually virulent form of influenza was due to visit the world without reference to the War; such epidemics having taken place in the past. But it seems also certain that the conditions brought about by the War vastly increased the resulting mortality. It is hard to believe that the war-caused deaths among civilians were not considerably more than the deaths in army and navy, but this belief hardly rests on scientifically admissible evidence.

The effect of the War on industrial accidents is almost equally uncertain; chiefly because the statistics for the pre-war period are too fragmentary to form a workable basis of comparison. Accidents move with the ups and downs of business activity, and therefore the years 1916 to 1920, inclusive, would naturally show large numbers. Aside from this, the figures give some support to the idea that the War temporarily interrupted a somewhat irregular downward trend of industrial accidents. The number of lives chargeable to the War on this account, however, can hardly be more than a very few thousand at most. Even if we add the normal rate of accidents for the

likely to be included. The Veterans' Administration estimate of total deaths from all causes among the veterans is 460,000. A comparison of this figure with the latest normal mortality tables indicates that the excess of deaths above normal is far less than the official estimate of service-connected deaths. Therefore the writer's figure of 170,000 is retained as an estimate of deaths caused by the War.

labor devoted to war work, it seems probable that the total would not rise above 10,000 deaths. The true loss attributable to the War on this account is the excess of actual accidents above those that would have occurred at the rate of industrial activity that would have prevailed if there had been no war; and this is of course still more conjectural. So far as laborers were injured or killed at war work who would otherwise have been injured or killed on work devoted to the uses of peace, the social loss consists of the worth of the commodities lost to peace uses rather than the accidents themselves, since these would have occurred in any case.[12]

To sum up, the total loss of life chargeable to the War directly and indirectly is uncertain, between the limits of about 160,000 and over half a million. A total of 300,000, military and civilian, would be a moderate guess—but merely a guess. As to the number of births, there is no certainty that the War, in its ultimate outcome, produced any shortage from normal rates. It did, of course, cut off the bulk of our normal immigration. But declines in births and in

[12] The United States Department of Labor has issued figures of fatal and nonfatal industrial accidents in the United States from 1917 on; but Secretary of Labor Davis in 1924 stated that the true numbers were not known, and estimated fatalities at 21,000. He placed total industrial accidents at 2,453,418, with a wage loss of over one billion dollars. *See* the Department's *Monthly Labor Review*, December, 1922, pp. 159 ff.; January, 1924, p. 146; November, 1924, p. 193. Figures published for metal mines, quarries, smelting, and ore dressing show no evidence of excess war mortality. In coal mines, 1914–16 shows less mortality than 1909–13, and 1917–18 shows a relapse to about the figures for 1909–13. In coke ovens, 1917 and 1918 show several thousand deaths above what appears to be the general trend. A special study for the iron and steel industry shows a substantial downward trend in accident frequencies with a heavy relapse in 1916, which was by far the worst year in the whole period of our neutrality and participation. The official figures for the whole country show nonfatal accidents reaching their peak in the post-war boom of 1920, while fatal accidents reach a maximum in 1918. See *Statistical Abstract, 1920,* pp. 266–271; *Monthly Labor Review,* X, 1457 ff., 831 ff., also *Statistical Bulletin,* Metropolitan Life Insurance Co., May, 1922, pp. 6–8.

One may roughly estimate that accidental deaths in this country occur one-third in industry, one-third in homes, and one-third elsewhere. Army and navy deaths during the year-and-a-half of war were probably equal to about two years' normal accident death toll for the whole country. It is stated that automobiles alone are now killing, in two years' time, more persons than were actually killed in action in our armed forces.

immigration cannot be reckoned as economic losses to a country situated as is the United States. Indeed, they may be among the enabling causes of our remarkable post-war prosperity. Since the problem of general civilian losses is so baffling, we must needs focus our main attention on the losses of persons in the armed services.

Despite the great advances in medicine and hygiene, disease still claimed more lives than battle, for the whole of the American forces, though not for the expeditionary force. The other countries suffered far heavier losses from battle than from disease, though their disease rates were undoubtedly, on the average, considerably heavier than ours. This war was unusually deadly in battle casualties, even in proportion to the vast numbers engaged, and the fact that ours were less than our disease losses is the result of the relatively small proportion of our total forces that reached the front, and the relatively short time they were engaged. Ayres gives figures showing a progressive decline in disease mortality per thousand troops per year in successive American wars, as follows: Mexican War, 110; Civil War (north), 65; Spanish War, 26; World War (expeditionary force to date of armistice), 19.[13] The rate for all the forces and for the whole period of service would be considerably less.

The character of disease losses has also changed. Scurvy, dysentery, and cholera, which took a heavy toll of deaths from our armies in the early part of the nineteenth century, have been conquered.[14] Typhoid, which ravaged our camps in 1898 and caused 85 per cent of the deaths, has been virtually eliminated, while in its place pneumonia (apparently charged with all fatal endings of influenza cases) accounted for 83.6 per cent of all disease deaths to May 1, 1919.[15] Tuberculosis, slower in its effects, accounted for many later deaths, and for more than one-third of the government hospital patients through 1925. From that time on, neuro-psychiatric cases, often slow to develop and with a very low death rate, have replaced tuberculosis as the leading group of hospital cases, accounting for 14,941 out of a total of 30,311 in 1930. Of 16,219 actual or suspected World War cases, they constituted 68.4 per cent.

But if the deadly toll of disease is a diminishing threat, there is

[13] Ayres, *op. cit.*, p. 124.

[14] *Vital Statistics of the United States Army during the World War*, by Maj. Albert G. Love, Military Surgeon, August, 1922, p. 3.

[15] Ayres, *op. cit.*, p. 126.

reason to think that modern war is finding new ways of disabling men for after-life, and that this part of the burden is increasing. The bare figures of sick and wounded give, of course, little clue to this lasting burden of disability they represent. Something over 10 per cent of the army's wounded, or 25,187, were discharged from the service as unfit because of wounds, and 179,578 were similarly discharged because of disease and nonbattle injuries; a total of 204,765, to the end of 1919.[16] By the end of the fiscal year 1922 there had been granted 351,940[17] claims for disability compensation, of which 174,024 were still active, to which should be added 92,597 men eligible to compensation but receiving vocational training and maintenance instead, making a total of over 266,000 cases still "active." Eight years later, 139,464 fresh awards had been granted, though the total of active awards had declined slightly, to 256,022. There are also 23,517 statutory tuberculosis awards rated "no disability." Nine hundred thousand disability claims had been filed and over half of these had been granted, or one for every ten men who saw even a day's service. Among the claims rejected were many genuine war disabilities, but rated at less than 10 per cent impairment of earning power and therefore not entitled to compensation. Evidently there has been a large turnover of cases, and disabilities have continued to develop years after the end of the War. Of the 226,484 disability awards active in 1926, 17 per cent had effective dates later than 1922, indicating that the disability developed more than four years after the end of hostilities, or more than three years after the bulk of the forces were mustered out of the service.[18] Similar figures for later years, if available, would swell this number.

The responsibilities assumed by the Government have taken various forms. These include insurance, compensation for death and disability, the "adjusted service compensation," hospital care, and outside medical and dental treatment. Since 1921 these have been centralized in the Veterans' Bureau; and the result, despite shortcomings and abuses, on the whole has been the most businesslike system this country has yet employed for the care of veterans and their

---

[16] From the report of the Surgeon-general's office, above cited, p. 1183. The Veterans' Bureau gives a figure of 251,916, presumably for a longer period and for all branches of the service. *See* 1922 Report, p. 18.

[17] The 1929 Report shows 355,712 through 1922.

[18] U. S. Veterans' Bureau, *Annual Report*, 1926, p. 247.

dependents. One result has been that, for the number of deaths that would have occurred in any case, government insurance and compensation were substituted for the far more inadequate provision which would have been made by the individuals themselves. To this extent the War represented a positive gain, as a partial offset to its heavy losses. The same is true, to a less extent, of those who would in any case have suffered sickness and disability, especially as the benefits of medical and hospital care have of late years been extended to cases not arising from war service.

Patients cared for by the Government in hospitals have formed a large and continuous burden, though with a high rate of turnover. In 1929 the turnover was 202 per cent, and in earlier years it was higher. In that year 81,136 patients were discharged, the average term being under 90 days.[19] Hospital patients reached their greatest numbers in March, 1922, when there were nearly 31,000, though the average for the year was short of 29,000. From then on the cases due to World War causes declined quite steadily, to 15,237 at the end of 1930, with 922 under observation to determine the cause of disability.[20] This decline has been largely balanced by the admission, from 1925 on, of cases not due to war service, now numbering 12,631 among the World War veterans. This has brought the 1930 total up to 31,311 of whom 28,850 are World War veterans. There are 1,208 Spanish War veterans, 79 Civil War veterans, and 174 veterans of other service.[21]

From now on, the Government's hospital bill will be less and less a gauge of war injuries and more and more a form of postponed recompense for mere service. On the other hand, the decline of war cases in the future will probably be far slower than in the past, and may cease entirely. As we have seen, over 68 per cent of them are now of the neuro-psychiatric type, which grew steadily up to 1926 and has not since declined. And these are proverbially long-lived cases. Further construction of hospital facilities, amounting to $15,000,000, was authorized in 1928 to enable the Government to care for these cases in its own institutions. This work is still going on, and an additional $15,950,000 has been authorized for future construction.

Vocational training and rehabilitation was a regular part of the government program for the war-handicapped. In all, over 330,000

[19] *Ibid.,* 1929, pp. 52–63.   [20] *Ibid.,* 1930, p. 53.
[21] *Ibid.,* 1928, pp. 1–2.

were rated as eligible, 180,000 entered training, and 128,000 completed training and were rated as rehabilitated. This work was at its height in 1921–23, with a maximum of 102,000 in training, and was virtually ended in 1927.[22] The work was done in existing institutions, in Veterans' Bureau schools, and in actual productive establishments. The trainee received his regular pay if still in service, a maintenance allowance, or, in one class of cases, the regular disability compensation. A study of pre-war and post-war wages of trainees indicates that they were typically able to earn more dollars than before the War, but not enough, on the average, to keep full pace with the rise either of prices or of prevailing wage-rates.[23] In other words, as might be expected, their handicaps were not completely overcome, and one can only conjecture to what extent they were mitigated.

On this service the Veterans' Bureau alone spent nearly 500 millions, to which possibly 30 millions should be added as a share of its general overhead. This would be over $4,000 per completed case. More than one-fifth of the work was done by other agencies before the establishment of the Veterans' Bureau.[24] And the men themselves gave their time, for what it may have been worth. All in all, rehabilitation may have cost as much as $6,000 to $7,000 per completed case; and yet it seems probable that it was worth what it cost. If the average man entering training had lost 43 per cent of his earning power (the average rating for all disability awards was rather above than below this) and if "rehabilitation" meant restoration to 90 per cent, this would mean $500 a year to a person at the $1,500 earnings level. And this would well repay the cost of training. If restoration were only to 80 per cent, this would mean $345 per year and might not be regarded as profitable on a strict actuarial basis, though none the less worth doing for the community.

The gain went presumably to the veterans themselves, and the Government saved nothing on its compensation bill, as the awards were based on the impairment of earning power which the type of injury in question would normally produce in the veteran's former occupation, and were not reduced in the case of veterans who were able to do better than this, either in their original occupation or in some other. This fact must be borne in mind when we come to using

[22] U. S. Veterans' Bureau, *Annual Report*, 1930, p. 17.

[23] *Ibid.*, 1923, p. 412; 1928, pp. 34–35.

[24] Based on monthly numbers in training, 1926 Report, p. 276.

the official percentages of disability as a gauge of the losses of earning power actually suffered by the men. To just the extent that rehabilitation succeeded in raising earnings above the normal for each type of injury, these percentages exaggerate the actual loss of earnings. For such disabilities as it has enabled the sufferers to remove, the Government pays twice; once in the cost of rehabilitation and once in compensation based on an "average" condition. All of which is quite proper and commendable, but adds to the difficulties of drawing a social cost-sheet; for if government pays twice, society suffers only once, though it may suffer more than either of the Government's payments can adequately measure.

Death compensation is paid to members of the immediate families of persons who died while in service, or afterward from causes connected with service. Parents and children are entitled to benefits only during actual dependency. In June, 1930, benefits were being paid to dependents of 90,954 veterans, the dependents numbering approximately 135,000. There were 21,754 widows, 32,746 children, and 65,205 cases with parent or parents, indicating a probable 80,000 or more parents.[25] The monthly compensation is 2½ millions, or at the rate of 30 millions per year. Parents apparently receive about $200 annually per person, and others at the rate of some $190 to $200 per adult consuming unit. This may be reckoned as something between half and two-thirds of the share these persons would have had in the income of a "normal" household supported by a breadwinner with an income of $1,500. Of course, this basis of reckoning is too mechanical to reflect what happens when a widow tries to maintain a home for two small children on $45 a month, or when another widow unburdened by children, and with the basic allowance of $30 a month, takes a commercial position and possibly even succeeds in earning more than her husband had done. Compared to the French widow's pension of $67.60 a year, ours is munificent; though, even so, France with her 630,000 war widows and orphans must spend several times as much as we do for this purpose.[26]

[25] Veterans' Bureau, *Annual Report,* 1930, p. 77. In the 1928 report the actual number of parents was given as 78,821, there being 63,057 awards involving parent or parents. At the same ratio 65,205 awards would mean 81,500 parents, but it seems that time must reduce the number of cases in which both parents survive.

[26] French figures from "The War Debts," an address by J. F. B. Mitchell, issued September, 1929.

What of the deaths not represented in these 90,954 awards? Over 22,000 more have been on the compensation rolls in the past, and their terminations represent for the most part the death of a beneficiary or the remarriage of a widow. (The reports do not show how many widows have remarried without terminating the award because there were other dependents surviving.) It seems probable that there were in the general neighborhood of 40,000 war widows, of whom 2,000 or more may have died. More than half the rest are still on the compensation rolls, and of the others the major part may be supposed to have remarried.[27] There remains an uncertain number of war-related deaths—presumably at least 75,000—which have never appeared on the death compensation rolls. While there are many reasons, the main one is probably absence of dependents entitled to compensation. This marks them as bachelors whose parents are not dependent (or have died). Which means that the major part of these cases are still likely to come on the rolls as the parents reach old age. A large minority of the terminated awards may be revived for the same reason. On the other hand, most of the children will soon graduate from dependency—few seem to have done so as yet. There will thus be a natural shift in the beneficiaries, the number of children diminishing while the number of parents increases.

Disability compensation is payable to all suffering from service-connected disabilities rated at not less than 10 per cent impairment of earning power, at the basic rate of $100 per month for permanent total disability, and $80 for temporary total disability. Partial disabilities are rated according to the percentage impairment of earning power normally resulting from such injuries, and are paid that percentage of the base rate. There are additional benefits for dependents, with the result that the total compensation is perhaps 10 per cent above the basic rates. There are 80 cases rated as double permanent total—where the need of a regular attendant is taken into the reckoning.[28] The rating of a case as permanent means not merely that the disability cannot be completely cured, but that the degree of disability is not likely to change, so that the veteran can count on his

---

[27] Miss Weeks has compiled terminations of awards by causes, but with the handicap that for several years death and disability are not separated. Indications point to a possible 9,000 terminations of death awards owing to remarriage of widow.

[28] Veterans' Bureau, *Annual Report,* 1930, p. 76.

income with reasonable assurance.[29] Many of the "temporary" cases will remain permanently on the lists. The Bureau is shifting them to permanent rating as rapidly as may be, and nearly 69 per cent of the cases were in 1928 on the permanent basis. There were then 257,536 veterans receiving compensation, rating on the average 43.7 disability and receiving benefits at the rate of $139,000,000 per year or $540 for the average award.[30] The 1929 total is 262,138.

The character of these disabilities is significant of changes in the nature of warfare and of advances in medical treatment. As against some 50,000 killed in action or died of wounds there are 56,000 still receiving compensation for neuro-psychiatric disabilities, over 56,000 for tuberculosis, and about 150,000 for "general medical and surgical conditions," including nearly 18,000 respiratory diseases other than tuberculosis. Amputations, so numerous in former wars, account for less than 8,000.[31] It is not without significance that neuro-psychiatric disorders have disabled more men than were killed by the enemy, while these and respiratory diseases have disabled more than the total of deaths in service. Undoubtedly many tuberculous veterans have been saved who would have died under earlier methods of treatment; but trench warfare has vastly increased the number of these cases.

Before judging the adequacy of this compensation we must note that percentage ratings are based on impairment of earning power at the veteran's former occupation, whereas many have found occupations where their handicaps count for less. And for every two veterans on the rolls, one has completed vocational rehabilitation. Some of these last are not drawing compensation, but the greater part are undoubtedly still doing so, and on the basis of a greater impairment of earning power than they now actually suffer. And we must note the additional provision that comes from other sources, especially war insurance.

[29] On the other hand, a considerable number of insurance awards, for "permanent and total" disability, have been terminated by reason of recovery. In 1929 these cases had mounted up to 3,677. *See* 1929 Report, pp. 80, 82.

[30] As of June 30, 1928—*see* Veterans' Bureau Report for that year, pp. 76–77. Averages are aggregative, the group reported as 10 per cent to 19 per cent being rated at 15 per cent, and so on. "Statutory awards" and retirement pay for disabled officers render later figures not strictly comparable.

[31] *Ibid.,* 1928, pp. 73–76; 1929, pp. 69–73.

Veterans permanently and totally disabled are receiving benefits from term or automatic insurance to the number of nearly 13,000, or some 39 per cent of the number of compensation awards in that class.[32] And insurance of these types is being paid on some 145,000 deaths in all (not all war deaths, of course), many of which must surely be assigned to war causes, though the exact number cannot be determined. Of those receiving death compensation, nearly three-quarters are receiving insurance from the Government in addition.[33] Most of these are term policies yielding the beneficiaries on the average about $50 per month for twenty years. The Government offered these policies to all the armed forces at net premium rates, in amounts from $1,000 to $10,000. Over 4½ million took out policies to an average amount of $8,756. The full $10,000 policy pays $57.50 per month for twenty years, and the beneficiaries are not limited to those entitled to compensation awards. Such insurance at such rates was, of course, not self-supporting; and it has been estimated that the Government has undertaken obligations amounting to 951 millions beyond what the premiums cover.[34]

In 1924 provision for veterans was increased by the "adjusted service compensation."[35] This of course benefited the disabled along with all the rest, and also the dependents of those who had died. The maximum award was $500 for home service and $625 for foreign service, and the average would come to less than $400. In addition, as already noted, about half the veterans were entitled to State bonuses of approximately $150. Amounts over $50 took the form of a 20-year endowment policy for the amount each man's "bonus" increased by 25 per cent would buy, applied as a single premium. On this basis the average "bonus" means a policy of nearly $1,000. The Government thus rendered itself liable to claims which might total

[32] This insurance is payable only to those disabled for any occupation, while disability awards are on the basis of disablement in the man's original calling.

[33] Veterans' Bureau, *Annual Report,* 1928, pp. 77–78.

[34] *Ibid.,* 1922, p. 24. Obligations commuted at 3½ per cent interest. Some term insurance was renewed beyond this date, but as the veterans' death rate returned to normal the insurance became approximately self-supporting.

[35] The award was on the basis of $1.00 per day of home service and $1.25 for foreign service, up to the above maxima. The basic pay of the private soldier was thus more than doubled retroactively, in the form of endowment insurance.

over 4 billions, with a discounted worth in 1924 of something over half that amount.[36] To date (1929) 3,650,093 claims have been granted, the total in cash payments and certificates amounting to slightly over 3½ billion dollars.[37] The discounted worth of the obligations, with an allowance for claims still to come in, may be roughly estimated in the neighborhood of 2 billions as of 1924. The fiscal burden is to be equalized by annual appropriations to an interest-bearing fund, sufficient to provide for the obligations and to be completed in 1946. Such appropriations for the first five years have totaled $560,000,000, or $112,000,000 per year in addition to some direct payments not passing through the fund. It is estimated that recent extensions will result in a need for appropriations of over $150,000,000 a year from now on.[38]

In all, it may be estimated that the Government has spent 3½ billions or more on account of service losses of life and health, to the end of the fiscal year 1930, not counting any costs while the men were still in service.[39] Adjusted service compensation would add more than 700 millions (including an allowance for a share in the general expenses of the Veterans' Bureau). But this, while a war cost, is not due to loss of life and health. It is a continuing fiscal outlay to pay for a social cost incurred while the War was being fought. Medical and hospital care of nonservice cases, and costs incidental to converted insurance, still further increase the Veterans' Bureau budget. As fiscal outlays they were no doubt occasioned by the War, and they may be classed with the adjusted service compensation as forms of postponed payment for service.

The future, of course, can at best be conjectured. Some help can be had from the experience of Civil War pensions, but very large allowances must be made for the differences between the two cases.

---

[36] Excluded from the award were: officers of the rank of army captain or navy lieutenant or higher, all commissioned officers on home service, and all men released from the draft.

[37] Veterans' Bureau, *Annual Report*, 1929, p. 30.

[38] *Ibid.*, p. 34. No increase in the appropriation was made for 1930.

[39] Based on the Veterans' Bureau items in the Treasury Department's estimate of war costs to 1927. Outlays for 1928 and years prior to 1922 from Veterans' Bureau, *Annual Report*, 1929, pp. 99–100; subject to omissions and adjustments indicated in the text. It is especially true of insurance items that actual disbursements by the Bureau and true expenses to the Government do not agree.

These differences are great enough to justify us in expecting a radically different outcome—otherwise the outlook would be decidedly disquieting. Civil War casualties, for the north alone, were far heavier than the American losses in the World War; roughly twice as many killed and wounded and three times as many deaths from disease. Yet the present legacy of compensated disability is more than twice the number on the Civil War disability pension roll for the corresponding period, in numbers receiving compensation. The Civil War pension list grew from 123,000 in 1875 to a peak of 419,000 in 1891.[40] If our present roll grows in the same way,[41] we should in 1945 be compensating 875,000 disabled veterans and spending, at present rates of compensation, some 475 millions a year for this alone, indicating a total veterans' budget for that year of some three-quarters of a billion. But the total list of Civil War pensioners kept growing until 1902, when it was just short of 1 million. And the money payments kept on growing until 1921, when they were just short of 250 millions. We were then paying over twice as much for Civil War pensions as for death and disability compensation for the World War. In 1926 we were still paying more in pensions for a war ended sixty-one years before, than for the World War, only eight years in the past. (The comparison does not include insurance or medical or hospital care or vocational rehabilitation with maintenance, and hence is not a fair one except as indicating what we may expect in the future.)

In trying to make these facts throw light on the future veterans' costs, we shall do well to ignore the dollar magnitude of the Civil War pensions and focus attention on the number of awards. The earlier rates of payment were originally quite inadequate, and there were increases which made them more adequate, and other increases which were called for to neutralize the shrinking dollar. The World War veterans' budget starts on a scale of adequacy which precludes the likelihood of extreme or radical increases of basic rates in the fu-

[40] The earlier figure is from the *Statistical Abstract,* the later figure from Devine's Carnegie Endowment study, "Disabled Soldiers and Sailors," p. 35. After 1890 the "invalid" rolls include nonservice disabilities, and fluctuate around 750,000 for the next ten years, after which they again decline.

[41] Possibly the total number of compensation awards is not comparable to the Civil War pensions, and permanent disabilities might be a more nearly comparable figure. One fears that neither is exactly comparable.

ture, and it is so organized that there are certain decreases that can be counted on. By reasoning without allowance for these facts it is possible to prove, fallaciously, that we shall be paying out 4 billions a year in 1975 for the World War veterans. Actually, there is room to hope that by 1975 the burden will be under 100 millions and that by 1985 it will have virtually disappeared if it is so managed as to be limited to the span of life of the veterans' own generation and not spread over the succeeding generation also, through pensions paid to relatively young widows who have married aging veterans.

Aside from this question, uncertainty as to the future number of compensation cases centers on the growth of the disability roll. And this depends on a further question: to what extent are the present numbers an evidence that the World War produced an aftermath of disability far larger than did the Civil War, in proportion to the casualty lists? And to what extent are they merely the result of the fact that we have been prompter in recognizing the existing cases and establishing contact with them? Both factors have been at work.

Most of the Civil War wounds were from bullets, while those of the World War were predominantly from high-explosive shells, which have more crippling effects. And almost exactly half of our present disability awards are for tuberculosis, other respiratory diseases, and neuro-psychiatric disorders; all of which are peculiar to the modern warfare of trench and barrage, gas, and high explosive. Also, modern medical science has undoubtedly revealed many injuries that were not traceable to war causes under earlier conditions, and the law now ranks as compensable any case, for example, of tuberculosis shown to have arisen before January 1, 1925, thus taking in many cases which would have been excluded from the Civil War pension lists until after the Act of 1890 admitted disabilities not due to service.

There can be no question that the World War will leave behind more disabilities than the Civil War in proportion to the casualty lists. It has already proved that. Its list is already greater, in proportion to casualties, than reached by the Civil War roll; it is still growing and has sixteen years still to go before reaching the date corresponding to the Civil War maximum. So far, from half as great a casualty list, the World War has produced over twice the recognized disabilities the Civil War produced (for the north) in the corresponding period of time. Yet it is difficult to suppose that it really produced over four times the Civil War proportion of disabilities to casualties. Double the proportion perhaps; but more is hardly plausible.

The probability is that at least half the discrepancy is due to the fact that the Civil War pensioners were slower in getting on the rolls, while the Veterans' Bureau has made systematic and sustained efforts to make contacts with all the men and acquaint them with their rights, with the result that there is now probably no very great number of eligible cases not in the records. Hence our list will not grow as much as the Civil War list did—that is fairly certain—and may reasonably be expected to grow less than half as much. In other words, we may expect our ultimate disability list to be no larger than the Civil War list and probably smaller, despite the fact that at present it is over twice as large as the Civil War list at a corresponding date. It seems also possible that the maximum, which by Civil War experience should come in 1945, may be reached some few years earlier. The present rate of growth in disability compensation awards fits in with this conclusion. It seems to point to a maximum somewhere between the extreme limits of 300,000 and 500,000 cases, with the probabilities in favor of 325,000 to 350,000. A check on this estimate can be found in the fact that the larger part of future additions to the disability rolls must come from previous awards not now active, or from rejected claims that may be reconsidered. An inspection of the causes for termination and rejection leads to the conclusion that only about one-fourth of the rejections, and a majority of the terminations, are for causes leaving room for future reconsideration. Allowing for deaths, one may estimate at 225,000 to 250,000 the total of claims out of which future reinstatements or reconsiderations must come.[42] Actually, a large part of this number could probably be ruled out of the realm of practical possibilities by anyone directly acquainted with the conditions. Many are disabilities ranked as less than 10 per cent, which may in future become more serious, but are not likely ever to be as serious as the average case. Uncertain as these figures are, they lend some support to the view that 500,000 may be taken as the limit of reasonably possible future increase, with the probable figure considerably lower.

[42] The reports do not make it possible to compute exactly the number of terminated disability awards and disallowed claims to date. The former probably number 186,000, the latter may number 400,000 in all.

After the maximum is definitely past, the natural death rate will bring about a fairly steady decline and in four more decades, or by 1985, active disability awards should have virtually come to an end. If the provisions of law are broadened to include nonservice disabilities, that will of course check the decline, but will have little effect on the duration of the whole burden. This, of course, is naturally a matter on which no predictions can be made.

Death benefits will be governed by two sets of forces. There will be future deaths which will be ranked as service connected, chiefly from among those with disabilities already so recognized. And there will be changes among the beneficiaries as children grow up and parents become dependent or die. Toward the end, widows will remain as the chief beneficiaries. Undoubtedly many past deaths not now represented by awards will furnish grounds for claims in the future as parents become dependent with advancing age. Awards for future deaths may or may not be numerous, depending on the standards used in determining whether war service was a contributing cause, but the average future death will involve far more dependents than the average so far, as the unmarried youths of 1918 have now acquired families.

The Civil War figures seem to indicate that the awards for actual, war-caused deaths will not increase as much as the roll of disability. The long-sustained size of the Civil War death-pension roll is due to something quite different: namely, the granting of the service pension, part of which continues to the surviving widow. The result is a large volume of pensions to widows much younger than their husbands. And there is no good reason for copying this feature of the Civil War pension policy.

One thing has already been done which must tend to reduce the incentive for a woman to marry an aging veteran for the sake of his pension: the service pension has been replaced by endowment insurance policies. If the widow's right to compensation continues to be limited to deaths in which the War was a contributing factor, there should be little question of marrying for the sake of pensions. If further safeguards were needed, the widow's pension right could be made to terminate at the time her husband, if he had lived, would have been seventy-five or possibly eighty years old and therefore past contributing to her support out of his earnings. If such a right were granted to a comparatively young widow, it would often be more useful if actual payment were deferred and the amounts allowed to accumulate at interest toward an annuity in those later years when it would in all probability be more needed. Such a limited pension right would cover all loss suffered by reason of death, and still set a definite time limit on the fiscal burden.

Can we now proceed to predict the amount of this future war outlay? Not with any approach to exactness, of course, and only on the assumption of present laws and policies. On this basis, however, something may be forecast as to the time when the outlay will be likely to reach its maximum, the amount of this maximum, the shape of the curve of decline from this maximum, and the time when the burden will come to an end. This forecast is embodied in the accompanying three charts. Chart XII traces the growth of the number of Civil War disability pensions and superimposes on it the World War disability awards for approximately corresponding dates, 1919 being taken as equivalent to 1865. From 1928 three lines are projected

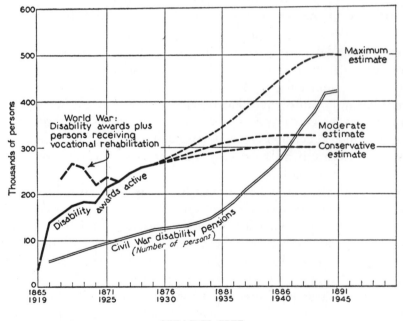

CHART XII.

*Civil War Pensions Compared to World War
Disability Awards.*

forward, representing a conservative estimate, a moderate estimate, and a maximum estimate of possible future growth. As there is probably no one figure in the World War experience that exactly corresponds to the Civil War pension list, permanent disabilities deserve separate mention. They started far below the Civil War line, and have risen well above it. The chart also includes an estimate of the additional number entitled to compensation but who received for a time vocational rehabilitation, with maintenance, instead.

Chart XIII shows the continuing war outlays for care of veterans, analyzed into five main divisions. The outlay for compensation is then projected forward on a curve based on the "moderate" curve of probable growth of disability, it being assumed that death awards will follow the same type of curve as disability. This seems a fair assumption. Outlays for hospital and medical care, and for salaries and expenses, are roughly estimated, being of secondary amount. Outlays on account of military and naval insurance, and adjusted service compensation, have their future course determined by existing contractual rights and laws, and must substantially come to an end by 1946. The war insurance is mainly in the form of twenty-year annuities, while the adjusted service compensation is mainly provided for by contributions to a fund which must be complete in 1946. The chart serves to present to the eye the way in which these outlays are scheduled to pass out of the national budget. It is, of course, possible that the termination of the twenty-year war life-insurance annuities will give rise to a demand for more liberal death compensation. If this should take place, it could not by itself involve a very heavy increase of the total expenditures so long as it was confined to war-caused deaths.

The total expenditure represented by this "moderate" curve is approximately 20 billions, while the curve representing the maximum limits of future growth indicates a total expenditure of something like 25 billions. If there were no question of new legislation and enlarged rights, 20 billions would seem a fair estimate. In view of the moral certainty that there will be enlargements of rights in the future, it is morally certain that more will be spent. There will also be expenses not strictly chargeable to taking care of war injuries, such as costs incident to the post-war insurance into which the veterans have been encouraged to convert their war insurance policies, or medical and hospital care for nonwar injuries. Some of

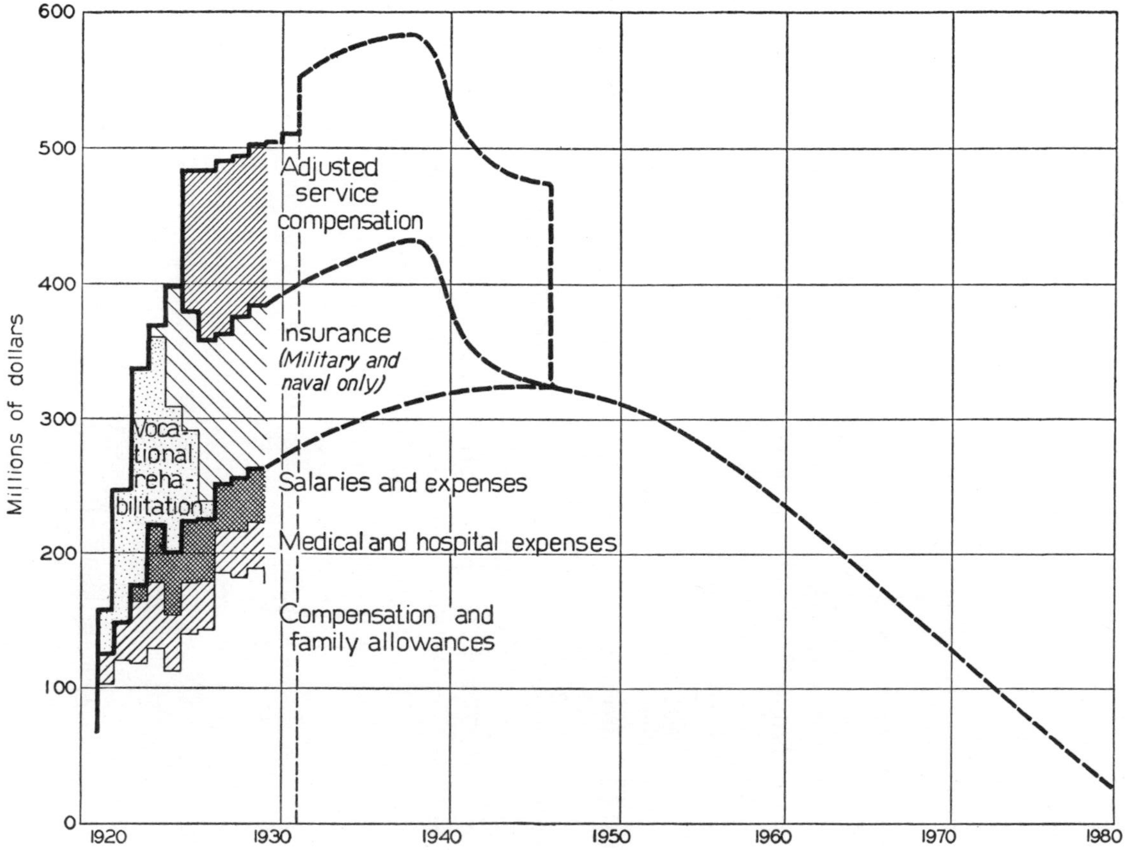

CHART XIII.

Veterans' Bureau Expenses Analyzed, with Forecast.

Millions of dollars

600
500
400
300
200
100
0

1920   1930   1940   1950   1960   1970   1980

Adjusted
service
compensation

Insurance
*(Military and
naval only)*

Vocational
reha-
bilitation

Salaries and expenses

Medical and hospital expenses

Compensation and
family allowances

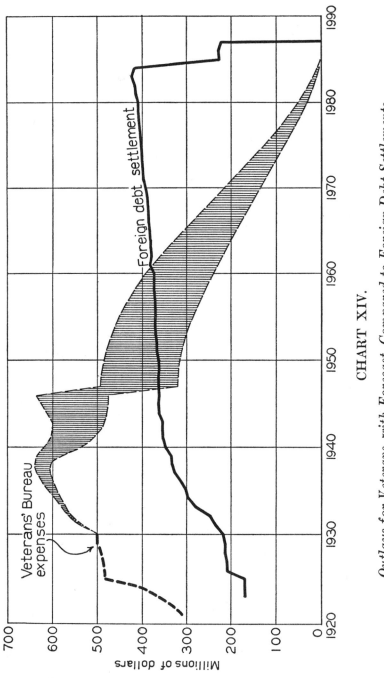

CHART XIV.

Outlays for Veterans, with Forecast, Compared to Foreign Debt Settlements.

these, at least, are excluded from the estimate of war costs in the Veterans' Bureau budget presented by the Secretary of the Treasury in his official estimate of the money cost of the War, which has formed the basis of the figures given in Chart XIII. There are also some veterans' activities not yet centralized in the Veterans' Bureau up to 1929. Taking all these things into account, 20 billions is almost certainly a low estimate.

It is an interesting coincidence that this estimate coincides so closely with the gross sum of payments due to the United States from foreign countries under the war debt settlements. In Chart XIV these two series of fiscal sums are presented, using the "conservative" estimate of veterans' outlays. Up to 1946 the veterans' budget is far the greater; after that year it stands a very good chance of being the smaller, though our maximum estimate remains higher for some fourteen years after that date. And the debt settlements reach their highest levels during the decades when the veterans' budget should be dwindling to nothing. Whether the veterans' budget is smaller or larger as a gross sum, as a discounted future expectation it is larger on any rational basis of estimate. From the standpoint of the fiscal costs of the War to the Government, perhaps the best treatment of these two sums stretching away into the uncertain future is to offset them against each other, though one cannot but feel that the international payments are a far more uncertain quantity than the minimum estimate of veterans' expenses. They represent really a maximum. The actual payments may fall short of this, but cannot exceed it.

This enormous sum is about equal to the whole gross fiscal cost of the War to the armistice with the original principal of the foreign loans included and no deduction for realizable assets remaining. It is almost as large as the net cost of the War to a year and a half after the armistice, after deducting for foreign claims and other realizable assets.

This, however, is all in the realm of money outlays by government. It remains to be seen whether this money outlay is a fair measure of the underlying burden to the national economy. Has the Government adequately compensated the disabled and dependent? Has it perhaps overcompensated them? Ought it to try to make its total of compensations exactly equal the economic losses suffered by the beneficiaries, or is this an inapplicable standard?

CHAPTER XIV

DEATH AND DISABILITY: FINANCIAL COSTS
VS. ECONOMIC BURDENS

THE money spent by the government on account of war deaths and
disabilities is, of course, not the ultimate cost of death and disability
to the nation; it is merely the recompense paid on account of it, and
the fiscal cost of the services incidental to that recompense. The recompense, considered by itself, is a transfer of funds from taxpayers
to veterans and their dependents, in which the net cost to the nation
is the cost of collecting the taxes and administering the transfer. The
basic objective fact in the underlying economic cost is a loss of productive power resulting in a loss of economic income. More important, though not exactly measurable, is the effect of this loss of
objective income on those who suffer it. The administering of compensation necessarily involves a moderate increase in the objective
cost to the nation, for the sake of a large reduction in the severity of
the human incidence. Thus it is worth doing, apart from any question of justice to veterans and their dependents.

Whether the recompense is large or small does not affect the nature of the original loss, though it affects the weight of its incidence
and its after-effects. Miserly compensation means that most of the
loss is left on the shoulders of those least able to bear it, and only a
small part taken up by the rest of the community. This makes the
burden bear heavier than it need to. Lavish overcompensation means
that government acts as an agency to collect funds from the taxpayer and enrich the beneficiary. And this, aside from being undesirable in itself, may add a further source of loss in the idleness to
which it may tempt the beneficiaries in the future. In this case the
nation's main loss will be the idleness, not the subsidies that caused it.

Compensation should, then, bear some approximate relation to the
economic loss suffered by those who are still here to receive compensation. But compensation does not aim to pay to each individual
widow the exact amount she has lost by the death of her individual
husband, who may have been destined, had he lived, to make millions
or to end in the poorhouse; who might have had one year or sixty

years of life ahead of him if the war had passed him by. Compensation is justifiably based on need rather than on individual losses. This being the case, there is no very cogent reason why the total amount of compensation should exactly equal the total sum of economic losses suffered by the beneficiaries.

Compensation based on need naturally follows a scale somewhat below the average income which the men might normally have been expected to earn; otherwise great numbers of the beneficiaries would be actually better off, economically, on account of their losses. On the other hand, compensation lasts during the whole life of the beneficiary, while the income it replaces would in many cases cease sooner. Of the disabled, many would have ceased to earn income before their deaths if there had been no war. The system of compensation virtually insures the beneficiary against these contingencies, and this would make up for a compensation scale based on something decidedly less than average annual earnings.

Benefits received from vocational rehabilitation are over and above standard compensation, and the man who succeeds in improving his earning power suffers no reduction in his compensation scale. Thus if compensation alone were enough to make up for normal loss of income, compensation plus benefits from vocational rehabilitation would be more—or actual loss of income less. And there is no reason why total compensation and total loss of income should be exactly equal after allowing for the benefits of rehabilitation. This would be an injustice to the man whose injury did not permit of improvement through vocational training.

Another reason for a discrepancy is this. The death loss caused by the war is the net excess of war deaths above the normal mortality which would have occurred in any case. And the same applies to disabilities. Actually, these normal deaths and disabilities cannot for the most part be segregated, and compensation is necessarily based on the gross total of war deaths and disabilities without deduction for normal mortality or disability rates. It includes, therefore, a form of free insurance against the normal probability of death during the term of service. The same principle applies to post-war deaths and disabilities from causes connected with war service. A certain percentage of these cases would have died or been disabled if there had been no war; but there would be no justice in singling out these cases and refusing them compensation; and in any case there is no way of doing it. It is probably better to pay compensation in two cases for which the war is not statistically responsible, rather than refuse it in one case of which the war was the real cause.

The principle can be illustrated by an exaggerated example. Suppose that every veteran's life were shortened one year by injuries or exposure. Then every veteran's death would be due to the War in some degree which it would be impossible to determine, and all in equal degree, so that if any were compensated, all should be. And there would be no way to determine except by difficult or doubtful actuarial reasoning, some time later, that these deaths represented, on the average, only one year's shortening of life; while even this would prove nothing of individual cases. To compensate each case for one year's loss of life only would be an absurdity; and any scheme of compensation would be bound, if it cared for dependents at all, to care for them during dependency. And the amount of the compensation could hardly bear any relation to the actual loss suffered by reason of premature death.

The problem is a real one, for many veterans are dying of causes with which the War had something to do: in fact, a large part of the deaths among the disabled since the close of the War are true war casualties. For purposes of social statistics, the best measure of the number of war-caused deaths would be the number of deaths in excess of the normal mortality for the age-group in question, with whatever allowance can be made for the fact that the group was originally above the average in health. But such an estimate would, of course, be of no use in determining which particular deaths should be regarded as war casualties for purposes of compensating the surviving dependents. For this purpose a quite different method must be followed, and if the results of the two methods agreed at all closely, it would be a coincidence. To sum up, proper compensation has some relation to the social burdens of death and disability, but there is no reason why the two should be equal.

It goes without saying that compensation cannot square the whole account, since it cannot reach those who have given their lives. A little reflection will show that attempts at quantitative estimates of the underlying loss to the community are subject to the same limitation. They can find no economic equivalent for the worth of a man's life to that man himself—none that will stand rational scrutiny. The very attempt smacks of a sort of solemn statistical levity. So also with the sufferings of the crippled or of the victims of psychopathic disorders: these as direct human costs, in and of themselves, are beyond the reach of measurement. They are simply and literally incalculable.

We cannot, for example, take a person's private consumption as the measure of what that person has lost by his own death; nor of what the world has lost. For with the consumption vanished also the necessities it served. The same holds true of what is gained or lost by a person's being born or not being born: his personal consumption is not the measure of any value we can recognize as significant. Did the life that is lost represent a surplus of pleasure over pain, or will the life that is to come represent such a surplus? No one can say. If we could find the surplus above the "necessities of life"—that arbitrary and varying quantity—we should still not have captured the "psychic surplus," or deficit.

It is proverbial that "all that a man has he will give for his life," and we might take the surplus of income above bare necessities—if these can be measured—as representing all that a man has to give in such a hypothetical bargain. This of course only applies to persons already born. There are cases where a somewhat similar choice is exercised on behalf of an unborn infant—by potential parents in cases of birth control. But here the minimum standard is commonly set well above the bare necessities of life. And in estimating the surplus of income above necessities care must be taken to deduct the claims of all future dependents, including unborn children, as well as those of dependents now in existence. The result, in the average case, would be so small that to take it as measuring the worth of a man's life to the man himself would be rather an impertinence than a useful economic index. It seems far better frankly to leave this quantity out of account.

There is one sense in which the surplus of a person's normal consumption above his necessities might have a value to the nation as a whole. It might be taken as a very imperfect index of the net economic power available for national purposes in case of some future emergency, such as war. Strictly speaking, the important quantity would be, not peace-time income, but the product that could be gotten out of the individual under war conditions, and this, as we have seen, is not the same thing. And "necessities" would mean, not any physical minimum, but the amount which it is nationally expedient or necessary to leave the individual for his own consumption in such a national emergency. A valuation on this principle would be dependent on a number of uncertain future contingencies, and its dollar value, if appropriately discounted, would be very small; while its national importance, if the contingency occurred, would be large out of all proportion to the ordinary peace-time value of the dollars in which it must needs be measured. Hence it is best simply to recognize its existence, without attempting to measure it and add it to a value in dollars that represent ordinary peace-time consumption.

For a nation with vulnerable land frontiers exposed to imminent danger of attack by other powers of equal or greater strength and resources, this element of aggregate net economic power available in national emergencies is of vital importance, even if this importance cannot be accurately measured in dollars. For a country situated as is the United States, it is undoubtedly outweighed by other social considerations. For us, the level of *per capita* well-being is properly paramount over considerations of aggregate economic power for war.

A large population may in and of itself have some value; but this is a matter that appears differently to different persons. To some, membership in a more populous nation is a source of direct gratification; while to others, preoccupied with evils of congestion and difficulties of mass self-government, increasing density of population beyond the present level is rather a source of concern. Our inquiry must be limited to a more specific problem.

Has the nation, *since* the War—and this means ultimately the individuals who have composed it *since* the War—been richer or poorer by the loss of life and health due to the War, and how much? The answer to this question will not tell us how much we ought to be willing to pay to save life or to avert injury; but it will tell us how much we can afford to pay without being economically poorer as a result. It simply recognizes the fact that the value of life and health in themselves, to the person living that life or possessing that health, is a problem too deep for the purely economic level of inquiry. And it falls back on the changes which particular kinds of losses of life and health bring to pass in the economic status of surviving persons. These are tangible and measurable quantities, granted the necessary data. They concern persons who are in the world in any case, and no question is raised or need be raised whether their lives represent net surplus or net deficit. The death of a soldier deprives them of a father, a husband, a son to support their old age; and this makes their economic status that much worse than it would otherwise have been. This deterioration of economic status is a fact which can be estimated without involving us in insoluble problems of the standard of national well-being or whether life as it is represents a state of surplus or of deficit in an absolute sense. It is for that reason and not from hardness of heart that we shall view the cost of death from the standpoint of the survivors: those who are here to experience changes in economic well-being which do not carry life or death with them: those who are here to be recompensed if they have suffered losses.

There are two questions that face us when we probe beneath the money expenses of the Government. One concerns the specific loss suffered by the disabled or the dependents of the dead. How great is this loss, and is the compensation reasonably commensurate? This is a relatively definite matter of earnings, and of the portion thereof which has been lost by these survivors. Another question is: how much poorer is the nation as a whole by reason of these losses? This is at bottom a matter of wealth produced and consumed by the whole economic system. In this study we shall take the personal earnings of the men as furnishing, with some minor adjustments, the key to the answer to both questions: as the gauge of their contribution to the national dividend as well as to the upkeep of themselves and their families.

This requires some defending, in view of the many persons and groups who have some interest or other of an economic sort in the average life. A man has a value to his employer, to the State as a citizen and taxpayer, to any organizations he may help support; possibly even to the consumers of the goods he produces. On the other hand, to those who are his competitors in the markets his room may be better than his company, from the purely economic standpoint. Moreover, the other values mentioned are not all positive. The average citizen is not only a source of revenue to the government but an occasion of expenditures as well. And while some contribute to charitable and other organizations, that is precisely because others need relief, and these others are sources of expense. The value of the citizen to such organizations depends on which kind he is: the nonexistent "average person" may bring neither gain nor loss. Balancing these positive and negative quantities against each other, the resultant will depend on the question whether a larger or smaller increase in population means increasing or decreasing efficiency and economy in the actual economic work performed by industry and government. Does the individual contribute to the "national dividend" more or less than is taken out by reason of his presence? This last, as we shall see, is not quite the same as the amount he takes out for his own personal consumption.

The *per capita* product of industry is greater than the wages paid, and out of the excess come the profits of the employer and the returns to capital. Does the loss of a worker, then, mean a loss of his *per capita* share of the gross product and not merely of his wages? This might be the case if the loss of life were so great that the population was materially reduced, and the result was idle plants and idle machines. Even so, this effect would only last until population, in its resumed growth, caught up with productive equipment and capital adjusted itself to the modified conditions. And even in the interim, a more probable effect would be that many persons would enter industry who would otherwise have remained in the home, and the cost would take the form mainly of the sacrifices of their industrial labor rather than of a loss of gross product. Wages might be taken as a measure of these sacrifices.

On the other hand, the actual condition of employment in our post-war economy suggests that more workers might merely have added to the numbers of unemployed without increasing product to any material extent. This, however, is extremely doubtful even as a short-run effect, and certainly does not represent the long-run adjustment.

What has actually happened has been a continued growth of population on which the losses of the War made little or no impression. And if the numbers engaged in manufacturing industry have during a large part of the post-war period shown an actual decline, this has been due to other causes than war casualties. There has been a substitution of capital for labor, in the form of increasingly elaborate and automatic mechanical equipment, and the nature of this substitution furnishes the key to the productive worth of laborers. In such substitutions as these, both labor and capital work under "diminishing returns"; and this fact distinguishes these substitutions from the more immediate effects of adding or subtracting laborers in a plant already fixed and adapted to definite methods of production and with a definite productive capacity. The employer tends to use the method which is cheaper for the work in hand, substituting capital for labor if it will do the work at a lower cost than the laborers' wages. And where this process works under the most favorable competitive conditions, there tends to be a close correspondence between the additional or "marginal" product of additional labor and its wages, or between the "marginal" product of capital and its cost to the employer. Under hypothetical conditions of perfect fluidity, the wages and the marginal product would be equal.

Actually, the effect of the loss of some laborers at any particular point in industry might well be simply the hiring of others to take their places, if their jobs did not happen to be among those where a further substitution of capital for labor is hanging in the balance, waiting for some push from the forces of demand and supply to decide the issue. But the effects do not end here. This substituting of labor for labor, if it takes place to a material extent, is not likely to mean merely a permanent reduction of the number of unemployed, but rather less labor working somewhere else in the system. And the place where the labor can be best spared will be the place where capital can most easily be substituted. This in turn draws capital which might otherwise have been employed in still a different place in the economic system, where it would have been worth its cost, which in turn tends to approximate the wages of the labor it was called on to replace. With all the uncertainties of this process of shifting and incidence, the most workable assumption is that the loss to industry as a whole from the loss of a worker is measured by his wages. In short, the principle of "marginal productivity" has sufficient application to this situation to justify us in taking wages as the best available measure of the loss to industry from the death of possibly 170,000 workers.

One factor of which this does not take account is the fact that a member of an established working force, if he has really found his place there, has a peculiar value and cannot be exactly replaced by the first worker whom the hiring machinery may be able to pick up in the market. To this extent the worker does have a value to his employer and to industry beyond his wages. The loss due to this disruption of a going force is of the general sort recognized by employers as the "cost of labor turnover." For most workers it is not large, and a few hundred dollars would undoubtedly cover it even in types of work where it is well above the average. Of course, the workers who bulk largest in the ordinary turnover of hiring, firing, and leaving are precisely those rolling stones who have least special value to an employer. And violent death does not select these types. But this whole matter is discounted by the fact that the men who went to war left their places when they entered the service, and these places had to be filled somehow, with the result that the reabsorption of the service men involved further problems of turnover. If one did not come back, the problem of turnover was more likely to be made easier than harder. Therefore it seems justifiable to ignore this special value of a worker to his employer when considering the economic loss from service deaths. A larger problem, quantitatively, is that of finding places for partially disabled men, and here employers may have borne a considerable burden, whose amount can only be conjectured.

If the average worker or citizen has a value to others besides his employer or his industry, it must be that his presence contributes in some way to greater efficiency in the actual work of the country. In other words, the work of the country must be in a stage of increasing efficiency with increased scale of operations. Sometimes it is possible to judge quite confidently whether a country is in a stage of increasing or decreasing efficiency in relation to total population. Few would probably question that China today, by this standard, is overpopulated, or that the United States before 1850 was underpopulated. But as to which class we belong in at present, a confident answer is not so easy.

Extractive industries are undoubtedly handicapped as agriculture is forced on to irrigated land, or the best and most accessible forests and coal deposits are used up. But "mass production" in manufacture and transport is still probably a source of economy: one of the reasons why we are a wealthy nation. Which element is more important one can only conjecture; and therefore it is not safe to assume that the life of an average worker has any important indirect value, positive or negative, to industry as a whole.

The value of the citizen to the State as a taxpayer proves on analysis to be simply a special case of this general principle. If the citizen's presence makes the national economy more efficient, then the State can take more in taxes with less sacrifice to the mass of taxpayers. Or if the business of government itself is a case of "decreasing costs" with larger-scale production, so that it is cheaper *per capita* to govern many people than few, then the presence of added citizens means that equally effective government can be furnished with lower taxes. As the whole national economy properly includes the work of government as one of its parts, this question is an integral part of the larger one already touched on.

So far as government itself is concerned, all the evidence goes to show that any economies that may result from large-scale operation (and there are many) are outweighed by the added duties imposed by the more complex relationships of a denser and more concentrated population. Government itself does not seem to be a business of decreasing costs; hence the average citizen taxpayer may be said to add about as much to the costs of government as he contributes toward defraying them. To sum up, a worker's personal earnings seem a fair gauge of his contribution to the national economy.

And that part of his earnings which would have gone to his surviving dependents is a fair index of the economic loss suffered by the community—the degree to which this (present) community is poorer by the worker's death. Of course it follows that those who take rather than give—who consume without producing—have, so long as they do so, a negative economic value. Aged nonproducers are in this class and so are dependent children, though only temporarily.

Children who will be producers have a future value, *but it is a value mainly to dependents who are potential rather than actual.* The child's life has value to *his* potential children. But if he dies in childhood they cannot be said to lose anything measurable. They simply lose the chance to be born into a disturbed and disturbing world; and that is a privilege on which we can set no money value. The child's life has some value to his parents, but this must be balanced against the cost of rearing the child to maturity. For the typical boy, there is also the girl he would have married if he had lived. She is a real person, and she has lost her future husband (whom she may never have seen). The ultimate incidence of this casualty probably carries a balance of loss, but it is vague, conjectural, unmeasurable, and often neutralized.[1] The immediate effect of the death of a child is to improve the economic condition of the family by reducing expenses, though with two qualifications. The household establishment is geared to a family of a certain size and some of the expenses may not shrink readily. And in an increasing number of cases the loss of one child is likely to cause another to be born, since the size of the family is kept down for economic reasons. In such cases the loss is the cost of bearing and rearing the child.

From this fragmentary discussion of a very far-reaching topic, one thing should be sufficiently evident. There is no one general "value of a human life," valid for all circumstances and for all purposes. A birth brought about or prevented is one thing, and a death quite a different thing; and the death of a bachelor is quite a different thing from the death of a member of an established family whose organization as an economic "going concern" may be disrupted thereby. And an immigrant admitted or excluded is still another thing. The present immigration law clearly regards human life added to the country in this form, beyond very moderate limits, as a national liability and not an asset. If the law is a valid criterion, the worth of such human lives to the country is a minus quantity, whatever may be true of their value in terms of tangible product, as we have attempted to sketch it.

Furthermore, worth varies with age, sex, family status, and state of employment. The adult mainstay of a dependent family has a large economic value; the old person retired from service has, in the cold-blooded economic terms we are using, a negative value: and the child is an immediate liability, while his value as a future asset raises difficult questions of principle. The wiping out of a family with a

[1] Of course the ultimate incidence of such a death is untraceable. The girl who would otherwise have married John Smith is very likely to marry Thomas Jones. Thereby she may save him (or in the ultimate issue William Brown) from being a bachelor, but increases by the same token his economic burdens. Or she or some other girl may remain unmarried, in which case there is some doubt whether her economic status is worse or better than if she had found a mate to "support" her while she did housework instead of working for pay outside the home. A large disproportion between the sexes, such as results in a country which has felt the worst war can do, must needs operate mainly to increase the number of single women. The American casualties were not great enough to make it at all certain that they operated in this way.

normal quota of dependents and workers would involve costs of burial and a moderate cost of industrial readjustment; but aside from this it could hardly be said to impose any economic burden on the remaining community; at least in the United States. But take the same number of persons, of the same ages, sexes, and economic conditions, from as many *different* families, and each death *may* involve an economic loss to the remaining members of the family affected.

The particular group with which we have most concern is a highly selected one, consisting almost entirely of males, most of them little over twenty at the outbreak of the War, with the normal quota of dependent or potentially dependent parents but with relatively few wives or children to suffer direct economic loss by their deaths. This last was a matter of selection in the draft, which preferred for immediate service those without dependent families. In the main, we may assume that these young men had simply not yet acquired the families which they would have acquired a little later; but to some slight extent there was undoubtedly selection of those who were destined for various reasons never to have families, or to have small ones. We shall see later that this makes some slight difference in estimating the economic loss suffered by the dependents who were left.

This is the group in which the war deaths and disabilities were concentrated. The general civilian population probably suffered a slightly increased industrial accident rate by reason of the unfamiliar and dangerous processes in war industries; and also suffered heavily from the influenza epidemic, which was probably intensified by war-time conditions. But the precise degree to which the War should be held responsible for this epidemic can only be vaguely conjectured. And this country suffered no such civilian mortality and damage to civilian health as did those countries which felt the actual heel of invasion or the pinch of blockade. Thus the losses come from three groups: service persons, industrial workers, and unselected members of the general population. The "value of life" in each case is different. In point of fact, it is not so much the value of life that concerns us as the cost of death.

Numerous estimates of the general economic value of a human life have been made, usually on the basis of capitalizing future earnings minus future consumption. This formula has a simplicity which commends it; but we shall see that it is not entirely suited to the purpose in hand. Bogart cites Sir Robert Giffen's estimate of $3,000, applicable to the losses of the Franco-Prussian War and therefore presumably not applicable to the population in general. He also cites Alfred Marshall's estimate of $1,000, Dr. Farr's of $1,500, and J. S. Nicholson's of $6,250; all for the population of England. The latest and most elaborate estimate cited by him is that of M. Barriol published in 1910–11, which places the average social value of an individual in the six leading countries at the following amounts:[2]

United States of America	$4,720
England	4,140
Germany	3,380
France	2,900
Austria-Hungary	2,720
Russia	2,020

The American figure is equivalent to about $8,000 in post-war dollars of the period 1923–28. There is also a highly elaborate post-war analysis, also by an eminent actuary, Dr. Louis Dublin, computing the value of males at different ages and in two different income-groups.[3] The method is to find the discounted worth of future income less personal consumption. On the basis of these studies he values the male population of this country at 1,144 billions, or approximately $19,000 per male of all ages. Men of the age of most of the American soldiers, in the "$2,500 group," are valued at more than $30,000 on the basis of the latest life-tables.[4] Estimating females at one-half the value of males, which Dublin regards as extremely conservative, would make the average value of an individual approximately $14,250.

These estimates are so amazingly in excess of all the others as to

[2] For the citations of all these estimates, *see* Bogart, *Direct and Indirect Costs of the Great World War*, 1919, p. 275.

[3] *See* especially, "The Money Value of Life and Life Extension," by Dublin & Lotka, *Amer. Jour. of Pub. Health*, XVII, 549–557, June, 1927; also *Statistical Bulletin*, Metropolitan Life Insurance Co., August, 1926.

[4] This $2,500 group is a statistically constructed group whose maximum earnings are reached somewhere between the ages of 40 and 45, and amount to $2,500. Their average earnings when employed are approximately $2,100. It is this group which Dublin takes as representative in computing the value of the whole male population. The present writer prefers an average of $1,500, in dollars of the buying power of 1923–28, to represent the personal earnings of the average male.

raise some questions as to the reliability of the whole process. Yet the discrepancy between Barriol's $4,720 and the $14,250 which corresponds to it in Dublin's reckoning can substantially all be accounted for. As already noted, the $4,720 grows to about $8,000 when converted into post-war dollars.[5] And in the same period real income per worker apparently grew nearly 20 per cent, so that we should expect an identical estimate at present to show a result as high as $9,600. The chief reason why Dublin's figure is higher than this is that it is based on an income scale about 40 per cent too high to represent average personal earnings for the whole population. Adjustment for this would bring his figure to about $10,000 ($10,180, to be exact). It would be brought still lower by the use of a more liberal discount rate than the 3½ per cent which Dublin uses in finding the present worth of future earnings. A higher discount rate would of course make the capitalized values smaller. On the other hand, the value he assigns to women is, as he says, conservative. These adjustments of Dublin's calculation seem to point to something close to the convenient round figure of $10,000 as the present worth of personal earnings minus personal consumption for the average member of the American population.[6] The difference between this and $9,600 is negligible. Thus Dublin's figures and Barriol's are in sufficient harmony to afford ground for confidence in the technical integrity of the process followed.

But there are some further deductions to be made before this figure can stand as a measure of the economic loss which premature death causes to the remaining members of the community. It represents, as Dublin notes, the share of the dead person's future earnings which would have gone to his dependents, actual *and potential*. It includes, in other words, the income which would have been consumed by children who would have been born, but were not. A major part of the loss from the death of an unmarried soldier, calculated on the Dublin basis, is the loss suffered by these nonexistent children whom he might have had if he had lived. And we have already discussed this question and shown reasons for confining our study of economic losses to persons who are actually here to suffer losses of an economic

[5] This does not take account of the fall in prices accompanying the depression of 1929–30.

[6] For the data and computations on which the above analysis is based, *see* Appendix B.

sort. The question makes a considerable difference, because most of the service men were young and unmarried. The dependents they actually left behind were only a part of those they would have had if they had lived; and hence the share of income which these actual dependents lost was only a part of the whole "net income" as calculated by Dublin's process. These men were selected in the draft precisely for the purpose of minimizing economic losses.

To eliminate these supposititious losses of nonexistent persons requires a complete recomputation from the basic data, by a more elaborate process than that followed by Dublin. An abridged form of such a computation is shown in Appendix B, in which the same standard population is used, but the data are sampled by five-year intervals to avoid prohibitive labor. As might be expected, the results are in fairly close agreement with Dublin's for the later ages when the family has reached its final size; but are much lower for the earlier ages. While there are arbitrary quantities and assumptions necessarily introduced, the writer believes that the general character of the process and of the result agrees with common sense in assigning the highest value to the man nearing forty, with a full-sized family, rather than to the man of twenty-five who is just married or on the point of marrying and has no children at all. And the writer believes that this estimate, rough as it is, comes nearer to a scientifically valid measure of economic values lost by premature death than can any blanket estimate of income minus personal consumption. The result is shown in the following table, which also shows Dublin's results, reduced to correspond with the lower earnings-scale here taken as representative.

Age	Value per surviving male (Dublin's scale reduced to $1,500 average earnings)[7]	Value per surviving male, revised computation
2	8,040	0
7	11,330	67
12	15,350	1,900
17	19,780	5,255
22	22,350	5,400
27	22,680	15,300
32	21,550	17,000
37	19,780	18,133
42	17,400	16,850
47	14,460	13,300
52	11,180	10,040
57	7,930	6,730
62	4,855	4,475
67	2,000	2,355
72	—547	137
77		—2,140
82		—2,747
87		—2,160

As will be seen, there is no great difference in the values at the ages when the family is at full size, what difference there is being due mainly to an unavoidable difference in the method of reckoning shares going to dependents. The method of selecting one year to represent a five-year period also produces some distortion upward, which could be eliminated in a more complete computation. The average value per male in Dublin's scale (reduced) is $13,430, while the elimination of merely potential dependents brings the average value in the revised computation down to $7,740 for the hypothetical static population used in the computations. Actual age-distributions would show more children and fewer old people, but would probably not greatly change the total result. If females were reckoned at two-thirds the value of males, the average for the whole population would be about $6,450. Whatever death toll the War is responsible for among the general civilian population may be con-

[7] Dublin's $2,500 group (average income about $2,100) multiplied by five-sevenths. Dublin uses a discount rate of $3\frac{1}{2}$ per cent, which seems unduly low for the purpose. The revised computation uses 4 per cent, but this makes little difference, especially as the method used in the revised computation, selecting one year to represent a five-year period, results in smaller discounts than if every year were separately computed.

sidered to have cost this much for every life lost, in addition to the direct costs of the fatal illness and of burial. So far as the War increased the mortality from industrial accidents, it affected a group whose average "economic value" is probably from $10,000 to $11,000; but the worth of those actually killed by war work and war working conditions may have been materially different from this average.

But nearly all the known war deaths were among the service men, who were, as we have seen, a highly selected group, not only as to age, but especially as to number of dependents. For this group the most complete data available relate to the 85,634 death awards active June 30, 1928. Even among service deaths these were a selected group, since all those who had no compensable dependents were automatically excluded. These men had a total of 125,455 dependents. In 1930 there were 90,954 awards with probably some 135,500 dependents. The average number of dependents for each award is trending upward with the addition of older men. The 1930 awards involved 10,347 widows without children, 11,407 widows with children, 32,746 children, and parent or parents in 65,205 cases representing probably about 81,000 parents in all.[8]

It is not difficult to make up an imaginary army which will fairly well represent these cases, though it will be necessary to add certain types not found in the standard population so far used. By including the married man of twenty-two (childless), unmarried men of ages up to forty-two, and the childless married man of twenty-seven, we can give this imaginary army precisely the dependents of the actual 90,954 (leaving the number of parents undetermined), and something approaching their probable age-distribution, though the oldest are not represented. The result is as follows:[9]

[8] Based on ratio of parents to awards involving parents in 1928, with allowance for reduced proportion of cases where both parents survive.

[9] This table gives the correct number of children, and the total number shown as married is equal to the total number of widows plus the number of cases in which children were left motherless.

Age at death	Status	Number	Unit worth	Total worth in thousands
17	Single	880	$ 5,255	$ 4,625
22	Single	31,857	5,400	172,000
27	Single	9,386	5,270	49,500
27	Married, childless	11,501	6,200	71,300
27	Married, 1 child	12,442	15,300	190,500
32	Single	10,788	4,775	51,500
32	Married, 2 children	4,876	17,000	82,900
37	Single	3,696	4,700	17,380
37	Married, 3 children	1,612	18,133	29,230
42	Single	2,577	4,975	12,800
42	Married, 4 children	1,429	16,850	24,080
		90,954		$705,815

This gives these service deaths an average economic importance to dependents of about $7,760. If the same value attaches to the rest of the estimated 170,000 deaths caused by the war among the service men, the total would be over 1,300 millions. If these additional deaths were prevailingly those with less burden of dependency, and therefore involved only three-quarters as much economic loss on the average as the deaths represented by awards, the total would be 1,165 millions. Including burial costs and similar items, 1,200 millions seems a fair estimate.

To this must be added a similar estimate of loss from disability, which may be conservatively reckoned at approximately 3 billions as of the end of the war; making a total of something like 4.2 billions capitalized loss of earning power due to death and disability and affecting actual survivors. It is interesting to note that on this basis disability is two and one-half times as heavy an economic burden as death.

These sums, however, are "present worths," discounted at 4 per cent, and as has already been indicated, the whole principle of discounting is of doubtful appropriateness as applied to such social totals.[10] The undiscounted loss of income which these totals represent is a total of about 8.7 billions, extending over a period of from sixty to seventy years from the end of the war.[11] For some thirty years after the end of the war the average annual loss (with moderate allowance for future death and disability) may be estimated at from

[10] *See* Chapter VI, above, pp. 93–94.   [11] *See* Appendix B, Table IV.

200 to 220 millions, after which it will taper off probably quite rapidly. If there is a large future growth in the number of disabilities due to the war, the annual losses, and the total, will both be larger than this. A reasonably liberal estimate might place the total at around 10 billions, allowing for future increases.

This is a large burden, though not large enough to constitute a serious drag on the economic power of a nation like the United States. Comparing it with the current federal expenditures for the veterans, we find that compensation and family allowances alone fall short of equaling the estimated loss in income by possibly 15 per cent though in view of the fact that compensation is for life, while earning power ends sooner than this, the two amounts may be nearly equivalent in real value. Including the cost of administering veterans' relief, and of medical and hospital care for injuries actually due to the War, the true social cost of war death and disability may be estimated at some 260 millions annually; or over half the present budget of the Veterans' Bureau. In terms of ultimate aggregate burdens (undiscounted) these additional social costs may mount up to 2 billions or more, bringing the total social cost of death and disability up to some 11 to 12 billions, which is half to three-fifths of the estimated total expenditures of the Veterans' Bureau.

The remainder represents, in the main, subsidized insurance and adjusted service compensation, together with medical and hospital care for nonwar ailments and the share of administrative costs chargeable to these activities. These, as already noted, represent various forms of deferred service compensation. One reason urged for such deferred service compensation, at least for the "soldiers' bonus," is the fact that the service men were working at low government pay while their fellows were making higher incomes in civilian work; and thus the service men made an actual economic sacrifice. The attempt to measure this sacrifice is peculiarly difficult. The statistics do indicate some sacrifice of this sort, but not a large one. For 1917–19, the difference between the earnings of the army, navy, and marine corps on the one hand, and what they would have earned at average employees' compensation in all industries on the other, amounted to about $35 per year per man. This indicates a difference of about $40 between the service men's pay-and-subsistence and rewards in *other* occupations.[12] On this basis the total economic sacri-

[12] Figures are derived from King, *op. cit.,* pp. 56, 60, 152, 164, 361, 364.

fice to be compensated would amount to about 230 million current dollars, or from 240 to 250 millions in post-war dollars. The Adjusted Service Compensation, reckoned as worth over two billions at the time it was granted, would pay this back eight times over. State bonuses alone, to those who received them, afforded threefold compensation.

Such a mechanical comparison has, however, a very doubtful meaning, for various reasons, including the form which the compensation took, the circumstances under which it was, or will be, received, and the fact that it was paid to a selected group. In Professor King's estimates a large proportion of the service compensation—over 40 per cent in 1918—consists of the allowance for free subsistence furnished to soldiers and sailors. This was reckoned by Professor King on a basis of about $220 per man in 1913 dollars, converted into dollars of the current year on the basis of index numbers of the prices of food and clothing. For 1918 it amounted to $375 per man.[18]

The question naturally arises whether this subsistence, whatever it may have cost, was worth this much in view of the fact that the living it represented was one of great physical hardship and discomfort. This question is not one of statistical analysis, and no definite answer can be given. If the allowance for subsistence were arbitrarily cut in two on this account, the economic sacrifice of the service men would be more than trebled. If subsistence were ignored entirely, the economic sacrifice would amount to 2½ billions, and the Adjusted Service Compensation and State bonuses together would still pay it back in the aggregate.

A further question is whether the actual average of wages and salaries in private industry is a fair standard by which to estimate what the service men could have earned if they had stayed in private life. Some few of them—mostly officers—would have been entrepreneurs and not wage or salary workers. All of them were a selected group. They were selected by eliminating the least fit, and by further exempting those whose services were most needed for essential war production. This double selection ruled out some of the most valuable and many of the least valuable. And they were selected by age. This may have made little difference in the case of the less skilled laborers, who reach their full earning power early, but for

[18] Based on a letter from Professor King giving the total figures used.

skilled workers and salaried employees it meant taking men who had not yet reached average earning power. Thus it is difficult to say whether the service men represented a group whose average earning power was more or less than the general average of wage and salaried workers.

Another and more intangible element is the fact that the early years of a high-grade worker are important out of proportion to the earnings he makes in those years, because they are the years in which he is forming his skill or laying the groundwork of later success. To take him from his calling in those formative years may disrupt his career, and in any case is likely to cost him more than the bare earnings he sacrifices for those years alone. As an offset to this, the army and navy are becoming more and more a collection of skilled crafts; and service has undoubtedly increased the earning power of many an enlisted man. For the sake of its own efficiency, the army employed psychologists to devise trade tests the purpose and effect of which were to give men with craft skills the chance to go on exercising and developing those skills. Despite which, one hears such stories as that of an officer to whom was assigned as a cook a man who could not cook but was a competent accountant, and as a clerk a man who knew no bookkeeping but was a good cook. He solved the problem by letting the "clerk" earn his pay in the kitchen and the "cook" earn his in the company office, but not all misfits could be so providentially canceled against each other. On the whole, it seems probable that army service represented more of handicap than of help to the later economic adjustments and careers of the service men, but this can hardly be proved; the matter is one of the intangibles which cannot be subjected to measurement.

To sum up, so far as statistically measurable economic sacrifices go, 2 billions of adjusted service compensation repays them several times over, without counting the other billions that have been spent and will be spent in the future on Veterans' Bureau services not due to war injuries. If these payments are justified it must be on grounds of intangibles which cannot be reduced to sums of dollar values.

One further question will be asked. Is the human loss, on the part of the dependents, heavy out of all proportion to the dollars in which we are forced to measure it? This is quite true whenever the loss falls on the dependents without mitigation or relief. The dollars typically represent the loss of the entire income that furnished the very necessities of life; and therefore they are not the "marginal dollars" of economic theory, but dollars of indefinitely greater value.[14] But we have to deal with a system of insurance and benefits which compensates the immediate dependents and, to that extent, passes the burden on to the taxpayer, in whose budget the dollars become "marginal." Slightly higher taxes deprive him of his least important items of consumption, to save the immediate sufferers from being deprived of everything, down to the most important. If this compensation were perfect, then we might regard these dollars as on a par with any other dollars. As it is, in general, the compensation seems sufficiently adequate so that no widely prevalent life-crippling hardships remain to mock the use of such a yardstick; and we may fairly employ it. But to the extent that compensation is not exact, the human losses are more than the dollars fairly measure.

[14] "Marginal," in this case, refers to the condition before the losses were incurred.

CHAPTER XV

THE WAR AND AGRICULTURE

THE main character of the effect of the War on agriculture has already been indicated, but it may be worth while to give some at least of the outstanding features of the story, as well as of its sequel, which is not yet ended. In general, the War found us a country of decreasing export surpluses, a stationary agricultural population, and moderately increasing physical output of farm products, due to increasing efficiency of farm labor, equipment, and organization. Output was approximately keeping pace with the growth of our total population.[1] And the prices of farm products were advancing faster than those of other commodities, by a substantial margin, and had been doing so for over a century.[2]

The War did not radically change these movements so far as concerned agricultural population and physical output. Maxwell's adaptation and continuation of Day's index indicates a slackened rate of growth of output since the period 1913–15.[3] (Single years mean little; for example, weather conditions made yields per acre abnormally large in 1914 and 1915.) On the other hand, Wolman's study indicates a more rapid increase during the six years from 1918–20 to 1924–26 than for either of the preceding decades.[4] One fact on which not even statistics can cast doubt is the huge increase in exports which took the place, temporarily, of the former decline, and did not reach its peak until 1921–22. As for prices, 1914 and 1915 saw no increase, 1916 saw them rising, but outstripped by other types of products, 1917 saw them soaring and taking the lead in the upward movement, 1918 to 1920 saw them ranging above twice their pre-war level, while other products were catching up with them. Nineteen twenty-one saw them plunge back to only 16 per cent above their pre-war level, while other products suffered far less de-

---

[1] Based on Day's index of agricultural production.

[2] *Recent Economic Changes*, pp. 623–624; also L. C. Gray, in *Proceedings, Amer. Academy of Pol. Sci.*, June, 1931, p. 51.

[3] *Review of Economic Statistics*, 1926, pp. 144–152.

[4] *Recent Economic Changes*, pp. 452 ff.

flation; and the succeeding years have seen this disadvantage continue, though somewhat diminished. Economists before the War would have called it a necessary and normal tendency for agricultural prices to rise faster than those of other things, partly because of the fact of diminishing returns from increased scale of agricultural production, and partly because the methods of production resulting from the industrial revolution and mass production have had less chance to revolutionize costs of production in agriculture. This view is supported by the trend of the whole period from 1800 to 1913 in the United States, as shown in two index numbers prepared by the Bureau of Agricultural Economics of the Department of Agriculture.[5] The price-level of farm products in 1913 was exactly that of 1801, while the corresponding level for nonagricultural commodities had fallen 50 per cent. The difficulties and pitfalls of such a comparison are obvious, in view of the fact that so many of the present nonagricultural commodities are wholly new. But if the charts are taken at their face value, they show that the purchasing power of farm products, in terms of other products, had doubled in a little over a century. The post-war period saw the gains of some thirty years wiped out, and they have not yet been restored.

The war-time demand for American food products was accentuated by one circumstance which made it more than an accurate register of world shortage. Supplies from Australasia and Argentina were not available to serve the European need, because the scarcity of shipping made these long hauls prohibitive. The increase in prices did not occur at once on the outbreak of the European war, partly because of unusually large crops of wheat and cotton in 1913 and 1914, and partly because the demand for cotton at first declined instead of rising. The world crop of wheat was also large in 1915, and the disappointing financial results led to no more than normal American crops in the next two years, with the result that prices soared upward. Cultivators suffered an actual loss on the 1914 cotton crop, estimated at 50 to 75 million dollars, and also on a large part of the 1917 potato crop, this last being due to a shortage of cars to move the crop to market. These were the chief dark spots in

[5] See L. C. Gray, loc. cit.; cf. also Recent Economic Changes, pp. 626–627.

the war experience of American agriculture.[6] The course of prices for the five chief cereals is indicated in the accompanying chart.[7]

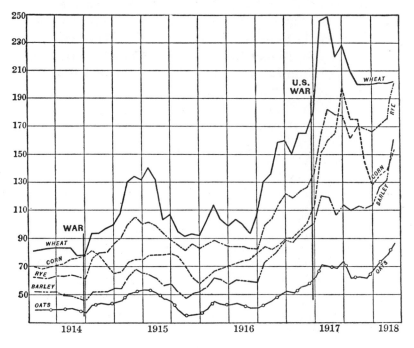

CHART XV.

Prices of Grain—United States.

The war effort is also shown in increases of crop acreage. Between 1914 and 1918 the acreage of our fifteen principal crops increased from 301 millions to 351 millions.[8] By 1924 about half this increase had apparently disappeared from crop cultivation.[9]

As for the after-effects of the War, they have not yet been liqui-

[6] These facts and figures are taken from B. H. Hibbard, *Effects of the Great War upon Agriculture in the United States and Great Britain,* "Carnegie Endowment Series," No. 11, 1919, especially pp. 29–31, 41–44.

[7] Chart XV from *ibid.,* p. 26.

[8] Hibbard, *op. cit.,* p. 49.

[9] *Statistical Abstract of the United States, 1925,* pp. 632–633, table of total crop acreages. These figures are not quite comparable with those of Hibbard.

dated. The prosperity of the immediate war years has passed, and has been succeeded by a prolonged depression which has continued as a large dark spot in our post-war prosperity, and has not been confined to this country. This depression is the result of economic forces which would have acted independently of the War, but the War has undoubtedly increased the difficulties of the necessary adjustment. The situation can perhaps be summed up in a single phrase: production outstripping demand.

As a result, the relation of the prices of the things the farmer buys to the prices of the things he sells has been disturbed, unfavorably to the farmer, after being changed in his favor during the War itself. The Bureau of Agricultural Economics of the United States Department of Agriculture has constructed index numbers of the prices of things farmers sell, and of things they buy, starting with 1910 and using the average of the period 1910–14 as a base. The ratios between these numbers give an important indication, though not a complete or infallible one, of the part played by price changes in making prosperity easier or harder for agriculture. In 1915 and 1916 the ratio fell to 95; agricultural prices were lagging behind the others. In 1917 the ratio leaped to 118, and remained above 100 through 1919, while agriculture prospered hugely. In 1921 the ratio fell to 75, and for the years 1921–29 it averaged a little over 85, while agriculture struggled with deep depression.[10]

From one standpoint, American agriculture is suffering from too much efficiency. Output has increased, with no increase of personnel; but there is not the same capacity for expansion in the world's consumption of farm products as of others. In fact, there is probably less than in any other major branch of production. Recent studies bear out the well-known proposition that a large crop typically sells for less total return than a small one;[11] and this can hardly fail to be more true of a general increase in agricultural production than of an increase in a single crop, which has more chance to displace rival agricultural products.

[10] These indexes and ratios are reproduced in *Recent Economic Changes,* p. 548.

[11] Cited in Seligman, *Economics of Farm Relief,* p. 67, footnote. The proposition that a shortage has more effect than a surplus seems to be mainly a distortion of proportionate changes due to reporting both increases and decreases as percentages of the initial amount.

As the population in general gains power to produce, and corresponding power to consume, it is inevitable that they will not consume proportionately more food by bulk, though they will naturally become more particular about grading, packing, and preparation. They will not wear proportionately more cotton in their clothes—cotton being the chief textile material produced by American agriculture—but may turn to other and more expensive materials. In fact, styles during this period have called for decidedly less goods than formerly, while silk and rayon have to some extent taken the place of cotton. And the very methods by which our increased production has been gained have involved a lightening of muscular effort in the day's work, and have thus reduced the natural requirements of the worker's diet, in terms of calories. We do not need to eat so much, and we seem to be eating less; certainly less meats and cereals, though more fruits and vegetables.

As for export demand, our agricultural exports had long been declining when the War suddenly reversed the movement, and then left us to endure the shrinkage all over again but more rapidly and painfully. Exports of our five chief cereals were 530 million bushels in 1897–98, declined to 168 million bushels in 1913–14, grew to 533 millions in 1921–22, and shrank again to 210 millions in 1925–26.[12] Thus a shrinkage that required some fifteen years at the pre-war rate was recapitulated in four years. In the meantime, wheat production in western Canada, the Argentine, and Australia has expanded as only young and undeveloped regions can expand, and Argentine beef exports have grown to nearly 2 billion pounds a year, while ours have virtually disappeared.

Agricultural efficiency has increased since the beginning of the present century, as measured by physical output per worker, at a rate comparable to that of manufactures, mining, and transportation. And the increase is to a large extent due to the same group of causes: mechanization. The tractor, the combine, corn-shellers, cotton pickers, and many other types of agricultural machinery have multiplied greatly and saved large amounts of labor. With this has gone the development of large farms, the farm of a quarter-section or even of a whole section in the subhumid region being inadequate to support a family, while in some types of farming proper machinery enables two men to handle an area of four sections with some

[12] *Recent Economic Changes*, pp. 551–552.

help at certain seasons. This means a decrease of personnel in such regions, while the taking up of some new land, the raising of other land from range to crop uses, and the general growth of more intensive types of cultivation have kept the total agricultural personnel approximately constant since the beginning of the present century, though since the War there has been a decline of 5 per cent. This in itself means a considerable flow of population from the farm, since this population has not lost the capacity of natural increase.

It is indeed a notable fact that, from the period 1908–10 to 1924–26, agricultural output per worker increased 44 per cent while that of manufactures increased only 33⅓ per cent. It is not without significance that of the four major branches of production—agriculture, manufactures, mining, and transportation—manufactures, the most prosperous, increased its output per worker the least in this period. That of agriculture increased 20 per cent in the first decade of the period, and another 20 per cent in the succeeding six years. That of manufacturing actually decreased 1 per cent in the first decade, as the result of war disturbances, and in the next six years recorded its recovery and post-war advance in an increase of 34½ per cent.[13] The figures for agriculture, however, are slightly misleading, owing to the fact that mechanization has to some extent brought the machine-making, machine-repairing, and oil-producing industries, not classed as agricultural, into the service of farm production. Including a fair quota of the workers in these industries, farm output per worker would not be quite so large.

Mechanization has also had one unfavorable effect on agriculture in reducing the need for feed for farm animals. "It has been calculated that not less than twenty millions of acres have in the last few years been in this way made available for the increased production of other crops."[14]

What part has the war played in all this? Hardly a major rôle, though it has had some effect. It afforded some stimulus to mechanization, though that was bound to come; and also to the effective spread of more efficient and scientific methods of production. And it relieved for a time the pressure of inadequate markets, thus tending to retard the ultimately necessary adjustment.

[13] These figures are taken from, or based on, tables given in *Recent Economic Changes,* p. 452.

[14] Seligman, *op. cit.,* p. 21.

The increase of one-sixth in the acreage of our principal crops, followed in five or six years by a shrinkage some half as great, naturally involved waste of effort and of capital outlay. And no such tangible indexes can really measure the hardships of those drawn into an untenable position in a calling which is proverbially not so much a business enterprise as a "way of life," and as such peculiarly resistant to the adjustments called for to adapt it to commercial changes.

One factor in the situation can fairly be charged to the War: namely, the abnormal boom and subsequent violent slump in agricultural land values. Some such reversal might have occurred without the War, but it would have been far milder. Farmers who bought land at the high prices of 1920, and incurred the high mortgage rates of 1920 to pay for it, suffered a calamity for which the War was directly responsible. The situation was made worse by a sequence of floods and droughts which reduced many farmers to destitution, forcing them to become dependent on relief. While these catastrophes are naturally not chargeable to the War, still, as in so many other cases, it bears some responsibility for the state of economic weakness which made the disasters so hard to meet and accentuated the seriousness of their results.

In general, the effect of the War on agriculture was the reverse of its effect on the country as a whole, save that in both cases it meant more hard work during the emergency. For the country as a whole it meant privation during the emergency and probably some partial recompense in the way of heightened prosperity afterward. For agriculture it meant prosperity during the emergency and heightened privation afterward. This difference in order of sequence is not an unimportant one; indeed, one present-day writer has found in such differences the whole distinction between virtue and vice, alleging that drunkenness would become virtuous if the headache came first and the feeling of elevation afterward. However that may be, the application to the present instance is somewhat marred by the fact that both sequences have ended—if the present is the end—in an accentuated depression.

The consequences of the agricultural depression have been manifold and widespread. One result has been the unsuccessful attempt at governmental stabilization of grain prices. This has left the United States Government with large stocks on its hands, salable only at a heavy loss, and hardly salable at all without wrecking prices which are still in a weak and tottering state. The mere financial deficit involved is no light burden. The losses have spread from farmers to many other groups in our economic organism. In sections predominantly agricultural, such as Iowa, widespread bank failures have been only one symptom of general community prostration. And the loss of buying power on the part of the farmers has been felt in a loss of demand for the goods and services of other groups in general, in all sections of the country. The nation has a stake in agriculture which makes its weakened condition a matter of moment to the whole community.

CHAPTER XVI

THE WAR AND THE RAILROADS

THE character of the war business was such as to place a peculiar strain on the railroads. The increase in general production was accompanied by an increase several times as great in railroad traffic, both freight and passenger, but especially freight. This traffic was concentrated in the eastern section of the country, and this, together with failure to unload cars with ordinary promptness, brought about unprecedented congestion of terminals and tracks in this section and enormously increased the difficulty of the task. Added to this, the winter of 1918 was marked by unprecedented cold and a series of blizzards in the eastern section which threatened at times to stop the running of trains completely.[1] This task was laid upon a railroad system the capacity of whose equipment had for two years previous been almost at a standstill, as well as being somewhat undermaintained.[2] A two-year decline in traffic, covering the fiscal years 1914 and 1915, had not witnessed the building up of reserves of capacity to meet subsequent increases. As a result, the growth of traffic in 1916 brought freight car shortages which, instead of being spasmodic and mostly confined to October, the month of heaviest movement, were continuous throughout the year. For the last four months of 1916 they averaged well above 100,000 cars, and this condition continued through the whole of 1917 and the first months of 1918.[3] The war task of the American railroads was obviously one of the greatest magnitude and difficulty.

The reasons for the condition of the roads at the outbreak of the War were largely financial. In 1911 their economic condition took a turn for the worse. The gradual increase in net earnings which had marked their economic stabilization came to an end, and earnings fluctuated uncertainly with some signs of a downward trend, while the cost of new capital had risen, causing serious difficulty in raising

[1] See W. D. Hines, *War History of American Railroads,* Carnegie Endowment; "Social and Economic History of the World War," American Series, 1928, pp. 39–40.

[2] *Ibid.,* p. 109.   [3] See *ibid.,* p. 267.

the funds needed for expansion. The various rate-increase proceedings of this period are full of evidence to this effect. From 1914 to 1916 the number of freight cars and locomotives actually declined, and while their total capacity increased, the increase was only about 2 per cent in two years as compared to an increase of 80 per cent in the ten years preceding.[4]

In 1916 the character of the difficulty changed. The largest traffic yet handled by the roads brought net earnings to a new high peak, but the pressure of business made it difficult to put cars and locomotives in the shops for repairs. And new equipment took time to order and to build. Largely on this account there is regularly a lag of about a year between an upturn of traffic and the corresponding upturn of equipment ready for service on the roads. Inadequacy of yards and terminals requires even more time to overcome.

In 1917 the roads faced continued car shortages, terminal congestion, and the complete disappearance of reserves of serviceable locomotives. Costs were rising and the necessity of large wage increases was in prospect, while the nature of the machinery for rate regulation precluded prompt increases of rates and ensured that, when received, they would represent conditions at least a year in the past and hence would fall hopelessly behind the needs created by the rapid rise of costs then going on. Efficient handling of the traffic emergency required coördination and the sacrifice of the competitive interests of individual roads, as well as the financing of new equipment which many of the roads could not handle for themselves. Much was done under the Railroads' War Board, but more was needed. To this situation government operation was a logical and well-nigh inevitable answer and the roads were in public hands for twenty-six months from January 1, 1918, to March 1, 1920.

The Federal Administration handled this terribly difficult situation, on the whole, with efficiency and with as high a degree of success as could have been expected. The companies were guaranteed earnings equal to the average of a "test period," consisting of the three years ending June 30, 1917. Financial policies then proceeded with-

---

[4] A chart of freight traffic and equipment, appearing in the *Railway Age*, January 6, 1923, p. 20, is reproduced in the present writer's *Economics of Overhead Costs*, p. 263. Where not otherwise specified, it may be understood that the source of figures in this section is the Interstate Commerce Commission's *Annual Statistics of Railways*.

out the need of safeguarding the earnings of particular properties, or of the roads as a whole. Rates were raised by a blanket increase without attempt to adapt them to the precise needs of the roads in particular regions, and wages were increased without being limited by the need of preserving a fair rate of earnings. The rise in rates was far less than the rise in railroad costs and far less than enough to counterbalance the general shrinkage of the dollar. Thus railroad transportation became relatively cheap, supported by government subsidy, this seeming to be the least burdensome method of meeting the difficulty, involving the least obstruction to the carrying on of war business.

New locomotives and freight cars were ordered, but no new passenger cars, as it seemed physically possible to meet the passenger demand with existing equipment. Every effort was made to keep the whole plant in good repair, though shortage of materials and labor prevented the renewing of rails and ties at customary rates. Carloads and trainloads were increased and traffic routed by the shortest and most available routes without regard to competitive interests of carriers. Incidentally, this probably had some slight effect in increasing freight receipts per ton-mile, as these had been diluted by the competitive hauling of freight over roundabout routes at rates governed by the charges of more direct routes. Such savings, of course, were available only up to the point of congestion of the more direct routes. Elimination of competitive duplication of passenger service was estimated by the Railroad Administration to have saved $60,-000,000 in 1918, while unified ticket offices, cutting down of advertising, and other similar economies from unification of a sort susceptible of fairly definite estimate amounted in all to $110,000,000, or about 2¾ per cent of total operating expenses for the year. Other economies were claimed, but were not of a measurable sort, and, if they existed, were swallowed up in the effects of terminal congestion, shortage of materials and of competent labor, and the tussle with the 1918 winter.

The question of the efficiency of the public administration of the roads is clouded by partisan controversy. It is bound up with the equally controversial question of undermaintenance of the properties. The extreme claim that the roads were returned to their owners in broken-down condition may be dismissed as fantastic; on the other hand the official "accounting test" of maintenance which showed net overmaintenance of $177,000,000 is not to be taken seriously, being a measure of expenditures and not of results. The main fact seems to be that there was undermaintenance, which was settled for $203,-000,000, but the amount of which can never be measured because there was no detailed appraisal of condition at either the beginning or the end of federal control.

The condition at the beginning was itself one of undermaintenance, chiefly affecting the moving equipment and mainly due to financial difficulties. During federal operation up to the armistice maintenance of cars and locomotives was quite well taken care of, with partial exception of passenger cars, where safety and not elegance was the standard set. Renewals of rails and ties, however, fell behind, largely owing to shortage of labor and materials. In the later months of federal control there was deliberate conservatism in maintenance owing to a desire to see to it that the Government did not lose in the bargain with the roads. It was felt that the roads could collect for undermaintenance, while there was little confidence in the effectiveness of the Government's corresponding remedy for overmaintenance. Thus it was thought well to be on the safe side.[5]

The Federal Control Act of March, 1918, required the Government to give back the roads in as good condition as they were received. The standard contract made with the companies formulated an alternative test of the Government's obligation, requiring maintenance expenditures equal to those of the "test period," 1914–17, with due allowance for changes in prices and labor costs and in the amount and use of the property. This was the basis of the official "accounting test," already mentioned, and it was undoubtedly unfair to the companies, since war conditions "resulted in there being frequent repairs at large cost without satisfactory permanent results."[6]

As to actual conditions, former Director-General Hines admits shortages of renewals of rails, ties, and ballast, and deterioration of appearance and finish of passenger cars though not of safe running condition, also some deterioration in freight cars. On the other hand, he claims that locomotives were in somewhat better condition when

[5] For matters dealt with in this and the preceding paragraph, see Hines, op. cit., pp. 111–120.

[6] Ibid., p. 110.

returned to the companies and ran more miles before needing major repairs.[7]

In addition to the need of maintaining the plant in good running order, there is the element of depreciation resulting from age, bringing units of equipment nearer the time of permanent retirement. On this score the war was responsible for abnormally low retirements, resulting in an increase in the average age of cars and locomotives. It was only in this way that the total capacity of freight cars and locomotives was increased, in the face of inability to furnish as many new units as would have been needed for this purpose if old ones had been retired at normal rates. Fiscally, such irregularities are neutralized by adequate and regular depreciation charges which go on regardless of any particular year's retirements and build up larger reserves in proportion as retirements in any year are smaller than normal. Thus the companies did not lose on this account except as depreciation charges may have been inadequate. These charges are calculated on the basis of the book cost of the property, and the cost of post-war replacements was, of course, greater. Thus the companies were left with the need of making replacements at increased prices, part of the excess being, in effect, charged against costs of operation and part added to capital account. During the Federal Administration retirements of cars and locomotives fell short of normal by approximately one year's quota, and this condition prevailed to a less extent through 1917, 1920, and 1921. In 1923 an abnormally large volume of retirements wiped out the major part of the shortage.

On the whole, it is safe to conclude that the recorded expenses of operation during federal control fell short of the amounts properly chargeable against this period by at least the sum of admitted undermaintenance. This amounts to something over 2 per cent of total operating expenses for the entire period. There is a further adjustment of similar character amounting to $101,000,000, consisting of the war-time increase of prices on materials and supplies received from the companies, used and not replaced. These two adjustments together would add some 3.3 per cent to total operating expenses. The question remains whether these costs, with these allowances, show evidence of inefficient operation. The conclusion must be that they do not, unless the especially large rise in railroad wages and

[7] *Ibid.*, pp. 113–115.

prices of railroad equipment and supplies in themselves represent inefficiency in resisting the bargaining pressure of the groups concerned. Such an accusation would be hard to prove.

Freight costs per revenue ton-mile exceeded those of the test period by 49 per cent in 1918 and 81 per cent in 1919; passenger costs per car-mile by 53 per cent in 1918 and 73 per cent in 1919.[8] If the adjustment of 3.3 per cent were evenly distributed, these increases would be approximately 54 per cent and 87 per cent for freight and 58 per cent and 79 per cent for passenger traffic. Average earnings of railroad workers rose 81.5 per cent and 82 per cent for the same years.[9] Meanwhile, hours worked per employee were decreasing, especially for 1919, so that compensation per hour increased materially more than compensation per employee. There seems no doubt that a properly constructed index of unit expenses of items entering into railroad costs would show that the cost items increased in expensiveness more than the increase of operating expenses per unit of traffic. On the other hand, a similar index of general wages in all occupations and general wholesale prices of all commodities would show a materially smaller rise than that of railroad operating expenses. Passenger costs would make a materially better showing if passenger-miles instead of passenger train car-miles were taken as the unit, owing to the increase in passengers per car. But this is only in part a real economy; in large part it represented less comfortable service.

Another indication is the amount of traffic handled per employee-hour. Freight and passengers can be combined in a rough-and-ready fashion by adding the number of revenue ton-miles to three times the number of revenue passenger-miles—a compound unit which has been used on occasion by railroad statisticians. The number of these compound units per employee-hour is as follows:

1916	1917	1918	1919	1920	1921	1922	1923
89.8	94.6	93.6	100	101.2	101.2	103.4	106.8

This shows an almost continuous increase, and indicates no great departure under federal operation from the trend for the whole period. Some part of this upward trend is due to the increase in average

[8] Hines, *op. cit.*, p. 214.
[9] Data from King, *op. cit.*, p. 147.

length of haul, and might be eliminated by a more elaborate traffic index.[10]

If instead of personnel we take total tractive capacity of locomotives as an index of the capacity of the mechanical equipment, the same results are evident. Tractive capacity of locomotives increased slightly faster than personnel, but in the first period, to 1917, traffic increased more than six times as fast, while in the second period, from 1917 to 1919, tractive capacity increased decidedly faster than traffic.

The main causes of this behavior are well known. Up to a certain point, increased traffic can be handled without proportionate increase in labor-power or equipment, but after the limits of the capacity of plant and equipment are reached, any attempt to carry more brings congestion, calling for large increases in labor, while the utmost effort can produce very little increase in traffic handled. The War brought about this condition in those regions where the traffic was concentrated, and especially near the Atlantic ports, where cars were piled up for long distances inland with no possibility of being promptly unloaded and sent on their way. Traffic in 1920 was heavier than at the war peak, and was still congesting the available facilities, but it was more widely distributed; the congestion was not so heavily concentrated at the Atlantic seaboard, and the railroad plant as a whole was able to accomplish more with little or no increase in hours worked.

To sum up, it appears that heavy carloads and heavy trainloads, aided somewhat by specific savings from consolidation, made up for the many unfavorable features of the situation, and that railroad accomplishments rose moderately in proportion to labor-time and materials used. The entire unit cost, however, rose more than that of labor and commodities in general.

This being the case, the federal "deficit"—more properly the shortage of earnings compared to the "test period"—represents not so much a high cost of railroad service in ultimate terms of efforts and materials, as a disproportionate rise of railroad wages and the prices of railroad supplies, and especially a failure of rates to keep pace with the general shrinkage of the buying power of money. It

[10] The writer has tentatively constructed such an index by averaging the one used above with tons, giving tons a weight of one-quarter of the whole. The conclusions given in the text are not materially affected.

was not, in the main, that the true or social cost was abnormally high, but that part of it was financed through the federal treasury and added to the war debt, instead of being financed entirely by rates and fares. Fiscally, of course, this "deficit" is one of the costs of the War to the Government. But for the nation as a whole it represents simply a shifting to a different group of persons of part of the cost of railroad operation, the greater part of which was devoted to ordinary peace-time ends. More accurately, the burden is not shifted to a wholly different group of persons, but to very much the same group of persons in a different capacity and with a different distribution of the load. People paid less freight rates and must ultimately pay more taxes.

It is worth noting that a German economist once concluded, on theoretical grounds, that this procedure would increase the economic benefits secured from railroads, the maximum being reached if rates covered only "variable costs" and the rest were paid out of taxes. He did not recommend the adoption of the plan, since the taxes would themselves be a burden not to be regarded lightly. But to say that the burden would outweigh the somewhat conjectural gains does not mean that the whole "deficit," or necessary subsidy, would be a social loss. If a 25 per cent lowering of rates increased business 5 per cent, the net social gain might be no more than about 8 per cent of the whole fiscal sacrifice. If the direct costs and incidental burdens of laying extra taxes were less than 8 per cent of the net yield, it would be a good bargain. To us, in the war emergency, the balance seemed to swing in this direction; future taxes were preferred to drastically increased rate burdens. The figure of 8 per cent, which is merely illustrative, is reckoned on the assumption that added traffic costs half the amount of the previous rates while the average "value of service" rendered to it is midway between the old rates and the new. This may underestimate the cost of added traffic under existing conditions, and may also err in ignoring the cumulative effects of a stimulus to business. But in any case, economic gains or losses are presumably only a minor fraction of the fiscal "deficit" involved.

Part of this "deficit," however, represented the unpaid costs of efforts and movement of materials and persons actually devoted to war service. This was the part for which war business was responsible. This portion cannot be segregated or accurately estimated. If the nation devoted one-fourth of its resources to war in 1918, this was probably responsible for materially more than one-fourth of that year's railroad traffic. Some of it, such as troop movements, was cheap traffic, but much of it was the most expensive business the roads had, causing the heaviest congestion. The proportion of war business in 1919 was, of course, smaller. So doubtful are the elements of the problem that any quantitative estimate may be out of order, but one-fourth of the total shortage of net return during the Federal Administration might be a reasonable estimate of the amount of true war costs not otherwise taken care of, which it represents. The same principle is applicable to the period of the six months' guaranty in 1920, which cost the treasury $530,468,000,[11] but which contained only a very small proportion of actual war business.

The total cost of the Federal Railroad Administration is summarized by former Director-General Hines at $1,123,500,000.[12] The added cost of the six months' guaranty would bring the total to $1,653,968,000. The treasury's estimate of the cost of war-time control of transportation systems, less assets remaining, was $1,564,-804,444. Hines's estimate is itemized as follows. Shortage in net operating as compared with standard return (all roads), $668,000,-000. Various adjustments, chiefly settlements of claims for under-maintenance, $204,000,000. Compensation to carriers in excess of standard return, $105,000,000. This includes $47,000,000 due to reckoning January and February, 1920, as one-sixth of a standard year, whereas normal net earnings during these months are considerably below the annual average. Director Hines is thus claiming that the standard return should have been figured on the basis of these months' normal quota of a year's earnings. If this had been done, much of the difference would merely have been shifted to subsequent months when the six months' guaranty of earnings was in operation, thus increasing the cost of this guaranty. Increased price of materials and supplies (to the extent that amounts returned to the companies were short of amounts received from them), $101,-000,000. This item has already been explained. Deficit of American Railway Express Company, $36,000,000; miscellaneous nonrailroad items, $88,500,000; capital expenditures for war purposes, $11,-000,000; expenses of Railroad Administration subsequent to return of the properties to the companies, $19,000,000; less credits for interest collected, $73,000,000. At a rough estimate, the true cost

[11] Hines, *op. cit.*, p. 223.   [12] *Ibid.*, pp. 315–318.

represented by all this to the national economy may be placed in the neighborhood of $400,000,000, including the whole of the nonrailroad items, administrative expenses subsequent to federal control, and capital expenditures for war purposes, and approximately one-fourth of the shortage of railroad net return and of other items of similar purport.

As we have seen, capital expenditures for additions and betterments had, prior to 1916, been falling short of the needs of expanding traffic. During the Federal Administration they undoubtedly continued to do so, though the number of dollars expended was greater than the average rate for the six years preceding federal control.[13] The year 1919 saw no such expenditures made except such as were necessary to the safe handling of existing traffic. The Federal Administration did not feel called on to embark on a program of expansion for roads so soon to pass back into private hands; and had it felt so inclined, it would have been balked by the delay and parsimony of congressional appropriations. It did offer to carry out any programs which the companies would approve and finance; but this offer was availed of to only a slight extent, for reasons which it may be possible to conjecture.

Despite the substantial increase of rates which ushered in the return of the properties in September, 1920, the roads faced a long and difficult period of economic rehabilitation. These rates were designed to cover increases in wages which had been granted earlier in the year, amounting to over $618,000,000 annually. But the depression which followed made it impossible to earn a fair return at these rates and at the same time made it evident that business would not stand higher rates; in fact a reduction was needed to stimulate revival. Reductions of wages in 1921 canceled the major part of the 1920 increases, at the cost of a strike in the shop crafts. And late in 1921 rates were ordered reduced about 10 per cent, the roads acquiescing despite the fact that existing rates were not yielding a fair return.

Under these conditions the roads faced the task of reducing operating expenses and making good the shortage of maintenance, of retirements and replacements, and of additional capital expenditures for additions and betterments. This last was needed, not only to provide sufficient capacity to handle normal growth in traffic, but to

[13] Hines, *op. cit.,* p. 127.

provide the means necessary to a reduction of operating expenses and a consequent recovery of net earnings. This was accomplished largely by means of heavier trainloads, which required not only more powerful locomotives but stronger and better roadbed and longer sidings.

This process was begun in 1922 and made large headway in 1923, coincident with the revival of general business activity. During the six years 1921–26, the roads made capital outlays of over 3½ billions, and raised efficiency of operation above the levels previously achieved, either by the Federal Administration or by the private managements before 1918. The course of the decline and recovery of earnings can be seen in the following figures of percentage returns on book value of road and equipment.

1916	1917	1918	1919	1920	1921	1922	1923	1924	1925	1926
6.16	5.26	3.51	2.46	0.09	3.07	3.83	4.66	4.54	5.09	5.36

The roads were now in sound condition. They had built up reserves of equipment which furnish a safeguard against inability to handle peaks of traffic. And while they had never quite earned the return of 5¾ per cent set by the Interstate Commerce Commission as a fair standard, they had been able to attract needed capital without real difficulty. From 1921 on, their rates have been stabilized at levels which almost match the general rise in money costs of living since the pre-war period, and while the wages they pay have risen more than this, they have made up the difference, as have other industries, by increasing output per worker. By 1926, they seemed to have passed out of the penumbra of the war, so far as traceable effects are concerned. Their chief concern was with the inroads of motor-vehicle competition. These have been heavy, but do not seem to threaten the health of railroads in general.

The present depression has renewed their financial difficulties. Their net earnings have shrunk more than those of industry in general, largely owing to the impossibility of contracting expenses proportionately with declining volume of traffic. As a result, the issue of increased rates is again before the country. The effects of the War, then, are not yet fully liquidated.

In a sense, the effects of such a major episode are endless. The return of the railroads was the occasion of a thoroughgoing revision of the federal railroad legislation, setting up by far the most comprehensive scheme of regulation we have yet had and grappling with the problems of labor, capital issues, strong and weak roads, and consolidations as well as with the basic problem of fair rates and fair return. The outcome of this legislation is still unfolding itself. But conditions would probably have forced very similar measures if there had been no war, and any effects the war may have had on these developments must be relegated to the limbo of untraceables.

CHAPTER XVII

SHIPPING AND SHIPBUILDING

THE effect of the War on shipping and shipbuilding may be summarized in four periods. The first effect of the outbreak of hostilities in 1914 was a brief depression due to the temporary decline of trade and paralysis of merchant shipbuilding, which was not then recognized as an essential war activity. Then came a period of intense demand for shipping, while tonnage dwindled under the submarine attacks. This lasted until the American government shipbuilding program got well under way early in 1918. Merchant ship construction in England fell far below normal, since labor and materials were severely limited and were heavily preëmpted by naval construction. Not until 1918 did it recover nearly to its pre-war volume.[1] And construction in this country increased little until 1917.[2] In that year our yards had the novel experience of building ships for foreigners to the number of 41, with a total gross tonnage of about 125,000.

The actual war-casualties of American shipping—the direct occasion of our entering the War—were a minor item in the total of war costs on shipping account. The total "losses by enemy action" from August 1, 1914, to the armistice amounted to 115 vessels totaling 322,946 tons gross register.[3] Total losses of allied and neutral countries were about thirty-six times as great.[4] Even at war-time costs of construction, the value of these American ships lost must have been below $100,000,000, and the value of cargoes possibly an equal

[1] See Fayle, *The War and the Shipping Industry*, Carnegie Endowment; "Economic and Social History of the World War," British Series, 1927, pp. 17, 245–254. *Cf.* also Statement of Lloyd George to House of Commons, August 16, 1917. Reprinted in Clark, Hamilton & Moulton, *Readings in the Economics of War*, Chicago, 1918, pp. 368–369.

[2] *Statistical Abstract of the United States, 1920*, p. 369, figures for seaboard construction. Building in 1915 was low, 1916 showed about 30 per cent increase but less than 1913 and 1914, 1917 more than doubled the record of 1916, 1918 more than quadrupled it, 1919 exceeded it twelvefold and 1920 between fourteen- and fifteen-fold.

[3] *Report, United States Shipping Board*, 1919, p. 37. Salter's estimate is 339,069 gross tons. See *Allied Shipping Control*, pp. 355–359.

[4] Salter, *Allied Shipping Control*, pp. 355–359.

amount. There was also loss of life, but the total numbers were so small as to have no perceptible effect on the estimates already made of war mortality, with their large margins of uncertainty. The losses of ships from enemy action were considerably smaller than losses due to ordinary marine risks. From these latter causes we lost in the same period 278 vessels totaling 405,400 gross tons: many, of course, in trades not exposed to submarine attack. In April, 1918, American and British building began to outstrip losses and ushered in the period of rapid increase in tonnage as shown in the accompanying chart.[5]

ALLIED AND NEUTRAL SEAGOING TONNAGE

Lost and Built

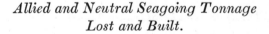

CHART XVI.

Allied and Neutral Seagoing Tonnage
Lost and Built.

At the end of fighting, the American building program was still in its early stages and it continued to pour out millions of tons. With the transfer of German ships to the Allies and Germany's rapid building to replace these losses, the result was an enormous oversupply of tonnage and a long depression both in shipping and in shipbuilding. American shipbuilding remained well below pre-war levels

[5] From *War Industries Board Price,* Bulletin No. 3, p. 34. *Cf.* also Clark, Hamilton & Moulton, *op. cit.,* p. 376.

from 1924 through 1927. Since then the stimulus of federal loans and mail contracts has brought about some increase.

The rivalry of the various shipping nations, especially in the continued building of special types such as tankers, has provided a fair volume of business for the shipyards, though less than the pre-war rate of activity. But while this has mitigated the depression for the shipyards, it has at the same time prolonged and emphasized the oversupply of general shipping resulting from the War. As it has turned out, the type of ship which the War called forth in such great numbers is not the one which the demands of post-war trade would have naturally called into being as the dominant type. It is the "tramp freighter" type, whereas ocean trade since the War has been coming increasingly into the hands of companies operating regular lines, with vessels of larger size and finer character. This, of course, increases the surplus of idle "tramp" tonnage, and emphasizes the economic wastefulness of the war-time construction.

The extreme war demand for shipping did not long survive the War itself. The transporting and maintaining of our own forces abroad constituted a demand which absorbed, at its peak in January, 1919, over 3½ million deadweight tons of shipping, largely American.[6] This was probably not far below the amount actually turned out up to that time under the United States Shipbuilding Corporation. This fleet dwindled more rapidly than it had grown: in four months it had decreased by nearly half; and two months later the heavy part of our return troop movement was practically over, only 133,000 men being left in France.[7] Meanwhile the American shipbuilding program went on of its own momentum, despite such cancellations as were found practicable, deliveries reaching their peak in September, 1919, with 810,386 deadweight tons. The construction program came to an end in May, 1922, with total deliveries of 13,627,311 deadweight tons (or possibly 9 million gross tons), the greater part of which was idle. The vessels built or acquired by the Shipping Board totaled 14,706,217 deadweight tons.[8]

The effect of this on the world's shipping supply was enormous, increased as it was by post-war building in other countries. In 1919 the world's ocean shipping was only very slightly greater than in

[6] *See* Ayres, *The War with Germany,* pp. 37, 39, 40.

[7] *Ibid.,* p. 15.

[8] *Report, United States Shipping Board,* 1929, pp. 126–127.

1914. But by 1923 it was 36 per cent greater.[9] More than two-thirds of this increase was American. Meanwhile demand had fallen off, being estimated at 80 per cent to 85 per cent of the pre-war level. The result was registered in 9 million gross tons of idle shipping out of a total of 57.9 million gross tons for the world as a whole in 1923. This also implies reduced cargo work for the shipping which remained active. Of the idle shipping about 5⅓ million gross tons were American.[10] By 1928 the total idle tonnage had fallen to about 4⅓ million gross tons of which nearly 3 million was American, and some 2 million belonged to the Shipping Board.

America had gained what many Americans had earnestly desired: a merchant fleet commensurate with its commerce, and a carrying trade more or less commensurate. Our ocean fleet had leaped upward from 1.8 million gross tons in 1914 to 12.4 million in 1923, second only to Great Britain's 19 million and between three and four times the tonnage of the next largest national fleet. Deducting idle tonnage, our active fleet was still over 7 million gross tons against Great Britain's 18 million, and was twice as large as that of any other country. This relative position we have approximately maintained. Our total tonnage has shrunk but our active tonnage has increased to about 7¾ million. The remaining idle tonnage may well be rated as for the most part obsolete and no longer worth keeping in the lists of world's merchant tonnage. Many of these ships were admittedly not adapted to the commercial demand—especially the wooden ships, which were a war measure pure and simple and were early disposed of. And others have been economically impracticable from the first. Many more simply were not needed.

By June, 1929, the Shipping Board had gotten rid of nearly 10 million deadweight tons, and still held 4,850,837 tons, of which only 2 million tons were active. Thus the Shipping Board holds a reserve of nearly 2.8 million deadweight tons or possibly 1.8 million gross tons of idle shipping, some of which at least is potentially serviceable

---

[9] E. S. Gregg, in *Recent Economic Changes,* p. 309. Figure for 1919 from *Statistical Abstract of the United States.*

[10] Gregg, *op. cit.,* p. 310. These figures for world shipping are in gross register tons, whereas the previous figures for the American war building program were in deadweight tons. A ship of 5,000 tons gross register might typically rate at from 7,500 to 9,000 tons deadweight. The latter is a measure of actual cargo capacity.

even though out of date. Of the vessels sold in the years 1923–28, in-clusive, something like 35 per cent were scrapped and the rest went into private employment. The question has been raised whether there should not have been more scrapping.[11] The Board has been criticized by private shipowners for keeping this idle tonnage and throwing it into the market whenever a strengthening of demand afforded an opportunity. This, it was claimed, tended to perpetuate a demoralized rate situation by a variety of competition no commercial concern could afford.

The War was the last great day of the tramp freighter. Since then, its importance has declined relative to the liner. And it is the liner that receives the public assistance in the form of mail contracts: a fact which of course strengthens any tendency there may be in that direction. Thus we have a rather paradoxical situation. The legacy of a huge fleet built for war purposes has precipitated us into a position in which a strong urge toward public assistance has been inevitable in order to give our marine, now that chance has forced one upon us, a tenable economic position. Yet the war-time ships are largely unsuitable to this post-war demand, and fresh construction is called for.

Some slight degree of subsidy might have been afforded by selling the Shipping Board vessels at materially less than the prevailing market price, but this does not seem to have been done to any considerable extent. Indeed the collapse of marine values to $30 to $40 per deadweight ton in 1923 left little room for large aid by this method. The Shipping Board vessels cost the Government from about $60 per deadweight ton up to the neighborhood of $300.[12] The $60 is typical of contract costs on vessels which were requisitioned unfinished, while the $300 represents a rather extreme war figure. The whole budget of the Shipping Board, spread over the total tonnage acquired, gives a comprehensive cost in the neighborhood of $250 per deadweight ton, though costs of construction alone were nearer $200, equivalent to perhaps $300 per gross ton. Present construction costs in American yards run in the neighborhood of $400 per gross ton for vessels of a faster and more expensive type, mainly combination passenger and freight ships.

---

[11] *Ibid.*, p. 313.

[12] Crowell, *Government War Contracts*, Carnegie Endowment; "Preliminary Studies of the World War," No. 25, 1920, pp. 204–205.

The Shipping Board seems to have been slow in following the market downward, keeping its prices at first above the declining market level, and so not only preventing large sales but handicapping the purchasers, with the result that some failed, and ships came back on its hands.[13] Some of the earlier sales were made at prices above $200 per deadweight ton, but it was one thing to fix such a price and another thing to collect it in time payments from the purchaser. Actual receipts from the bulk of sales (which may differ considerably from nominal prices) have ranged typically around $25 per deadweight ton, while the remaining fleet stood on the Shipping Board books in June, 1929, at an average valuation of about $16 per ton.[14] In view of the age and character of the ships, these values may not be materially below the general market level, though they represent an abnormally large depreciation from original cost.

The Merchant Marine Act of 1920 contained various forms of indirect assistance to shipping and shipbuilding, most of which have apparently been ineffective or allowed to remain dead letters.[15] Loans to aid construction, and mail contracts, were provided for, and these have been carried further under the Act of 1928. These, the most effective forms of aid, have naturally applied to new construction of vessels adapted to line service. They have not served as means of redeeming the war-time shipping from wasteful idleness: they can only be urged on grounds of salvaging and perpetuating the commercial position in which the war shipping placed us. The idle ships themselves seem to be waste in any case.

It is worth noting that the best of our ships seem to gravitate to the protected trade from coast to coast through the Panama Canal. The movement of American vessels through the canal has grown enormously since the War, taking a huge jump upward in 1923. It suffered a decline during 1916, but in 1918 it was back at the level of 1915, and by 1927 it had multiplied eightfold. This increase has absorbed a very appreciable part of our ocean-going tonnage, largely in coastwise trade. And since our total employed tonnage has been about holding its own relative to that of other countries, it would appear that our shipping engaged in the competitive high-

[13] *See* Gregg, "Failure of the Merchant Marine Act of 1920," *Amer. Econ. Rev.,* XI, 602–603, December, 1921.

[14] *Report, United States Shipping Board,* 1929.

[15] Gregg, "Failure of the Merchant Marine Act of 1920," *op. cit.,* pp. 604–608.

seas trade has been slowly declining despite some increase in our total shipping. This situation has not yet reached a stable equilibrium. It remains to be seen whether the present policy of loans and mail contracts will prove an adequate support. And so far as it is dependent on this kind of aid, our enlarged merchant marine is far from an unmitigated economic gain. We are subsidizing construction which costs us around $400 per gross ton to compete with foreign ships in a rather strenuous rivalry.

World shipbuilding has naturally been depressed following the immediate post-war increases in certain countries. For the four years 1923–26 inclusive, it averaged about 70 per cent of the pre-war rate. American building has done somewhat better than this, averaging nearly 80 per cent of its pre-war rate for the years 1924–27 inclusive; but the showing would not be so good if the pre-war period were extended back of 1910, as the years 1906–8 were years of very large construction. Construction on the Atlantic coast has fallen off heavily, that on the Pacific coast has slightly more than held its own, that on the Great Lakes has declined slightly, and that on western rivers has considerably increased. In general, temporary stabilization has been reached at a level below that of the immediate pre-war period, leaving the war increase of plant capacity to be scrapped or stand idle and most of the three hundred thousand war-time shipbuilders to find other employment.

In conclusion, does the shipping and shipbuilding situation here outlined represent a national asset or a national liability? Are the ships still held by the Shipping Board worth the $16 per ton at which they are valued, or are they perhaps a net liability as long as the idle ones involve some maintenance outlays? Are the other capital assets of the Shipping Board worth their book value (which considerably exceeds that of the ships) or would this capital be of more service if released to other uses? Were the vessels sold worth, to the purchasers, the prices paid? And if they were worth something to the purchasers, did this value merely represent the opportunity to take away from others freight which these others had the capacity to handle in any case, and could have handled more economically if there had been fewer ships with fuller cargoes?

Final and accurate answers to these questions are not to be had. On the credit side there is the probability that the abnormally low ocean freight rates which have prevailed have stimulated some commerce which might not otherwise have moved. On this there may be some "consumers' or producers' surplus" to be reckoned with as a net gain; the commerce was worth more to someone than the freight rate or else it would not have moved. On the other hand, it was not worth very much more than the freight rate or else it would not have required cutthroat rates to move it. Aside from this, the low freight rates are a gain to the shippers at the expense of the carriers. And the sharing of a limited tonnage among more vessels than are reasonably needed to carry it represents a real loss in efficiency.

It would seem reasonable, also, to charge some interest on the post-war commercial assets of the Shipping Board, and add this to the operating deficits. A fair scheme would seem to be to charge interest on the selling price of assets which have been sold, for the period during which they were held; and interest on the book value of assets remaining. This might add a matter of $150,000,000, more or less, to the cost of the War on account of shipping.

All in all, it appears probable that there is a liability balance in the post-war shipping situation; certainly from the standpoint of world economy if not from that of American national economy. This means that the three billions and more actually spent fall short of measuring the social cost of the War on shipping account.

The War also had its effect on the traffic of our inland waterways. Tonnage on the Great Lakes, as represented in freight movements through the Sault Ste Marie canals, reached a peak in 1916 which it has never since quite equaled. The depression of 1921 struck this traffic with peculiar severity, reducing it to less than 53 per cent of the 1916 peak. It subsequently recovered to about the 1918 level, and well above that of any years prior to 1916. The chief decline has been in lumber.

The War brought the Federal Government into the business of hauling freight, mainly on the lower Mississippi and Warrior rivers, also to a slight extent in intracoastal service and for a short period on the New York Barge Canal. On the Mississippi and Warrior rivers —the latter serving the Birmingham coal and iron district—the attempt has been to demonstrate the economic practicability of barge traffic with modern types of equipment, which the Federal Barge Lines installed. Thus the avowed aim is to stimulate private business. On the Warrior River the traffic of the federal lines, after growing to nearly 400,000 tons in 1927, has declined to 254,555 tons

in 1929. In the meantime, however, the Tennessee Coal and Iron
Company has begun using the river for the hauling of its own products. On the Mississippi the traffic of the Federal lines grew to
1,555,000 tons in 1928, but declined to about 1,400,000 tons in
1929. In no case was there any significant increase during the War
itself, and the Federal equipment was not sufficiently developed to
produce substantial results until 1920 or 1921, while even at the latter date terminal developments were incomplete. It might be said
that in this case the War furnished the occasion for an economic ex-
periment which had little bearing on the furthering of the War itself, but was mainly for the benefit of future transportation and for
proving the worth of the channel improvements already made by the
Government. On the lower Mississippi (from Memphis to New Orleans), there has been during this period a very great development
of private business, the total traffic between Vicksburg and New
Orleans increasing from 2,400,000 tons in 1917 to over 11,000,000
tons in 1926, in which year the Federal lines on the Mississippi carried a total of slightly over 1,000,000 tons.

The Federal Barge Lines were under the Federal Railroad Administration while it was in operation and were then transferred to
the War Department. In 1924 the service was placed in the hands of
a publicly owned corporation, and has since then showed better operating results. Both the Federal Railroad Administration and the
War Department showed operating deficits of about $1,000,000 per
year, covering the first seven years of federal operation. The first
whole year under the corporation still showed a large deficit, but a
surplus appeared in 1926 and 1928. Deficits appeared in 1927 and
1929, due to the burden of the recently established service in the
upper Mississippi. From 1925 to 1929 the corporation has had an
average net income of $81,892.39 per year, though 1929 showed a
deficit of $109,728.93 after deducting depreciation. The lower Mis-
sissippi service (where governmental stimulus is least needed) has
regularly showed net earnings, carrying the deficits on the other
services. These figures take no account, of course, of interest and
taxes on the investment, amounting in 1929 to about $18,000,000 in
plant and equipment, or nearly $21,000,000 of total assets.[16] Taking
these into account, even the lower Mississippi lines would not appear

[16] For these figures *see* Hines, *op. cit.*, p. 150, and Annual Reports of Inland Waterways Corporation.

a lucrative investment. A fair charge for these elements for the whole period from 1918 through 1929 would bring the total sacrifice up to more than $20,000,000 on the whole service. The sacrifice in 1929 would amount to fifty cents or more per ton of freight handled, in addition to freight earnings amounting to approximately $3.00 per ton.

Further capital items for the benefit of the service include municipally built terminals, and of course the channel improvements paid for by the Federal Government. Eighteen cities on the Mississippi have terminals built or building representing an investment of something like $25,000,000.[17] Where the federal lines make use of these, compensation is paid on a scale which is stated as affording ample return "wherever freight flows freely over them."[18] The implication seems clear that not all the municipal terminals have proved profitable, though some are stated to have earned good returns.

It is probably impossible to estimate how much of the increase in river traffic is the result of these federal activities, and only a detailed study of the very varied traffic would afford a basis for estimating the benefits received by shippers, producers, and others in excess of freight rates paid. In general, where such a large volume of traffic has been developed, there is a fair possibility that the benefits may be worth the sacrifices incurred. In any case, the sacrifices, and whatever benefits have sprung from them, are among the incidental results of the War.

[17] *Annual Report of Inland Waterways Corporation,* 1929, pp. 10–11.
[18] *Ibid.,* p. 21.

CHAPTER XVIII

THE NORTHERN MIGRATION OF NEGROES

ONE of the definite effects of the War was a wave of negro migration to northern industrial cities, which has resulted in an approximate doubling of the pre-war negro population of the northern states. Between 1915 and 1925 the northern negro population increased by probably something like a total of 700,000 in excess of the pre-war rate of increase. Between 1915 and 1928 it is estimated that some 1,200,000 negroes moved north, though not all of them remained.[1] In 1910 the northern negro population was 1,036,000, and for the previous decade it had been increasing at the rate of about 16,000 per year. In 1916 the first wave of war migration started, and by 1920 the northern negro population had grown to 1,551,000, indicating a movement of well over 400,000 in five years. Local school censuses and test counts point to the conclusion that this rate of increase was maintained, or nearly maintained, in the next five years.[2] And since the rural negro population of the northern states has been actually declining, it can be said that the whole movement, or more, went to the cities.

In the meantime, while the total negro population of the south still showed a slight increase between census years, the increase was so small as to make it probable that there was an actual decrease from 1916 on. And the rural population showed a decrease, even from 1910 to 1920, indicating a larger decrease from 1916 on. Southern negroes also are moving cityward.

The causes of this movement are largely economic, though partly of other sorts. Cotton growing was facing difficulties. The ravages of the boll weevil were increasing during the war years, reaching their height in 1920–21 and causing heavy reductions in yield per acre. Social conditions in the south also created restlessness, and the development of negro publications tended to intensify this and make it

[1] Charles S. Johnson, "The Changing Economic Status of the Negro," *Annals of the American Academy of Political and Social Science*, CXXXX, 131, November, 1928.

[2] Charles S. Johnson, *The Negro in American Civilization*, p. 17. Figures for 1900, 1910, and 1920 are from the United States Census.

more articulate. But the opportunity for the great exodus was created by the demand for labor in northern industries brought about by the War, coupled with the virtual disappearance of immigration from abroad. Changes in the northward movement of negroes have been definitely correlated with changes in foreign immigration, increasing when it fell off, and *vice versa.*[3] They have thus constituted a small and partial offset to the changes in the larger movement of foreign labor to our industrial centers.

The northward movement came in two waves, with the depression of 1921 intervening. For the first wave, the demands of war production may claim a large share of the responsibility; for the second the War can still be held responsible, *via* the sharp curtailment of immigration which followed it, and which it may be said to have precipitated. Both the restriction of immigration and the northward movement of negroes might have come later in any case, but the War certainly hastened and intensified both changes.[4]

One economic effect has been to raise the material standard of living of the negroes, both those who went north and those who remained behind. This is partly offset by the increase in material needs resulting from the change to the more rigorous climate of the north, and from rural to city living conditions. It is estimated that the cost of the New York city government, as indicated in the 1931 budget, lays a burden of $434 on an average family of five—more than the entire annual income of many rural families. Indeed, the increase in material wants and expenses due to city living conditions is one general offset to the increased *per capita* income which our population as a whole has been enjoying. After all due allowance has been made for this, however, a material raising of standards of living remains.

The effect of the exodus on the condition of the southern negro seems to have been wholly for the better. There were attempts to keep negroes at home, and to prevent propaganda and recruiting for the northward movement; but these seem to have exercised slight

[3] Johnson, *The Negro in American Civilization,* p. 36.

[4] In a monograph entitled *The Mobility of the Negro,* shortly to appear in the "Columbia University Studies," Mr. E. E. Lewis of Howard University undertakes to determine the relative importance of the two main elements underlying the negro exodus from the southeastern region, using methods of statistical correlation. He concludes that the push of bad agricultural conditions outweighed the pull of industrial opportunity, for the region covered by his studies. He deals with the exodus, without regard to destination.

restraining effect.[5] The actual decline of the rural negro population created a serious labor shortage; and the effort to combat this took its more permanent and significant form in efforts to improve conditions. Wages rose, naturally, but there was also a general formation of interracial committees for the promotion of closer and more harmonious relations and the removal of grievances.

Hundreds of these committees have been formed, under the leadership of the Commission on Interracial Coöperation. As a result, today "intelligent white and colored men know more about each other than at any time since the Civil War." The committees are working for legislation, schools, civic improvements, more efficient police protection (an element in the prevention of mob violence), hospitals, and "the elimination of petty injustices and discriminations that are the worst feature of the race stuation in the south."[6]

Another effect of the changing conditions has been to hasten the decline of the plantation system in southern agriculture, with its perpetuation of semidependent conditions for the negro cultivators. The ultimate effect may well be to stimulate the development of the more diversified agriculture of which the south stands in so much need. In general, the position and treatment of the negro in the south appear to have materially improved.

In the north, aside from increased wages, the results of the movement were not so uniformly favorable. The increased industrial competition and general friction between the races led to trouble, including bloody race riots in East St. Louis, Chicago, and elsewhere. The living quarters the negroes were able to find were naturally in the least desirable sections of the towns—sometimes in vicious districts. Congestion at first was often quite serious. As the black belts formed and extended their boundaries, there was widespread unsettling of real estate values. Residential segregation of the races was undoubtedly sharpened, since one or two negro families in a white district now constituted a more serious menace than formerly, and stimulated efforts to secure their removal for the protection of the character of the district. Near the borders of an existing "black

---

[5] *See* Emmett J. Scott, *Negro Migration during the War,* Carnegie Endowment for International Peace; "Preliminary Economic Studies of the War," No. 16, especially Chapter VII.

[6] Will W. Alexander, *The Negro in the New South, Annals,* CXXXX, 152.

belt" this was a much more serious matter, and methods of protection were less refined. As the advance guard of the negroes secured a definite foothold, values fell heavily, followed often by some measure of recovery as the district was abandoned to the colored residents.

The northward movement has definitely brought the negro into industrial employments. One unfortunate element was the fact that the first entry of negroes was often made in the capacity of strike-breakers, with the natural result in the form of intensified hostility and resistance. "Steel workers in Pittsburgh increased from less than 100 in five plants in 1910 to 16,900 in 23 plants in 1923—21 per cent of all steel workers in the district. Ten per cent of all iron molders in Chicago are Negroes. In Detroit, there were 11,000 Negro workers in the Ford plant, before its remodeling for the new Ford car, and about the same proportion in the present organization."[7]

One result of the movement has been a reduction in employment of negro women and children. Many women formerly working on the soil are now not listed as gainfully employed. Families moving into northern states were forced to keep their children in school, though improved conditions in the south are also responsible for the marked decrease of negro child labor.

Though the negroes earn low wages, they seem to be in general no less self-sustaining than the foreign-born whites, as judged by the percentage in almshouses. This percentage is, however, heavily concentrated in the northern states, indicating that the 2 million and more of negroes who are attempting to gain an economic foothold in these states do constitute a dependency problem out of all proportion to their numbers.[8] On the other hand, "the Metropolitan Life Insurance Company alone has 2,500,000 Negro policy holders, over one-fifth of the entire negro population, representing eventual assets close to a billion dollars."[9]

Another phase of the movement is the stimulus given to the struggle of the negro for recognition in the ranks of organized labor. Negroes have gained a foothold in labor unions, but are rather typically kept in segregated locals, and these frequently have no

[7] Charles S. Johnson, *Annals, op. cit.*, p. 133.

[8] Niles Carpenter, "Feebleminded and Pauper Negroes in Public Institutions," *Annals, op. cit.*, pp. 69, 73.

[9] Charles S. Johnson, *Annals, op. cit.*, p. 135.

direct representation in governing bodies, being represented through white locals.[10] The northern migration has undoubtedly made this issue more active.

To sum up, the War has forced on the north something like twice as large a share of the national problem of color as it had borne previously, creating large massed and segregated negro populations in the northern urban centers. This has created friction and some serious trouble; but on the whole it does not seem clear that it has been a misfortune for the nation as a whole. For the negro it has meant on the whole a step in the long journey toward freedom and an independent social and economic position—not without its setbacks and hardships. For the whites, it has meant all the difficulties of adjustment attendant on this same process.

[10] *See* Abram L. Harris and S. D. Spero, *The Black Worker.*

CHAPTER XIX

MUNITIONS AND ALLIED INDUSTRIES

Explosives.

THERE is surely a share of the irony of history in the fact that the Great War broke out in Europe two years after the court order for the dissolution of the American "Powder Trust." In the light of the outcome, there was one feature of that dissolution order for which our Government had cause to be thankful during the time we ourselves were engaged in the struggle. While there was a division of plants and business in dynamite and black sporting and blasting powders, the production of military and sporting smokeless powders was left in the hands of the duPont Company. The outcome was that the Government got its smokeless powder during the War at less than pre-war prices; this being made possible partly by the economies of mass production and partly by the use of plants already put in operation to supply the Allies during our neutrality.

Thus the plants that supplied our own war needs were not only in full production when this country declared war, but their cost had been substantially written off out of the profits of the business done for our Allies. Hence there was no need to burden the production for our own Government with any of the abnormally high overhead charges which such a temporary emergency necessarily involves. These facts serve to explain what must have been a unique record in the production of major war supplies. It is difficult to conceive how the war need could have been more successfully met under competition—indeed it is hard to see how smaller competing businesses could have met the war emergency as well, either in promptness of expansion or in economy of production and uniformity of product.

The ultimate result has been an undreamed-of expansion of the duPont interests, reaching out widely into allied fields and culminating in the control of General Motors. A great industrial family has become a much greater economic dynasty.

The production of military explosives required new plants, as the plants producing for commercial purposes were not adaptable to the military types of product. As a result, $220,000,000 was spent for new construction, or nearly 2⅔ times the pre-war "gross capital" employed by the company.[1] Total volume of business including construction, during the entire war period, reached $1,049,000,000, and 1,466,761,219 pounds of military explosives were produced for the Allies and the United States Government. Some two-fifths of the allied munitions came from the duPont enterprises. Military products, which had contributed only some 5 per cent of the company's income, became the dominant factor, and workers and product increased more than tenfold.[2] The sum of $141,000,000 was distributed to stockholders, though Mr. Pierre S. duPont has stated that "taxes paid to the United States Government not only absorbed the entire profit of the company on powder sold to our Government, but, in addition, they wiped out all of the profit made on these powders during the preceding twenty years."[3] The apparent discrepancy between these statements may be explained by the fact that a munitions tax was levied on production for the Allies before we entered the War, and this business was presumably more profitable than that for our own Government.

While the war-time expansion was great and rapid, the company did not neglect preparedness for the return to peace, experimenting with peace-time products for the utilization of the basic materials and intermediate products going into military explosives. These materials—nitric and sulphuric acids, ammonia, glycerine, alcohol, coal-tar intermediates, cotton, and wood pulp—are now used in making a variety of products. One of the war explosives plants has been turned to the making of dyestuffs, using a number of these materials. But in addition to this well-known resource, there are paints, rayon, pyralin, leather substitutes, and a number of other products.

A large part of the equipment for war explosives has not been susceptible of use in these ways, and much new capital has been required for the post-war shift. That the capital has been forthcoming with something to spare is evidenced by the expansion of the duPont interests, especially the purchase of an interest in General Motors, leading ultimately to control. This represents a sort of partial or

[1] M. S. Rukeyser, *Rev. of Revs.*, April, 1928, p. 376.

[2] "War Doesn't Pay," by Pierre S. duPont, *The Nation's Business*, October, 1921, p. 10.

[3] *Ibid.*, p. 9.

secondary integration, as the production of automobiles affords an outlet for such products as paints, varnishes, and fabrikoid, as well as for the forces devoted to engineering development and construction. The duPont organization, in short, has come out of the War larger and stronger than it went in, and the major capital wastes were written off from the business of the neutrality period and are, in a sense, not chargeable to our own participation at all. In this respect this company was unusually fortunate; though their own efficiency and forehandedness played a large part in bringing the fortunate outcome to pass.

Other industries have not fared so well. In general, war supplies which the Allies made for themselves without calling heavily on us, and which we strove to bring into quantity production during our nineteen months of belligerency, afforded less opportunity for war profits and a heavier rate of obsolescence. Some never got into quantity production before the armistice, and the investment was, in the outcome, largely lost.

Small Arms.

In the production of small arms, two outstanding examples may be taken: the Remington Company at Bridgeport and the Winchester Repeating Arms Company at New Haven. These companies met the problem of reconstruction in different ways. The Remington Company built in 1916 "the largest small-arms plant in the world next to Krupps," a $12,000,000 plant employing 18,000 persons.[4] This plant was sold at the end of the War to the General Electric Company, which has transformed it to the production of its varied forms of electrical equipment. Such a transformation obviously involves a scrapping of much of the more specialized machinery, though some of the basic metal-working equipment retains its usefulness. The situation afforded the General Electric Company an opportunity to secure buildings with capacity in advance of immediate demand, in an industry where demand is sufficiently predictable to make this advantageous when it can be done on favorable terms. In the spring of 1922 the General Electric Company was using 30 per cent of the floor space, and expected to be using it all in three years.

[4] S. H. Bunnell, *Iron Age,* May 25, 1922, p. 1434.

The Winchester Repeating Arms Company elected to keep its New Haven small-arms plant and to develop the manufacture of general sporting goods including cutlery, fishing tackle, flashlights, and other articles. Naturally it was not possible in a few months or a few years to develop sufficient demand to utilize fully the capacity of a large military small-arms plant.

The outcome of these and other experiences in war supplies has been to add to the tasks and costs of military preparedness the activity of war planning for industrial mobilization, in charge of the Assistant Secretary of War.[5] Procurement plans are prepared and revised as necessary, with the dominant idea of reducing the time required to reach quantity production. The country is divided into districts and contact is maintained with producers who must be relied on for supplies. District chiefs in the various supply branches may be civilians serving at a dollar a year. Specifications are placed in the hands of potential producers, requirements are estimated and apportioned on the basis of plant surveys, and plans are made for plant conversion and expansion where necessary, with consideration of the problem of what is to become of such enlarged plants after the emergency.

A further feature which it has been proposed to add to the post-war preparedness program is the policy of "educational orders" for munitions, distributed among numerous concerns in relatively small amounts without being strictly governed by the results of competitive bidding. An Assistant Chief of Ordnance is said to have estimated that the resulting preparedness to produce even small amounts might save three or four months' time in bringing munitions into quantity production: a process that consumed from fifteen to twenty-four months in 1917–18.[6] Such a policy would make the peace-time supplies a little more expensive, and would constitute a relatively inexpensive insurance against the stultifying condition revealed at the outbreak of the Spanish-American War, when it was said that only one firm was equipped to make wagons to army specifications; and Theodore Roosevelt had to break the bonds of regula-

[5] See "War Planning and Industrial Mobilization," by Maj. A. B. Quinton, Jr., Harvard Business Rev., October, 1930, pp. 8–17.

[6] Brigadier General Ruggles, cited by Robert Dougan in The Nation's Business, March, 1930, p. 144.

tions to secure wagons for his regiment of "rough-riders."[7] "Educational orders" naturally involve some added expense, but this expense is a part of the logical procedure if we are to have an army at all. For its primary function is to serve as a nucleus for the most rapid possible expansion in the event of war.

Dyestuffs.

The War forced the United States into the production of dyestuffs by cutting off supplies from Germany, which had previously held a virtual monopoly in this industry. As a result, our supplies for some years were very inadequate and of extremely uncertain quality. In 1916 the textile industry narrowly escaped curtailment for lack of dyes, and was forced to many expedients to eke out available supplies. One obstacle to development lay in the fact that there were many German-owned patents in this country which were held unused. After our entry into the War, these patents were taken over and placed in American hands by the Alien Property Custodian, thus greatly facilitating the development of the industry. By the end of the War our domestic production was meeting the domestic demand quite adequately as to quantity, and was rapidly approaching satisfactory quality. Our industry had had protection more effective than the most stringent tariffs; and this had been sufficient to overcome the natural handicaps to starting a new industry. Tariff protection had also been furnished, but it is doubtful if it had any great effect. We had been forced to disregard the prestige of the German products, and the belief that our coal-tars were not of the requisite quality. The supposed decisive superiority of German chemical genius in this field was, temporarily at least, discounted by the appropriation of the German patents.

The question remained whether the new industry could survive German competition after the War. Aside from the natural urge to protect any industry once established, if not fatally handicapped, the War had greatly strengthened the desire for national self-sufficiency as a means of guarding against the disturbance resulting from the cutting off of sources of supply in time of war. But stronger than this was the consideration that dyestuffs and explo-

[7] The writer is here relying on personal recollection of a contemporary article.

sives are allied products, in the sense that they require many of the same intermediate products in their manufacture. As a result, a strong dyestuffs industry affords a valuable starting point for expansion in the production of military explosives, and is regarded as one of the "key industries" from the standpoint of economic preparedness for war, as well as for the textile industry.

On the coming of peace, the policy of emergency protection was continued, to be followed by substantial safeguards in the tariff act of 1922. Under these safeguards, production has expanded, and we are now exporting more than we import, though the industry is mainly carried on for the domestic market. Naturally, this state of affairs imposes some burdens on the consumer; presumably considerably more than the tariff duties collected on the small amounts which come in over the tariff wall. The precise amount of such burdens is hardly susceptible of measurement; but as dyes constitute a relatively small part of the cost of the goods they enter into, the burden is not heavily felt, even though its aggregate amount may be substantial.

While prices are above the pre-war level, the excess does not seem to be more than the rise of prices in general. The Tariff Board's index of domestic dye prices stood at $1.26 per pound in 1917, at 60 cents in 1922, and averaged 41 cents for 1926–28.[8] Prices in 1913, for imported dyes, as judged by one large and representative sample, averaged in the neighborhood of 33 cents per pound.[9] This does not seem to leave much room for heavy increases of price due to the protective duties, when the general shrinkage of the dollar has been allowed for.

As for the burden on the ultimate consumer, the whole value of our domestic consumption of dyestuffs—about 75 million pounds at 41 cents per pound—comes to a little over 30 million dollars per year. This may be compared to more than 5 billions' worth of textile mill products for 1925, most of which were dyed. The figures include some duplication, but on the other hand they leave out 1½ billions of value added to materials in the making of the textiles into wearing apparel before reaching the final consumer, not to speak of corresponding items for other final products as they reach the consumer. It appears that the total price of dyes is a fraction of 1 per cent—

[8] *Annual Report of Tariff Commission*, 1929, p. 56.
[9] *Tariff Information Series*, No. 2, p. 20.

possibly half of 1 per cent—of the ultimate price of the consumable products into which they go.[10] The cost to the consumer of sustaining the domestic dye industry is a fraction of that fraction. It is merged in the general burden of protection, which has been increased as a result of the War. This total burden is not negligible, but the part due to dyestuffs may fairly be considered so.

In this connection it is appropriate to mention the great dam, power plant, and nitrogen fixation enterprise at Muscle Shoals. This was a war enterprise, which did not reach the stage of production in time to contribute to the contest. Parts of it are capable of peace-time service, but its ultimate destiny has not yet been decided. The fertilizer plant, which was to furnish the peace-time outlet for the nitrogen produced, has already been rendered obsolete by the developments of the art.

Glass.

One industry greatly stimulated and permanently affected by the War is the production of glass. At least two small divisions of the industry, those of optical and photographic glass, are essential to the production of growingly important military equipment—field glasses, telescopic sights, range finders, periscopes, and cameras for making maps from airplanes. For the most part, however, the effect of the War resulted from the cutting off of our normal commercial supplies from Germany, France, England, Austria, and Belgium. Belgium was before the War our largest source of imported plate and window glass.

Before the War, this country possessed a fairly strong glass industry, but one which was mainly devoted to the commoner grades of product and left the higher qualities to be imported from abroad.[11] The strength of our industry, as is so often the case, lay in mechanical equipment and methods, its weakness in scientific research and that knowledge of the essential chemistry and physics of its product which is essential to the higher achievements of quality, reliability, and precision.

In the making of optical glass, the Bausch & Lomb Optical Com-

---

[10] This impression is also borne out by a table showing the cost of dyes in cents for various garments. *See* United States Tariff Commission, *Annual Report*, 1926, p. 36.

[11] *Tariff Information Series*, No. 5, p. 10. The statements in this section are mainly based on the findings of this survey.

pany was a pioneer, building an experimental plant as early as 1912. By the end of 1914, foreign supplies were becoming uncertain, and two other concerns, Keuffel & Esser and the Spencer Lens Company, began experiments in the field, as did also the Bureau of Standards. By the time of our entry into the War, the situation was critical, and the geophysical laboratory of the Carnegie Institution at Washington placed an experimental detail in the Bausch & Lomb plant, later extending their work to the Spencer Lens Company and the Pittsburgh Plate Glass Company, which became the largest producer. By 1918, large quantities were being produced, equal in quality in most respects to the best European product. This development of the necessary knowledge and technique was gained only at very considerable expense.

Optical glass was admitted free of duty before the War, but since 1922 has been protected.[12] There was a flood of imports after the War, but this reached its height in 1920, and had declined very heavily before the duties went into effect. Since then they have fluctuated at levels below 10 per cent of the domestic production. Prices, strangely enough, reached their minimum in 1923, after the imposition of the duty. While domestic output has been maintained, the number of producers has declined. In 1926 there were but two and in 1929 the Tariff Commission was informed that there was but one. In such a case, lacking domestic competition, the fairness of the protective duty becomes a peculiarly critical matter for the consumer, whom the War has blessed with the burden of supporting one more tariff-protected industry. Fortunately, the whole amount at stake is small; a few million dollars would buy our entire annual consumption. The small size of the industry presumably accounts for the abandonment of competitive production. These abandonments by concerns which invested capital and development expenses during the War undoubtedly involve some loss of capital, chargeable as one of the social costs of the War.

In all, twelve new branches of the glass industry were established in this country during the War: optical glass, laboratory or chemical ware, gauge tubing, watch crystals, glazing glass, oven glass, glass brick, siphon bottles, photographic glass, high-grade picture glass, and glass for spectacles. Other branches of manufacture re-

[12] Data for this paragraph are from *Summary of Tariff Information,* 1929, pp. 551–552.

ceived material stimulus. Between 1914 and 1917 total imports declined from $8,200,000 to $2,225,000, while exports increased from $3,700,000 to $5,500,000; a net change of nearly $16,000,000 without allowing for changing prices. This represented, however, a small proportion of our total domestic production, which was very nearly on a self-sufficing basis.

Tariff protection had been reduced under the Act of 1913, standing at an average level of about 37 per cent *ad valorem* in 1914. Protection was made higher under the Act of 1922. The domestic industry has increased along with the general expansion of American business, and imports remain a relatively minor item. The demand for plate and window glass has grown, not only with the increased building operations following 1921, but also as a result of increased standards of lighting.

Special Metals and Minerals Group.

A group of minor metals and minerals particularly affected by the War includes antimony, chromite, graphite, magnesite, potash, pyrites and sulphur, quicksilver, and tungsten.[13] All of this group except potash have direct military uses, and potash was an "essential" war product. In each case we were dependent on foreign supplies before the War, and the War resulted in stimulating domestic production in the face of handicaps in respect to cost of production. In several cases this situation was purely temporary and we have gone back to our condition of dependence on imports, with no attempt at protection of domestic production. In this class may be placed chromite, potash, and pyrites. Some potash is capable of being extracted as a by-product from the dust of cement mills and blast furnaces, but apparently not enough to satisfy our demand. A certain amount was extracted from kelp during the War, and the equipment for this purpose was a loss after the coming of peace. Antimony might also be placed in this class, as there is little home production except as a by-product of lead and of recovery from scrap; sources which yield about half our requirements. Domestic smelting of foreign ores declined after 1918, but is protected by a moderate duty. In the cases of antimony, chromite, and potash, our

[13] For this group see *Tariff Information Series,* No. 21, also *Summary of Tariff Information,* 1929.

deposits are not sufficient to sustain a permanent industry, and are better kept as reserves for emergency use.

In some cases the war development has actually strengthened our industry, while in others the mere lapse of time has brought nearer the exhaustion of the richest or most advantageous foreign sources of supply, and made it appear that our industry may soon be able to compete effectively. In some cases the amount of capital invested may in itself have been an effective argument for sustaining the industry by protection. In any case, the War has left us a legacy of new protection, or increased protection, in graphite, magnesite, manganese, quicksilver, and tungsten, and low protection for the smelting of antimony. The Government also afforded special relief by authorizing the Secretary of the Interior to "adjust and liquidate" net losses (not over $8,500,000) suffered by reason of production undertaken in patriotic compliance with the Government's requests, for the sake of supplying the needs of the nation. Producers of manganese, chromite, tungsten, and pyrites benefited by this relief measure.

CHAPTER XX

OTHER INDUSTRIES

Textiles.

THE textile industry has had troubles since the War, and the War played a certain part in bringing on some of these troubles, but there is no way of assigning to it its share of responsibility. The War increased the demand for textiles and stimulated the increase of plant capacity. The industry has since been suffering from a surplus of productive capacity. But this condition is complicated by so many contributory factors that it might serve as an example of the difficulties of tracing cause and effect in such historical sequences.

One is the change in fashions of women's clothing, whereby far less yardage of goods is needed. This was partly a matter of the short skirt, introduced during the War as a measure for economizing materials, with the aid of the Parisian style mentors. The style mentors are now lengthening the skirts again—this measure has been urged for the relief of overproduction—and apparently are encountering more resistance than in the original upward movement.

But if the skirt goes down again, women's burden of clothes will still be a lightened one, for there have been other changes in matters which were inscrutable mysteries to our Victorian forefathers. Would these changes have come in any case? If so, would they have come as soon? Are they due to something in the spirit of the age; a general urge toward feminine emancipation; and if so, did the War hasten the growth of this spirit, and of its material manifestations and its material incidence on the textile industry? To ask these questions is to leave them unanswered!

Cotton and wool textiles have suffered from the shift to more showy fabrics—silk and the newly developed rayon. To what extent is this due to the same spirit of emancipation, to what extent to general prosperity, and to what extent to the contagion of conspicuous consumption by the War's *nouveaux riches?* To what extent is it simply the result of the development of the cheap synthetic rayon fabric? So far as the sale of rayon has cut into the sales of the older textiles, it is interesting to note that this was used as a means of salvaging some of the productive capacity and organization which went into military explosives during the War. Thus the problem of surplus producing capacity for explosives was solved, in part, by developing an alternative product of synthetic chemistry which cuts into the sales of another overequipped industry which is itself troubled by the legacy of war-time expansion. The specter of overequipment is not exorcised but it haunts a different victim.

The difficulties of textiles in New England are in part simply the result of the attempt to maintain the industry in a traditional location at the same time that natural advantages are leading to a strong development in the South. This is something with which the World War had little or nothing to do: we must go back to the Civil War to trace ultimate causes of this movement. It is a part of the post-reconstruction rise of an industrial South.

To sum up, some part of the difficulties of overequipment in the textile industry seem to be due to the War, though no one can say what part.

Coal.

Another industry which suffered after the War from the aftermath of war-time expansion is the bituminous coal industry. But the effect of the War is mixed with numerous other elements which are probably of more importance, especially in prolonging the condition. The industry suffers chronically from more productive capacity than the market will absorb, and from irregular operation for this and other reasons. There is no need to deal with this industry here, as it has been so fully treated in the reports of the United States Coal Commission.

Construction.

Within the construction group of industries, are different groups with somewhat different stories to tell. From the standpoint of source of demand, we think of public works, industrial construction, and private residences. From the standpoint of supply, the grouping is somewhat different. Road building differs more from the erection of post offices than the latter does from the putting-up of an office building, or an apartment building. And the private apartment building differs more from a frame house than from industrial or public buildings that approximate its own type.

In general, the War created a shortage of residential housing, and a falling behind normal growth in roads and other public works. The effect on demand for industrial construction was not so simple, but at any rate the years succeeding the War have seen ample and increasing growth. Activity in the building of roads was probably intensified for a time by the fact that the War had seen expenditures reduced to a minimum. After which we apparently forgot that this was a special condition and went on building at an increasing rate. The mechanization of the processes has, however, prevented direct employment of labor from increasing in harmony with output.

Construction of residential housing felt the stimulus of an existing shortage, but more slowly, being held back by the effect of the emergency laws limiting rentals. Some construction went on even while these laws were generally in force, and the shortage of housing has been made good and possibly turned into a surplus. This has certainly been the case in some districts. This means that there was a supernormal volume of building after the War to balance the subnormal volume during the conflict; but the process of catching up has been spread over a number of years. One incidental effect of the rent laws has been to stimulate the preference for selling houses rather than renting them. In the case of apartments this has led to the development of coöperative ownership. It seems fair to say that all traceable effects of the War on the construction industries have been long since liquidated and that no visible aftermath remains.

The Tariff.

One major economic phenomenon in this country, symptomatic of economic and other conditions, is the tariff. We have seen the sequel of the War in respect to tariff protection in a number of minor industries; and it is typical of the larger story. The War played a subtle joke upon the Democratic party by causing the reduced tariff of 1913 to be followed by a cataclysm which cut off more imports than any tariff has ever done, and afforded far more ruthless protection. It furnished all the stimulative effects of a high tariff and some—in the shape of eager foreign demand for our products—which tariff walls do not afford, but are likely to prevent.

The outcome has been the natural one. The War of 1812 led to protection for reasons partly similar. In the present instance the new industries that have been brought into existence by the cutting off of imports are of less importance than the intensification of the long-standing discrepancies between the American and the foreign economies as to money prices, wage rates, and—so it was feared—production costs. Depreciated and fluctuating currencies added to the motive for higher protection. And for the first time the agricultural interests seem to have accepted the protectionist prescription for their difficulties. The result was the Tariff of 1922; "a tariff with rates higher than any in the long series of protective measures of the whole period"[1]—with the exception of its successor, just enacted. "The special conditions of 1921–22 led to an extreme of protection which few had thought possible."[1]

The effects of this tariff protection may be seen in the figures of imports compared to home production, as given by the Tariff Commission. Running over these figures one is impressed by the consistency with which imports are kept down to a very small percentage of our total consumption, whenever there is a strong domestic industry in the field at all. We are striving for national self-sufficiency wherever it seems reasonably practicable to establish it. In this, of course, we are but following the general course of the industrial nations of the world.

The balance sheet of protection, for national benefit or detriment, can hardly be drawn on a scientific basis. The new element in the present situation, aside from the conversion of the agricultural interests to the benefits of protection, is the conversion of numerous bankers and industrialists to the dangers which may be concealed in it, chiefly the danger of limiting the market for our products, both by placing too great obstacles in the way of the natural means of payment, and by stirring other countries to raise their barriers against our goods. Whether this is one of the causes of our present depression is, of course, a hopelessly controversial question.

Conclusion.

The foregoing brief summary of after-effects of the War lends force to the view voiced by some observers that the War has left us, in common with Europe, overindustrialized. Yet when one thinks also of the widespread "overproduction" and depression in agriculture, the conclusion is inescapable that this diagnosis is too simple.

[1] Taussig, *Tariff History of the United States* (7th ed.), p. 453.

There is no escape to be sought by shifting from industry to agriculture. If the diagnosis be changed to "general overproduction," this is surely beside the mark for countries as poor as those of post-war Europe. And even in this country the unemployed could use vastly more goods of standard sorts than the economic system permits industry to produce.

There cannot be too much productive power, in a country that has mastered the problems of what to produce and how to match the supply of productive forces with effective demand for products. But as no country has mastered this problem, there may be too much productive power for the system we have of bringing supply and demand together. That is one reason for the view that our international credits on account of war debts may be only fictitious gains to our national economy: our power to produce and consume being limited by our imperfect machinery for matching supply with effective demand. This general condition, however, aside from the war debts, and some specific dislocations, is to be charged mainly against technical progress rather than the War. This country would have been trying to produce things in any case, and it would hardly have raised more agricultural products if there had been no war. In all human probability it would have had no more favorable balance of trade, as a relief from the danger of overproduction. It would have had periods of prosperity and depression, though the prosperity might not have been as intense and sustained as that of 1923–29, and the depression or depressions very likely not as severe as the major crisis from which we are now suffering. But all this is conjectural.

With all the overequipment and resulting partial idleness of plant capacity the rather stubborn fact remains that we have produced and consumed more *per capita* than ever before. Presumably we shall do so again, after recovering from the present depression. No doubt some part of the post-war prosperity was due to temporary causes and lacked a sound basis; but that will be an extremely difficult matter to prove, one way or the other. The foreign trade situation up to 1929 relieved us, as has already been shown,[2] of the effects of the *impasse* that results when a nation has an industrial system built to sell exports to foreigners, and the foreigners then take to producing the same goods for themselves.

[2] *See* especially Chapter XII above, p. 174, *cf.* also p. 177.

The facts are not at hand as to the extent to which wasteful duplication of productive facilities has resulted from such international rivalry for export markets on the one hand and self-sufficiency on the other. Our present tariff policy is, of course, spurring the world in that direction. A more self-contained economic system the world over may force us to some readjustments.

The War, as we have seen, gave an enormous stimulus to manufacturing in this country. Some departments were depressed, some converted to war uses, some vastly expanded, and some new industries taken up. After the War, the depressed nonessential industries resumed activity, while the surplus productive capacity in the expanded lines sought new outlets—sometimes at each other's expense, as we have seen. The net effect, however, has been the development of new products tending to enlarge the scope of consumption and absorb some at least of our supposed surplus of producing power.

The problem presented is indeed a difficult one. When we solve it, we shall have rid ourselves, not only of the unfavorable after-effects of the War, but of the far older and larger problem of industrial depressions and unemployment. Toward the solution of this problem, the War can hardly be said to have made any contribution, unless by bringing the evil more sharply into our consciousness it has increased our determination to make headway in dealing with it.

CHAPTER XXI

A FINAL SUMMARY

THE particular industries and phases of post-war experience which have been sketched in the chapters just preceding constitute the weak spots and those affording problems of post-war adjustment. After concentrating attention on them one may well wonder how the nation as a whole can have been ranked as prosperous beyond all precedent at precisely the period when it was handicapped by these weak spots and wrestling with these problems. Therefore it is well to remind ourselves that the nation nevertheless *was* prosperous beyond all precedent, in terms of aggregate and *per capita* product and income, however unevenly this prosperity may have been distributed.

The problem of the effect of the War on this prosperity may be set forth in two questions: have we been richer or poorer since the War than we should have been if the world had remained at peace; and have we been richer or poorer than we should have been if the War had come as it did, but we had remained neutral? The first question can be answered, after a fashion and with all necessary reservations, by an appeal to "normal" trends, prolonged into the post-war period; the second question involves so many uncertainties that it is virtually unanswerable.

As to the first question, it is possible, though far from certain, that the peak of our post-war prosperity was not only the highest in our history but higher than anything we should have experienced if there had been no war. But it is also morally certain that the depressions of 1921 and 1930 cut deeper than any that would have occurred if the War had not disrupted the economic life of the world. And with every week that the present depression continues, the moral certainty increases that the effect of the War in deepening our depressions outweighs its conjectural effect in heightening our post-war boom; and that we have on the average been poorer since 1919 than we should have been if peace had continued. It is even possible that we have been poorer since 1922.

The question of the effect of our participation in the War, assuming the existence of war in Europe in any case, is hopelessly conjectural because it depends on what would have happened had we remained neutral. Would the Central Powers have won the War, and if so, what effect would that have had on our international position? Such questions are probably idle. What seems fairly certain is that our exceedingly profitable neutral trade would have been seriously hampered or crippled, and we should have emerged without the enormous volume of debts owing to us which are hampering the resumption of normal economic relations at present. This might have been a blessing in disguise. And Europe would still, after the War, have been in urgent need of our funds and our goods, which we should have been in a position to supply. Hence there is no adequate reason for supposing that our prosperity would have been any less than it has actually been. Whatever the outcome of the War if we had not entered it, Europe could hardly have been worse disorganized than the Peace of Versailles left it, nor international economic relations more disrupted.

Perhaps the main reason for thinking that the peak of our postwar prosperity was higher than we should have enjoyed if there had been no war consists in the fact that Europe had such need of our goods that she bought them on credit and so enabled us to continue marketing a large export surplus in spite of the fact that we were now a creditor nation and would naturally be receiving an excess of goods rather than sending it out. Thus the process was cumulative, Europe falling increasingly into our debt. We have seen in an earlier chapter that such a credit demand affords, while it lasts, probably the greatest possible stimulus to production; but it is in its essence a temporary condition. The present state of Europe indicates that the process is coming within sight of the natural limits set by the credit capacity of the European nations. From now on, we must probably get on without a large part of this extra and temporary stimulus; and therefore we may have to resume, after the present depression, from a lower level than the post-war trend hitherto would indicate. This is especially true if the international debt situation remains unchanged, since it constitutes a serious obstacle to the resumption of normal international trade relations.

This whole international debt situation has entered upon a new chapter with the "Hoover plan" for a one-year moratorium, on which negotiations are being carried out as these pages receive their final revision. This proposal constitutes the first practical recognition on the part of the United States of the fact that German reparations and interallied debts are, after all, bound together; and also that the terms of the settlements cannot, under all conditions, be literally carried out. Whether the temporary concessions made now will be sufficient, from the bare standpoint of preserving Europe from fiscal and political shipwreck or whether some more permanent adjustment will be necessary—this remains to be seen. The recent fall in prices has automatically increased the real burden of the debts by an enormous amount. And the whole situation increases the uncertainty as to whether it will prove practicable for us to collect the full amount of the payments due us under the terms of the Young Plan. There can be no question but that full collection would be an evil for the civilization of which our country forms a part.

And even granting fiscal repayment as practicable, it is far from certain that we can collect these sums in a form which will mean a net addition to the wealth our nation would otherwise be producing and consuming. There is a large probability that at least part of our collections may, directly or indirectly, displace domestic production rather than add to it. If Europe sends us goods, some of them will compete with our own industries which are now working at part capacity for lack of markets. And if Europe cannot send us goods, she can buy less from us, thus tending to reduce the output of our export industries which are in a similar condition. Our balance of trade is now being maintained by a reduction of Europe's purchases from us: a situation from which we do not gain. Thus the collections harm Europe without clearly and certainly benefiting us. In short, on these doubtful matters of our post-war prosperity as affected both by domestic and international conditions, the balance sheet of the War probably shows a loss, though this may not be susceptible of proof.

There remains our domestic war debt, and the very real and tangible billions of losses from death and disability, whose fiscal counterpart is found in the budget of the Veterans' Administration. This last is the chief clear and demonstrable burden to the national economy remaining from the War. The paying off of 23 billions of war borrowings, with possibly 13 to 14 billions of interest, disbursed to our citizens after being collected from our citizens as taxes—this involves burdens on our national economy, no doubt. But it is not a net loss of 23 billions nor of 36 or 37 billions. Whatever net burdens there may be, they are, if the contentions of earlier chapters are sound, not capable of demonstration or measurement. Aside from the aftermath of death and disability, the measurable national effects were for the most part borne while the struggle was going on. In that respect we were the most fortunate of the major participants.

We were fortunate, first of all, in the period of our neutrality. Instead of plunging at once into the conflict, we had some two years—discounting the preliminary depression—in which we sold munitions at high profits and received a general stimulus to our own production through the diffused and cumulative effects, with the result that we were able to consume more and at the same time to save enormously more; building up without felt abstinence the greater part of the productive plant for munition-making which was of actual service in fighting the War. In general, productive equipment which we had to instal after our own entry into the War produced little effective output before the armistice; and if we had had to rely solely on such equipment, we should not have been able to congratulate ourselves so heartily on our performance.

The year 1916 was notable not only for general prosperity, but especially for the number of very large incomes and the size of the few largest.[1] "Profiteering" was not yet effectively limited by war taxation. The rich had plenty of funds, either to pay as taxes, to subscribe to government bonds, or to devote as capital to essential war production.

From our entry into the War to the end of the fiscal year 1921 this country spent, through Federal, State, and local governments and private agencies, very nearly 40 billion dollars on war demands of one sort or another, of which possibly 35½ billions was on account of the World War, and the rest mainly pensions to veterans of former wars and the normal peace-time outlays of military and naval establishments. Of the 35½ billions some 32 billions represented outlays of goods and services by the national economy as a whole, and not mere fiscal transfers such as payment of interest on the public debt to our own citizens. These war-time dollars may be thought of as roughly equivalent in buying power to post-war dollars of 1922–28. About half of this effort was concentrated in the calendar year

[1] See *The National Income and Its Purchasing Power,* pp. 171, 177; *Income in the United States,* pp. 351–357.

1918, constituting more than one-fourth of our national income in that year.

We have estimated that some 13 billions of this war cost came out of increased productive effort during the years 1917–19, as compared to the arbitrarily chosen standard of the *per capita* level of 1915; and 19 billions came out of decreased consumption, by the same arbitrary standard. The years 1920–21 witnessed a shrinkage in the national output of wealth which would go far toward wiping out the increase in the years 1917–19. Indeed, over the whole period from 1917 to 1922, and allowing for a normal upward trend, it is more than doubtful if the War caused any increase in our national volume of production above what it would otherwise have been, by way of compensation for its costs. On that basis the cost all came out of decreased consumption, but the retrenchment was spread over a longer time than the war effort.

The increased output in 1917–19 was made possible largely because, in spite of fewer workers attached to private employments, there were more persons actually at work in them. This came about simply through lessened unemployment. Furthermore, those in essential industries put in a great deal of overtime. In human terms as well as in money terms, this was more than usually costly output.

The workers who produced it naturally did not receive their full share of the increase—naturally, that is, in view of the need of diverting over one-fourth of the whole to the Government. The purchasing power of salaries shrank by billions, inflicting on this class the most pinching economic burdens borne by any major group. The *total amount* of salaries increased, even in buying power, simply because there was such an increase in numbers working for the Government. As for wages, wage *rates* probably failed to keep full pace with rising costs of living, but annual earnings per worker showed some gains, because workers were more fully employed. In this form of added work done, wageworkers made a contribution which the figures of national income fail to show.

Farmers gained over 5 billions in the years 1917–19, and might be said to have been paying for it ever since. Business incomes, including corporate savings, mounted enormously, though only a moderate increase found its way to individuals as interest and dividends. The true worth of these corporate savings it seems impossible to measure, owing to uncertainties as to the real meaning of net incomes reported in a time of great inflation, and the difficulty of choosing an appropriate index number to deflate them. In any case, the shrinkage of consumption came for the most part out of salaried workers and security holders. The latter paid, not through shrunken incomes, but in loans and taxes. And, of course, they retained their equities in an increased corporate surplus, and some billions of government bonds, on which they probably received as interest something more than they had to pay as taxes to meet this same interest on the bonds held by themselves and their neighbors.

Besides the economic outlays, made at the time the War was fought, in the shape of increased efforts and decreased consumption, there were also valuable coal and ores taken out of the ground and destroyed. Such costs as these bear on the future, and their amount is hardly measurable. But our estimated 32 billions was disposed of at the time. What was left over included a mass of fiscal obligations requiring us to collect money as taxes and disburse it as interest or other forms of payment, all to the same general body of citizens from whom the taxes came, though not in the same proportions. The more material post-war burdens for the nation as a whole consisted of the task of demobilizing industry from war and remobilizing it for peace; and the burden of the dead and injured.

The task of paying off our war borrowings, principal and interest, will probably require a total volume of financing amounting to over 36 billions, which will presumably be disposed of not much later than 1950.[2] The longer it takes, the larger the total amount of interest financing. By that time, if no further concessions are made to foreign countries, we shall have received 5 or 6 billions from them as debt settlements, reducing the burden on our own taxes from war-debt financing to some 31 billions or more.

Assuming that the income tax bears the burden, this amounts to collecting the 31 billions mainly from the wealthy and well-to-do and distributing it to a group whose average wealth is still greater. We might have saved ourselves this necessity by trebling our taxation during the War—if we could. The total amount of tax financing would have been far less than we shall ultimately have to carry out, and this in itself would have been an advantage to our national economy, though nothing remotely approaching the full amount of

[2] This estimate of 36 billions does not include the principal of the reborrowings made necessary by the present depression.

the interest charges we should have avoided. But the feat was impossible; or if possible could have been done only at the cost of imposing crippling burdens on business, or on the masses of the people, or both. The taxes of the rich could not have been trebled, for the simple reason that they were already paying more than one-third of their incomes. The *added* burden would of necessity have fallen with crushing impact on the small and medium-sized incomes. Thus the post-war interest payments represent, on the whole, the lesser of two evils.

The economic burden of death and disability, so far as it can be measured at all, consists first of loss of income to the disabled and to the dependents of the dead to an amount which we have estimated at about 8.7 billions for the present numbers, and which is likely to grow by new cases, possibly to 10 billions. Besides the loss of income there are services involved in administering the relief, as well as hospitalization, vocational rehabilitation, and other services. The total social cost is necessarily considerably more than the bare loss of income. For one thing, it cost a great deal more to administer a transfer of funds from taxpayers to veterans than from taxpayers to bondholders. And there is an inevitable tendency to add to the relief of strictly war losses, taking on the relief of disabilities or other misfortunes not caused by the War. With this there need be no quarrel, so long as it is kept within reasonable bounds.

Thus it seems not unreasonable to estimate that adequate relief, economically administered on present principles, can be had for a total fiscal cost of not much more than 20 billions. This is probably a minimum figure; as for a maximum, none can be set so long as legislative bodies retain the power to grant increased privileges and benefits, and to extend the duration of claims beyond the normal lifetimes of the veterans. If we follow the Civil War precedents in these matters, the total burden will be far more than 20 billions.

In the ordinary course of events, this fiscal burden should have passed its peak by 1946, by which time the war-time life insurance annuities will have terminated and the fund to finance the adjusted service certificates is to be completed, thus removing two major divisions of the expense budget. From that time on the total burden should dwindle fairly rapidly as the number of claimants diminishes from natural causes. It is only on this assumption that it is possible to estimate a total as low as 20 billions. This is entirely consistent with adequate relief of losses actually due to the War though it may not be enough to finance the measures of relief which will be found politically expedient.

By 1950 or soon thereafter, our war debt will, in all human probability, be paid off. By that time, if the outlays for veterans' relief remain fairly conservative, and if no unexpectedly great increase in compensable disabilities occurs, and if the present debt settlements with foreign nations are carried out—three large "ifs"—our Government will have no further net fiscal burdens left from the World War. From then on the debt settlements will exceed the probable cost of veterans' relief, and will go on increasing as the veterans' relief dwindles. From that time on the War may be a source of net income to our Government, if we have the hardihood under those conditions to collect it.

As we have seen, the national outlay of goods and services, made at the time of the War, amounts to an estimated 32 billions, while the aftermath includes debits and credits which may, in the long run, offset each other, if the foreign debts are collected, and if the collection actually benefits our national economy. Even on this basis, the balance up to 1950 will show a shortage of several billions, to be added to the original 32. In addition, there are the vast sums rated in this study as "fiscal transfers."

The whole account could be treated in another way, ignoring the debts due us from abroad on the ground either that they cannot be collected, or that the fiscal collections are likely to yield our national economy no benefit. There is a fair case already for the proposition that, including their share of responsibility for the present depression, the debt payments received to date have done our national economy more harm than good. On this basis we have the 32 billions already reckoned, plus something like 10 billions representing loss of income to actual persons through death and disability, plus actual costs of medical and hospital benefits and of administration of the compensation system. Besides these 42 billions there is an even larger volume of "fiscal transfers." This includes, on a conservative estimate, some 10 billions of compensation to veterans and dependents beyond war losses as reckoned above. A considerable part of this is, as we have already seen, an unavoidable incident of any just scheme of compensation. Other fiscal transfers will include probably some 38 billions, mostly principal and interest on our domestic war debt.

The net burden on the national economy represented by these "fiscal transfers" is, of course, far less than the total of 48 billions, and is wholly beyond scientific computation.

So much for the tangible economic quantities. What of the intangibles? Has the War been a gain or a loss to us in other than dollar values? Any such discussion is necessarily subjective in its standards, to some extent at least; and the best course may be to discuss it frankly from the standpoint of the writer's own predilections. The attempt to discuss it objectively from the standpoint of generally accepted canons faces almost insuperable difficulties. One can hardly adopt the standards of President Harding's "normalcy" as measures by which to judge of normalcy's worth, *sub specie aeternitatis*.

For one thing, the War gave us a proven sense of capacity for national accomplishment which was decidedly lacking before 1917. Then, we were a nation of self-confident people, but we were not a self-confident nation. Too many untested elements had gone into our melting pot. Those of native stock felt that they could answer for themselves and the elements to which they were accustomed, but what of the others? Our ability to control racially heterogeneous masses and masses impregnated with the newer types of radicalism: this was a matter of real doubt. There was question even of the physical hardihood and courage of the Uncle Sam of the machine age. Few would have predicted that we could put two million men in France and twelve hundred thousand on the battle front in successful struggle with Germany's veterans.

We could not have done it with our own resources alone—not in 1918—let us always remember that. Yet it is also good to remember that the thing was done. American-made artillery was lacking and American-made airplanes were few, but our men proved their worth. Our unity under strain was adequate to meet the situation. If the writer adds that he would not have wished it to be much greater, he will merely reveal the fact that he regards the war psychology as a necessary evil in its suppression of normal dissent, hardly less than in its propaganda of uncritical hating. We may feel proud of our performance without rejoicing in these accompaniments of it.

There are curious contradictions in the outcome. The American Federation of Labor, which had seemed only waiting for Gompers' death to pass into more radical hands, returned to the Gompers

standard and elected a man of his general stamp of policy to succeed
him. This looks like a move to the right. And yet American socialism,
because it supported the War and because Bolshevism gave us something more radical to compare it with, came for a time at least to be
viewed as almost conservative. And this looks like a shift to the left.
In the morals of the sexes, increased radicalism is clearly evident,
and the War may well have hastened this movement, though it did
not create it.

The moral effects of war to those who saw service are more important, but harder to determine, than gains or losses in dollars and
cents. On the whole, it seems fair to say that neither the idealism nor
the depravity of war appear to have produced a lasting effect on the
great majority, so far as their everyday conduct is concerned. Some
have probably found the army life damaging to their fitness for the
responsibilities of an individualistic existence. There is plenty of the
economic motive in army life, but it operates on a genially preda-
tory plane: one must watch one's kit against one's buddies. For the
private, the atmosphere is one of irresponsibility in matters most
closely corresponding to the burdens and demands of business or
industry.

There is some disposition to make the War directly to blame for
the recent real or supposed crime waves. This, of course, is a matter
that can hardly be proved. It seems fair to assign the War some responsibility, but mainly of an indirect sort. It may well have helped
to make some of the veterans intolerant of the restraints of industry,
or otherwise to unfit them for its requirements; and a man unfitted
for regular economic existence is a potential recruit to the irregular
existences. In some, the fact that they had been hardened to the use of
firearms and the taking of life may have shown itself, in the course of
a criminal career, in increasingly reckless killings. But modern gun-
men are so young that if we are to blame the War for them we must
blame its effect on the minds of children. Probably a larger measure
of responsibility for the cheapness of human life in certain quarters
is to be charged against the organized and illegal liquor traffic (itself a result of the War) together with the comparative immunity
from punishment and the general weakening of the older moral
sanctions.

While speaking of the excesses of lawlessness, it is well not to for-
get the excesses and occasional lawlessness that were shown by officers

of the law at the height of the post-war campaign against radicals and reds. This has placed some serious blots on our record as a free people. It was one of the least tolerable sides of "normalcy"; and its excesses were directly chargeable to the war psychology. They might well have stimulated an increase of radicalism, had not other forces decreed its decline.

In general, some reaction against Wilsonian idealism was probably only natural. But the violence of the reaction that actually occurred was probably a phase of something wider; a moral letdown after undue strain, possibly reinforced by the generally callous attitude which war promotes and which is described by the phrase, "hard-boiled." It was such an attitude that bred the scandals of the Harding administration; and it is highly probable that the War had some responsibility both for developing this attitude and for letting it make its way into high places. The parallel of Grant's administration is too pointed to be overlooked. But we must not yield to the temptation to blame everything we do not like on the War.

On the whole, the morale of the labor situation appears to have improved during and since the War, except from the standpoint of the revolutionary. There has been more willingness to coöperate, and the growth of employees' representation in one form or another is undoubtedly a step in advance, though complicated by the use of company unions to weaken the power of national organizations of labor. The open shop movement probably did not succeed in doing enough harm to outweigh this element of progress. The accommodative spirit of labor seems even to be surviving the effects of the depression of 1930, despite what use radical propaganda has been able to make of that catastrophe. If another such catastrophe comes without definite steps being taken to protect labor against the resulting economic shipwreck, we shall only have ourselves to blame if the attitude of labor becomes less peaceful and tolerant.

Another result of the War was a strengthening of the forces making for more tolerant treatment of trusts and industrial combinations. Whether this is a force for good or ill is perhaps a matter which no one man should undertake to determine. To date, probably, it has on the whole made for increased industrial efficiency without obviously or grossly oppressive price tactics.

In international affairs, the sequel of the War in this country seems to have been an increasingly stubborn insularity, resisting an inescapable trend toward sharing in world affairs. The fact that this resistance is less strong on the eastern seaboard may be a mitigating factor, or it may only be a cause for the development of an ill-omened sectionalism between the eastern seaboard and the interior. The result has been partially to debar us from the one greatest compensation the War has had for the states of Europe: the development of organizations for international coöperation and adjudication. The Kellogg treaties indicate that we are ready to lend support in our own way, and may mark the shift to a more hopeful attitude. And the present writer would be far from undertaking to decide in just what form we may best make our contribution—if only all contribution be not refused.

Our post-war insularity includes—with those who cultivate it—a thoroughly thick-skinned attitude as to what other peoples think of us. To those who hold this attitude consistently, our post-war unpopularity may perhaps be no conscious loss. But this attitude of abnormal insensibility is itself a loss of a rather grave sort: a harmful defense mechanism against the losses we have actually suffered. For we have lost something; in the foreign reactions to the collection of the war debts, to the invasion of other countries by American capital, to our own intensified tariff exclusiveness. We have not been very actively loved in the past, perhaps; but now we seem to be actively resented, for reasons not difficult to understand. This is a real loss; which can probably be repaired in proportion as we coöperate in the machinery which has been set up for the constructive handling of international problems.

But it is impossible to canvass all the effects of the War, and still more impossible to assess their worth and weight. It was a great calamity; one of which we did not feel enough of the weight to make us appreciate what the rest of the world has borne and suffered. Perhaps one of the most pregnant commentaries on the episode is the fact that our enormous economic outpourings did not bring our real sacrifices within the same range of magnitudes with those of Europe. For us, the remaining material burdens are light relative to our strength, and the most important things are the imponderables.

Here also the War was a calamity, though with compensations. It did not literally turn the clock of progress back a decade or a generation: the effect was not as simple as that. In some things we have gone far backward; while in others the introduction of useful ideas may actually have been hastened. We have learned things, as men must from any great experience; but too often we seem to have learned the wrong things. And we might have had better experiences to learn from. Perhaps all we can be sure of is that nothing has remained untouched by the War. Everything that has happened has happened differently because of it.

APPENDIX A

TREASURY ESTIMATE OF WAR EXPENDITURES

Money Cost of the World War to the United States Government to June 30, 1929.*

[Net expenditures of the United States Government after deducting the estimated value of certain assets acquired]

	Expenditures	Fiscal years 1917 to 1921 Receipts	Assets June 30, 1921 (partly estimated)	Net war cost
EXECUTIVE				
Relief, protection, and transportation of American citizens in Europe	$ 743,776.21	$ 58,694.40	$ 20,000.00	$ 665,081.81
National security and defense, executive, various commissions	15,031,044.90	......	......	15,031,044.90
Expenses, trading with the enemy act	359,998.53	29.90	......	359,968.63
INDEPENDENT OFFICES				
Alien Property Custodian	2,662,729.41	2,688.22	1,363.17	2,658,678.02
Committee on Public Information	2,452,152.39	26,001.21	2,653.65	2,423,497.53
War Trade Board	5,675,384.09	124,902.35	7,606.74	5,542,875.00
War Industries Board	1,957,774.78	154,010.17	3,638.42	1,800,126.19
European Food Relief	94,942,644.91	......	......	94,942,644.91
Council of National Defense	1,924,316.43	267,243.90	23,775.79	1,633,296.74
National Advisory Committee for Aeronautics	739,087.08	......	58.60	738,978.48
Vocational Rehabilitation, including national security and defense	135,745,808.09	4,604.59	2,000.00	135,739,203.50
Federal control of transportation systems (revised to June 30, 1929)	2,276,872,649.03	1 532,959,703.67	2 109,795,290.45	1,634,117,654.91
Federal control of telegraph and telephone systems	13,214,266.47	107,563.44	......	13,106,703.03
Food and Fuel Administrations	21,092,024.77	7,572,642.85	......	13,519,381.92

* From *Annual Report of the Secretary of the Treasury*, 1929, pp. 527–530. This table is based on table for 1927 without revision of receipts and assets remaining June 30, 1921, except in cases specifically noted.

1 Receipts to June 30, 1929, after deducting expenditures since 1921.   2 Assets of June 30, 1929.

	Expenditures	Fiscal years 1917 to 1921		Net war cost
		Receipts	Assets June 30, 1921 (partly estimated)	
Capital Issues Committee	147,966.09	5,346.49	......	142,619.60
Exports Administrative Board	250,000.00	......	......	250,000.00
Federal Reserve Board: Expenses, trading with the enemy act	12,495.38	......	12,495.38	......
State, War, and Navy Department buildings: National security and defense	36,907.23	......	19,604.00	17,303.23
Federal Trade Commission: National security and defense and trading with the enemy act	759,486.13	2,195.96	245.16	757,045.01
Interdepartmental Social Hygiene Board: Protection of military and naval forces and national security and defense	1,028,573.84	308.87	1,845.59	1,026,419.38
United States Employees' Compensation Commission: Expenses in France and national security and defense	80,691.57	45.62	......	80,645.95
Railroad Labor Board	430,597.84	......	......	430,597.84
WAR EMERGENCY CORPORATIONS				
United States Sugar Equalization Board (Inc.)	5,000,000.00	30,000,000.00	[3] 11,370,621.39	[4] 36,370,621.39
United States Housing Corporation	66,500,000.00	7,659,294.11	[5] 30,145,523.40	28,695,182.49
United States Shipping Board Emergency Fleet Corporation (includes United States Shipping Board)	3,316,100,269.06	69,212.27	[6] 280,504,525.98	3,035,526,530.81
War Finance Corporation (revised to June 30, 1929)	500,000,000.00	......	[7] 564,577,716.68	[4] 64,577,716.68

[4] Credit, deduct.

[3] Covered into Treasury on July 15, 1926.

[5] Of this sum $22,438,834.31 was covered into the Treasury during the fiscal years 1922–1926.

[6] Assets as of June 30, 1926 (less continuing costs 1921–1926; figures as of June 30, 1929, not available).

[7] Of this sum $499,000,000 was covered into the Treasury during the fiscal year 1925, and $990,000 during the fiscal year 1929, as a repayment of capital stock. In addition thereto $64,352,768.79 was covered into the Treasury during the fiscal year as miscellaneous receipts "Earnings of War Finance Corporation." If the Treasury made an interest charge against the corporation on net payments (advances) from the Treasury the apparent profit of $64,577,716.68 would be practically wiped out.

United States Grain Corporation	500,000,000.00	450,000,000.00	[8] 25,000,000.00	25,000,000.00
INTERIOR DEPARTMENT				
National security and defense, war materials investigations, etc., adjustment and payment of mineral claims	4,316,697.94	220,652.23	......	4,096,045.71
POST OFFICE DEPARTMENT				
National security and defense, espionage, and trading with the enemy acts	245,266.89	......	......	245,266.89
STATE DEPARTMENT				
National security and defense and other war appropriations	17,063,675.94	24,638.42	70,000.00	16,969,037.52
DEPARTMENT OF AGRICULTURE				
National security and defense, procuring nitrate of soda, stimulating agriculture, etc.	17,378,838.42	1,014,346.71	949,500.00	15,414,991.71
DEPARTMENT OF COMMERCE				
National security and defense, military research, etc.	7,093,658.50	369,127.20	1,071,500.00	5,653,031.30
DEPARTMENT OF LABOR				
National security and defense, expenses interned aliens, war employment service, etc.	12,118,716.67	104,359.27	51,000.00	11,963,357.40
DEPARTMENT OF JUSTICE				
National security and defense, expenses of aliens, etc.	2,941,688.84	58,137.20	96,800.00	2,786,751.64
TREASURY DEPARTMENT				
Bureau of War Risk Insurance	504,773,249.00	....	....	504,773,249.00

8 The sum of $25,000,000 was covered into the Treasury during the fiscal year 1922; on account of the remaining $25,000,000 of its capital stock the Grain Corporation turned over to the Treasury certain foreign obligations received by it.

	Expenditures	Receipts	Assets June 30, 1921 (partly estimated)	Net war cost
		Fiscal years 1917 to 1921		
Expenses of loans	74,769,610.47	......	......	74,769,610.47
Auditing accounts abroad	1,084,546.99	......	......	1,084,546.99
Expenses trading with the enemy act	5,019.10	......	......	5,019.10
National security and defense	4,320,638.55	......	......	[9] 4,320,638.55
Collecting war revenue, tax on estates, munitions, excess-profits tax, etc.	69,617,965.39	......	......	69,617,965.39
Hospital facilities, service, etc. (Public Health Service)	73,109,956.85	......	......	73,109,956.85
Hospital construction (Supervising Architect)	110,000.00	......	......	110,000.00
Coast Guard (see S. Doc. No. 397, 65th Cong., 3d sess.)	8,256,181.00	......	......	8,256,181.00
Other activities under Treasury Department	4,028,493.23	......	......	4,028,493.23
Sale of property, office material, etc. (all departments)	......	1,838,826.68	3,758,000.00	[4] 5,596,826.68
WAR DEPARTMENT				
Quartermaster Corps:				
Pay of the Army	2,819,195,163.64	......	......	2,819,195,163.64
General appropriation (supplies, services, and transportation; barracks and quarters; construction and repair of hospitals; horses for Cavalry, Artillery, and Engineers; inland and port storage and shipping facilities)	6,873,420,115.48	......	......	6,873,420,115.48
All other	88,737,158.99	......	......	88,737,158.99
Medical Department	316,653,619.96	......	......	316,653,619.96
Signal Service:				
Increase for aviation	519,099,186.83	......	......	519,099,186.83
All other	445,909,364.65	......	......	445,909,364.65

[4] Credit, deduct.

[9] This includes $4,465,301.58, representing cost of site and building now occupied by the Veterans' Bureau, less certain credits.

Ordnance Department:				
Ordnance stores, supplies, ammunition, equipment, etc.	575,321,328.31			575,321,328.31
Armament of fortifications	3,203,479,956.17			3,203,479,956.17
Manufacture of arms, automatic rifles, armored motor cars	469,919,699.99			469,919,699.99
All other	189,377,285.21			189,377,285.21
Engineer Department: Bridges, depots, electrical installations, operations, fire control	633,271,951.84			633,271,951.84
National Guard (Militia)	33,822,344.47			33,822,344.47
War miscellaneous (military)	115,362,044.92			115,362,044.92
Sale of surplus war supplies and surplus property		536,571,711.38	294,401,819.54	[4] 830,973,530.92
Due from German Government account of army of occupation (June 30, 1927)		61,313,643.18	158,000,000.00	[4] 219,313,643.18
Transfer of supplies, materials, and equipment to other departments without cost		383,688,380.35		[4] 383,688,380.35
Total War Department	16,283,569,220.46	981,573,734.91	452,401,819.54	14,849,593,666.01
NAVY DEPARTMENT				
Office of the Secretary:				
Pay, miscellaneous	29,624,157.85			29,624,157.85
Aviation, Navy	185,301,332.24			185,301,332.24
All other	2,447,962.19			2,447,962.19
Bureau of Navigation: Training stations, outfits, recruiting, transportation, etc.	95,514,379.65			95,514,379.65
Bureau of Ordnance: Ammunition, armament, batteries, stores, torpedoes, etc.	502,692,026.19			502,692,026.19
Bureau of Yards and Docks	212,751,627.78			212,751,627.78
Bureau of Medicine and Surgery	37,694,883.16			37,694,883.16
Bureau of Supplies and Accounts:				
Freight	44,346,599.91			44,346,599.91
Fuel and transportation	133,872,964.01			133,872,964.01
Maintenance	54,100,822.67			54,100,822.67

[4] Credit, deduct.

		Fiscal years 1917 to 1921		
	Expenditures	Receipts	Assets June 30, 1921 (partly estimated)	Net war cost
Pay of the Navy	613,134,005.34	. . . . . .	. . . . . .	613,134,005.34
Provisions	205,314,070.11	. . . . . .	. . . . . .	205,314,070.11
Naval supply account fund	143,276,476.56	. . . . . .	. . . . . .	143,276,476.56
Reserve material	2,007,016.51	. . . . . .	. . . . . .	2,007,016.51
Bureau of Construction and Repair	144,014,058.27	. . . . . .	. . . . . .	144,014,058.27
Bureau of Steam Engineering	134,095,303.94	. . . . . .	. . . . . .	134,095,303.94
Naval Academy	9,263,459.90	. . . . . .	. . . . . .	9,263,459.90
Marine Corps	165,049,397.04	. . . . . .	. . . . . .	165,049,397.04
Increase of the Navy: Construction, machinery, armor and armament, torpedo boats, destroyers, etc.	10 731,900,271.35	. . . . . .	. . . . . .	10 731,900,271.35
Increase of compensation, Naval Establishment	27,205,433.20	. . . . . .	. . . . . .	27,205,433.20
Temporary concrete office buildings, Navy and War Departments	7,175,489.45	. . . . . .	. . . . . .	7,175,489.45
Sale of war supplies and surplus property	. . . . . .	24,438,785.70	55,000,000.00	4 79,438,785.70
Total Navy Department	3,480,781,737.32	24,438,785.70	55,000,000.00	3,401,342,951.62
MISCELLANEOUS				
Increase of compensation civilian employees	147,416,619.18	. . . . . .	. . . . . .	147,416,619.18
Interest on war debt (1918–1921)	2,746,640,992.03	. . . . . .	. . . . . .	2,746,640,992.03
Foreign obligations (June 30, 1927)	11 9,598,236,575.45	1,743,930,406.81	12 7,470,000,000.00	384,306,168.64
Total	40,021,689,942.45	3,782,587,503.15	9,004,887,583.94	27,234,164,855.36

4 Credit, deduct.

10 Exclusive of approximately $400,000,000 expended under the act of Aug. 29, 1916, which provided for a three-year building program.

11 Represents obligations acquired for cash advances under Liberty bond acts.

12 Payments to be received under the various funding agreements have been discounted so as to show their present value on a basis of 4 per cent per annum, payable semiannually. The debts of Austria and Greece have been included on a similar basis. Obligations acquired in connection with the sale on credit of surplus war material and relief supplies are included.

Fiscal years 1922 to 1929

CONTINUING COSTS

Veterans' Bureau:

	Fiscal years 1922 to 1929
Salaries and expenses	290,092,095.44
Hospital facilities and services	35,718,556.78
Medical and hospital services	255,463,495.48
Military and naval compensation	1,189,481,872.62
Military and naval family allowance	683,385.52
Vocational rehabilitation	493,990,008.62
Military and naval insurance	663,085,288.78
Adjusted service, certificate fund	560,000,000.00
Adjusted service, dependent pay	36,050,040.36
Total Veterans' Bureau	[13] 3,524,564,743.60
Interest on war debt	[14] 6,748,088,779.44
Hospital construction (Supervising Architect)	[15] 17,001,442.13
Settlement of war claims act of 1928	[16] 50,140,293.16

Total money cost of the World War to the
United States to June 30, 1929 . . $50,361,435,200.78 $3,782,587,503.15 $9,004,887,583.94 $37,573,960,113.69

[13] Fiscal year 1922, $329,092,702.77; 1923, $362,855,651.98; 1924, $396,984,419.08; 1925, $483,261,139.23; 1926, $484,481,070.75; 1927, $492,292,610.87; 1928, $474,952,662.22; 1929, $500,694,486.75.

[14] Fiscal year 1922, $968,620,027.01; 1923, $1,034,178,428.77; 1924, $917,883,165.09; 1925, $862,158,336.50; 1926, $815,307,516.39; 1927, $771,604,629.45; 1928, $715,657,257.91; 1929, $662,729,418.32.

[15] Fiscal year 1922, $8,204,064.49; 1923, $6,441,975.67; 1924, $1,976,148.77; 1925, $317,438.89; 1926, $50,383.29; 1927, $22,731.94; 1929, [4]$11,250.92 (deduct).

[16] Fiscal year 1928, $50,000,424.16; 1929, $139,869.

NOTE.—The President, under proclamation dated Nov. 14, 1921, declared the end of the war with Germany to be July 2, 1921, the date on which the joint resolution of Congress terminating the state of war was approved. The figures contained herein are on the basis of warrants issued. They make allowance for estimated normal expenditures under the War and Navy Departments on a peace-time basis, receipts on account of the sale of war supplies and surplus Government property, and assets held on June 30, 1921, a large part of which has subsequently been converted into cash and covered into the Treasury, the remainder being estimated. Necessarily some of the figures represent approximations, since no cost records relating to the war were maintained.

APPENDIX B

CALCULATIONS OF ECONOMIC LOSS THROUGH DEATH AND DISABILITY

THE estimate here made of the economic "worth" of a human life (in the sense of loss due to death) is a departure from that made by Drs. Dublin and Lotka, and uses their basic data.[1] Their figures give the discounted present worth, at all ages from birth to age seventy-five, for the group we are considering, of future earnings minus future personal consumption. The result is taken to show the economic worth of a man, not to himself but to his dependents, *actual and potential*. The purpose of the modified study here undertaken is to eliminate the values accruing to the purely potential dependents: that is, those whose very existence is potential. In the case of a man dying at the age of twenty, not yet married and having no children, Dublin's method includes the value he would have had to his wife and the children who would have been born to them if he had lived. These children do not exist and never will exist, and for that reason the present study undertakes to rule out their interest and estimate only the loss suffered on account of this death by persons actually existing. On this basis the future wife has a recognizable interest, but the future children do not.

Their share nevertheless enters into the calculation, but in a negative way. Considering the young married man who has as yet no children, there are two living persons in the family, the man and his wife —also their parents, whose interest will ultimately be reckoned with. But if the man had lived, his wife would not have enjoyed half his income, because in that case there would have been children to support, and her share would be correspondingly reduced. What we have to reckon is her share, and that of the parents, in the man's income when distributed among a family of normal size and composition. Furthermore, account is taken of the fact that while the childless widow is deprived of financial support, she is also typically freed

---

[1] Since this appendix was written, their material has appeared in book form. *See* Dublin and Lotka: *The Money Value of a Man,* 1930. For convenience, the method is referred to as Dublin's in this discussion.

from the burden of maintaining a family home, and this constitutes a very material credit, mitigating the purely economic loss.

The type of estimate indicated by these considerations involves matters of judgment and guessing which prevent it from being as accurate as Dublin's reckoning of income minus personal consumption. But it seems that a rough and approximate estimate of the factors logically pertinent to the problem in hand is preferable to a more formally accurate calculus which includes factors not logically pertinent to it.

Dublin's calculation proceeds in the following way. He starts with 100,000 children born, and computes the number surviving at all ages, using recent mortality data which give longer life expectancies than the standard American Life Table. He also estimates the percentage of these survivors who are gainfully employed. He constructs a scale of earnings for a gainfully employed person through the successive years of his working life, the rate increasing with age and experience up to a maximum and then declining. Studies have so far been published for the "$2,500 group" and the "$5,000 group." The $2,500 group is one whose maximum earnings per employed individual are $2,500 per year, while the average throughout the working life is approximately $2,100. And it is this group on which we shall base our calculations, scaling down the amounts to correspond with average earnings of $1,500 per year. From these data the aggregate earnings of all the survivors at every age are then computed. Individual cost of living is also estimated, and total cost of living for all survivors. From these figures can be secured the total "net" income of all the survivors at each age. These amounts are then discounted and added together so as to give the present worth of the 100,000 newborn infants, the 92,606 infants of one year, and so on down to the 30,941 surviving at age seventy-five. Dividing this aggregate net worth of each age-group by the number in each group, the result is the actuarial "net worth" of one man at any age.

In his study of the "$5,000 group," Dr. Dublin introduces one difference of treatment. Instead of deducting personal consumption on the basis of a scale of necessary expenditures considered appropriate to the income-group, as he did for the $2,500 group, he apportions the total income on the basis of a scale of adult consuming units in the family. This scale assumes that the man marries at the age of twenty-five, and obviously treats the wife as one full adult unit, but the amounts allowed for children of different ages can only be inferred from the family totals. There is also an allowance for savings, sufficient to yield a fair retirement income from the interest alone. And these savings become, in effect, part of the excess of income above personal consumption which is discounted to find the net worth of the breadwinner to his dependents. This seems justifiable, since the savings ultimately pass to his heirs, with compound interest except for the years when the breadwinner is himself living on the income. And for these years, when the breadwinner is consuming but not producing, he is credited with a negative value which at least roughly balances the amount of interest of which his heirs fail to receive the benefit.

The proposed modification of Dublin's method requires more computation, for reasons which will readily appear. And to avoid a prohibitive burden the observations are taken at five-year intervals, using ages two, seven, etc., to represent the mid-points of five-year groups. It also becomes necessary to follow the method of dividing the income among the members of the family on the basis of adult consuming units. Then, instead of treating the whole surplus above personal consumption as net value, it becomes necessary to calculate for each age the interest of dependents then living in the future income. It is this which increases the number of computations necessary.

For the unmarried male, the persons having a recognizable interest in his future earnings are his future wife and his parents. The parents' interest is, of course, a minus quantity for the years they must support him, and a much-discounted positive quantity for the later years when the parents may, in turn, be receiving support from their son. For the childless married man the potential wife has become an actual widow, and we must consider whether her interest is modified by that fact. Her interest in the current year's income is that of one adult out of two. Her interest in the income of ten to fifteen years hence is the interest of one adult in what would by then be a full-sized family containing, on Dublin's reckoning, from 3.8 to 4.3 adult consuming units.

The birth of the first child adds one more living dependent who has an interest in the man's future earnings, and something to lose by his death, and so increases the worth to living dependents of all his future instalments of income. Having added one child to his

family, the "worth to living dependents" of his income at, for instance, age forty is larger than it was before the child was born, by
just the amount of the child's share. The second child has a similar
effect, and the third, by which time we have the "standard" family
of five, and his net worth to his living dependents, in case of death
thereafter, will be something like the full amount shown by Dublin's
calculation: total income less personal consumption.

The birth of the first child also changes the economic status of the
widow for the worse, since she now has a home to make for the child.
The death of the husband deprives her of financial support without
freeing her from the burden of home-making; and is thus a much
heavier economic loss than for the childless widow. Further, some
account must be taken of the number of wives who die before their
husbands and therefore have no interest surviving the husband's
death; also of the fact that the widow's loss terminates with the
widow's own death. It also terminates with her remarriage, but the
present study has balked at that particular detail of hypothetical
family history, and given the value of human life the resulting
benefit.

All the other matters mentioned, however, are given some representation in the computation which follows.

The general method is to start with Dublin's 100,000 born, and set
down in the first column the number of survivors at ages two, seven,
twelve, etc., and in the second column the total earnings of these survivors, using five-sevenths of the figures for Dublin's $2,500 group.
The third column gives the number of adult consuming units in the
assumed normal family, and furnishes the key to the division of the income and the computation of the dependents' interests, though with
various adjustments which will need some detailed explanation. This
scale of adult consuming units is only one of many parts of the process depending on judgment and estimate. Next comes the estimate
of the interest of survivors in the successive years' income of an unmarried person, followed in successive columns by the discounted
worth of this series at different ages. Next comes the interest of survivors in the successive years' income of a married man of twenty-
seven with one child, followed by their discounted worth at age
twenty-seven. The process is repeated for the man of thirty-two with
two children, the man of thirty-seven with three children, and the man
of forty-two with his maximum family, which we are representing as

averaging 3½ children and a percentage of dependent parents. This column serves as a basis for calculating discounted worths for all subsequent ages, since all the dependents are now represented and there is no further change in the list of claimants to shares in the man's income.

The sum of the "discounted worth" column for any age, say twenty-seven, gives the total worth of the 83,692 persons who are supposed to survive to that age: or would do so if the table gave figures for every year instead of every fifth year. A fair approximation is had by summing the columns as they stand and multiplying by five. This method gives a result which is somewhat exaggerated, and also slightly distorted as between age-groups, but it may serve as a first approximation. The general scheme of computation is shown in Table I, opposite page 302.

The scheme of adult consuming units in the family is shown in Table II, below, which also shows Dublin's scheme for purposes of comparison. While Dublin's scheme allows a larger aggregate of consuming units, the difference is largely apparent, as the present computation assumes that children from sixteen to twenty are still members of the family and that some of them are dependent on their parents for support, but balances this against the fact that the majority are earning something, and some are earning more than their expenses and actually contributing to the net family income. Separate inclusion of dependent children of sixteen years and more would increase the total consuming units for the last four age-periods, bringing it much closer to Dublin's figure. The allowance for the

TABLE II

Adult Consuming Units in Family.

Age	Man and wife	First child	Second child	Third child	Fourth child (½)	Parents	Total	Dublin's total ($5,000 group)
27	2.00	.50	..	..	..	..	2.50	2.2
32	2.00	.60	.50	..	..	..	3.10	3.0
37	2.00	.80	.60	.50	..	..	3.90	4.0
42	2.00	..	.80	.60	.25	.25	3.90	4.3
47	2.00	..	..	.80	.30	.30	3.40	3.5
52	2.00	..	..	..	.40	.30	2.70	2.9
57	2.00	..	..	..	..	.10	2.10	2.4

fourth child is reduced, on the assumption that only half the families will have as many as four children.

In calculating the interest of dependents in the person's income, the basic method is as follows. If, for instance, we are dealing with a married man, aged twenty-seven and with one child, and wish to find the dependents' interest in the income he would have at the age of thirty-seven, we find that the total consuming units in the family at that age will be 3.9, of which the wife and the first child represent 1.8. Then 1.8/3.9 times the "total earnings of survivors" at age thirty-seven (which is $131,400,000) gives $60,700,000 as the total interest of dependents. The discounted worth of this at age twenty-seven is $41,000,000. This represents the total worth of 83,692 men surviving at age twenty-seven to their then-existing dependents, in respect of the income the survivors of these 83,692 would earn ten years later. Dividing $41,000,000 by 83,692 gives approximately $496 as the worth of one man living at age twenty-seven, in respect of his prospective earnings ten years later.

Variations on this basic procedure are adopted to meet special features of the problem. Children of two, seven, and twelve are sources of expense and not income and are therefore represented by minus quantities. These minus quantities are taken from Dublin's figures of expenses for his $2,500 group, reduced by the factor five-sevenths and further reduced to correspond to the numbers surviving at these ages. In these cases the average expense for the entire five-year period is taken, since the mid-year of the period would not represent it closely enough. At age seventeen, it is assumed that income and expense balance. And at age twenty-two, it is assumed that the survivors at that age employ $20,000,000, or nearly $234 apiece, either as contributions to present family expenses above their own upkeep, or as savings which will ultimately accrue to the benefit of their dependents.

For subsequent years, dependents' interest in the unmarried person is calculated by the basic formula, with the modification that the potential wife is accorded only half the interest of an adult. This assumes that, if the potential wife remains unmarried, she loses the support she would have received from her husband, but also escapes the very real economic duties and burdens of home-making and housework. She can take a position in store or factory and receive wages for work which may be no more exacting than that she would have done in the home. She may really improve her strictly economic status, though in the typical case we are assuming that she loses something.

In certain special calculations where a man leaves a widow but no children, we have followed the same logic. But it seemed fair to assume that the actual widow loses more than the merely potential wife, as she suffers an actual change in her conditions of living, and these have a certain inertia about them. We have therefore represented her loss by a three-fourths share of an adult unit for the first five years after her husband's death, and after that by a one-half share. The widow with children is counted at one full adult unit. She loses that much income by her husband's death and is not freed from the burdens of home-making. Even after the children are all self-sustaining her share is still reckoned on the same basis, since the housewife who has raised a family of children cannot take an industrial or commercial position as easily as a young person who has never had that drain upon her energies, nor can she be sure of standing the pace.

Strictly speaking, the loss a widow suffers from the death of her husband in respect, let us say, to his income of ten years hence is conditioned by the actuarial probability that *both wife and husband* would, under normal expectation, be alive ten years hence.[2] Those wives who would normally die before the tenth year cannot be said to lose the tenth year's subsistence. On the other hand, the loss may be more than would be reckoned on a basis of bare joint life expectancy of one man and one woman, because of the effect of remarriages. A conservative treatment of this factor would simply cancel remarriages of widowers against remarriages of widows and ignore the whole matter. A more liberal treatment might admit some doubt whether these elements fully cancel, in their ultimate incidence, and might give the "value" of the husband's life the benefit of this doubt. The computation in Table I adopts this liberal attitude, and credits the wife's interest with more than would result from a bare joint life expectancy of wife and husband, but less than would result from

---

[2] There may be room for some philosophizing on the subject of the normal life expectancy of the husband who is already dead; but the logic is inevitable if one is to treat this problem at all. The war deaths are an accomplished fact, and the question is: if these particular deaths had not occurred, what would have been the expectancy of life and income?

assuming that every wife lives as long as her husband. So long as there are dependent children, no discount at all is made for mortality of wives, on the general ground that the economic loss from the death of the head of the family is not less if he leaves orphaned children than if he leaves a wife to care for them. Someone must bear the burden if the wife is not there to do it.

The allowance for the interest of dependent parents is one of the most difficult features of the problem, because of the lack of adequate figures as to the extent of such dependency. The recent survey by Abraham Epstein places the number above the age of sixty-five who are partly or wholly dependent at two millions in the United States.[3] The parents of the generation represented in our army of 1918 will number more than this when they reach corresponding age. The number of adult consuming units allotted to dependent parents in the present calculation is sufficient to provide full maintenance for well over 4 million adults in place of the 2 million of Epstein's estimate; and hence may be regarded as liberal. In fact, it is more than enough to take care of the entire excess of expenses over earnings for all the aged as Dublin figures it, reckoning each aged person at one full adult consuming unit. This is figured on the further assumption of a stationary population in which the adult males surviving out of 100,000 born are responsible between them for the whole support of the survivors of the previous generation of parents, who numbered at birth 200,000. Since the actual population is growing, and some parents are supported by daughters, this assumption is a liberal one.

This method of computation yields negative values for children aged 2. This would be a valid result if the death of an infant had no relation to the birth of others. But there are undoubtedly many cases in which the size of the family is limited by economic considerations, and in many of these cases the death of an infant results in permitting one more to be born. In these cases the death results in an economic loss equal to the amount spent in bearing and rearing the first child. In this sense the life of the infant has a positive value. Balancing these cases against those of the other type, it has seemed fair to ignore the negative values for the very young resulting from the standard computation scheme.

[3] Survey published by League for Industrial Democracy, reported in *New York Times,* January 6, 1930.

TABLE III

Undiscounted Loss of Income Due to Deaths. Based on Active Death Awards June 30, 1928.

Age at death	Status	Number	Loss of income at given number of years after death, in thousands of dollars														
			0	5	10	15	20	25	30	35	40	45	50	55	60	65	70
17	Single	880		176	212	180	146	144	152	162	180	141	88	35	—39	—42	—17
22	Single	31,775	6,350	7,650	6,510	5,275	5,210	5,500	6,030	6,510	5,080	3,177	1,270	—1,396	—1,524	—603	....
27	Single	11,538	2,780	2,366	1,916	1,893	1,996	2,192	2,366	1,846	1,154	462	—508	—554	—219	....	....
27	Married, childless	9,341	3,980	1,913	1,550	1,532	1,616	1,774	1,913	1,494	934	373	—411	—448	—177	....	....
27	Married, 1 child	12,498	9,040	8,313	7,580	5,275	5,800	6,120	5,450	3,960	2,625	1,100	—550	—612	—237	....	....
32	Single	9,788	2,004	1,625	1,605	1,693	1,860	2,004	1,565	979	392	—430	—470	—186	....	....	....
32	Married, 2 children	4,332	3,778	3,510	2,916	1,928	2,123	1,888	1,373	911	381	—191	—208	—82	....	....	....
37	Single	1,708	284	281	296	325	350	274	171	68	—75	—82	—32	....	....	....	....
37	Married, 3 children	1,102	1,075	988	826	540	480	349	231	97	—49	—53	—21	....	....	....	....
42 and up	Single	1,968	323	340	374	403	315	197	79	—87	—94	—37	....	....	....	....	....
42 and up	Married, 4 children	704	691	568	479	307	223	148	62	—31	—34	—13	....	....	....	....	....
		85,634	30,316	27,730	24,264	19,351	20,119	20,590	19,392	15,909	10,494	4,447	—842	—3,243	—2,196	—645	—17

Total undiscounted loss, 185,658 × 5 = 928,290 (in thousands).

Estimate for 90,954 awards in 1930, 1 billion dollars.

Including 79,046 additional deaths at three-fourths average loss, total estimated loss is 1,650 millions.

This computation scheme furnishes the basis for Table III, which reckons the loss from the 85,634 deaths represented in the compensation awards active June 30, 1928. Column IV gives the discounted "worth" of these lives and the succeeding columns give the undiscounted loss of annual income to dependents at five-year intervals.

In certain respects this computation scheme is liberal, notably in its allowance for dependent parents and for the interest of the potential wife, and in its treatment of the deduction for the probability of the wife dying before her husband. In other respects, it may not be liberal enough. There is some lack of elasticity in family expenses where the establishment is geared to a family of a certain size, and the loss of one member may not remove all the expenses represented by his *pro rata* share of the family total. For this reason the table may underestimate the loss due to death. Moreover it deals only with members of the immediate family, whereas there are other parties who have a real interest. More distant relatives receive some support; and there is in the aggregate a large volume of contributions to various public works and activities of general benefit which cannot fairly be dismissed by saying that those who contribute to these things merely balance those who passively receive benefits or impose burdens. All in all, we may take the computation for what it is: a very tentative estimate, erring now on one side and now on the other, but giving a fairly reasonable approximation to a quantity which does not lend itself to much more accurate measurement.

This computation also affords the basis for reckoning the losses from disability. Here the method is to take the percentages of reduction in earning power represented in the active disability awards of 1929, and apply them to the gross incomes indicated in Dublin's table for the survivors at successive future ages. The results appear in Table IV. This procedure is also too liberal in some respects and not liberal enough in others. It makes no deduction for improvement in actual earning power through rehabilitation work, in case that was worth more than it cost. On the other hand, it omits all disabilities rating less than 10 per cent, which are excluded from compensation. It omits many cases of disability due to the war, where the sufferer has not been able to furnish proof of the origin of his condition; and on the other hand it includes many cases in which an automatic presumption of war origin was admitted, but among which there is a considerable percentage which would have suffered disability if there had been no war. When one takes into account the great uncertainty of the future course of disability, any estimate becomes extremely tentative and doubtful.

The $1,500 income-scale, which is the basis of all these calculations, represents the conditions of the period of post-war prosperity. For present scales of money prices and wages, this represents a substantial overestimate. Future trends, of course, cannot be predicted with certainty.

TABLE IV

Disability awards active 1929 *Assumed age in 1929*	*Assumed number at each age*	| *Total earnings of survivors, in tens of thousands of dollars, in*									
		1929	*1934*	*1939*	*1944*	*1949*	*1954*	*1959*	*1964*	*1969*	*1974*
32	50,000	7,880	8,100	8,075	7,430	6,625	5,670	4,420	3,020	1,530	306
37	110,000	18,220	18,290	16,810	14,990	12,820	10,000	6,840	3,465	693	..
42	75,000	12,940	11,900	10,610	8,980	7,070	4,840	2,451	491	....	..
47	27,138	4,520	4,030	3,446	2,683	1,838	922	186	....	....	..
Total	262,138	43,560	42,320	38,941	34,083	28,353	21,432	13,897	6,976	2,223	306

Grand total of earnings of survivors:
(Five times sum of columns in above table)   . . $11,604,550,000
Total loss at 44.2 per cent disability[4] . . . . $ 5,125,000,000
Estimated loss prior to 1929   1,940,000,000

Total undiscounted loss from disability   7,065,000,000
Total undiscounted loss from death . . . .   1,650,000,000[5]

Grand Total   . . . . $ 8,715,000,000

[4] In the 1929 report of the Veterans' Bureau, p. 24, the average rate of disability is given as 32 per cent, which obviously refers to partial disability only, as may be verified by the analysis into 10 per cent groupings on the following page. Combining this with the total disabilities gives an average of 44.2 per cent.

[5] *See* Table III, above.

Age	Survivors of 100,000 born	Total earnings of survivors, $00,000 omitted	Adult units in full family	Interest of dependents (whole group)	Unmarried males Discounted worth at 4 per cent at ages 7	12	17	22
2	91,350	....	..	—200	....	....	....	....
7	89,490	....	..	—264	—264	....	....	....
12	88,625	....	..	—289	—237	—289	....	....
17	87,499	361	..	0	0	0	0	....
22	85,691	893	1.	200	111	135	164	200
27	83,692	1,205	2.5	241	110	134	163	198
32	81,691	1,286	3.1	205	77	94	114	138
37	79,355	1,314	3.9	166	51	62	76	92
42	76,382	1,318	3.9	164	42	51	62	75
47	72,813	1,212	3.4	173	36	44	53	65
52	68,482	1,081	2.7	190	33	40	48	59
57	62,635	925	2.1	205	29	35	43	52
62	55,437	721	2.	160	18	23	27	33
67	45,975	493	2.	100	10	11	14	17
72	34,199	250	2.	40	3	4	4	6
77	22,417	50	2.	—44	—3	—3	—4	—5
82	11,574	....	2.	—48	—3	—3	—4	—5
87	4,385	....	2.	—19	—1	—1	—1	—1
Total	1,141,692				12	337	919	924
					5	5	5	5
					60	1,685	4,595	4,620
Worth per survivor					67	1,900	5,255	5,400

	Discounted worth at ages					
57	*62*	*67*	*72*	*77*	*82*	*87*
. . . .	. . . .	. . . .	. . . .	. . . .	. . . .	. . . .
. . . .	. . . .	. . . .	. . . .	. . . .	. . . .	. . . .
. . . .	. . . .	. . . .	. . . .	. . . .	. . . .	. . . .
. . . .	. . . .	. . . .	. . . .	. . . .	. . . .	. . . .
. . . .	. . . .	. . . .	. . . .	. . . .	. . . .	. . . .
. . . .	. . . .	. . . .	. . . .	. . . .	. . . .	. . . .
. . . .	. . . .	. . . .	. . . .	. . . .	. . . .	. . . .
. . . .	. . . .	. . . .	. . . .	. . . .	. . . .	. . . .
. . . .	. . . .	. . . .	. . . .	. . . .	. . . .	. . . .
. . . .	. . . .	. . . .	. . . .	. . . .	. . . .	. . . .
. . . .	. . . .	. . . .	. . . .	. . . .	. . . .	. . . .
436	. . . .	. . . .	. . . .	. . . .	. . . .	. . . .
260	317	. . . .	. . . .	. . . .	. . . .	. . . .
142	172	210	. . . .	. . . .	. . . .	. . . .
49	59	72	88	. . . .	. . . .	. . . .
—20	—24	—30	—36	—44	. . . .	. . . .
—18	—22	—27	—32	—39	—48	. . . .
—6	—7	—9	—11	—13	—16	—19
843	496	216	9	—96	—64	—19
5	5	5	5	5	5	5
4,215	2,480	1,082	47	—480	—318	—95
6,730	4,475	2,355	137	—2,140	—2,747	—2,160

TABLE I

...putation Scheme: Value of a Human Life to Surviving Dependents.

Married one child — Int. of dependents	Married one child — Disc. worth at age 27	Married two children — Int. of dependents	Married two children — Disc. worth at age 32	Married three children — Int. of dependents	Married three children — Disc. worth at age 37	Int. of dependents	42	47	52
....	....	....	....	....	....	....	....	....	....
....	....	....	....	....	....	....	....	....	....
....	....	....	....	....	....	....	....	....	....
....	....	....	....	....	....	....	....	....	....
....	....	....	....	....	....	....	....	....	....
723	723	....	....	....	....	....	....	....	....
665	546	872	872	....	....	....	....	....	....
607	410	810	665	977	977	....	....	....	....
422	234	673	455	896	736	981	981	....	....
464	211	445	246	749	506	807	663	807	....
490	184	490	223	490	272	681	460	560	681
436	134	436	163	436	199	436	242	294	358
317	80	317	98	317	119	317	144	176	214
210	44	210	53	210	65	210	79	96	116
88	15	88	18	88	22	88	27	33	40
—44	—6	—44	—7	—44	—9	—44	—11	—13	—16
—48	—6	—48	—7	—48	—8	—48	—10	—12	—15
—19	—2	—19	—2	—19	—3	—19	—3	—4	—5
	2,568		2,777		2,876		2,572	1,936	1,373
	5		5		5		5	5	5
	12,842		13,885		14,382		12,862	9,683	6,865
	15,300		17,000		18,133		16,850	13,300	10,040

INDEX

Accidents, industrial, 185
Adjusted Service, certificate, 181; compensation, 118, 188, 194–195, 201, 223–224, 284; *see also* Bonus
Aftermath of the War, *see* War aftermath
Agriculture, 2, 10–14, 41, 59, 141, 144, 153, 170, 178, 227–234; product per worker, 144; effect of war on, 229; affected by post war depression, 230; output per worker, 231–232; prices, 230; mechanization, 231; exports, 231; plantation system, 259
Airplanes, 54, 286
Aldrich-Vreeland Act, 21, 23
Alexander, Will W., 259
Allies, loans to, *see* Loans
American Federation of Labor, 20, 47, 168, 287
American Library Service, *see* War work
American Railway Express Company, *see* Railways
Anti-trust laws, *see* Trusts
Armed forces, numbers in, 34, 53–54; subsistence of, 40, 88–89, 224; demobilization of, 52; post-war expenses of, 54; pay and subsistence, 130; *see also* Army and Navy
Armistice, 53
Armories, 119
Arms, small, 264–266; Remington Company, 264; Winchester Repeating Arms Company, 264, 265; *see also* Guns
Army and Navy, 34, 40, 52–54, 69, 86, 88–89, 101, 110; intelligence tests, 49; trade tests, 49; post-war expenditures, 58; pay of, 127; pay and subsistence, 130; post-war budget as affected by war, 141–104; *see also* Armed forces
Artillery, *see* Guns
Assets, productive, 55
Atlantic Seaboard, congestion of, 12
Automobiles, 174
Ayres, Col. Leonard, 30, 35, 44, 119, 182, 187, 249

Balance of trade, United States, *see* Trade
Barge Lines, Federal, 254–256
Barriol, M., 217
Baruch, Bernard M., 26

Bausch and Lomb Optical Company, 268
Bogart, E. L., 7
Bolshevism, 60, 172, 287
Bond issues, 118; *see also* Liberty Bonds, Loans, Borrowings, Debt
"Bonus," 108, 131, 223; federal soldiers, 118–119; soldiers, *see* Adjusted Service certificate, Adjusted Service compensation
Bonuses, state, 118–119, 121, 224
Borrowings, 31, 71–72, 79, 101; government, 72, 100, 127; domestic, 74, 76, 128; inflation through, 81; interest on war debt, 88; from corporations, 123; war, 114, 283, 285; *see also* Loans, Debt
Bridgeport, Conn., 43
Bryan, W. J., 18
Budget, workers, 50; war, 87; pre-war, cf. post-war, 101–105
Bunnell, S. H., 264
Bureau, of agricultural economics, 228, 230; of labor, 103, 113
Business, executive: characteristics, 19; profits and losses, 73
Buying power of Europe diminished by war, 179

Cantonments, 146
Capital, export of, 17, 22, 62–63, 178; expansion during neutrality, 26; private capital, salvage of, 56; private capital, invested for war purposes, 56; increase of, 125
Carnegie Institution, 269
Carpenter, Niles, 260
Casualties, 181–182, 185, 187, 197–198; Civil War, 196
Census of occupations, 1920, 140
Cereals, 229
Civilian war work, 34–35; women, 45
Civil War, 187, 197–200, 284; pensions, 195–196, 200; wounds, 197
Clarkson, 43
Coal, 178; British, 2; rationing, 47; industry, 59, 169, 273; Tennessee Coal & Iron Co., 255
Commerce, United States Department of, 63
Commission on Interracial Coöperation, 259
Company unions, 60
Compensation, 205–207; railroad em-